Konstantin Sheiko
in collaboration with Stephen Brown

NATIONALIST IMAGININGS OF THE RUSSIAN PAST

Anatolii Fomenko and the Rise of Alternative History
in Post-Communist Russia

With a foreword by Donald Ostrowski

ibidem-Verlag
Stuttgart

Bibliografische Information der Deutschen Nationalbibliothek
Die Deutsche Nationalbibliothek verzeichnet diese Publikation in der Deutschen Nationalbibliografie; detaillierte bibliografische Daten sind im Internet über http://dnb.d-nb.de abrufbar.

Bibliographic information published by the Deutsche Nationalbibliothek
Die Deutsche Nationalbibliothek lists this publication in the Deutsche Nationalbibliografie; detailed bibliographic data are available in the Internet at http://dnb.d-nb.de.

Coverpicture: Reflecting the dilemma confronting the medieval warrior in Vasnetsov's famous 1882 painting 'Knight at the Crossroads', Russian nationalists hope to influence Russia as it chooses whether to turn east (Asia), west (Europe), or move ahead along its own special path.
Source:
http://www.hunter.cuny.edu/classics/russian/russianlinks/vasnetsov-warrior-compressed.jpg

∞
Gedruckt auf alterungsbeständigem, säurefreien Papier
Printed on acid-free paper

ISSN: 1614-3515

ISBN-10: 3-89821-915-1
ISBN-13: 978-3-89821-915-0

© *ibidem*-Verlag
Stuttgart 2009

Alle Rechte vorbehalten

Das Werk einschließlich aller seiner Teile ist urheberrechtlich geschützt. Jede Verwertung außerhalb der engen Grenzen des Urheberrechtsgesetzes ist ohne Zustimmung des Verlages unzulässig und strafbar. Dies gilt insbesondere für Vervielfältigungen, Übersetzungen, Mikroverfilmungen und elektronische Speicherformen sowie die Einspeicherung und Verarbeitung in elektronischen Systemen.

All rights reserved. No part of this publication may be reproduced, stored in or introduced into a retrieval system, or transmitted, in any form, or by any means (electronic, mechanical, photocopying, recording or otherwise) without the prior written permission of the publisher. Any person who does any unauthorized act in relation to this publication may be liable to criminal prosecution and civil claims for damages.

Printed in Germany

Soviet and Post-Soviet Politics and Society (SPPS) Vol. 86
ISSN 1614-3515

General Editor: Andreas Umland, *Catholic University of Eichstaett-Ingolstadt*, umland@stanfordalumni.org

Editorial Assistant: Olena Sivuda, *Dragomanov Pedagogical University of Kyiv*, sivuda@ukrcognita.com.ua

EDITORIAL COMMITTEE*

DOMESTIC & COMPARATIVE POLITICS
Prof. **Ellen Bos**, *Andrássy University of Budapest*
Dr. **Ingmar Bredies**, *Kyiv-Mohyla Academy*
Dr. **Andrey Kazantsev**, *MGIMO (U) MID RF, Moscow*
Prof. **Heiko Pleines**, *University of Bremen*
Prof. **Richard Sakwa**, *University of Kent at Canterbury*
Dr. **Sarah Whitmore**, *Oxford Brookes University*
Dr. **Harald Wydra**, *University of Cambridge*
SOCIETY, CLASS & ETHNICITY
Col. **David Glantz**, *"Journal of Slavic Military Studies"*
Dr. **Rashid Kaplanov**, *Russian Academy of Sciences*
Dr. **Marlène Laruelle**, *EHESS, Paris*
Dr. **Stephen Shulman**, *Southern Illinois University*
Prof. **Stefan Troebst**, *University of Leipzig*
POLITICAL ECONOMY & PUBLIC POLICY
Prof. em. **Marshall Goldman**, *Wellesley College, Mass.*
Dr. **Andreas Goldthau**, *Stiftung Wissenschaft und Politik*
Dr. **Robert Kravchuk**, *University of North Carolina*
Dr. **David Lane**, *University of Cambridge*
Dr. **Carol Leonard**, *University of Oxford*

Dr. **Maria Popova**, *McGill University, Montreal*
FOREIGN POLICY & INTERNATIONAL AFFAIRS
Dr. **Peter Duncan**, *University College London*
Dr. **Taras Kuzio**, *George Washington University, DC*
Prof. **Gerhard Mangott**, *University of Innsbruck*
Dr. **Diana Schmidt**, *University of Bremen*
Dr. **Lisbeth Tarlow**, *Harvard University, Cambridge*
Dr. **Christian Wipperfürth**, *N-Ost Network, Berlin*
Dr. **William Zimmerman**, *University of Michigan*
HISTORY, CULTURE & THOUGHT
Dr. **Catherine Andreyev**, *University of Oxford*
Prof. **Mark Bassin**, *University of Birmingham*
Dr. **Alexander Etkind**, *University of Cambridge*
Dr. **Gasan Gusejnov**, *University of Bremen*
Prof. em. **Walter Laqueur**, *Georgetown University*
Prof. **Leonid Luks**, *Catholic University of Eichstaett*
Dr. **Olga Malinova**, *Russian Academy of Sciences*
Dr. **Andrei Rogatchevski**, *University of Glasgow*
Dr. **Mark Tauger**, *West Virginia University*
Dr. **Stefan Wiederkehr**, *DHI, Warsaw*

ADVISORY BOARD*

Prof. **Dominique Arel**, *University of Ottawa*
Prof. **Jörg Baberowski**, *Humboldt University of Berlin*
Prof. **Margarita Balmaceda**, *Seton Hall University*
Dr. **John Barber**, *University of Cambridge*
Prof. **Timm Beichelt**, *European University Viadrina*
Prof. em. **Archie Brown**, *University of Oxford*
Dr. **Vyacheslav Bryukhovetsky**, *Kyiv-Mohyla Academy*
Prof. **Timothy Colton**, *Harvard University, Cambridge*
Prof. **Paul D'Anieri**, *University of Kansas, Lawrence*
Dr. **Heike Dörrenbächer**, *DGO, Berlin*
Dr. **John Dunlop**, *Hoover Institution, Stanford, California*
Dr. **Sabine Fischer**, *EU Institute for Security Studies*
Dr. **Geir Flikke**, *NUPI, Oslo*
Dr. **David Galbreath**, *University of Aberdeen*
Prof. **Alexander Galkin**, *Russian Academy of Sciences*
Prof. **Frank Golczewski**, *University of Hamburg*
Dr. **Nikolas Gvosdev**, *Naval War College, Newport, RI*
Prof. **Mark von Hagen**, *Arizona State University*
Dr. **Guido Hausmann**, *Trinity College Dublin*
Prof. **Dale Herspring**, *Kansas State University*
Dr. **Stefani Hoffman**, *Hebrew University of Jerusalem*
Prof. **Mikhail Ilyin**, *MGIMO (U) MID RF, Moscow*
Prof. **Vladimir Kantor**, *Higher School of Economics*
Dr. **Ivan Katchanovski**, *University of Toronto*
Prof. em. **Andrzej Korbonski**, *University of California*
Dr. **Iris Kempe**, *Heinrich Boell Foundation Tbilissi*
Prof. **Herbert Küpper**, *Institut für Ostrecht München*
Dr. **Rainer Lindner**, *Stiftung Wissenschaft und Politik*
Dr. **Vladimir Malakhov**, *Russian Academy of Sciences*
Dr. **Luke March**, *University of Edinburgh*

Prof. **Michael McFaul**, *Stanford University, California*
Prof. **Birgit Menzel**, *University of Mainz-Germersheim*
Prof. **Valery Mikhailenko**, *The Urals State University*
Prof. **Emil Pain**, *Higher School of Economics, Moscow*
Dr. **Oleg Podvintsev**, *Russian Academy of Sciences*
Prof. **Olga Popova**, *St. Petersburg State University*
Dr. **Alex Pravda**, *University of Oxford*
Dr. **Erik van Ree**, *University of Amsterdam*
Dr. **Joachim Rogall**, *Robert Bosch Foundation, Stuttgart*
Prof. **Peter Rutland**, *Wesleyan University, Middletown*
Dr. **Sergei Ryabov**, *Kyiv-Mohyla Academy*
Prof. **Marat Salikov**, *The Urals State Law Academy*
Dr. **Gwendolyn Sasse**, *University of Oxford*
Prof. **Jutta Scherrer**, *EHESS, Paris*
Prof. **Robert Service**, *University of Oxford*
Mr. **James Sherr**, *Defence Academy of the UK, Swindon*
Dr. **Oxana Shevel**, *Tufts University, Medford*
Prof. **Eberhard Schneider**, *University of Siegen*
Prof. **Olexander Shnyrkov**, *Shevchenko University, Kyiv*
Prof. **Hans-Henning Schröder**, *University of Bremen*
Prof. **Yuri Shapoval**, *Ukrainian Academy of Sciences*
Prof. **Viktor Shnirelman**, *Russian Academy of Sciences*
Dr. **Lisa Sundstrom**, *University of British Columbia*
Dr. **Philip Walters**, *"Religion, State and Society," Oxford*
Prof. **Zenon Wasyliw**, *Ithaca College, New York State*
Dr. **Lucan Way**, *University of Toronto*
Dr. **Markus Wehner**, *"Frankfurter Allgemeine Zeitung"*
Dr. **Andrew Wilson**, *University College London*
Prof. **Jan Zielonka**, *University of Oxford*
Prof. **Andrei Zorin**, *University of Oxford*

* While the Editorial Committee and Advisory Board support the General Editor in the choice and improvement of manuscripts for publication, responsibility for remaining errors and misinterpretations in the series' volumes lies with the books' authors.

Soviet and Post-Soviet Politics and Society (SPPS)
ISSN 1614-3515

Founded in 2004 and refereed since 2007, SPPS makes available affordable English-, German- and Russian-language studies on the history of the countries of the former Soviet bloc from the late Tsarist period to today. It publishes approximately 20 volumes per year, and focuses on issues in transitions to and from democracy such as economic crisis, identity formation, civil society development, and constitutional reform in CEE and the NIS. SPPS also aims to highlight so far understudied themes in East European studies such as right-wing radicalism, religious life, higher education, or human rights protection. The authors and titles of previously published and forthcoming manuscripts are listed at the end of this book. For a full description of the series and reviews of its books, see www.ibidem-verlag.de/red/spps.

Note for authors (as of 2007): After successful review, fully formatted and carefully edited electronic master copies of up to 250 pages will be published as b/w A5 paperbacks and marketed in Germany (e.g. vlb.de, buchkatalog.de, amazon.de) and internationally (e.g. amazon. com). For longer books, formatting/editorial assistance, different binding, oversize maps, coloured illustrations and other special arrangements, authors' fees between €100 and €1500 apply. Publication of German doctoral dissertations follows a separate procedure. Authors are asked to provide a high-quality electronic picture on the object of their study for the book's front-cover. Younger authors may add a foreword from an established scholar. Monograph authors and collected volume editors receive two free as well as further copies for a reduced authors' price, and will be asked to contribute to marketing their book as well as finding reviewers and review journals for them. These conditions are subject to yearly review, and to be modified, in the future. Further details at www.ibidem-verlag.de/red/spps-authors.

Editorial correspondence & manuscripts should, until 2011, be sent to: Dr. Andreas Umland, ZIMOS, Ostenstr. 27, 85072 Eichstätt, Germany; e-mail: umland@stanfordalumni.org

Business correspondence & review copy requests should be sent to: *ibidem*-Verlag, Julius-Leber-Weg 11, D-30457 Hannover, Germany; tel.: +49(0)511-2622200; fax: +49(0)511-2622201; spps@ibidem-verlag.de.

Book orders & payments should be made via the publisher's electronic book shop at: www.ibidem-verlag.de/red/SPPS_EN/
Authors, reviewers, referees, and editors for (as well as all other persons sympathetic to) SPPS are invited to join its networks at www.facebook.com/group.php?gid=52638198614 and www.linkedin.com/groups?about=&gid=103012

Recent Volumes

77 Galina Kozhevnikova in collaboration with Alexander Verkhovsky and Eugene Veklerov
Ultra-Nationalism and Hate Crimes in Contemporary Russia
The 2004-2006 Annual Reports of Moscow's SOVA Center
With a foreword by Stephen D. Shenfield
ISBN 978-3-89821-868-9

78 Florian Küchler
The Role of the European Union in Moldova's Transnistria Conflict
With a foreword by Christopher Hill
ISBN 978-3-89821-850-4

79 Bernd Rechel
The Long Way Back to Europe
Minority Protection in Bulgaria
With a foreword by Richard Crampton
ISBN 978-3-89821-863-4

80 Peter W. Rodgers
Nation, Region and History in Post-Communist Transitions
Identity Politics in Ukraine, 1991-2006
With a foreword by Vera Tolz
ISBN 978-3-89821-903-7

81 Stephanie Solywoda
The Life and Work of Semën L. Frank
A Study of Russian Religious Philosophy
With a foreword by Philip Walters
ISBN 978-3-89821-457-5

82 Vera Sokolova
Cultural Politics of Ethnicity
Discourses on Roma in Communist Czechoslovakia
ISBN 978-3-89821-864-1

83 Natalya Shevchik Ketenci
Kazakhstani Enterprises in Transition
The Role of Historical Regional Development in Kazakhstan's Post-Soviet Economic Transformation
ISBN 978-3-89821-831-3

84 Martin Malek, Anna Schor-Tschudnowskaja (Hrsg.)
Europa im Tschetschenienkrieg
Zwischen politischer Ohnmacht und Gleichgültigkeit
Mit einem Vorwort von Lipchan Basajewa
ISBN 978-3-89821-676-0

85 Stefan Meister
Das postsowjetische Universitätswesen zwischen nationalem und internationalem Wandel
Die Entwicklung der regionalen Hochschule in Russland als Gradmesser der Systemtransformation
Mit einem Vorwort von Joan DeBardeleben
ISBN 978-3-89821-891-7

To my mother Emily, father Boris, sister Natasha and niece Alexandra back in Russia

Contents

Foreword by Donald Ostrowski   9

Introduction   11

I   Russian Nationalism   35
    I.1   The Search for Identity: East or West?   35
    I.2   Nationalism and Post-Communism   51

II   The Rise of Alternative History   63
    II.1   Russian History's Discontents: Lomonosov, Morozov, Fomenko   63
    II.2   Prester John, Columbus and the Russian Horde   73
    II.3   The Competition for Ancestors and Alternative History   82

III   Russian History and its Forgeries   97
    III.1   Historians, Sources and Interpretations   97
    III.2   Normanists and Anti-Normanists   114
    III.3   Uncovering the Plot Against Russia   128

IV	Farewell to the Mongols	143
	IV.1 Mongol Rule in Russia – Vice and Virtue	143
	IV.2 Russia's Pastoralists: Pechenegs, Qipchaqs, Mongols, Tatars	147
	IV.3 Sources	154
	IV.4 Eurasianism	165
	IV.5 The Blonde Genghis Khan	171
	IV.6 Asiatic Russia: Myth and Reality	173
	IV.7 Foreign Conquest or Civil War	177
	IV.8 The Myth of Mongol Terror	180
	IV.9 Steppe Warriors	186
V	Russia's Medieval Near Abroad	189
	V.1 From Confrontation to Cooperation	189
	V.2 Four Battles	197
	V.3 The Romanov Falsification of History	205
VI	The Four Ivan the Terribles	213
	Conclusions	233
	Bibliography	237

Foreword

Alternative or alternate history is a merger of science fiction and historical fiction in that it attempts a speculative reformulation of history, along the lines of 'what if history were different?' These alternative histories often find willing believers among those untrained in critical historical thinking. *The Da Vinci Code* by Dan Brown, for example, never claimed to be more than fiction, yet it had tens of thousands of readers convinced the conspiracy described in it was historical fact. Anatolii Fomenko and other 'new chronology' historians in Russia do pretty much the same thing as Dan Brown did, except (a) they claim to believe in their own speculative fiction (which places them in the category of cranks) and (b) they ratchet up the conspiracy to include all world history and all serious academic scholars.

Konstantin Sheiko's book is a well-written, well-researched discussion of the phenomenon of the 'new chronology' history in Russia since the fall of the USSR. Sheiko focuses on the writings of Anatolii Fomenko, but also discusses other 'pseudo-historians' as 'a problem in history' in order to try to understand what the context for their popularity is. Their books sell in the hundreds of thousands while serious academic historians sell merely in the hundreds. The main argument of the 'new chronology' historians is that history has been falsified to deny Russia and the Russians their proper place in history. By eliminating much of the Middle Ages and, among other things, the Mongol invasion, by claiming that Russia was founded before ancient Greece and Rome, and by placing the writing of the Old Testament after the writing of the New Testament, along with other 'reformulations', Fomenko proposes an ultra-patriotic view of history in which the Russians dominate at every turn. Christopher Columbus, for example, was a Russian agent when he discovered the New World, and so forth.

As context for his analysis, Sheiko presents the most recent serious scholarship on Russian history and contrasts Fomenko's and other 'new chronology' historians' refashioning of it. According to Sheiko, the 'new chronology' historians are able to capitalize both on the Soviet claim that outsiders falsified Russian history and on the subsequent distrust of the Soviet version of things. In rejecting both the foreign version and the Soviet version, the 'new chronology' historians, thus, are able to find a gullible audience ready to believe in an egregiously contorted reformulation. The astrophysicist Carl Sagan in his book *Broca's Brain* (1979) argued that it was incumbent upon serious scholars to refute the theories of the cranks and charlatans; otherwise, if they ignore those theories, they concede the public forum to them by default.

In this light, Sheiko has done historical scholarship an important service. Sheiko's work on this topic is impressive. He is up to date on the latest scholarship and does well in summarizing the theories of Fomenko and the other 'new chronology' historians in a fair and clear manner, which is not an easy task. He also is able to refute their claims through appeal to evidence, logical argument, and elegant interpretation.

Donald Ostrowski
Cambridge, Mass.

Introduction

Since the fall of Communism in 1991, Russian historians have engaged in a process of rewriting, rediscovering and reinventing Russia's past. They have been joined by an army of popular and amateur historians who write about the past often in the hope of influencing contemporary politics and public opinion. This book concerns a group of writers whose focus is the past and whose work, amateur rather than scholarly, is part of the present contest to establish a new identity for post-Communist Russia.

A central question for post-Communist Russian identity is the relationship between Russia and its imperial heritage. Vera Tolz has pointed out that for Russia, the process of nation building has been complicated by the fact that:

> Russia has traditionally been the centre of an empire, and therefore confusion over the 'just borders' of the new state is greater among politicians, intellectuals and even ordinary people than is the case in the non-Russian newly independent states...what is important to note is that the early creation of an empire (well before the process of Russian nation building began), the empire's land-based character and the resulting high level of mutual cultural influences and assimilation between conquerors and conquered to some extent blurred the feeling of difference between the imperial people and other subjects of the empire.[1]

Another distinguishing feature of Russian identity, according to Tolz, is that the majority of intellectuals in Russia see the broadly defined 'West', rather than non-Russians of the former Soviet Union, as 'the constituting other' in opposition to which Russia seeks to understand itself. According to the historian Alexander Yanov, Russians have always been divided into those who viewed Russia as part of the European tradition and those who favour a special path or *Sonderweg* for Russia. For many Russian patriots, there was a clash of civilisations, a war between individualistic Romano-German Europe

---

1   Vera Tolz, *Russia* (London: Arnold, 2001), 70-73.

and the more spiritual and collectivist world of Orthodox Russia.[2]

Vladimir Shlapentokh has noted the importance of what he describes as the 'greatness syndrome' to the Russian sense of identity. Historically, Russians have compared the status of their state to the greatest power of the day - France in the eighteenth century, Britain in the nineteenth century and the United States in the twentieth century. Shlapentokh noted opinion polls in the mid 1990s that suggested 75% of Russians were nostalgic for the Soviet Union and its superpower status. About the same number looked forward to the reappearance of Russian greatness in the future.[3]

These three broad themes of imperial heritage, opposition to the West and the search for greatness are of crucial importance for the writers whose work is the subject of this book. These writers are engaged in the process of imagining a new Russia, although they regard this new Russia as the recovery of something ancient and essential. They have become popular at a time when Russia's identity is up for grabs, and when it is by no means clear whether Russia's present rulers will succeed either in building a Western-style nation state or in reestablishing Russia as the powerful international actor it was in centuries past.

Anatolii Fomenko (1945-) is a renowned mathematician who belongs to the academic staff of Moscow State University. Fomenko is a member of Russia's Academy of Sciences, a professor with a doctorate in applied physics and mathematics, head of the Mechanical-Mathematical Department of Moscow State University and author of one hundred and eighty scientific works. He has written twenty-six monographs and textbooks in his specialist field of mathematics. Fomenko was awarded Russia's State Award in 1996 for his scientific achievements.[4]

---

2   Alexander Yanov, 'Russian nationalism in Western studies: misadventures of a Moribund paradigm,' *Demokratizatsiia* 9:4 (Fall 2001): 552.
3   Vladimir Shlapentokh, 'Is the greatness Syndrome Eroding?' *The Washington Quarterly* 25:1 (January 1, 2002): 132.
4   Anatolii Fomenko and Gleb Nosovskii, *Novaia khronologiia i kontseptsia drevnei Rusi, Anglii, Rima. Fakty, statistika, gipotesy* II volumes (Moscow: Moscow State University press MGU, 1995, 1996); Anatolii Fomenko, *Novaia khronologiia Gretsii. Antichnost' i srednevekov'e* II volumes (Moscow: MGU, 1996); Anatolii Fomenko and Gleb Nosovskii, *Imperiia: Rus', Turtsia, Kitai, Evropa, Egipet. Novaia matematicheskaia khronologiia drevnosti* (Moscow: Faktorial press, 1996, 1997, 1998, 1999); Anatolii Fomenko and Gleb Nosovskii, *Rus' i Rim. Pravil'no li my poinimaem istoriiu Evropy i Azii?* II volumes (Moscow: Olimp, AST print house, 1997); Anatolii Fomenko and Gleb Nosovskii, *Novaia khronologiia Rusi* (Moscow: Faktorial press, 1997); Anatolii Fomenko and Gleb Nosovskii, *Matematicheskaia khronologiia bibleiskikh sobytii* (Moscow: Nauka, 1997); Anatolii Fomenko, 'Smysl

Fomenko's interest in astronomy and its application to chronology caused him to undertake what would prove to be a commercially successful journey into popular history writing. He began his historical research in the 1970s but only came to prominence outside of mathematics after the collapse of Communism. Fomenko is the founder and leading light of the 'New Chronology' movement whose efforts to rewrite Russian and world history have generated much amusement but also great controversy inside Russia.

Together with his colleague, Gleb Nosovskii (1958-), whose qualifications include a PhD in physics and mathematics, Fomenko embarked upon a wildly speculative rewriting of Russian history. They have spawned a significant number of like-minded amateur historians, many of them scientists turned pseudo-historians like themselves.[5] Among their supporters is Gary

---

russkogo dela v sokhranenii Imperii,' *Nezavisimaia Gazeta*, 21 November 1996; Anatolii Fomenko and Gleb Nosovskii, *Rekonstruktsia vseobshchei istorii* (Moscow: Delovoi Ekpress, 1999); Anatolii Fomenko and Gleb Nosovskii, *Bibleiskaia Rus'* II volumes (Moscow: Faktorial press, 1998, 2000); Anatolii Fomenko and Gleb Nosovskii, *Rus'-Orda na stranitsakh bibleiskikh knig* (Moscow: Anvik, 1998); Anatolii Fomenko and Gleb Nosovskii, *Vvedenie v novuiu khronologiiu, kakoi seichas vek?* (Moscow: Kraft+Lean, 1999); Anatolii Fomenko, *New Methods of Statistical Analysis of Historical Texts. Applications to Chronology* III volumes (New York: Edwin Mellen Press); Anatolii Fomenko and Gleb Nosovskii, *Rekonstruktsia vseobshchei istorii. Issledovania 1999-2000* (Moscow: Delovoi ekspress, 1999); Anatolii Fomenko and Gleb Nosovskii, *Kakoi seichas vek?* (Moscow: Aif-Print, 2002); Anatolii Fomenko, Gleb Nosovskii, *History: Fiction or Science* VII vol. (Paris, London, New York: Delamere, 2003).

5   Among the many popular historians who corroborate Fomenko or criticise conventional historical accounts of Russian and world history are Anatolii Abrashkin, *Predki russkikh v drevnem mire* (Moscow: Veche, 2001); Anatolii Abrashkin, *Drevnie Rossy: Mifologicheskie paralleli i puti migratsii* (Nizhnii Novgorod: NNGU print house, 1999); Anatolii Abrashkin, *Chudo-Uydo: Istoriia odnogo perevoplashchenia* (Nizhnii Novgorod: NNGU print house, 1999); Anatolii Abrashkin, *Rus' sredizemnomorskaia i zagadki Biblii* (Moscow: Veche, 2003); Anatolii Abrashkin, *Tainy Troianskoi voiny i sredizemnomorskaia Rus'* (Moscow: Veche, 2006); Anatolii Abrashkin, *Sredizemnomorskaia Rus': velikaia derzhava drevnosti* (Moscow: Veche, 2006); Anatolii Abrashkin, *Skifskaia Rus'. Ot Troi do Kieva* (Moscow: Veche, 2008); Alexander Bushkov, *Rossiia kotori ne bylo* (Moscow: 'OLMA-Press', 1997); Alexander Bushkov and Andrey Burovskii, *Rossiia kotoroi ne bylo II, Russkaia Atlantida* (Moscow: 'OLMA-Press', 2001); Alexander Bushkov, *Rossiia kotoroi ne bylo III, mirazhi i prizraki* (Moscow: 'OLMA-press', 2004); Alexander Bushkov, *Rossiia kotori ne bylo IV. Blesk i krov' gvardeiskogo stoletia* (Moscow: 'OLMA-press', 2005); Alexander Bushkov, *Zemlia. Planeta prizrakov* (Moscow: 'OLMA-press', 2007); Alexander Bushkov, *Ivan Groznyi. Krovavyi poet* (Moscow: 'OLMA-press', 2007); Alexander Bushkov, *Chingiz-khan. Neizvestnaia Azia* (Moscow: 'OLMA-Press', 2008); Alexander Bushkov, *Rasputin. Vystrely iz proshlogo* (Moscow: 'OLMA-press', 2008); Alexander Bushkov, *Stalin. Krasnyi monarkh* (Moscow: 'OLMA-press', 2008); Alexander Bushkov, *Stalin. Ledianoi tron*

(Moscow: 'OLMA-press', 2008); Andrey Burovskii, *Nesbyvshaiasia Rossiia* (Moscow: Eksmo, 2007); Andrey Burovskii, *Ariiskaia Rus': lozh' i pravda o vysshei rase* (Moscow: Eksmo, 2007); Leonid Bocharov, Nikolai Efimov, Igor Chachukh and Igor Chernyshev, *Zagovor protiv russkoi istorii* (Moscow: ANVIK, 2001); Alexander Guts, *Mnogovariantnaia Istoriia Rossii* (Moscow: AST, 2000, 'Poligon', 2001); Alexander Guts, 'Mif o vosstanovlenii istoricheskoi pravdy,' *Matematicheskie struktury i modelirovanie* 1 (1998); Alexander Guts, *Podlinnaia Istoriia Rossii* (Omsk: OMGU, 1999); Alexander Guts, 'Modeli mnogovariantnoi istorii,' *Matematicheskie struktiru i modelirovanie* 4 (1999); Valerii Demin, *Otkuda ty, russkoe plemia?* (Moscow: Veche, 1996); Valerii Demin, *Tainy Russkogo naroda* (Moscow: Veche, 1997); Valerii Demin, *Giperboreia – utro tsivilizatsii* (Moscow: Veche, 1997); Valerii Demin, *Zagadki Russkogo severa* (Moscow: Veche, 1999); Valerii Demin, *Tainy zemli russkoi* (Moscow: Veche, 2000); Valerii Demin, *Giperboreia: istoricheskie korni russkogo naroda* (Moscow: Veche, 2000); Valerii Demin, *Zagadki russkikh letopisei* (Moscow: Veche, 2001); Valerii Demin, *Zvezdnaia sud'ba narodov Rossii* (Moscow: Veche, 2001); Valerii Demin, *Rus' giperboreiskaia* (Moscow: Veche, 2002); Valerii Demin, *Zagadki russkogo mezhdurech'ia* (Moscow: Veche, 2003); Valerii Demin, *Drevnee drevnosti: rossiiskaia prototsivilizatsia* (Moscow: Veche, 2003); Valerii Demin, *V poiskakh kolybeli tsivilizatsii* (Moscow: Veche, 2004); Iurii Petukhov, *Vechnaia Rossiia* (Moscow: Molodaia Gvardia, 1990); Iurii Petukhov, *Dorogami Bogov* (Moscow: Mysl', 1990); Iurii Petukhov, *Kolybel' Zevsa: Istoriia Russov ot antichnosti do nashikh dnei* (Moscow: Mysl', 1998); Iurii Petukhov, *Gibel' Rossii* (Moscow: Mysl', 1999); Iurii Petukhov, *Istoriia Russov 40.000 let do nashei ery* vol. I (Moscow: Mysl', 2000); Iurii Petukhov, *Russkaia Khazaria* (Moscow: Mysl', 2001); Iurii Petukhov, *Tainy drevnikh russov* (Moscow: Veche, 2001, 2002, 2003); Iurii Petukhov, *Rusy drevnego Vostoka* (Moscow: Veche, 2003); Viktor Kandyba, *Istoriia russkogo naroda* (St-Petersburg: Lan', 1996); Viktor Kandyba and Peter Zolin, *Real'naia istoriia Rossii* (St-Petersburg: Lan', 1997); Viktor Kandyba and Peter Zolin, *Istoriia i ideologia ruskkogo naroda* II volumes (St-Petersburg: Lan', 1997); Viktor Kandyba, *Zaprechshennaia Istoriia* (St-Petersburg: Lan', 1998); Iaroslav Kesler, *Russkaia tsivilizatsia* (Moscow: Eko-press, 2000, 2002); Iaroslav Kesler and Igor Davidenko, *Kniga tsivilazatsii* (Moscow: Eko-press, 2001); Iaroslav Kesler, *Azbuka i Russko-Evropeiskii slovar'* (Moscow: Kraft+, 2001); Iaroslav Kesler and Dmitrii Kaliuzhnyi, *Zabytaia Istoriia Moskovii. Ot stroitel'stva Moskvy do raskola* (Moscow: Veche, 2003); Iaroslav Kesler and Dmitrii Kaliuzhnyi, *Zabytaia Istoriia Rossiiskoi imperii* (Moscow: Veche, 2004); Igor Davidenko, *Lozhnye maiaki istorii* (Moscow: Eko-press, 2002); Vladislav Poliakovskii, *Tataro-Mongoly, Evrazia, Mnogovariantnost'* (Kaluga: GUP Oblizdat, 2002); Anatolii Storozhev and Vladimir Storozhev, *Rossiia vo vremeni*, book I, (Moscow: Veche, 1997); Sergey Valianskii and Dmitrii Kaliuzhnyi, *Put' na vostok ili bez vesti propavshie vo vremeni* (Moscow: Kraft+Lean, 1997); Sergey Valianskii and Dmitrii Kaliuzhnyi, *Drugaia Istoriia nauki* (Moscow: Veche, 2002); Sergey Valianskii and Dmitrii Kaliuzhnyi, *Drugaia Istoriia Rusi* (Moscow: Veche, 2002); Dmitrii Kaliuzhnyi and Alexander Zhabinskii, *Drugaia Istoriia voin* (Moscow: Veche, 2003); Sergey Valianskii, *Uslovia Vyzhivania Rossii* (Moscow: Kraft+, 2005); Murad Adzhi, *My – iz roda Polovetskogo* (Rybinsk: 1992); Murad Adzhi, *Polyn' polovetskogo polia* (Moscow: Pik-Kontekst, 1994); Murad Adzhi, *Taina Sviatogo Georgia, ili podarennoe Tengri* (Moscow: 1997); Murad Adzhi, *Evropa, Turki, velikaia step'* (Moscow: Mysl', 1998); Murad Adzhi, *Kipchaki* (Moscow: Novosti, 1999); Murad Adzhi, *Tiurki i mir: sokrovennaia Istoriia* (Moscow: AST, 2004); Murad Adzhi, *Aziatskaia Evropa* (Moscow: AST, 2006); Murad Adzhi,

Kasparov, one of Russia's most celebrated chess grand masters.[6] Kasparov's boast that 'I can spread any historian against the wall in a debate about Russian history' was typical of the pugnacious confidence of Fomenko's acolytes.[7] Alexander Zinoviev, one of Russia's best-known writers, has written a glowing introduction to one of Fomenko's latest publications.[8]

Fomenko's original claim was that conventional chronology was bedevilled with errors and deliberate falsifications. Conventional dating amounted to little more than the ill-informed guesses of early modern scholars like Scaliger, the famous Dutch scholar and astronomer, who, Fomenko alleged, added thousands of years to the story of civilisation and filled in the gaps with the mythology that we know today as ancient history.[9] For Fomenko, recorded history was not as old as previously thought, ancient history was a duplicate of medieval history, Greeks and Romans deserved far less attention than was usually accorded them, and the Bible's Old Testament was written after the New Testament.

The New Chronology project is far from modest. Fomenko's crowning achievement runs to seven volumes. It is based on research undertaken over thirty years. It turns out, according to Fomenko, that many historical figures are duplicates and triplicates, that is, copies of the one historical personage known in different contexts and eras by different names. Roman history is mostly the history of the Holy Roman Empire, which turns out to be the story

---

Dykhanie Armagedonna (Moscow: AST, 2006); Vladimir Shcherbakov, *Gde zhili geroi eddicheskikh mifof* (Moscow: 1989); Vladimir Shcherbakov, *Gde iskat' Atlantidu* (Moscow: 1990); Vladimir Shcherbakov, *Asgard – gorod Bogov* (Moscow: 1991); Valerii Khamtsiev and Alexander Balaev, *David Soslan, Friedrich Barbarossa, Alania ot Palestiny to Britanii* (Vladikavkaz: IR, 1992).

6   Davidenko and Kesler, *Kniga tsivilizatsii*, see Kasparov's foreword. Fomenko's endorsement of Kasparov's input is in the foreword to Fomenko, Nosovskii, *Novaia khronologiia i kontseptsia drevnei Rusi, Anglii, Rima. Fakty, statistikia, gipotesy.*

7   For Kasparov's endorsement, see Gary Kasparov, 'Chernye dyry istorii,' *Ogonek* 1, 2, 3 (January 1999).

8   See 'Introduction' to Fomenko *History: Fiction or Science* (Paris, London, New York: Delamere Publishing, 2003).

9   Fomenko, Nosovskii, *Bibleiskaia Rus'*, I, 21-24; for mathematical-statistical critique of Skaliger/Petavius see also Anatolii Fomenko, *Metody statisticheskogo analiza narrativnykh tekstov i prilozhenie k khronologii* (Moscow: MGU, 1990, 1996); Anatolii Fomenko, *Globalnaia khronologiia* (Moscow: MGU, 1993); Anatolii Fomenko and Gleb Nosovskii, *Geometrical and statistical methods of analysis of star configurations. Dating of Ptolemy's Almagest* (USA: CRC-Press, 1993); Anatolii Fomenko, *Empirical-statistical analysis of narrative material and its application to historical dating* II volumes (the Netherlands: Kluwer Academic publications, 1994); Fomenko and Nosovskii, *Kakoi seitchas vek?*, 16-33.

of Russia projected westwards and backwards in time. Jesus Christ was also known to history as Pope Gregory the Seventh and lived in Rome in the eleventh century. Only in the seventeenth century did the dating of conventional history and Fomenko's dates achieve unison.

Fomenko's new version of Biblical history, not surprisingly, drew fire from the Russian Orthodox Church. Having been labelled an anti-Christ in the early 1990s Fomenko soon became a celebrity academic, a status that eluded him as a mathematician. Books, television programs and the Internet proclaimed the birth of a new science. Professional historians scoffed, but instead of retreating to his scientific specializations, Fomenko broadened his attack on conventional history and in the process, generated book sales, a dedicated brotherhood of imitators and growing notoriety. Critics who have maintained their sense of humour have labelled Fomenko as 'the terminator' because so many accepted periods, events and personalities are expunged from his version of the past.

Fomenko trawled through the history of Eurasia, Byzantium, and Rome to show that historians all around the world appropriated the achievements of Russians to boost the prestige of their own national history. Arguably, Fomenko's greatest achievement is the invention of a Slav-Turk empire that allegedly dominated the first half of world history, that is, until the seventeenth century. This 'Russian Horde' as Fomenko named it, was based in the area that we normally associate with the Golden Horde founded by the Mongol khans in the thirteenth century.[10]

Fomenko's vision is an inspiring one for those who measure Russia's greatness by the amount of space it occupies on a map. He offers an account of the Russian state as if it were the history of all of Eurasia. Fomenko's writing is inspired, in part, by the work of the Eurasianists of the early twentieth century who first argued that Russia was neither European nor Asian but a distinctive society. The academic leader of this group, Nikolai Trubetskoi, argued that Asia was the natural home of Russia in much the same way that Europe was a traditional enemy.[11]

For most Eurasianists, the Mongols were misunderstood and undervalued. Lev Gumilëv, who has done more than any other Russian writer to popularize Russia's Asian identity, argued that the West deliberately

---

10 Technically, Golden Horde is the latter-day name applied by Russia to the Qipchaq Khanate.
11 Nikolai Trubetskoi, *The Legacy of Chengiz Khan and other Essays on Russia's identity* (Michigan Slavic Publications, 1991), 161-67.

engineered a 'black legend' to demonise the Mongols as savage barbarians. Ironically, Fomenko's legend is blacker still because he writes the Mongols out of the history of Russia altogether.[12]

Fomenko's claim, often repeated in the works of popular writers, is that the Mongols, or Tatars as the Russians called them, did not come from far off Central Asia but had always lived within the lands of European Russia along the Volga River and adjacent steppes. Genghis Khan had European features, spoke Slav and Turkic languages and never invaded Russia. While Gumilëv described a symbiosis of Russia and the steppe peoples, Fomenko's goal is to achieve what his thirteenth-century ancestors could not, the extermination of the Mongols from the historical record. According to Fomenko, the myth of the Mongol invasion was an invention of Church chroniclers and the Romanov dynasty, designed to glorify their own contributions to Russian history. Strictly speaking, these are not original claims because, as we shall see, there are earlier writers who have not accepted that Russia lived under Mongol occupation. Fomenko has made these claims popular among a contemporary Russian audience and added his own interpretation to the story of key moments in Russian history.

Conventional historians were at first unsure whether to regard Fomenko and his entourage as post-modern clowns or dangerous ethno-nationalists. For his critics in Russia, Fomenko is both an embarrassment and a potent symbol of the depths to which the Russian academy and society generally have sunk amid the economic disasters and political and military humiliations heaped upon Russia since the fall of Communism. But the critics do admit that Fomenko's writings are popular, especially in comparison to the works of conventional historians whose output often can find no commercial outlet at all. Fomenko's publisher boasts that three hundred thousand copies of Fomenko's works have been sold in an era when ten thousand is considered an excellent print run for popular history.[13] One of Fomenko's critics noted

---

12   See his Lev Gumilëv, *Drevniaia Rus' i Velikaia step'* (Moscow: Mysl', 1998).
13   This is the claim made in the publicity for the English translation of Fomenko, *History: Fiction or Science*, (Paris, London, NY: Delamere Publishing, 2003); In the 1990s in Russia, the printing of ten thousand copies was regarded as a sign of a book's popularity. See Viktor Shnirelman, *Who gets the Past? Competiton for Ancsestors among Non-Russian intellectuals in Russia* (John Hopkins University, 1996), 49. Print runs for other alternative writers are impressive enough in a country where books are a luxury for most people: Viktor Kandyba and Peter Zolin *Istoriia i Ideologia Russkogo naroda* was printed out in 10,000 copies; Murad Adzhi *My roda polovetskogo* and his other books were printed out in 10,000 copies; Alexander

that having made a tour of the Moscow's bookshops one would notice that the best shelves are occupied by the 'alternative' writers, while the serious works of past and present historians evade the eyes of the customer.[14]

Academic symposiums have been held at Moscow University to discuss and dissect the new scourge of 'Fomenkoism'. Internet sites proclaim Fomenko's view of world history in a variety of languages while popular radio stations have dedicated discussions to these 'modern' historians. A glossy, illustrated English-language volume has recently appeared to introduce a new world of readers to Fomenko.[15]

Conventional historians, having once ignored Fomenko, are now responding to the point where the most recent exposition of the 'anti-history' of Fomenko ran to three large volumes and more than thirty articles.[16] It

---

Bushkov's *Rossiia kotoroi ne bylo*, vol. I, 75,000 copies, vol. II – additional print of 7,000 copies; Leonid Bocharov, Nikolai Efimov, Igor Chachukh, Igor Chernyshev, *Zagovor protiv russkoi istorii*, 15,000 copies; Anatolii Abrashkin, *Predki russkikh s drevnem mire*, 7,000 copies. Alternative titles seem to compete well with conventional history books as the printed numbers of copies demonstrate: A. Sakharov, *Istoriia Rossii do 18 veka* II volumes (Moscow: AST, 2003), 10,000 copies; A. Sakharov, *Istoriia Rossii 17-18 veka* (Moscow: Rosman, 2003), 10,000 copies; Vadim Kozhinov, *Prorok v svoem otechestve. Russia 1803-1822* (Moscow: Eksmo, 2002), 5,100 copies; Boris Rybakov, *Rozhdenie Rusi (9-13th centuries)* (Moscow: Aif-Print, 2003), 5,000 copies; Dmitrii Ilovaisky, *Novaia dinastiia* II volumes (Moscow: AST, 2003), 5,000 copies; Dmitrii Ilovaisky, *Nachalo Rusi* (Moscow: AST, 2002), 5,000 copies; Dmitrii Ilovaisky, *Tsarskaia Rus* II volumes (Moscow, AST, 2002), 5,000 copies; Dmitrii Ilovaisky, *Sobirateli Rusi* (Moscow: AST, 2001), 5,000 copies; Dmitrii Ilovaisky, *Stanovlenie Rusi* (Moscow: AST, 2002), 5,000 copies; Sergei Oldenburg, *Samoderzhavnoe pravlenie 1894-1904* (Moscow: 2001), 5,000 copies; B. Soloviev, *Russkoe dvorianstvo*, (Moscow: Poligon, 2001), 5,000 copies; I. Popov, *Rossiia i Kitai: 300 let na grani voiny* (Moscow: Ast, Astrel', Ermak, 2001, 2004), 5,000 copies; Ruslan Skrynnikov, *Vasilii Shuisky* (Moscow: AST, 2001), 5,000 copies; Ruslan Skrynnikov, *Tri Lzhedmitriia* (Moscow: AST, 2001), 5,000 copies; Ruslan Skrynnikov, *Ivan Groznyi* II volumes (Moscow: AST, 2001), 5,100 copies; series of Lev Gumilëv, *Ot Rusi k Rossii*, 3 parts, (Moscow: 2000), 5,000 copies, additional print 17,000 copies; *Otkrytie Khazarii*, 5,000 copies; *Chtob svecha ne pogasla*, 5,000 copies; *Chernaia legenda*, additional print 15,000 copies; *Tysiacheletie vokrug Kaspia* II volumes (Moscow: AST, 2002), 5,000 copies.

14   See Alexei Laushkin, *Lozh' novoi khronologii. Kak voiuet s khristianstvom A.T. Fomenko i ego edinomyshlenniki* (Moscow: Palomnik, 2002).
15   Fomenko, *History: Fiction or Science*.
16   See Igor Nastenko et al., eds., *Istoriia i antiistoriia: Kritika 'novoi khronologii' akademika A. Fomenko* (Moscow: Yazyki russkoi kultury, 2000); Igor Nastenko et al., eds., *Antifomenkovskaia mozaika* 5 books (Moscow: Russkaia panorama, 2000, 2001, 2002, 2003); Dmitrii Volodikhin and Dmitrii Oleinikov in collaboration with Olga Eliseeva, *Istoriia Rossii v melkii goroshek* (Moscow: ManufASTura-Edinstvo, 1998); Laushkin, *Lozh' novoi khronologii; Astronomiia protiv 'Novoi Khronologii'* (Moscow: 2001); *Russkaia Istoriia protiv 'Novoi Khronologii'* (Moscow: 2001);

would be fair to say that the best way for many historians in Russia today to reach a popular audience is to write a response to Fomenko. In his own way, Fomenko has come to represent a significant part of what R.W. Davies described as the 'mental revolution' that has taken place within the former Soviet intelligentsia after the collapse of Communism.[17]

A book about a wildly speculative pseudo-historian who is still obscure in the West needs some further justification at this point. Certainly, the justification cannot be that Fomenko has contributed something important or new for historians to consider about history. Nor can much credit be taken for identifying the obvious mistakes, distortions and falsehoods that litter 'alternative' or pseudo history. What is interesting is that, while Fomenko seems to be a man of straw, his reconstruction of Russian history thrives despite and almost certainly because of the condemnation of his conventional colleagues.

Fomenko is an example of apocalyptic writing in a troubled land. But, this book will argue, Fomenko has roots in more mainstream thinking and his version of Russian history may well have resonances in the continuing debate about Russian identity. Fomenko is telling an old story about Russia in a slightly new way at a time when Russia is struggling to make the transition from empire to nation-state. He is the inspiration behind an underground war waged by self-styled 'modern' historians whose task is to recover – or steal, depending upon the reader's point of view – a usable past for the post-Communist world.

Fomenko is a case study in Orientalism. Edward Said pointed out that the production of academic knowledge and political power grew together, and that scholars often acted as the willing or naïve instruments of power and subordination. Historians, like explorers or missionaries, have, whether they are conscious of it or not, promoted the colonial enterprise by creating an image of the 'other' preparatory with or simultaneous to its conquest.[18] This may be literally true in the case of Fomenko. For his critics, Fomenko's ideas are providing fuel for those who would reconstitute a Russian Empire. It is not just modern-day Mongols who are deprived of part of their heritage. In

---

Sbornik Russkogo istoricheskogo obshchestva 3:151 (Moscow: 2000); also see Sergey Fatiushkin's impressive collection of web materials critical of Fomenko, Bushkov and Co: http://fatus.chat.ru/foma.htm (as of November 17, 2008).
17 See Robert William Davies, Soviet history in the Yeltsin era (Basingstoke: Macmillan, 1997), 49-75.
18 Edward Said, Orientalism (London: Penguin, 1995).

Fomenko's history, Ukraine and Belarus too have no identity outside of their connection to Russia. Pseudo-historians are unrepentant, noting that the Mongolian and Ukrainian peoples are sadly mistaken in the delusion that they were ever anything other than elements of the Russian Horde.

Fomenko sees himself as engaged in a war of ideas where ethno-nationalism is the tactic of his enemies. If Russia is to survive, conventional history has to be overturned and the truth allowed to surface. If, on occasions, his speculations are wide of the mark, this is only to be expected in an age when bold hypotheses are needed as the dark veil of historical ignorance is finally raised to reveal the lingering traces of the world's greatest empire.

Vladimir Tismaneanu has recently identified several threats to the emerging democracies of the post-Communist world. They include Leninist legacies, salvationist popular sentiments, the rhetoric of reactionary nostalgia, the fluidity of political formations, the crisis of values, authority, and accountability, and the tensions between individualistic and communitarian values.[19] Most of these trends and tensions are clearly visible in the writing of Fomenko and the emerging Russian pseudo-history he represents.

Fomenko himself may prove to be just a footnote in the post-Communist path of the decaying Soviet intelligentsia. Soviet Russia was famous for the training *en masse* of scientists, its public libraries and book culture, and its alleged commitment to rid scholarship of religion and other illusory ideologies. It is ironic therefore that Fomenko, a leading Soviet scientist and erudite amateur in the social sciences, should attempt to impart to the next generation a model of history that seems to transgress every rule of science. On the other hand, Fomenko's writing leans heavily upon a pattern of writing history that, as we shall see, emerged from the 'scientific history' of the Stalinist era. On the surface, Fomenko seems to represent a break with the past. In fact, his writing represents a convergence of different elements that crisscross the story or Russia's search for identity over the last three centuries.

To the West, Russia remains the riddle, puzzle and enigma described by Winston Churchill. Tim McDaniel has emphasized the importance to Russian self-identity of the search for Russian uniqueness.[20] Many Western

---

19 Vladimir Tismaneanu, 'Discomforts of victory: democracy, liberal values and nationalism in post-communist Europe,' *West European Politics* 25:2 (April 2002), 81-243.
20 Tim McDaniel, *The Agony of the Russian Idea* (Princeton: Princeton University press, 1996), 22-54.

commentators in the 1990s feared that Russia's history left it unprepared for life as a liberal nation-state. They predicted that Russia would follow the example of the Weimar republic, the depressing path travelled by Germany in the 1920s and 30s from infant democracy to an aggressive, nationalistic and racist dictatorship under the leadership of Adolf Hitler.[21] One of the more enduring debates about Russia since the fall of Communism was whether the darker predictions of the rise of National Socialism or national Bolshevism in Russia might plunge Europe and the world into new crises.

Weimar has been described as 'democracy without the democrats' and the same formula seemed to apply equally well to post-Communist Russia. According to a former member of Boris Yeltsin's post-Communist government, during the 1990s 'the very word 'democrat' became a swearword'.[22] Richard Pipes has argued that aggressive nationalism is the default state of Russian nationalism and the danger of a new wave of militarism and aggressive expansionism is ever present.[23] Many Russians, on the other hand, see themselves as an endangered species. The Moscow philosopher, Vadim Mezhuev, has described Russia as sinking slowly into non-existence.[24]

It may turn out that these fears are overstated. Sceptics point out that while new Russian revolutions are often predicted, Russia itself seemed relatively stable in the first decade of the twenty-first century, with a new and prosperous elite.[25] Extremist groups did not succeed in overturning the post 1991 settlement in the decade after the fall of Communism. On the other hand, poverty has remained a persistent problem, ethnic tensions are obvious throughout the Russian Federation, part of the former Soviet bureaucratic, scientific and military elite has been displaced and alienated, and Russia's post-Communist political system is often described as at best an illiberal democracy.[26] Russia's economic growth has not translated into votes for

---

21 See, for example, Rogers Brubaker, *Nationalism Refrained. Nationhood and the National Question in the New Europe* (Cambridge: Cambridge University Press, 1996), and Judith Devlin, *Slavophiles and Commissars* (Basingstoke: Macmillan, 1999), 204.
22 McDaniel, *The Agony of the Russian Idea*, 183.
23 Richard Pipes, 'Introduction' in Heyward Isham (ed), *Remaking Russia: Voices from Within* (Armonk: Sharpe, 1995), 5.
24 Quoted in Alexander Yanov, 'Russian nationalism in Western studies: misadventures of a Moribund paradigm,' *Demokratizatsiya* 9:4 (Fall 2001): 556.
25 For positive view of democratic progress in post-Communist Russia, see Leon Aron, 'Russia's revolution,' *Commentary* 114:4 (November 2002): 22-30.
26 For a negative view of democratic progress in post-Communist Russia, see Sarah

liberal political parties. Since 1991, the trend in voting patterns in Russia has moved away from pro-Western reformers, usually described as the political 'right' by Russian commentators. In Duma elections, politicians described as nationalists, conservatives, and so-called 'state-builders', dominate and they seem to have found a leader in the Vladimir Putin and his close ally and successor as Russian president, Dmitrii Medvedev. The mayor of Moscow, Iurii Luzhkov, noted that Russia has become a 'strange bird', lacking its right wing. Yegor Gaidar, the liberal Prime Minister in the first Yeltsin government expressed the view after the disastrous failure of liberals in parliamentary elections in 2004 that his greatest fear was 'a radical nationalistic wave with consequences difficult to predict'.[27]

Astrid Tuminez has made the point that radical nationalism was not a significant force in Russian elections in the 1990s even though the drift of politics was towards more statist and anti-liberal political parties. For her, nationalism comes in waves, showing that 'brief and limited power of aggressive variants of nationalism' have significant impacts at certain points in Russia's history and can occur after periods of calm.[28] Such an observation is compatible with an argument that bursts of nationalist energy are possible in Russia in the years to come.

These developments represent a justification for this book. The pro-Western mood of the late Communist period has given way to a more traditional Russian scepticism towards the outside world. Fomenko's history has become a kind of folk wisdom shunned in the academy but inspiring conversations about history at the popular level. This is because it appeals to those, like Fomenko himself, who managed, associated with or fantasized about a real empire, the Soviet Union, or its imperial predecessor. Russia has found the nationalism of Western Europe difficult to replicate and a growing chorus of voices in Russian politics is sceptical of Western political models in general. It is important to understand how the greatness syndrome manifests itself at a popular level and is transmitted from generation to generation. Few academics in present-day Russia have been more successful than Fomenko in repackaging the patriotic elements of Soviet ideology for a post-Communist

---

Mendelson, 'Russians' Rights Imperiled. Has Anybody Noticed?' *International Security* 26:4 (2002): 39-69.

[27] Quoted in 'Former PM decries Russian nationalism,' *United Press International* (January 28, 2004): 1.

[28] Astrid Tuminez, *Russian Nationalism since 1956. Ideology and the Making of Foreign Policy* (Lanham: Rowman and Littlefield, 2000), 16.

audience.

Fomenko feigns political impartiality, claiming that his research 'pursues purely scientific purposes and does not aim at any political, religious or societal goals'[29]. He evokes the image of an elder statesman who must struggle to restrain the young firebrands who are in agreement with him or inspired by his ideas. Fomenko makes no secret of the fact that there is an obvious enemy for Russia, the West. Here Fomenko repeats the complaints of eighteenth century Russian patriots, nineteenth century Slavophiles and Stalinist ideologists in the twentieth century. Fomenko's novelty lies in the way that he has added the empire of the Mongols to the geopolitical ambitions of the tsars and the international brotherhood of the Soviet Union to write a popular post-Soviet vindication of empire.

Understandably, most academics take a patronizing tone when dealing with the fantastic claims made by nationalists. Hobsbawm has described nationalist historians as the intellectual equivalent of poppy-growers supplying a gullible public with dangerous drugs.[30] Russians searching for imaginary parents or glorifying their past is nothing new. In her study of the rituals of socialist realism, Katerina Clark has noted that one of the favourite plots of Soviet novels of the 1930s was that of orphans in search of parents. The message was that 'the child without a father is...a child without an identity'.[31] The historian, Yuri Slezkine, who grew up in Russia, has recalled:

> Children often fantasize about discovering an enviable set of 'real parents'; nations can do something about it. One popular strategy is simply to lay claim to more prestigious progenitors (Noah's sons and Herodotus's distant tribes, e.g., have proven their usefulness on numerous occasions); another is to boost the status of existing ones (my own Russian ancestors, I learned in grade (sic) school, had invented the radio, airplane, steam locomotive, and light bulb, while also defending their neighbours from barbarian invasions).[32]

---

29 Nosovskii, Fomenko, *Rus-Orda na stranitsakh bibleyskikh knig*, 9.
30 Eric Hobsbawm, Introduction in Eric Hobsbawm and Terence Ranger (eds), *The Invention of Tradition* (Cambridge: Cambridge University Press, 1983), 13.
31 Katerina Clark, *The Soviet Novel: History as Ritual* (Bloomington: Indiana University Press, 2000), 135.
32 Yuri Slezkine, Who Gets the Past: Competition for Ancestors Among Non-Russian Intellectuals in Russia (book review),' *The Journal of Modern History* 70: 3 (September 1998): 754.

Nonetheless, the phenomenon of writers and readers throughout the former Soviet Union accepting these claims is a real one, in need of close investigation. It might be thought that this 'competition for ancestors', as Vladimir Shnirelman has dubbed it, would have exhausted the competing national groups of the former Soviet Union. In fact, judging by the sheer volume of publications, it seems to have generated even more interest not only just among Russian but also among all the former nations of the Tsarist and Soviet states.[33]

While their ideas about history are often simplistic or propagandistic, writers of pseudo-history can play a part in future developments. Liah Greenfeld has noted the distinctive role that Russian intellectuals play. While the 'spirit' of Russia is usually thought to reside in its people or *narod*, this spirit, 'paradoxically, was revealed through the medium of the educated elite, who, apparently, had the ability to divine it'.[34] Yitzhak Brudny views the key ingredient in the rise of nationalism as the manipulation of nationalist sentiment by elites.[35] To achieve this goal, however, there needs to be a popular history that can tell the Russians who they are. Valerii Tishkov's survey of ethno-nationalism in the former Soviet Union also noted the important role of political and intellectual elites in acting as a catalyst for extreme nationalism.[36] The historian, Anatolii Khazanov, has noted that a 'preoccupation with ethnic rather than civic national identity' has affected all former Communist countries, including the successor states of the former Soviet Union.[37] Commentators on nationalism often view ethno-nationalism as a sign that intellectuals are setting the agenda. If this is true, then it is important that we discover how the story of ethno-nationalism is told and how it has evolved.

On the other hand, it would be wishful thinking to suggest that Fomenkoism is no more than an elite construction. Fomenko's version of history is popular among a reading public disillusioned with Communism and

---

33 Victor A. Shnirelman, *Who Gets the Past? Competition for Ancestors among Non-Russian Intellectuals in Russia* (Washington: The Woodrow Wilson Center Press, 1996), 1-7.
34 Liah Greenfeld, *Nationalism: Five Roads to Modernity* (Cambridge: Harvard University Press, Mass, 1992), 261.
35 Yitzhak Brudny, *Reinventing Russia: Russian nationalism and the Soviet state, 1953-1991* (Cambridge: Harvard University Press, Mass, 1998), 1-4.
36 Valerii Tishkhov, *Ethnicity, Nationalism and Conflict in and after the Soviet Union. The Mind Aflame* (London: Sage, 1997), XIV.
37 Anatolii M. Khazanov, 'Ethnic nationalism in the Russian Federation,' *Daedalus* 126:3 (Summer 1997): 121.

the broken promises of consumer capitalism. It is deliberately aimed at keeping alive an imperial consciousness and secular messianism in Russia. Thus, Fomenko's history has a practical application in modern-day Russia and confirms that an imperialist discourse is alive and well, making more difficult Russia's evolution into a nation state.

This book lays no claim to testing definitively the truth or falsehood of the ideas put forward by Fomenko and his supporters. The claims range from the barely plausible to the ludicrous. The question I have set myself is not the accuracy of the claims made but why such seemingly fantastic histories have emerged with such vitality in post-Communist Russia. To me, the interesting question is why certain fantasies about history take upon a life of their own and others do not. Only part of the answer to this question relates to Fomenko and his motives. The real answer lies in explaining what it is about Fomenko that connects to a post-Soviet audience. To achieve that goal, it is necessary to understand what it is that Fomenko and his readers believe to be wrong with the conventional account of Russia's history.

I am interested in exploring Fomenko as a case study of the pseudo-history that has proliferated everywhere inside the former Soviet Union in the decade after the collapse of Communism. Its popularity suggests that there clearly is a role for those who claim to write history freed from its Romanov and Communist straightjackets. In the present political and ideological void in Russia, Fomenko's alternative history matters more than it might in a more stable country.

I have concluded that seven factors are especially important in explaining the success of Fomenko. In the first place, Fomenko taps into existing Russian self-identity, specifically the belief in the positive qualities of empire and the special mission of Russia. Secondly, Fomenko addresses the key issue of Russia's origins, important because Russians tend to believe that the past holds answers to the future. Thirdly, he has capitalized upon new knowledge about Russia's close relationship to Asia, long denied by Church chroniclers, Romanov propagandists and Communist functionaries. Fourthly, he addresses the present geo-political reality of Russia, which must deal with its relative weakness in relation to the West and its new Asian location. Fifthly, it inspires an audience among the dispossessed, especially the vast reading public that once formed the Soviet intelligentsia. Sixthly, he has borrowed heavily from previous attempts to establish a Russian identity, ranging from Slavophilism to Eurasianism. Seventh, Fomenko is reasonably ingenious in offering seemingly plausible answers to puzzling and hidden aspects of Russia's conventional history. Fomenko's ideas are popular not because of what he claims is his main concern, that is, rewriting world chronology, but because he finds in history a simple answer to the question of who the Russians are.

The writers under consideration here have a reasonably conservative view of the periods of Russian history and the turning points that shaped Russia's trajectory. There were three crucial moments – the foundation of a Russian state (Kiev Rus), barbarian invasion (the Mongols) and the Time of Troubles that brought the Romanovs to power. As the so-called State School historians of the nineteenth century told it, this was an inspiring tale of paradise (Kiev Rus), paradise lost (the Mongols and Time of Troubles) and redemption (the Romanovs). For Fomenko, this history is as much a mythology as the chronology and religion that underpinned it. Paradise was lost when the Romanovs came to power and only the enduring spirit of Russia has kept alive the flame of former greatness in the modern era.

In Chapter One, I examine the literature dealing with Russian nationalism to elucidate the recurring themes of Russian identity. The consensus in this literature is that Russians have mostly viewed themselves as an imperial nation, that is, that the Russian Empire and Soviet Union was in some sense the Russian nation-state. Russians do not view the concept of empire with the pejorative connotations that this word has in the west.

In Chapter Two, I introduce Fomenko's work and place him in the context of the proliferation of pseudo-history in the former Soviet Union. It is pointed out that pseudo-history is not a strictly Russian phenomenon but that the form that pseudo-history has taken in Russia reflects anxieties about Russian identity.

Chapter Three discusses the first of Russia's turning points. This is the Normanist controversy, an enduring obsession of Russian historiography. Slavophiles and Soviet historians deemed Normanism, that is, the notion that Vikings founded Russia's first state, as deeply insulting and historically inaccurate. Starting with Mikhail Lomonosov in the eighteenth century and continuing to this day, there is an anti-Normanist counter-argument, mostly dismissed in the West, which was shaped into its present form during the Stalin era. Anti-Normanism provides a model that the alternative writers can follow in their efforts to overturn what they regard as the equally implausible legend of Russia's defeat at the hands of invading Mongols in the thirteenth century.

Chapter Four focuses upon the second turning point, the Mongols. It examines the war of pseudo history against the East, manifested in the attempt to write the Mongols out of history. I argue that this is now an obsession in pseudo-history. The new war against the Mongols reflects deep dissatisfaction with Russian and Soviet history writing and capitalizes upon the fact that interpretations of the Mongol era are presently in a state of flux. Old certainties about a vicious 'Tatar Yoke' imposed upon Russia are under challenge and a new consensus about how to understand the relationship between Russia and the Mongols is yet to emerge. The same themes are apparent here as in the Normanist controversy but repackaged to prove that the Mongols were Russians, just like the Viking Rus before them.

Chapter Five continues the themes of Chapter Four by examining Fomenko's strange account of Mongol military history. Chapter Six describes the final turning point before the modern era, the so-called Time of Troubles that led to the coming to power of the Romanovs. Usually described as the period following the reign of Ivan the Terrible, Fomenko views this towering figure as four different tsars whose reigns spanned the 'real' Time of Troubles.

In my approach I am treating Fomenko as a problem of history. I am trying to explain why at the present time there is an audience for what he writes. To explain why his ideas are popular it is necessary to explore the historical debates about the Mongols or Kiev Rus. Fomenko rides a wave of conventional revisionist thinking about the Mongol era and assumes that his readers are reasonably knowledgeable about these debates. Because Russian and non-Russian scholarship are in a sense converging and share information more freely following the tearing down of the 'iron curtain', it is reasonable to claim that there are certain general trends emerging in the revisionist histories of Russia written by both Russian and non-Russian conventional historians since the fall of Communism. While desirable in itself, the revisionism of conventional history has created a space for pseudo-history.

It might be objected that Fomenko is a subject for literature or cultural studies, not history. Indeed some Russian historians have argued that the best way to deal with pseudo-history is through psychoanalysis and therapy. I appreciate that Fomenkoism is part of a literary tradition in Russia and when necessary do use some insights from disciplines outside of history. But to me, it is a matter of context and the historical approach. Explaining why a phenomenon has occurred when it did is a necessary first step to evaluating its broader significance for Russian history and its future. My aim is to show that, given Russia's legacy and present circumstances, it would have been surprising had something like Fomenkoism not emerged in the form that it has.

Fomenko publishes mostly as a co-author with Nosovskii. Nonetheless, the many critics of New Chronology assume that Fomenko is their principal opponent and this is the approach taken here. The references are usually to books co-authored with Nosovskii but in the book the name Fomenko will suffice as shorthand for Nosovskii and Fomenko.

More problematic is the fact that there is literally a New Chronology community that writes and publishes, sometimes agreeing and often disagreeing with one another about topics and details. Fomenko, in one of his more recent works endorses just two writers and warns that there are many others who invoke his name without his imprimatur. The writers endorsed by Fomenko are Alexander Bushkov and Alexander Guts. Other pseudo-historians examined as part of the research for this book share many of the ideas expressed by Fomenko. That is not to suggest that the broad field of pseudo-history is a unified or coherent body of writing because it is not. What the following brief portraits of the principal authors used for this book indicate is that pseudo-historians have a common enemy – conventional history, and a common goal – the recovery of Russian greatness. Beyond that, there is a great deal of divergence and competing imaginary pasts.

Bushkov is a popular detective and fantasy writer whose account of Russian history boasted an impressive print run of seventy-five thousand copies.[38] His theme is the alternative routes Russia might have taken if Moscow, the Romanovs and the Orthodox Church had not played such dominant roles. He imagined a Catholic Russia linked to the West and an Islamic Russia firmly planted in the Middle East as desirable alternatives. He is unique among the thirty alternative writers I examined for this book in that he is not outrightly hostile to the West.

Bushkov's principal theme is that Russian history has been falsified. This process began with Nestor, the alleged author of earliest medieval

---

38   Bushkov, *Rossiia kotoroi ne bylo I, II, III and IV; Zemlia. Planeta prizrakov; Ivan Groznyi. Krovavyi poet; Chingiz-khan. Neizvestnaia Aziia; Rasputin. Vystrely iz proshlogo; Stalin. Krasnyi monarkh; Stalin. Ledianoi tron.*

Russian chronicle. Since that time, historians have suppressed the obvious, including the facts that the Tatar-Mongols were ethnic Slavs, that the khans and tsars were often one and the same person and that Peter the Great was the most repressive tsar in Russia's history. Like Fomenko, Bushkov is adamant that there was no Mongol invasion. His account resembles Fomenko's so closely that the supporters of Fomenko accuse Bushkov of shameless plagiarism. In Chapter Four, I examine Fomenko and Bushkov together because their work overlaps to present the fullest picture of pseudo-history's counterattack against the Mongols.

Guts was trained in physics and worked on the problem of time before he turned his hand to writing Russian history.[39] According to Guts, the modern history of Russia is a lie in which conventional historians are complicit for failing to realize that, for example, Mongols were Russians, Cossacks formed a distinct estate as early as the twelfth century and that Russians were the Aryan progenitors of world civilisation. The title of Guts's most popular book, *Mnogovariantnaia istoriia Rossii* translates as the 'Multi-Versioned History of Russia'. Like Bushkov, Guts is intrigued by the historical counterfactual and endorses Fomenko's general approach but not his every detail. The interested student can take one of Guts's online history courses from Omsk University. These students will soon discover that they are learning history the Fomenko way.

Iaroslav Kesler is a Professor of Chemistry at Moscow University who argues that modern history has been falsified to deny the existence of a Slavic/Russian-speaking world empire whose centre was Constantinople.[40] The culture of Europe was Slavic until the seventeenth century. On the other hand, the Slavs fell under the sway of the Turks at that time; Peter the Great paid tribute to the Ottoman sultan, who was the most powerful ruler in Europe. Wars between Sweden, Poland and Russia in the eighteenth century represented conflict between the shards of the disintegrating Empire. While its military power rose and fell, Russia has always been the bearer of a higher form of civilization.

Anatolii Abrashkin is another scientist turned popular writer who confirms that traditional Russian history textbook is manufactured

---

39 Guts, *Podlinnaia Istoriia Rossii; Modeli mnogovariantnoi istorii; Mnogovariantnaia Istoriia Rossii.*
40 Kesler, *Russkaia tsivilizatsia; Kniga tsivilazatsii; Azbuka i Russko-Evropeiskii slovar'; Zabytaia Istoriia Moskovii. Ot stroitel'stva Moskvy do raskola; Zabytaia Istoriia Rossiiskoi imperii.*

mythology.⁴¹ For him, ancient peoples including the Aryans, Hittites and Cimmerians were known as Russians at different points of time. Russians are different from the remaining Slavs because they are above national pride. Russians were the real Imperial builders, while the rest of the Slavs, from Ukrainians to the Poles and Czechs, with the notable exception of the Serbs and Byelorussians were preoccupied with their petty statehoods and in the process harmed the Imperial cause, just as they are doing now.

Vladislav Poliakovskii's training is in physics.⁴² Like Fomenko, Poliakovskii believes that the dates we have for world and Russian history do not reflect true historical chronology. History describes the same event in multiple repetitions. For Poliakovskii, as for Fomenko, an outstanding case of a historical myth is the Tatar-Mongol wars. Sergei Valianskii and Dmitrii Kaliuyzny agree with Fomenko that world chronology, as we know it, is in error and that Russia's contribution to civilization has been consistently underestimated.⁴³

Viktor Kandyba and Petr Zolin represent an interesting team because the former is an alternative writer while the latter is a conventional historian who has steadily moved towards a wholesale rejection of conventional history. They contend that archaeology, linguistics, and other comparative sciences confirm that early civilizations have existed on the territory of the future Russian Empire from the late Palaeolithic and Mesolithic periods, 30,000-15,000 years ago. Ptolemy, using data from the first and second centuries AD, recorded the existence of nearly a hundred cities in the land north of the Black Sea, that is, Sarmatia or Scythia.⁴⁴ Greek mythology turns out to be a mere reflection of the actual history of Russia: Scythians like Achilles came from Russia to conquer Troy, that ancient centre of world civilization and classical neighbour of Russia, while the Russian Amazons defended Troy against the Greeks.

Alternative writers, on the surface at least, embrace a naïve, almost

---

41 Abrashkin, *Drevnie Rossy; Avesta v Russkikh perevodakh; Predki Russkih v etom mire; Rus' sredizemnomorskaia i zagadki Biblii; Tainy Troianskoi voiny i sredizemnomorskaia Rus'; Sredizemnomorskaia Rus': velikaia derzhava drevnosti; Skifskaia Rus'. Ot Troi do Kieva.*
42 Poliakovskii, *Tatary-Mongoly, Evrazia, Mnogovariantnost'.*
43 Valianskii and Kaliuzhnyi, *Put na Vostok ili bez vesti propavshie vo vremeni; Poniat' Rossiiu umom; Drugaia Istoriia nauki; Drugaia Istoriia Rusi;* Kaliuzhnyi and Zhabinskii, *Drugaia Istoriia voin;* Valianskii, *Usloviia Vyzhivania Rossii.*
44 Kandyba and Zolin, *Istoriia i ideologia russkogo naroda,* I, 296; see also Kandyba, *Istoriia russkogo naroda;* Kandyba and Zolin, *Real'naia istoriia Rossii.*

touching view of the power of history. For these writers, history really does matter. Alternative writers have suggested that Hitler would not have dared to invade Russia if it had not been for German historians' slander that insisted that the Slavs were nothing without German leadership and organization. Had German propaganda told the truth about how the Indo-Aryans originated in the lands between the Don and the Ural Rivers, Hitler's plans would have been different.[45]

Abrashkin, Kandyba, and Zolin have strong reservations about Fomenko's new chronology. Yet, like Fomenko, their accounts of history depends upon sweeping attacks upon old assumptions and dogmas and they embrace any and every criticism of the conventional wisdom. The same themes emerge again and again of Russia's ancient greatness, the myth of the Mongols, the Western (read Romanov) plot against Russian history, and the bias against Russia's Eurasian heritage found in Tsarist, Communist and Western literature.

Bushkov, Guts and Fomenko know each other's work well and form the inner circle of the pseudo-history under investigation here. I will use the term alternative writers or pseudo-historians when discussing this group even though they would be offended by both titles. Alternative is opposed to conventional, a category that comprises the vast bulk of Russian and non-Russian professional historians. I often cite the conventional literature to place in context or pass judgment upon the conclusions of alternative writers. When I use the term New Chronology, I have in mind just Fomenko's publications even though the enterprise has now spread globally and many writers are involved. When Fomenko, Bushkov or Guts are making an idiosyncratic point, I try to point this out. In general, my aim is not to alert the reader to the many debates within the field of pseudo-history. There are divergent opinions but these seem to me to be much less important than the general thrust of their work and its attack upon conventional history. With more space, more could have been written about the intricacies and nuances of these writers. Instead, I have had to restrict myself to a study of Fomenko as a case study in pseudo-history. My aim is simply to sample his work, put it in context and offer an explanation of the phenomenon.

The term pseudo-history is used because while Fomenko is concerned with the past, he does not write what trained historians would recognise as history. The title chosen for Fomenko's English-language debut, *History:*

---

45 Kandyba, Zolin, *Istoriia i Ideologia Russkogo naroda*, I, 303.

Science or Fiction, is revealing. Fomenko has invoked the positivist model of the nineteenth century that survived in Soviet Marxism of the twentieth century, where historical truth can be divined and retold as a series of propositions and laws. On the other hand, the suggestion that Fomenko's history is somehow science in comparison to the fiction of conventional wisdom will not convince many historians inside or outside of Russia.

A modern reader would not describe Fomenko's history as theoretically informed. He seems unaware either of modern scepticism about the fact/interpretation dichotomy made popular in the West by E. H. Carr in *What is History*[46] or the post-modern challenge to conventional history that began with works such as those of Hayden White that called into question conventional distinctions between history and fiction.[47] Fomenko assumes that the researcher can and should distinguish between history and fiction. On the other hand, his methods would not meet with approval from conservative theorists of history such as Keith Windschuttle who maintains that the professional training of historians and peer review of their work pushes history closer to the goal of establishing the truth of the past and of distinguishing what most probably happened from what could not have happened.[48] Fomenko is not a historian in this sense. He provides no fair-minded review of the historical literature about a topic with which he deals, quotes only those sources that serve his purposes, uses evidence in ways that seem strange to professionally-trained historians and asserts the wildest speculation as if it has the same status as the information common to the conventional historical literature.

Fomenko is aware that he has no academic training in history and that his view of the past is unconventional. He describes himself as a scientist who was forced to write history because conventional historians ignore the big questions. His account of the past is a rival to conventional history, not its continuation. Russian readers are unlikely to be put off by Fomenko's amateur status. Fomenko has a famous precedent in Lomonosov who also described himself as having been forced to write history because there was no other Russian willing and able to resist the lies told about Russian history in the eighteenth century. Professional historians in Russia are still tainted by

---

46 Edward Hallett Carr, *What is History?* (Harmondsworth: Penguin, 1964).
47 Hayden White, *Metahistory: the historical imagination in nineteenth-century Europe* (Baltimore: Johns Hopkins University, 1973).
48 Keith Windschuttle, *The Killing of History: how a discipline is being murdered by literary critics and social theorists* (Paddingtone: Macleay, 1994).

the memory of Soviet propaganda.

Fomenko's work often conveys the staccato beat of a chronicle with major issues passed over in silence followed by short vignettes about events that Fomenko thinks are important. Fomenko is not interested in gender, sexuality, classes or culture, the issues taken up by Western historians in recent decades. The pseudo-historian's past is a world of great men, geopolitics, the genealogy of royal families and the use of history as an instrument of power.

Finally, my book deals with Russia and my theoretical section examines theorists whose focus is Russian nationalism. It might have been better had Russian nationalism itself been examined more fully in the comparative light of, for example, the Habsburg, Ottoman or Yugoslav experiences. I plead lack of space and express the hope that the link between pseudo-history and the Russian search for identity emerges in this work. When describing Fomenko, who, as we shall see, is deeply enthusiastic about his homeland, I usually use the term patriot rather than nationalist. This is because I accept David Rowley's claim that there is little evidence of nationalism, in the Western sense of the term, in Russia. It is a matter that is investigated more thoroughly in the following chapter.

I   Russian Nationalism

I.1   The Search for Identity: East or West?

Fomenko entitled his major work *Imperiia* or Empire, a word that has much more positive connotations in Russia than it does in the West. Empire, for Fomenko and for many Russians, means the repository of political and economic power projected across a huge geographic era. This meaning is very different to Lenin's concept of exploited and subjugated colonial peoples. This positive view of the imperial past is reflected in the fact that the overwhelming majority of Russians have found it impossible to distinguish between Russia as nation-state and Russia as empire. Thus the term nationalism, in the context of Russia, is a problematic one.

The growing vitality of nationalism has been one of the most remarked upon aspects of the post-Communist history of Eastern Europe and the former Soviet Union.[49] The context for Fomenko is the collapse in 1991 of the Soviet Union, the Communist state that more or less occupied the territory inherited from the Tsarist Empire. The Soviet Union's principal successor state, the Russian Federation, is the world's largest state even if it is only half the size of its Communist and Tsarist predecessors. Politically and geographically, modern Russia occupies the same space today as it did approximately three hundred years ago in the era of Peter the Great. Since the collapse of Communism, Russian intellectuals and political commentators have sought out solid ground in order to make sense of Russia's new geography and its diminished place in the hierarchy of the world's great powers.

The Tsarist Empire and the Soviet Union were the world's largest multinational states. Soviet ethnographers counted 194 nationalities in 1926, 97 in 1939, 126 in 1959 and 92 in 1979.[50] For its supporters, the Russian Empire and its Soviet successor represented an alternative to the nation-state of Western Europe and to the exploitative and individualistic Western model

---

49   See Charles Kupchan, 'Introduction. Nationalism Resurgent' in C. Kupchan (ed.), *Nationalism and Nationalities in the New Europe* (Ithaca: Cornell University Press, 1995), 1-15.
50   Basile Kerblay, *Modern Soviet Society* (London: Methuen, 1983), 39.

of society.⁵¹ The demise of the Soviet Union came as a shock for the significant number of Russians who viewed the historic Russian state as a popular empire based on the principle of mutual respect that avoided the chauvinism and outright racism of other European empires.⁵²

To the dismay of those who saw the Soviet Union and the Russian Empire in positive terms, not one of the former Soviet republics, or former Tsarist provinces, chose unity or federation with Russia after 1991. Of the 104 named nationalities in the former Soviet Union, fifteen obtained statehood in 1991. The largest of the new states, the Russian Federation, is a patchwork of at least fifty-three ethnic groups. Meanwhile twenty five million Russians live in the 'near abroad', the smaller successor states that surround Russia.⁵³

With the break-up of the Soviet Union, Russia lost its recently acquired borderlands and its Slavic heartland of Ukraine and Belarus. It is by no means clear that the shrinking of the territory under the control of Moscow has come to an end. Secessionist movements in the Caucasus are the most obvious example of the potential for further disintegration.

For those who desire that Russia make the transition from empire to nation-state, this shrinking was a positive development. The Russian Federation is much more Russian than its Tsarist and Soviet predecessors. In the Tsarist and Soviet periods, Russians constituted only about half the population of the state whereas about 80% of the post-Communist Russian Federation is ethnically Russian. At the same time, Russia is more firmly placed in the Asian part of the Eurasian land mass than it ever was during Tsarist or Soviet times.

Some definitions are needed at this point. Katherine Verdery has claimed that 'concepts of nation and nationalism became so vast and so interdisciplinary over the last thirty years that they rivalled all other contemporary foci of intellectual production'.⁵⁴ It is into this huge literature that we need to delve for an understanding of Fomenko's mental universe.

Terms such as patriotism and nationalism are used frequently in this book. Patriotism seems less problematic and can be defined as strongly

---

51   McDaniel, *The Agony of the Russian Idea*, 22-23.
52   Tolz, *Russia*, 204-07.
53   Jeff Chinn and Robert Kaiser (eds), *Russians as the new minority: ethnicity and nationalism in the Soviet successor states* (Boulder: Westview Press, 1996), 3.
54   Katherine Verdery, 'Whither "nation" and "nationalism"?' *Daedalus* 122:3 (Summer 1993): 37.

positive feelings towards one's homeland.[55] On the other hand, Verdery has warned that assuming nation and nationalism to be the same is a simplification often found in the literature. She endorses Eric Hobsbawm who distinguishes between the nation as citizenship, 'in which the nation consists of collective sovereignty based in common political participation', and the nation as ethnicity, 'in which the nation comprises all those of supposedly common language, history, or broader cultural identity'.[56] The only agreement in the literature about nation and nationalism, according to David Rowley, concerns what nationalism is. Rowley argues that there is general acceptance of the definition provided by Ernst Gellner. According to Gellner, 'Nationalism is primarily a political principle which holds that the political and the national unit should be congruent'.[57]

The problem is that once we define nationalism in that way, there seems to be little application to Russia. Most scholars agree that nationalism did not develop in Russia as it did in the West. Rowley has argued that what we call Russian nationalism is usually Russian imperialism.[58] Hosking points out that Russian nationalism remained undeveloped because the imperial and Communist states were dedicated to the pursuit of a multi-national empire.[59] For Hosking, the most important fact about Russian history was that in Russia 'the empire has always oppressed the nation. State building has impeded nation building'.[60] Nationalism, a child of nineteenth and twentieth century Europe, had no opportunity to grow in Russia.

The peculiar nature of Russian self-identity has to be viewed in context. Nationalism was triumphant in Europe in 1918 everywhere except Russia. Khazanov points out that the Ottoman and Habsburg Empires were no less prone than Russia to nationalism because all three encompassed remarkable ethnic diversity, administrative and political borders that did not match ethnic or religious boundaries, and different levels of economic prosperity between regions and nations. Before World War One, ethnic minorities comprised

---

55 See, for example, David Brandenberger, *National Bolshevism: Stalinist Mass Culture and the formation of modern Russian national identity, 1931-1956* (Cambridge: Harvard University press, MA, 2002), 12-13.
56 Verdery, 'Whither "nation" and "nationalism"?' 37-38.
57 David Rowley, 'Imperial versus nationalist Discourse: the case of Russia,' *Nations and Nationalism* 6:1 24.
58 *Ibid.*, 25.
59 Geoffrey Hosking, *Russia and the Russians* (Penguin, 2002), 456-7.
60 Geoffrey Hosking, 'The Russian Myth; Empire and People', in Duncan and Rady (eds), *Towards a New Community: Culture and Politics in Post-Totalitarian Europe* (Hamburg and Munster: LIT Verlag), 37.

approximately half of most European states. By 1919, after the self-determination championed by Woodrow Wilson was selectively implemented, this figure was reduced to a quarter.[61] The Russian Empire, by contrast, more or less became the Soviet Union minus Finland, Poland, the Baltic States and Bessarabia. Thus, the Russians remained part of an imperial world, forming only half the population of the land they dominated. Other states, like former Yugoslavia, saw attempts to build a state from many nations, but there was nowhere anything that resembled the magnitude of the Soviet Union. Unlike the British Empire of the nineteenth century, the continental Russian empire and its newly acquired colonies formed a single territorial domain. Therefore it was more difficult for Russians than for the British to make distinctions between the peoples of metropolis and the peoples of the periphery.

Modern Western historians of Russia tend to think that patriotism was in short supply among Russia's lower classes until the twentieth century. A recent account of Russian and Soviet national identity noted that Russian peasants were local and religious in orientation.[62] Tolstoy, for example, claimed that he never heard any of his peasants admitting to patriotic feelings but only 'the most utter indifference or even contempt for every kind of patriotism'.[63] Sarah Davies in her study of letters written in the 1930s noted that ordinary Russians did not seem to have a clear idea of who they were except in terms of who they were not, that is Jews, Armenians and so on.[64]

This type of evidence is usually met with suspicion and disbelief by Russian patriots. For them, Russians have always been as enthusiastically loyal to their country as they are today. To prove that this patriotism was neither imagined nor invented, ancient examples of patriotism are often cited. Herodotus's account of Scythian renegades who adopted Greek customs and were then murdered by their countrymen for lack of patriotism is taken as evidence that Russian-style patriotism was alive and well in the era of classical Greece. Russian patriots use more recent examples to confirm the trend. They point to the classics of medieval Russian literature such as *The Lay of Igor's Host*, an appeal to a sense of collectivity among the peoples of Kiev Rus in connection to a military campaign against the neighbouring

---

61 Anatolii M. Khazanov, 'Ethnic nationalism in the Russian Federation,' 121.
62 David Brandenberger, *National Bolshevism: Stalinist mass culture and the formation of modern Russian national identity, 1931-1956*, 12-13.
63 *Ibid.*
64 Sarah Davies, *Popular Opinion in Stalin's Russia: terror, propaganda, and dissent, 1934-1941* (Cambridge: Cambridge University Press, 1997), 88-89.

Polovtsy in 1186. The unknown author of *The Lay of Igor's Host* lamented the death of Prince Igor, and summoned princes from beyond Kiev to come forward to fight for the land of Rus as if it were their land too.[65] These same patriots claim that anti-German feelings among the Slavs can be traced back at least to the famous plea made in 1659 by Krizanic, a Croat and Roman Catholic priest, who appealed to Tsar Alexis 'to succour the Trans-Danubians, Poles and Czechs, to begin to know their oppressed and shameful state and to think about the enlightenment of the people that they might take the German yoke from their necks'.[66]

Thus, there is a vast gulf in understandings of nationalism between its practitioners and its theorists. Most theorists of nationalism believe that nationalism is a strictly modern phenomenon. Brubaker noted that the idea that the nation or ethnic groups are primordial and eternal is completely dead among academics but is often resuscitated at a popular political level.[67] Gellner traced nationalism to the need for industrial society to find a means of connecting individuals who had abandoned the collectivist principles of the village. Anderson's imagined communities arose from the coming of print culture, which made it possible for utter strangers to think of themselves as kin.

Other well-known theorists like Anthony D. Smith and Adrian Hastings are willing to concede to the advocates of nationalism that the roots of the phenomenon, proto-nationalism, extend deep into history.[68] The pre-modern attachment to an *ethnie*, in Smith's view resembled and to an extent gave rise to the modern sense of national identity. Nations are different to *ethnies* because they are more complex and rely upon citizenship, economic integration, and a collective's consciousness of being part of a particular nation. Proto-nationalism is not in itself nationalism.

Smith described the nation as a 'named human population sharing an historic territory, common myths and historical memories, a mass public culture, a common economy and common legal rights and duties for all

---

65 'Slovo o pogibeli Russkoi zemli' in *Drevnerusskaia literatura* (Moscow: Shkola, 1993), 135.
66 See Michael Boro Petrovich, *The Emergence of Russian Panslavism, 1856-1870* (New York: Columbia University Press, 1956), 7.
67 Roger Brubaker, *Nationalism Reframed, Nationhood and the National question in the New Europe* (Cambridge: Cambridge University press, 1996), 15.
68 Adrian Hastings, *The construction of nationhood: ethnicity, religion, and nationalism* (Cambridge: Cambridge University Press, 1997).

members'.[69] Yael Tamir, for one, criticized this definition as confusing causes (for example, the historic territory) and the feeling itself. She prefers a much more subjective definition:

> A nation, then, may be defined as a community whose members share feelings of fraternity, substantial distinctiveness, and exclusivity, as well as beliefs in a common ancestry and a continuous genealogy. Members of such a community are aware not only that they share these feelings and beliefs but that they have an active interest in the preservation and well-being of their community. They thus seek to secure for themselves a public sphere where they can express their identity, practice their culture, and educate their young.[70]

This subjective notion of the nation finds no support in the definition offered by Margaret Canovan. Canovan argues that nations are important to the modern world because they generate the appearance of a family sharing common origins while also aspiring to be impartial to differences within that family. She agrees with Tamir that ethnicity should not matter to membership of a nation but still sees nations as something objective. As she puts it, the British own the complex legacy of the British nation, from the BBC to Shakespeare, and that is the case 'whether we embrace it with open arms or angrily repudiate it'.[71]

It would be possible for a discussion of competing definitions of the nation to continue ad infinitum given that nationalism's many scholars disagree over fundamentals as well as details. In the case of Russia, both subjective and objective definitions operate at the level of popular consciousness. As we shall see, surveys suggest that Russians do not rate bloodlines as a crucial factor in Russian nationality, preferring language and self-identity as markers of who is a Russian.

Russian identity is a distinctive puzzle within the wider debate. It is so puzzling that Tolz has recommended a close reading of all three main approaches to the study of nationalism to address the issue of Russian

---

69   Anthony D. Smith, *The Ethnic Origins of Nations* (Oxford: Blackwell, 1986).
70   Yael Tamir, 'The Enigma of Nationalism,' *World Politics* 47:3 (April 1995): 418.
71   Margaret Canovan, *Nationhood and Political Theory* (Cheltenham: Edward Elgar, 1996), 72.

nationalism.[72] The first approach is the primordialism common among practitioners of nationalism who believe that their nation has always existed. The second approach to nationalism is the 'nation as a modern phenomenon' idea championed by Anderson and Gellner. Most scholarly accounts of nationalism adopt a modernist perspective although it is now under challenge from post-modernists who stress the importance of discourses of nationalism and not simply the list of objective criteria modernists apply to test the presence of nationalism.

Rowley is an example of the post-modern perspective. He claims that Russians, on the surface at least, had all the pre-requisites for a nation according to modernist theorists of nationalism:

> A European people who make up a large homogenous population, who have inhabited a clearly defined homeland for more than a millennium, who have professed a common religion for 800 years, who speak a common language, who have fought many times against foreign enemies, and who have experienced economic and social modernisation that has gradually accelerated over the last three hundred years.[73]

Nonetheless, Russians lacked a discourse of nationalism and this is why in Rowley's opinion a Russia-dominated state has collapsed twice in the twentieth century - precisely because of a lack of nationalism. Rowley has argued that Russian nationalism finally emerged in the 1990s because a discourse of 'Russia for the Russians' at last came to be deployed by the Russian president, Boris Yeltsin in the last years of the Soviet Union. This last claim is, as we will see, strongly disputed by many historians who look upon Yeltsin's victory as evidence of anger at the Communist system rather than the triumph of a new discourse.[74]

Rowley is however certainly correct when he points out that none of Russia's rulers and only a minority of its political oppositions ever desired to hive Russians off into their own nation state or to assimilate or breed out the non-Russian element. The Russian state was for most Russians the natural

---

72   Tolz, *Russia*, 4.
73   Rowley, 'Imperial Versus Nationalist Discourse,' 24.
74   See for example, Astrid S. Tuminez, 'Nationalism, Ethnic Pressures, and the Break up of the Soviet Union,' *Journal of Cold War Studies* 5:4 (September 1, 2003): 81-90.

home of the Russian people, whom history had chosen and prepared to lead a multi-ethnic state. The fact that this state was an empire did not undermine that conviction. That Russians could successfully manage such an empire without racism or any other form of discrimination was at the heart of Russian self-belief.

The tsars promoted the idea of Russian greatness and, at least from the nineteenth century, took pride in the unity of the peoples of the Tsarist Empire under Romanov rule. Peter the Great is widely credited with having been the creator of the modern Russian state, the revolutionary who waged war against an outdated medieval system of government, church and customs. The service state that emerged was aimed at ensuring Russia's competitiveness in the struggle for mastery of northern Europe. Its principal legacy was a Westernised elite divorced from a mainly traditionalist and rural population.[75] Neither this elite nor Peter's successors could envisage Russia as anything other than an empire.

After Peter, it took another century for Russian rulers to formulate an official vision of what Russia was. Under Tsar Nicholas the First and his Minister for Education, Uvarov, the trinity of 'Autocracy, Orthodoxy and Narodnost'' was coined. *Narodnost'* or nationality, the third pillar of the Nikolaevan trinity, conveys a sense of unity of the peoples of Eurasia. *Narodnost'* is deliberately vague in the way it evokes a bond between the peoples of Russia and the land they occupy. It was in effect an antidote to nations within the Russian empire seeking their own states. Its aim was to bind the people of Russia together by stating that they were special and morally superior to the West.[76]

The first Russian historians – Tatishchev, Lomonosov and Karamzin - were fervent monarchists as well as patriots whose histories were directed towards explaining and justifying the emergence of imperial power in Russia. Tatishchev thought that Russia would develop into a single community rallied around the rule of law and monarchy.[77] Tatishchev's aim was to sell an image of empire to the newly acquired lands as the only way to consolidate Russia's restive frontier.[78] Lomonosov made it clear in a letter to Voltaire that history

---

75   McDaniel, *The Agony of the Russian Idea*, 10.
76   Nicholas Riasanovsky, *Nicholas I and official nationality in Russia, 1825-1855* (Berkley: University of California Press, 1959), 266-72.
77   Rudolph Daniels, *V. N. Tatishchev, Guardian of the Petrine Revolution* (Philadelphia: Franklin Publishing Company), 95.
78   Daniels, *V. N. Tatishchev*, 65.

should be written with criticisms of Peter the Great left out.[79] Karamzin, Russia's most popular nineteenth–century historian, praised the Romanovs who well knew that 'our ancestors, while assimilating many advantages which were to be found in foreign customs, never lost the conviction that an Orthodox Russian was the most perfect citizen and Holy Rus' the foremost state in the world'.[80] Nor did history writing fall under the influence of Western-style nationalism and its liberal underbelly in the remainder of the nineteenth century. Black's study of the state school historians of the nineteenth century concluded that Karamzin, Soloviev and Kavelin were united in their Great Russian patriotism and their opposition to liberalism, that 'ulcer of our landed society' in Soloviev's phrase.[81]

These were not historians likely to inspire nationalism of the type that swept Europe during and after the era of the French Revolution. There was patriotism but no liberalism of the type common among nineteenth century nationalists in Europe. At the same time, ethnic nationalism of the type criticized by Hobsbawm or Verdery did not flourish either. The tsars rejected any form of nationalism among their subjects as potentially dangerous to the regime. The resistance of Tatars and Bashkirs was put down with much severity and labelled as the rebellion of bandits and thieves. The Tsar was the steward of the peoples of this land, an image that tapped into the oldest form of customary practice or group instinct with the aim of enhancing the prestige of the monarch. This approach profited also from the belief that foreigners, whether from east or west, were evil. The iron curtain of medieval Russia that West European travellers wrote so much about encouraged the circulation of wild rumours in Russia about the West, contributing to xenophobia.[82]

Anderson and Nigel Harris look upon the russifying policies of Alexander the Third as evidence that Russian nationalism was a factor in Tsarist policies.[83] Rowley argues, however, that what is usually regarded as

---

79   See Walter Gleason, 'The Course of Russian History According to an Eighteenth-Century Layman,' *Laurentian University Review* 10:1 (1977): 26.
80   Edward C Thaden, *The Rise of Historicism in Russia* (New York: Peter Land, 1999), 17.
81   Joseph Lawrence Black, 'The State School Interpretation of Russian History: A reappraisal of its genetic origins,' *Jahrbücher for Geschichte Osteuropas* 21 (1973): 521.
82   Marshall Poe, *A people born to slavery: Russia in early modern European ethnography, 1476-1748* (Ithaca: Cornell University Press, 2000).
83   Benedict Anderson, *Imagined Communities* (London: Verso, 1983), 84 and Nigel

russification under Alexander the Third and Nicholas the Second from 1881 to 1905 was so half-hearted that it amounted to little more than an attempt to modernize the Russian Empire to ensure its loyalty and fitness for the next war.[84] Thus Russification was mainly directed at Ukrainians and Poles, not the peoples of the Caucasus or Central Asia. Tuminez has pointed out that 'Russification did not elicit great enthusiasm among Russians – even those who were ethnic nationalists'.[85]

The Russian tsars ended up with the worst of both worlds because the perception, if not the reality, of Russian chauvinism spurred nationalist sentiment at the periphery. Like so many Tsarist tactics, half-hearted Russification backfired when it provoked nationalist sentiment at the edges of empire in 1905 and 1917. As Seton Watson put it, 1905 was 'as much a revolution of the non-Russian against Russification as it was a revolution of workers, peasants and radical intellectuals against autocracy. The two revolts were, of course, connected: the social revolution was in fact most bitter in non-Russian regions, with Polish workers, Latvian peasants and Georgian peasants as protagonists'.[86]

On the other hand, Russia was not sufficiently russified to provide the necessary glue to hold Russia together in World War One. Dominic Lieven has pointed out that nationalism and pan-Slav sentiment were present among the factors that led Russia into World War One but was not the main factor.[87] As Nathaniel Knight has put it, 'Despite vigorous efforts to make autocracy national, nationality in Imperial Russia would never be an effective means of mobilization'.[88] When the Tsarist regime collapsed in 1917, it disappeared almost overnight as if it were a hollow shell. The historian Vasilii Rozanov wrote in 1917: 'Russia has collapsed in two or three days... it was more difficult to shut down the office of chauvinistic *Novoe Vremia*, than to shut down all of Russia...there is no Tsardom, no Church, no army... what is left behind? Absolutely nothing'.[89]

Harris, *National Liberation* (London: Penguin Books, 1992), 77.
84 Rowley, 'Imperial versus Nationalist Discourse,' 25-27.
85 Tuminez, *Russian Nationalism Since 1856*, 40.
86 Hugh Seton-Watson, *Nations and States* (London: Methuen, 1982), 87.
87 Dominic Lieven, *Russia and the origins of the First World War* (London: Macmillan Press, 1983), 37.
88 Nathaniel Knight, 'Ethnicity, Nationality and the Masses: Narodnost' and Modernity in Imperial Russia,' in David Hoffman and Yanni Kotsonis (eds), *Russian Modernity: Politics, Knowledge, Practices* (New York: St. Martin's Press, 2000), 59.
89 Vasilii Rozanov, *O Sebe i Zhizni Svoei* (Moscow: Respublika, 1990), 579.

There have been many opposition groups to the tsars but few signs of anything other than an imperial mentality. Nicholas the First's coronation in 1825 was the object of an assassination plot by Decembrists inspired by Western political ideas. Nicholas the First ordered the suppression of the demonstrators whose leaders were hanged or exiled to Siberia. Yanov finds in the Decembrist movement a 'liberal alternative to empire in Russia' and cites Sergei Trubetskoi's advocacy of federalism in the constitution to be introduced after a Decembrist victory.[90]

But while the Decembrists were influenced by Western ideas of representative government, their leaders showed no consistent loyalty to the establishment of Western-style liberalism in Russia. Pavel Pestel, the leader of the Southern Society, emphasised the unity of Russia, which was to be strengthened in the future once non-Slavs lost their identities and merged into a 'single united Russian people'.[91] In his own way Pestel was a nationalist who advocated the independence of Poland. Yet neither Pestel nor Trubetskoi could imagine Russia cut off from the bulk of the empire that the tsars had accumulated.

In Rowley's account, Russian Westernizers were often not liberals and usually were closet imperialists. Before 1991, the Provisional Government that replaced the tsar in March 1917 could claim to have been the only liberal government in Russia's history. Yet this government risked everything by aggressively committing itself to a new offensive in July 1917, inspired by the territorial rewards promised Russia after the defeat of the German, Austro-Hungarian and Ottoman Empires.[92] Leading Westernizers of this era, such as Pavel Miliukov, were as keen on Russia's imperial expansion as the tsars were. In the 1990s, the post-communist governments of Yeltsin and Putin went to war twice over Chechnya to prevent what they perceived to be the dismemberment of Russia at the hands of nationalist separatists. To achieve this goal of state unity at the expense of nationalism, Yeltsin and Putin were prepared to jettison their credentials as post-Communist liberal reformers. It is true that elites within Russia acted to abolish the Soviet Union in 1991 but this was a 'revolution from above' carried out without popular consultation.

This does not mean that this aspect of Russian mentality betrays a fondness for non-Russians. As we shall see, opinion polls suggest there is

---

90   Alexander Yanov, 'Russian nationalism in Western studies,' 555.
91   Tolz, *Russia*, 195-96.
92   Rowley, 'Imperial versus Nationalist Discourse,' 26.

considerable Russian hostility towards people from central Asia or the Caucasus. But there is an equally strong view that Russians brought development and civilisation to these areas and that, for example, if Chechnya did gain independence, Chechens should be entitled only to their allegedly traditional homeland in the mountains.

Russia did produce its own conservative romantics of the type that helped to create modern nationalism in Western Europe. These were the Slavophiles who railed against Western influence in Russia and the repressions carried out under the government of Nicholas the First. From its origins in the 1830s and 40s, Slavophilism became a way of life and a moral conviction. Slavophiles derived their inspiration from the image of a golden age of pre-Petrine Russia when there were few Western influences in Russia, the bureaucracy was relatively small, and the Tsar lived, at least in theory, as a demigod in harmony with his people.

Yet while critical of Peter the Great's reforms, the Slavophiles did not represent a nationalist alternative as they were firmly committed to the ideal of the Tsar and Orthodoxy as the foundations on which Russia was based as opposed to the political liberalism emanating from the West.[93] Slavophiles exalted Russia's natural qualities, arguing the spiritual superiority of Russia and that Moscow was a Third Rome. For Slavophiles, the world of the Orthodox Slavs was a single whole and its division into separate nation states unnatural.

Slavophiles most clearly propounded the idea of Russia as a nation of all eastern Slavs, united by common origin and culture.[94] In the nineteenth century, Russians tended to consider the Slavic parts of the Russian Empire as their domain and to relegate Central Asia and the Caucasus to the status of colonies. It was not just Slavophiles who saw Russia this way. Kliuchevskii wrote about Russians, Bielorussians and Ukrainians as if there were no differences between them, all part of a single Russia tied to the Russian land.[95] In the second half of the nineteenth century, some Slavophiles embraced pan-Slavism, putting pressure upon the Tsarist government to act

---

93   Rowley, 'Imperial versus Nationalist Discourse,' 27.
94   On the Slavophiles see N. L. Brodsky (ed.), *Rannie slavianofily* (Moscow, 1910), XXX-XXXVIII; on Pan Slavists see Mark Bassin, 'Russia between Europe and Asia: The Ideological Construction of Geographical Space,' *Slavic Review* 50:1 (1991): 13; Vladimir Soloviev, *Natsional'nyi vopros v Rossii* (St Petersburg, 1888), 41; Nikolai Berdiaev, *Sud'ba Rossii* (St Petersburg: 1918), 1.
95   Robert Francis Byrnes, *V. O. Kliuchevskii. Historian of Russia* (Bloomington: 1995), 225-229; Vasilii Kliuchevsky, *Kurs russkoi istorii volume* V (Moscow: 1989).

more strongly in defence of Slav interests in the declining Ottoman Empire.[96] This was a war not to align peoples and borders but an expanded Slav empire with Moscow at its centre.

Christopher Ely has argued that the Russian obsession with the beauty of their native land emerged in the nineteenth century as part of the attempt to establish an identity that was distinct from the West.[97] Slavophiles described the land as the soul of Russia.[98] Dostoevsky thought the Russian soul more capable than any other of achieving 'the idea of universal union and brotherhood'.[99] Berdiaev noted that not only have 'vast Russian plains and snowy plains always oppressed the Russian soul' but that Russian geography was an explanation of why individual liberty and social groups had played only a minor role in Russia's history.[100] Just as importantly, there were no natural frontiers to this landscape, encouraging the perception that whenever Russians occupied territory, it was, in fact, Russian territory for good historical reasons.

Very few Russians to this day have ever described themselves as nationalists. As Yanov has put it, 'even the most reactionary nationalist forces ... never call themselves nationalists, only "patriots"'.[101] Tishkov has pointed out that:

> In Russia, nationalism is understood exclusively as ethnic nationalism – and that with a strongly negative connotation. Indeed in the Russian language, the specific term 'ethnonationalism' did not exist: there were simply no other forms of nationalism under discussion.[102]

According to Yanov, the unpopularity of the term 'nationalism' owed its

---

96 David Mackenzie, *Imperial Dreams - Harsh Realities: Tsarist Russian Foreign Policy, 1815-1917* (Greensboro: University of North Carolina, 1994), 57.
97 Christopher Ely, *This Meager Nature: Landscape and National Identity in Imperial Russia* (University of Northern Illinois Press, 2002).
98 Nikolas K. Gvosdev, 'The Slavophiles speak to America,' *Journal of Church and State* 42:1 (Winter 2000): 5.
99 Quoted in Rowley, 'Imperial versus Nationalist Discourse,' 34.
100 Berdiaev, *Syd'ba Rossii, Opyty po Psikhologii Voiny i Natsionalnosti*, 62-63; see also Mark Bassin, 'Turner, Soloviev and the Frontier Hypothesis: The Nationalist Significance of Open Spaces,' *The Journal of Modern History* 65:3 (September 1993): 473-511.
101 Yanov, 'Russian nationalism in Western studies,' 562.
102 Tishkov, *Ethnicity, Nationalism and Conflict in and after the Soviet Union*, 230.

strength in Russia to Vladimir Soloviev, the religious philosopher who feared that Western-style nationalism was in fact xenophobic racism and therefore not a desirable alternative to the equally unhealthy Slavophile *Sonderweg*. Soloviev criticized Russia's foreign policy between the Crimean and Turkish Wars, especially the rise of pan-Slavism. Noting what he regarded as the militant, nationalistic and aggressive policies of the Tsarist government, Soloviev put himself in opposition to the chorus of hawkish Slavophiles who fervently supported wars against the West and the Turks, and who attempted to win support through religious and nationalistic propaganda.

Soloviev argued that the Slavophile route of development chosen by Russia's leaders in the nineteenth century inevitably led to self-destructive nationalism. According to Soloviev, this phenomenon was already in process at the beginning of the nineteenth century, and evolved in law-like fashion: a nation's self consciousness led to national self-satisfaction, which in turn led to national self-adoration and finished in a nation's self--destruction.[103] Meanwhile, Soloviev saw Russia as the key to a much broader problem, that of uniting the various Christians of the world in a single church. In this way, Soloviev himself advocated a messianic role for Russia just as the Slavophiles saw Russia as the light of the Christian world.

On the left, there were political thinkers who recognized the existence of separate nations and who criticized the Russian imperial idea. The anarchist Kropotkin certainly acknowledged the arguments put forward for the existence of nations when he wrote that there was: 'a kind of union between the people and the territory it occupies, from which territory it receives its national character and on which it impresses its own stamp, so as to make an indivisible whole both men and territory'.[104] According to Rowley, the populists of the nineteenth century could also be considered nationalists.[105] Lenin too was in his own way a believer in the reality of nations even if he despised nationalism. In 1917 Lenin seized his opportunity to appeal to the peoples of the Tsarist Empire promising them their rights on the grounds that 'all nations have the right to self-determination'.[106] Of course, there was a cynical side to these appeals given that Lenin looked upon nationalism as a transitory phase

---

103 For a concise and very sympathetic description, see Alexander Yanov, 'Russian nationalism in Western studies: misadventures of a Moribund paradigm,' 562-64.
104 'Kropotkin and the Anarchist Movement,' in J. Cahn and Eric Fisera, ed., *Socialism and Nationalism* vol. I (1987), 50.
105 Rowley, 27.
106 Quoted in Nigel Harris, *National Liberation* (I. B. Tauris, 1990), 88.

in history's movement towards Communism. As another leading Communist and Marxist, Piatakov, put it, 'once we unite the economy and build one apparatus...all this notorious self-determination will not be worth one rotten egg'.[107]

Yet, as Slezkine has pointed out, Lenin and Stalin were, surprisingly for Marxists, prepared to accept nations as the basic building blocks in the world in which they lived.[108] The Soviet government went out of its way to divide its territory into nationally based regions with their own language and, where possible, ethnic bureaucracy. For Lenin, as for Kropotkin or the Populists, nationalism was not however an end in itself.

Lenin was fortunate too that while Ukrainian or Georgian states emerged briefly after 1917, they proved unstable and were easily toppled. Lenin could rely upon the fact that the underdevelopment of nationalism made possible the reestablishment of a multi-national empire without the danger of new civil wars. At the same time the linking of territoriality and ethnicity in the form of union republics helped to ensure that nationality eventually gained a new importance in a 'state of all the people'.[109]

Under Stalin, Communist nationalistic ideology had a dual character just like its Tsarist predecessor. One side was anti-Western and promised the export of the Russian revolution. The other side focused upon the creation of a new type of individual who ideally would be nationalist in form but socialist in content. It was the reinterpretation of Nicholas the First's trinity, where autocracy was preserved in the form of Communist dictatorship, Orthodoxy was replaced with communist ideology, and *narodnost'* found expression in multi-ethnic 'new Soviet man'.

Brandenberger has pointed out that Soviet internationalism quickly degenerated into Russo-centric patriotism especially after 1937 when Stalin launched a propaganda barrage aimed at exposing the evil deeds of the German and Polish governments. Still, this was state building from above and not nationalism from below.[110] Part of this war against the West was a closer integration of the Russian east, that is, Central Asia, as well as the Caucasus and Siberia, into the Soviet mainstream. Stalin himself took every opportunity

---

107   Nigel Harris, *National Liberation*, 88.
108   Yuri Slezkine, 'The USSR as a Communal Apartment, or How a Socialist State promoted Ethnic Particularism,' in Geoff Eley and Ronald Grigor Suny (eds), *Becoming National: a Reader* (London: Oxford University Press, 1996), 204-06.
109   Ronald Suny, *The Revenge of the Past* (Stanford: Stanford University Press, 1993), 84-126.
110   Brandenberger, *National Bolshevism*, 109.

to be photographed posing with representatives of the Soviet borderlands as if all of Eurasia was united with him in resistance to the evil of the West.

Ultimately, the Soviet government created pliant republics on the territory of the former Russian Empire; no republic seceded from the Soviet Union until its collapse. Nonetheless, the very act of allowing Ukrainians or Georgians a homeland and the opportunity to use their native language contributed to the collapse of 1991 by creating obvious successor states. When the Soviet Union came to an end in 1991, it broke up into the fifteen national republics. On the other hand, the status of the Russian Socialist Federal Republic within the Soviet Union was unclear given that the Russians, unlike other nationalities, did not have their own Communist Party or educational institutions. Thus many Russians identified themselves with the Soviet Union as if it were their nation-state.[111]

Rowley has argued that the events of 1991 broke the pattern of Russian history and that Yeltsin was the first Russian politician to successfully deploy the discourse of nationalism.[112] Nationalism may have been an important factor in the end of the Soviet Union but historians are clearly split on this issue. As his experiment with a mixed market economy collapsed around him, Gorbachev found that political elites in the non-Russian republics of the Soviet Union resorted to ethnic nationalism as a first port of call once it was clear that Communism was nearing the end of its life. According to Khazanov 'loyalty to one's nationality was stronger than loyalty to the Soviet state. In all, nationalism in the communist countries remained a Trojan horse, hiding a number of possible outcomes. When communism collapsed, the unsolved problems immediately surfaced'.[113]

On the other hand, Brudny has argued that Yeltsin was not a nationalist at all and his discourse of Russia for the Russians was simply a manoeuvre against his rival, Gorbachev.[114] The evidence that his electoral success reflected the enthusiastic response of voters to a new discourse of nationalism remains controversial and many writers believe that the election of 1990 was nothing more than a vote against Gorbachev and seventy years of Communist rule.[115] Even Rowley acknowledges that it is by no means

---

111 Brudny, *Reinventing Russia: Russian Nationalism and the Soviet State, 1953-1991*, 7.
112 Rowley, 'Imperial versus Nationalist Discourse,' 35-36.
113 Khazanov, 'Ethnic nationalism in the Russian Federation,' 122.
114 Brudny, *Reinventing Rusia*, 262.
115 See Malia, Martin, *The Soviet Tragedy. A History of Socialism in Russia, 1917-1991*

certain that the present efforts to transform Russia into a nation-state will not be reversed at some point in the future. The fact that support for the nation state remained unstable for the remainder of the 1990s casts doubt upon Rowley's conclusion that, at the beginning of the decade, a change in Russian mentality had taken place.

I.2 Nationalism and Post-Communism

In her study of post-Communist Russian nationalism, Tolz has identified five nation-building projects under way in Russia since the fall of Communism in 1991. Proponents of these five projects envision Russia as an empire, as a union of the East Slavs, as a union of Russian speakers, as a biological entity or as a Western-style nation state.[116] Hosking has produced a similar list, arguing that the new post-Communist Russia must choose either to restore the Tsarist and Soviet empire, to reunite with Ukrainians and Bielorussians as a nation of eastern Slavs, to reconstitute Russia on the basis of Russian speakers, incorporating Russian- speaking areas like northern Kazakhstan in the process, or build a Western-style nation state dedicated to the principles of civic and not ethnic nationalism.[117] Only the Western-style nation state is a new idea in Russian history.

Russian writers have often evoked a sense of crisis and Messianism to argue the case for the new. Chaadaev, a champion of Russian Westerners, argued that Russia had given the world nothing of value because she had not yet created anything to give. The philosopher Herzen wrote of the defeat of the Decembrists that there was 'complete emptiness and vacuum' in a society 'that was disoriented and afraid. Where was the exit out of such a ridiculous and painful situation, where was it? There was no exit'.[118] For Lenin and the Bolsheviks, the Tsarist state was a grotesque hulk that had to be demolished in its entirety if a better Russia were to emerge.

The liberal reformers who dominated the first post-Soviet government of president Boris Yeltsin were similarly apocalyptic in their declarations about

---

(New York: The Free Press, 1994), or Astrid Tuminez, 'Nationalism, Ethnic Pressures, and the Break-up of the Soviet Union,' 81-136.
116   Vera Tolz, 'Forging the nation: National identity and nation building in post-Communist Russia,' *Europe-Asia Studies* 50:6 (September 1998): 993.
117   Hosking, *Russia and the Russians*, 56-7.
118   Alexander Herzen, *Byloe i Dumy* (Leningrad: 1947), 291.

Russia. They took seriously the euphoria embodied in the idea that the end of communism in 1991 represented the 'end of history' as Francis Fukuyama had declared in his work of the same title.[119] A miracle of the market economy was supposed to fix the mistakes of history through the invisible hand of competition. By the end of the decade, liberal reformers in Russia had lost the optimism of the early 1990s.

The first Yeltsin government embraced Western-style democracy not only in its enthusiasm for the market economy, but in its definition of what the Russian nation was. Since 1991, the Russian Federation has defined itself in civic terms – its members are Russian citizens or *Rossiiane*, and not ethnic Russians or *Russkie*. Anyone living on the territory of the Russian Federation at the time of the law's adoption on 28 November 1991 automatically became a citizen of the Russian Federation. It was hoped that economic success and a genuinely federal structure would ensure that nationalism would not tear apart the former Soviet Union as it had done the former Yugoslavia.[120]

According to Davies, in the years 1991-92, it seemed that the Communist era had been discarded forever by Russian intellectuals, such was the momentum of the pro-Western mood in the wake of the failed coup of 1991. Subsequent economic difficulties then caused disillusionment and a revival of interest in the Soviet past and its predecessors.[121] Liberal optimism after the collapse of Communism was partly inspired by the hope of a civic nationalism that would prove its strength before an expansionist ethnic nationalism had an opportunity to impose itself on the popular imagination. The dominant trend in Western thinking about nationalism regarded its subject as in important respects a social construction rather than an essential part of nature. It followed that the basic assumption of most Russians that national feeling was primordial and unchanging could be modified to suit the new capitalist, democratic Russia that was striving to prove that it was ready to take its place among the great powers in the post-Communist world.[122]

It is still not clear how successful this strategy will prove. Commentators point to the fact that economic and political reforms have changed to more state-oriented policies since the liberal heyday of the early 1990s. Brudny concluded that Russia's liberal reformers squandered their opportunity when their popularity was at its height in the early 1990s to develop an inspiring

---

119 McDaniel, *The Agony of the Russian Idea*, 178.
120 Tolz, *Russia*, 125.
121 Davies, *Soviet History in the Yeltsin Era*, VII.
122 Tolz, *Russia*, 207.

ideology to legitimise democracy, market capitalism, and the pre-imperial borders of Russia.[123] Recently, the two Russian liberal parties, the Union of Right Forces and Iabloko, failed to cross the threshold of five percent and, as a consequence, the economic revolutionaries of the early 1990s are no longer represented in the Duma. For critics, the dominating presence of Putin as President for much of the first decade of the twentieth century was clear evidence that Russia was reverting to its autocratic and imperial roots. According to former Prime Minister Gaidar, the contest now is for 'who will be most anti-Semitic, who will be blaming the non-Russians for Russian problems, who will be most anti-American'.[124] Critics of the 'shock therapy' approach taken by liberal economic reformers in the 1990s would respond that the reformers brought this development upon themselves.

The idea of shaping a Russian nation state might seem feasible to those who, following Gellner and Anderson, think that nationalism is modern, invented or imagined and therefore can be shaped, and not an unchanging and primordial fact. Irrespective of where nations come from, Russians have very little experience of conceiving Russia in terms of a voluntary association confined to a particular historic space. The combination of nationalism and liberalism was not a significant political force in Russia until the collapse of Communism.

Opinion polls suggest that factors other than citizenship are crucial to the self-identity of Russians. In her study, Tolz relied upon surveys conducted between 1992 and 1997 by the Moscow-based Public Opinion Foundation.[125] In a poll conducted in February 1995 by Igor Klyamkin, Russians throughout the Russian Federation were asked to name characteristics that they thought were `necessary for a Russian'. From the Klyamkin survey, the following answers were the most popular: to love Russia and view it as a homeland (87%), to know and love Russian culture (84%), to have Russian as a native language (80%), to regard oneself as a Russian (79%), to have Russian citizenship (59%), to be identified as Russian on an internal passport (24%), to have Russian parents (24%), to have Russian physical appearance (22%). These results seem consistent with other polls. It would seem that Russians

---

123 Brudny, *Reinventing Russia: Russian Nationalism and the Soviet State, 1953-1991*, 259-65.
124 Quoted in 'Former PM decries Russian nationalism', *United Press International* (January 28, 2004): 1.
125 Tolz, *Forging the nation: National identity and nation building in post-Communist Russia*, 993.

prefer a definition that is subjective and inclusive (love of Russia and its culture and knowledge of the language) rather than prescriptive and objective (genealogy or official status).

Slavophiles represent a group that seem well suited to capitalize upon the sentiments expressed in the poll cited above. Slavophiles argue for a Russia that includes traditional Slavic lands, Ukraine, Belarus and northern Kazakhstan. This movement's most famous spokesman, Alexander Solzhenitsyn, was hailed as 'a moral compass for the nation' when he returned to Russia in 1994.[126] Solzhenitsyn's orientation was Slavic. He thought it best if Russia, Belarus and Ukraine were to cut off the stagnant Asian underbelly.

Yet Slavophiles suffered some devastating blows during the 1990s. Many Russians were surprised and saddened that in Ukraine almost 75% of voting residents cast their votes in favour of independence in 1991. The process of nation building that has taken place in the 'Slavic' republics of Ukraine and Belarus has proceeded more quickly than many Russians expected. Solzhenitsyn's declining influence in the 1990s when he was fired from his increasingly unpopular weekly radio and television appearances, mirrored the decline of Slavophilism itself.

Ukrainian and Belarus historians actively promote the separate historical origins of the three East Slav peoples. The important implication of this view of history is that the merger with Russia in the seventeenth and eighteenth centuries did not mean the 're-unification of the indigenous Russian lands', as Russians would have it. For Ukrainian nationalists in particular, this was an imperial conquest, a destruction of two European and democratic states by a semi-Asiatic Russian despotism. Outside of Russia, those who fear Russian expansionism see Ukraine as especially significant. According to Brzezinski: 'It cannot be stressed strongly enough that without Ukraine, Russia ceases to be an empire, but with Ukraine suborned and then subordinated, Russia automatically becomes an empire'.[127]

An emphasis upon language is a more inclusive definition of Russia and potentially offers a basis for the emergence of a nation state of the type that Solzhenitsyn would approve. There is support in opinion polls for viewing Russians as a community of Russian speakers, regardless of their ethnic

---

126 Nina Khrushcheva, 'Solzhenitsyn's History Lesson,' *The Nation* 268:16 (May 3 1999): 32.
127 Zbigniew Brzezinski, 'The Premature Partnership,' *Foreign Affairs* (March/April 1994): 80.

origin. Because Russian was widely spoken in the Soviet Union from Ukraine to Central Asia, this vision of Russia potentially entails the recreation of a substantial part of the Russian Empire or Soviet Union. Apart from ethnic Russians, there seems little momentum in Ukraine, Belarus or Kazakhstan for this type of redrawing of borders to occur.

The exponents of a racial view of Russia included anti-Semitic groups like the 'Black Hundreds' of the early part of the twentieth century and some modern neo-Nazis. Commentators complain that neo-Nazism is a growing phenomenon in Russia. Racist groups target Central Asians and Muslim peoples of the North Caucasus even more than Jews who continue to find themselves the subject of hostility and suspicion. Nonetheless, the bloodlines argument still struggles to find support in Russia where most people accept that they were once part of a mingled host. Even Gumilëv who is usually cited as supporting the idea of race seemed confused about whether his category of ethnos is biological or cultural.[128] Most Russian patriots, Fomenko included, would claim that race is an irrelevant concept for multi-ethnic Russia. The Russians play a leading role in Eurasia because they are the most numerous and the most talented in terms of managing such a complex and challenging version of statehood and because the smaller nations welcome their rule. There is however, more potential for arguments about race in the smaller Russia of today and the popularity of Gumilëv may reflect the fact that he discusses race in an academic way, a taboo subject in Soviet times.

The remaining and seemingly the most popular of the models listed by Tolz is the imperial one. As Khazanov has put it: 'It was hard for Russia to free itself from the legacy of the empire, just as it was difficult for many Russians to free themselves from a certain empire-oriented psychology'.[129] The imperial model asserts that the Russians are, for reasons of geography and history, an imperial people whose nature is strongly shaped by their mission to create a supranational state. Imperial thinking is so pervasive that it overlaps with other categories. For Slavophiles, Russians were more spiritual than other peoples,[130] for Tsarist bureaucrats, Russia was a source

---

128   See Viktor Shnirelman, *Who Gets the Past?* (Washington D.C.: John Hopkins University press, 1996), 8.
129   Anatolii Khazanov, *After the USSR: Ethnicity, Nationalism, and Politics in the Commonwealth of Independent States* (Madison, WI: University of Wisconsin Press, 1995), 38.
130   George Fedotov, *The Russian Religious Mind* (Cambridge: Harvard University

of enlightenment for backward neighbours: and, for its generals, Russia provided protection in a hostile environment. The imperial idea is very strong in the works of Russian writers at least from the time of Peter the Great. They agree that building an empire was a historic necessity for Russia given its lack of natural frontiers and the dangers posed to it by its porous borders. This was a tolerant and philanthropic version of empire, 'the only such phenomenon in the world'.[131]

How can Russian patriots support such an opinion when the popular Western image of Tsarist Russia and the Soviet Union was that of a tyrannical despotism? For many Russians, the tsar's empire was widely appreciated and respected by the vast array of peoples who came to be part of the Russian Empire. As proof that this positive view of empire was not simple self-delusion, selective quotation from non-Russian sources is the preferred method of establishing Russia's unique talents in managing a multi-national state. Bismarck (1815-1898), who was Prussian ambassador in St.-Petersburg before he became German chancellor, wrote that:

> The English behave in Asia in a less civilized manner than the Russians... they are too nosy toward the indigenous populations, and try to keep their distance; on the contrary, the Russians are welcoming to the conquered nations, familiarize themselves with the indigenous way of life and assimilate with them.[132]

Among the British, there is Lord Curzon (1859-1925), once viceroy of India and British Foreign Minister, who echoed Bismarck when he wrote 'Russia has a remarkable skill of establishing loyalty and even maintaining good friendship with those whom they have conquered. The Russian becomes as a true brother, he is free of superiority and misconceptions that fuel hatred more than ruthlessness'.[133]

Whatever the truth content of these statements, they accord with the positive self-image many Russians have about their relationship to the non-Russian peoples of the empire and to their fellow Slavs to the west and south.

Press, 1966).
131 This quote is from the philosopher Il'in. See Tolz, *Russia*, 202.
132 Quoted in Vadim Kozhinov, *Istoriia Rossii, sovremennyi vzgliad* (Moscow: Charli, 1997), 75.
133 Quoted in Fedor Nesterov, *Svyaz' Vremen, Opyt Istoricheskoi Publitsistiki* (Moscow: 1980), 107-108.

Timo Piirainen, using interviews with Russian teachers in the mid 1990s, found that his interviewees almost universally thought of Russians as kind and generous, tolerant, and willing to see other's point of view. This self-image coexisted with a view that Russians love their motherland and that nationalism is contrary to the Russian character.[134] For many writers, Russia was a counterbalance to Western models of state building. It was this difference to the West that defined what Russia was.

Russian patriots are almost unique in viewing Russia this way. For advocates of national independence in the former republics of the Soviet Union, the disintegration of the Soviet Union was an inevitable outcome for Europe's last empire. According to the critics, the 'official nationality' of the nineteenth century and Soviet 'internationalism' of the twentieth century were masks that hid the chauvinism of the Great Russians. Russia was, in the phrase of Engels, a prison of the peoples and its demise was inevitable. Richard Pipes has described 'the so-called 'nationality question' in the Soviet Union as a euphemism for what is elsewhere known as imperialism and colonialism'.[135] The Soviet Union and its Tsarist predecessor were different to the United States where a multinational population arose from immigrants whose choice was to leave the countries in which they were born to seek opportunities abroad. The Soviet Union, and the tsars before them, by contrast, achieved ethnic diversity by conquering literally dozens of smaller nations. Russia established a colonial domain while portraying itself as a liberator setting free the less numerous peoples of the borderlands from their German, Austrian, Polish, Ottoman or Tatar enslavers. According to Szporluk, the Soviet Union was simply the Russian Empire.[136] In Benedict Anderson's words, it proved in practice impossible to stretch 'the short, tight skin of the nation over the gigantic body of the empire'.[137]

Russia can be looked upon as distinctive in the European context. This is because the Russian state was the Russian Empire long before nationalism became a powerful force in Europe. Many theorists note that empire is the default category for Russians when thinking about what Russia

---

134 Timo Piirainen, 'The Fall of an Empire, the birth of a Nation: Perceptions of the New Russian National Identity,' in Chris J. Chulos and Timo Piirainen, *The Fall of an Empire, the Birth of a Nation: national identities in Russia* (Aldershot: Ashgate, 2000), 161-95.
135 Richard Pipes, 'Russia's shuddering empire: the prospects for Soviet disunion,' *The New Republic* 201:19 (November 6, 1989): 52.
136 Roman Szporluk, 'After Empire: What?' *Daedalus* 123:3 (Summer 1994): 1.
137 Anderson, *Imagined Communities*, 82.

is. That is, it is not simply a case of homeland nationalism where the emphasis is placed upon reincorporating Russians who live outside of Russia.[138] Nor is it a case of Russification or expelling non-Russians within the borders. Russianness is related to the messianic ideal of presiding over the many peoples of Eurasia to the mutual benefit of Russians and non-Russians alike.

The popular image of Ivan the Terrible sums up the problem well. Maureen Perrie has described how in the Glasnost era, Russian democrats noted Stalin's admiration of Ivan the Terrible and his bloodthirsty purges during the *oprichnina* as embodying all that was wrong with Russia in both the distant and more recent past.[139] Yet Eisenstein's 1944 film about Ivan the Terrible seemed to strike a chord with the Soviet public because it adopted the positive image of 'a people's tsar' whose oprichnina destroyed the power of the greedy hereditary nobles or boyars and because Ivan the Terrible, by conquering Kazan in 1552, was portrayed as finally ending the threat to Russia posed by steppe nomads. These conflicting visions of history remain an important part of Russian cultural life to this day.

This imperial version of the Russian nation has attracted notoriety in the West. In 1993 when Duma elections were held, an alliance emerged between the rump of the Communist Party and a resurgent Russian nationalism.[140] After the Communists first peaked in the 1996 presidential election and then receded, concern in the West focused upon Eurasianism. Eurasianists celebrate Russia as a multi-ethnic, multi-confessional state, an ancient entity that has always existed even if its form or name underwent superficial changes. It is an appropriate name because Eurasia suggests a people who are different to Europeans and to Asians. According to Eurasianist mythology, multi-ethnic Russia embraced Slavic, Finno-Ugric, Tatar-Turkic and even Mongolian and Iranian peoples yet in some intangible way evolved into the Russian nation after centuries of interaction between these peoples. For most Eurasianists, the measuring stick for Russian greatness was Europe and not Asia. Russia needed Asia if it were to be a genuine competitor with the

---

138 Brubaker, *Nationalism Reframed: nationhood and the national question in the New Europe*, 111.
139 Maureen Perrie, *The Cult of Ivan the Terrible in Stalin's Russia* (Palgrave: New York, 2000), 2.
140 See, for example, Judith Devlin, *Slavophiles and commissars: enemies of democracy in modern Russia* (New York: St. Martin's Press, 1999), X-XVI.

West.[141]

There were at least three phases of Eurasianism. The first was a cultural movement best represented in Alexander Blok's poetic homage to the Scyths, the people described by the ancient Greeks who occupied the area north of the Black Sea. It does not matter to Russian patriots that historians came to the conclusion that Scythians most likely employed an Iranian and not a Slavic language. Everything else about them seemed Russian, including their passion for strong drink and bathhouses. Scyths had a reputation as fearsome warriors, the model of an Asian barbarian whose history could be traced back at least to 530 BCE when, Herodotus tells us, Scythian warlords having encountered the Persian army north of the Black Sea vowed to fight protecting not their riches but the burial mounds of their ancestors. This idea inspired the peoples of Eurasia to treasure and protect the land of their grandfathers.

As Blok's poem of 1918 put it when Russia lay seemingly prostrate before the German invader, 'Just try to fight with us!/ Yes we are Scythians! Yes we are Asiatics!/ With slanting and greedy eyes'. Blok expressed the essential elements of the artistic Scythians. Scythianism was a defiant rejection of the West, an assertion of Russia's right to satisfy its greed at the expense of the West, just as the Scythians relied upon their fearsome reputation to maintain independence in the face of the expanding Greek world. It is this version of Eurasianism to which Fomenko is closest embracing as it does a fascination with the strength of Asia but no great love for Asian peoples.

The second phase of Eurasianism was an academic movement formed mainly from émigré writers in the years following the Bolshevik conquest of power. Trubetskoi and his followers mostly lived outside the Soviet Union but sympathized with the Soviet goal of uniting the peoples of Eurasia. In the west, George Vernadsky wrote a positive account of the Mongols and related Russian nationality to its Mongol past.[142] Petr Savitskii embodied the extreme when he described Eurasia as one people in a biological sense given the process of genetic mutation that had taken place during centuries of interaction.[143]

---

141   Mark Bassin, 'Asia', in Nicholas Rzhevsky, ed., *Modern Russian Culture* (Cambridge: Cambridge University Press, 1988), 76-77.
142   See George Vernadsky, *The Mongols and Russia* (New Haven: Yale University Press, 1953).
143   See Tolz, *Russia*, 202.

A third phase comprised scholars writing near the end of the Soviet period and in post-Communist Russia. These scholars attempted to revise the history of the Mongols in a more positive light. Gumilëv argued that the peoples of the earth form various ethnies whose fortunes depend upon the passion or *passionarnost* of brilliant leaders who arise from time to time.[144] One such leader was Genghis Khan, the great Mongol conqueror of the thirteenth century.

Since the collapse of the Soviet Union, Eurasianism seems to have gained more supporters than it has ever had in the past. They have created alarm in the West. Shlapentokh has described the Eurasianists as an emerging totalitarian force in their worship of traditional Russian and eastern models of government.[145] Yanov has argued that a liberal and European Russia is a less likely outcome than an aggressive and Eurasianist one.[146] The political wing of Eurasianism is best articulated by political firebrands like Vladimir Zhirinovsky or Alexander Dugin, the latter claiming that Russia's task consists in 'taking over the Tatar geopolitical mission in the name of Eurasia' of confronting 'the Roman-German world whose pathological culture is a dead-end of degradation and decay'.[147]

Fomenko is closest to the Blok conception of Eurasianism. With the defection of Ukraine and Belarus in 1991, present-day Russia has lost some of its claim to the history of Kiev Rus, the first state of the East Slavs. The major centres of Kiev Rus, with the exception of Novgorod the Great, are now located in Ukraine, not Russia. After Kiev Rus came the Mongols, a dubious legacy for many pseudo-historians despite the prodigious efforts of Gumilëv to generate a positive image of the eastern invaders. Fomenko would prefer to look upon Asia as a crucial second-in-command to Russia in the war against the West and not, as Gumilëv would have it, an equal partner. Ultimately, the Mongols would have to go.

As Blok or Trubetskoi tried to do in the early part of the century, Fomenko is attempting to recruit Asia to the Russian cause in its battle against the West. For Fomenko, Slavophilism is a dead end because, with its emphasis upon ungrateful fellow Slavs, Slavophilism underestimates just how

---

144 Viktor Shnirelman and Sergei Panarin, 'Lev Gumilev: His Pretensions as a Founder of Ethnology and his Eurasian Theories,' *Inner Asia* 3 (2001): 1-18.
145 See, for example, Dmitrii Shlapentokh, 'Russia on the Eve. The Illusions and Realities of Russian Nationalism,' *The Washington Quarterly* 23:1 (2000): 173-186.
146 Alexander Yanov, 'Russian nationalism in Western studies,' 52.
147 Nikolai Trubetskoi, *Nasledie Chingizkhana*, 'Predislovie Alexandra Dugina' (Moscow: 1999), 10.

powerful an empire the Russian Horde once was. Eurasianism is simply too Asian. Fomenko's aim was to find another way to understand Russia's greatness. Most studies of Russian nationalism agree that Russia's path has been, and may well continue to be, unique. A strong sense of a benevolent imperial identity, of greatness past and present, and hostility to the West are common themes in the story of Russia's search for identity. As we shall see, Fomenko's pseudo-history capitalises upon these threads, without which it is difficult to tell a story to Russians about who they are.

II The Rise of Alternative History

II.1 Russian History's Discontents: Lomonosov, Morozov, Fomenko

Fomenko's writing about the past is expansive and diverse and because it has not yet attracted scholarly interest in the literature published in the West, requires some exposition. As Fomenko tells the story, his voyage of historical discovery began in 1973 when he was already a well-established mathematician at Moscow University and when Soviet science was at the height of its powers. Fomenko's career took its first tentative steps in a new direction after he read an article written by an American astronomer Robert Newton who had discovered strange deviations in the behaviour of the moon.[148] Newton's discovery provoked debate in the London Royal Society and British Academy of Sciences, but scientists could not explain the phenomenon. This problem prompted Fomenko to read closely the works of the self-taught astronomer and idiosyncratic polymath, Nikolai Morozov (1854-1946), which, Fomenko claims, he treated with suspicion at first, and which were difficult to find since they had been long forgotten in the Soviet Union.

Morozov is a hero of the alternative historians, a Socialist Revolutionary in his youth whose grandfather was a distant relative of Peter the Great. From 1881 to 1905, Morozov was in prison and used his time to study chronology, mathematics, chemistry and the Bible.[149] For Fomenko, it was Morozov who 'first created a scientific understanding of chronology and introduced important new methods of scientific chronological analysis'. Morozov had some strange ideas. Such was his hatred of the West that he believed that the Mongols actually struck Russia from the West, and not from the Orient as was commonly believed. Fomenko has noted, with some pride, that in 1946, Morozov and Joseph Stalin were two of only three honorary members of the

---

148 Fomenko, *History: Fiction or Science?*, XXX.
149 For an account of Morozov, see *Nikolai Aleksandrovich Morozov 1854-1946*, vstupitel'naia stat'ia Semena Vol'koficha (Moscow: Nauka, 1981), and Semen Vol'fkovich, 'Nikolai Aleksandrovich Morozov, ego zhizn' i trudy po khimii,' *Priroda* 11 (1947).

USSR Academy of the Sciences.[150]

In 1924-1932 Morozov published his last and most comprehensive work, the seven-volume *Khristos* where he elaborated upon his criticisms of conventional chronology and attacked Christianity. According to Morozov, early chronologists had made major errors, and the gaps in their history were papered over with mythical events or repetitions of stories they had already used in connection with other peoples or places. Morozov claimed with good reason that ancient sources used by historians were rarely originals. Instead all we have are copies of copies. For Morozov, these were most likely written during the Renaissance. The so-called Dark Ages that linked classical civilization to the Middle Ages were understandably opaque to the early moderns. According to Morozov, these centuries never existed. They were a figment of the West's imperial imagination.

Using the astronomical table from Morozov's book and applying Robert Newton's mathematical research, Fomenko discovered that the inconsistency and deviations in Newton's calculations concerning the moon could be resolved.[151] This left a much bigger question of global chronology, since the allegedly wrong calculations for the moon were based upon data for earlier lunar eclipses. Fomenko read the work of Immanuel Velikovsky (1895-1979), the Russian-born popular writer who confirmed the strangeness of ancient history. In the modern world, there is more or less continuous progress in civilization even if it is a team effort with sometimes Europe, sometimes the Arab world and sometimes Eurasia or China leading the way. In the ancient world there are gaps and circles where the otherwise curious and competent human race seemed to have fallen backwards in civilizational terms. Velikovsky's notion that catastrophes, even meteor showers, might explain the dark and stagnant periods of ancient history, was not good enough for Fomenko.[152] In the 1980s and 1990s Fomenko promoted the search for a true world chronology in research projects, public appearances, articles, and books.

Fomenko is not the first scientist to question world chronology. Isaac Newton (1643-1727), the great English mathematician and scientist, wrote *The Chronology of Ancient Kingdoms Amended* in which he took issue with the chronology of the ancient Greeks and used astronomy to recalculate well-

---

150   Fomenko, *History: Fiction or Science*, 16.
151   Nosovskii and Fomenko, *Kakoi seichas vek*, 6-7.
152   Guts, *Mnogovariantnaia istoriia Rossii*, 289-90.

known events. Thus, Newton thought that the siege of Troy needed to be moved two hundred years forward from 1183 BCE to 965 BCE. Newton concluded that national vanity caused the Greeks, Latins, Babylonians, Assyrians, and Egyptians, to extend the timelines of their histories.[153]

Fomenko is immodest enough to view himself as part of a tradition established by Isaac Newton. But his real teacher is Morozov who came to the conclusion that two individuals, Scaliger and Petavius, were responsible for the conventional textbook of European and world history. The villain is Scaliger, or Joseph Justus dell Scala (1540-160), the most celebrated scholar of his era. A student of astronomy and history, Scaliger applied textual criticism to ancient Roman works, wrote about ancient astronomy and attempted to make sense of the often contradictory chronology found in the work of Greeks, Romans, Persians and Egyptians.

Fomenko praised Morozov and enthusiastically agreed with his conclusion that Scaliger's ancient chronology was artificially extended. But the pupil found his teacher to be a flawed genius whose works needed substantial correction. Morozov criticized world chronology only for the periods before the sixth century AD. Morozov, in Fomenko's opinion, underestimated the extension of world chronology by one thousand years.

Fomenko insists that his new dates are the result of a complex statistical-mathematical research of the so-called quantitative features of ancient texts and chronicles. What that means is not exactly clear. The calculations are difficult for the non-specialist to follow and the endless tables are no doubt designed to intimidate as much as to impress. On the other hand, the practical implication of Fomenko's method for the historical narrative that we have today is relatively easy to follow. The alternative historical narrative confirms that this is indeed a radical and unlikely

---

[153] Fomenko also counts among his predecessors more obscure critics of conventional chronology such as de Arcilla, a sixteenth century professor of Salamanca University, Jean Hardouin (1646-1729), the French scientist, theologian, archeologist, philologist, historian, and numismatist, who worked as a director of the French Royal Library, and Peter Krekshin (1684-1763), Peter the Great's personal secretary, who wrote a book highly critical of the conventional wisdom about Roman history. Fomenko is in partial agreement with the German Robert Baldouff, a philologist who criticized ancient sources, which, he believed, were written in the middle ages, and with Edwin Johnson (1842-1901), a British historian who thought that existing chronology should be dramatically shortened. Wilhelm Kammeyer (?-1959) is another scientist and lawyer, who developed a method to determine the authenticity of ancient official documents, and discovered, at least to his satisfaction, that a great portion of the allegedly antique and early medieval texts were latter-day forgeries.

reordering of what Fomenko calls the 'consensual history'. The simplified examples he gives rest incongruously alongside the complex mathematics that supposedly underpins this new chronology.

As Fomenko argues, Scaliger's history loops backwards on three occasions, thus creating three chronological shifts of 330 years, 1050 years, and 1800 years. As a consequence the same event is potentially replayed three times. Morozov and Fomenko agree that the Biblical events are much younger than we think. Morozov dated them to the third to fifth centuries AD.[154] According to Fomenko, the main events of the Bible took place in the eleventh and twelfth centuries, which gives a difference of one thousand years compared to Morozov's calculations, and 1800 years compared to Scaliger's chronology.

The events described in the Bible or Scaliger's history mostly did happen, but the chronologists have placed them in the wrong place and time in history. They are a historical mirage or 'phantom' events for Fomenko, in the sense that these events reflect some true picture of past events, but the reflection offers only fleeting clues as to the true timing or location of the event in question. As a renowned scientist, Fomenko could use his scientific prestige to put forward an argument that carbon dating was too unreliable to contradict his more extravagant claims.[155]

For Fomenko, historians and scientists alike tended to be conservative and supportive of the status quo and failed to ask the radical questions.[156] Happily for his readers, Fomenko believes that most dates from the seventeenth century to the present are more or less correct. Happily for Russian nationalists conventional ancient history that marginalised Russia's part in ancient events, needed to be rewritten.

To flesh out his account, Fomenko provided a steady stream of alleged examples of false dating and duplicates. The examples cited by Fomenko include the account of the Peloponnesian War by Thucydides, and the three eclipses in the first, eighth and eighteenth years of the war mentioned by the Greek writer. Looking at this evidence, the astronomer Petavius found the starting point for the Peloponnesian War in 431 BCE. Morozov and Fomenko

---

154 Nikolai Morozov, *Otkrovenie v groze i bure: Istoriia sozdaniia Apokalipsisa*, ed. by V.Sablin, (Moscow: Byloe, 1907); *Proroki. Istoriia vozniknoveniia bibleiskikh prorochestv, ikh literaturnoe izlozhenie i kharakteristika* (Moscow: ob. Sytina, 1914); *Khristos. Istoriia chelovecheskoi kultury v estestvonauchnom osveshchenii*, VII volumes (Moscow-Leningrad: 1924-1932).
155 See Fomenko, *History: Fiction or Science?*, 74-90,
156 Nosovskii and Fomenko, *Bibleiskaia Rus'*, I, 92-104.

IMAGININGS OF THE RUSSIAN PAST   67

instead decided that the eclipses that Thucydides sighted could only have taken place in the thirteenth century AD and that it was only then that the Athenians and Spartans took to fighting. Fomenko finds it incredible that a grammatically complicated and factually rich account such as that of Thucydides, the only one we have detailing the whole of the Peloponnesian War, could have emerged in the fifth century BCE 'when writing materials had been scarce and expensive – the Mesopotamians use styluses to scribble on clay, the Greeks aren't familiar with paper yet, and write on pieces of tree bark or use sticks for writing on wax-covered plaques'.[157]

Why was the name of Tacitus, the celebrated historian of Rome, seldom mentioned before the Italian Renaissance? Here, Fomenko repeats a suggestion already made in the nineteenth century, that the works of Tacitus were a modern forgery. This was no reappearance of interest in a long-lost writer but a first appearance for Tacitus, a historical duplicate for Poggio Bracciolini, the Renaissance writer who provided such detailed descriptions of the Rome of his day. Why do medieval Italians refer to the fourteenth century as the trecento or three hundreds and the sixteenth century as the cinquecento or five hundreds? The Italians wisely ignored a millennium that did not exist.[158]

Fomenko is struck by the high quality of some maps from the early sixteenth century where the eastern coast of both Americas is stunningly accurate and there seem to be accurate glimpses of Greenland, the west coast of the future United States and even Australia. Yet there are other maps from the same era of much poorer quality such as the maps by Hans Rust dating from 1480, or the Venetian Pietro Coppo that appeared in 1528. Venetians were considered to be first class seafarers, but, on Coppos's map, only the Mediterranean is more or less accurately depicted, while the rest of the world is horribly misshapen in comparison to modern maps. According to Fomenko, Rust's and Coppo's maps were undoubtedly true maps of that period, while the higher-quality maps allegedly dating to the sixteenth century were in reality composed in the nineteenth century when knowledge of the world was more or less complete.[159] The genuinely old maps were removed from circulation because of the inconvenient information that could be found

---

157   Fomenko, *History: Fiction or Science?*, 98.
158   *Ibid.*, 25.
159   *Ibid.*, 242.

on them.[160]

Some of that inconvenient information related to what Fomenko calls the Russian Horde and what the West knew as the Golden Horde or Grand Tartaria. Fomenko argues that this mysterious Eurasian empire began in the 1300s when the person whom we currently know as Ivan Kalita, founded not Moscow, as conventional historians believe, but the Russian Horde dynasty.[161] The period of the Russian Horde effectively came to an end only with the Times of Troubles in the seventeenth century, when a new pro-Western pretender, Mikhail Romanov, overthrew the last legitimate tsar of the Russian Horde dynasty, Boris Godunov.[162] The Russian Horde was a multinational entity that once occupied an area roughly comparable to that of ancient Scythia/Sarmatia, the Hunnish conquests, Tsarist Empire, and the Soviet Union. Russia's original homeland was not the Ukrainian rivers or the north-eastern forests near Moscow but the steppe adjacent to the Black and Caspian Seas, to which Fomenko attaches the complex label of the Dnepr-Volga-Don-Ural basin.

Conventional historians often describe the regional and tribal names of groups that have lived in Russia as if they were separate and unrelated peoples–Scythians, Sarmatians, Huns, Goths, Bulgars, then Polyane, Duleby, Severyane, Ulichi, Drevliane, Polovtsy, Pechenegs, and, much later, Cossacks, Muscovites, Ukrainians, Byelorussians. Within each and every group there are often many gradations. For Fomenko, we should see a single ethnos lurking behind mythical and historical names.[163]

The term Mongol, for example, does not refer to the modern Mongol people or to the area we now call Mongolia. As for the 'Mongol' invasion, this was more a civil war between northern and southern factions of the Russian Horde. The Mongols were not a racial type distinguishable by their language, appearance or bloodlines. Relying upon Gumilëv, Fomenko has argued that Mongols of the Borjigin clan, including Genghis Khan, were tall, white-skinned, fair-haired and blue-eyed.[164] As Gumilëv told the story, Mongolian mythology suggests that the mother of this clan was impregnated by the spirit

---

160 Nosovskii and Fomenko, *Bibleiskaia Rus*, II, 157-169.
161 Nosovskii and Fomenko, *Novaia khronologiia Rusi*, 67.
162 *Ibid.*
163 Nosovskii and Fomenko *Imperiia*, 319.
164 Gumilëv, *Drevniaia Rus' i velikaia step'*, 395, 398. Dmitrii Ilovaiskii, the popular anti-Western nineteenth century historian also emphasized that Genghis Khan was most probably of European appearance. See Dmitrii Ilovaiskii, *Stanovlenie Rusi* (Moscow: Charli, 1996), 499.

of a white youth.¹⁶⁵ The proto-mother of the Mongolian ethnos gave birth to three sons. Bodonchar was born from this union, became a famous hunter/warrior and subjugated neighbouring tribes. Many famous Mongols linked their genealogy to Bodonchar, including the Borjigin clan of Genghis Khan. The name 'Borjigin' meant blue-eyed. Blue eyes and blonde, or red, hair were, it seems, considered as proof of a blood connection to Bodonchar.¹⁶⁶ This sort of evidence was confirmation for Fomenko of the extent of the empire of the Russian Horde and the fact that its influence extended well to the east, incorporating Mongolia itself.

Russia's history was indeed ancient. Among the suspect sources Fomenko believes to be genuine is *Kniga Velesa*, a work that first appeared in an émigré journal published by the eccentric folklorist and writer Iurii Miroliubov in the 1950s and purportedly based on oral traditions. According to Fomenko, Kniga Velesa was the work of ninth-century pagan priests of Novgorod and plausibly related the migration of ancient Russians through Siberia to the southwest of Asia, chased southwards by the encroaching ice age. According to specialists, Kniga Velesa is an obvious forgery.

According to Fomenko, it is not just individuals who can have a fluid identity but Russia itself. The kaleidoscope of nationalities and peoples living on Russia's territory represented an ethnos that was bilingual and well-travelled. Conventional historians admit that the famous fifteenth-century Russian traveller Nikitin could move freely in the Muslim world, knowing Russian, Persian, Turkic and Arabic. Why would that not be true of other educated Russians of the fifteenth century when the Slav-Turk Empire was at its height, asks Fomenko? As for the language of the early Slavs, it seems to have lacked the differentiation that would occur later. In the 860s, the missionary brothers were sent from Byzantium to convert the Slavs and who eventually developed in Bulgaria a single Cyrillic alphabet based on Greek that came to be widely used.¹⁶⁷ This Slav language was, of course, proto-Russian as much as it was a generic Slav tongue.

The empire of the Russian horde imagined by Fomenko was terrifying to its enemies, that is, the West, but a Cossack-style military democracy for the Slavs and Turks. The civilian population, Fomenko speculates, used to elect their princes through the democratic instrument of the assembly or

---

165 Gumilëv, *Drevniaia Rus' i velikaia step'*, 394-95.
166 *Ibid.*
167 Hosking, *Russia and the Russians*, 37.

veche. The prince was a civilian leader responsible for the welfare of the city. The armed forces were known as hordes and were stationed on the borders and headed by khans or, to use the Russian word for the same term, tsars. There were occasional civil wars if, for example, an ambitious civilian ruler tried to usurp too much authority. Tsar-Khans often launched punitive raids against civilian leaders or one another. This is the source of the confusion in the West where these civil wars came to be known erroneously as the invasion of Russia by the Mongols. This story is also a model of how many Russians view the best qualities of the Russian character.

It has been pointed out that the allegedly Marxist scholarship of the Soviet academy showed a surprising degree of interest in ethnogenesis, a subject widely regarded as lacking in scientific credentials in the West. Ethnogenesis was understood in the Soviet Union as 'the process of development of the main characteristics of an ethnic community, including the physical characteristics of its members, language and other cultural features'.[168] Both Gumilëv and Fomenko understand the ethnos as in some sense biological but also a state of mind. While the imperial core was Slav and Turkic, loyalty to Russia and hostility to the West were sufficient qualifications for membership of this ethnos. There were no racial demarcations and no religious animosity, claims Fomenko, between Turk and Slav in the medieval world because Islam and Orthodoxy represented a common religion. The modern analogy is a Cossack warrior community where ties of blood are less important than attitude, loyalty and martial skill.

For Fomenko, the confusion over the name of Genghis Khan's empire resulted from the fact that the term 'Mongol' is a corruption of 'Mogol' and should be translated as 'Great', as it is in certain languages, and not used in reference to a specific area or people.[169] Karamzin for example, called the Tatar-Mongols 'Mogoliya', missing the 'n'. Other writers referred to it as 'Mogulistan'.[170] Fomenko emphasizes the fact that 'Tartar' means 'horror' or 'hell' in Greek. According to Fomenko, 'Tatar-Mongol' meant 'Great Horror', the reaction of the West to the raids of the Russian Horde. This name originated in Western Europe and found its way into Byzantine sources where it was used to describe various invasions and wars. Eventually the names 'Tatar' and 'Mongols' stuck to particular ethnic groups, making them

---

168 Viktor Shnirelman, *Who Gets the Past?*, 1-2.
169 Nosovskii and Fomenko, *Novaia khronologiia Rusi*, 65.
170 *Ibid.*

respectively the Tatars and the Mongols, as we know them today. An analogy would be the Russians who began life as the Slavs and whose descendants attracted different names (Great Russia, Russia Minor and White Russia). Fomenko delights in revealing for his readers illustrations from medieval European books where the modern Russian lands are referred to sometimes as Russia, sometimes as Muscovy and sometimes as Tartaria and sometimes as all three. The European illustrators of the medieval period often depicted those who lived in Muscovy and Tartaria in traditional Cossack, Tatar, or Muscovite attire.

Of course, the Russian chronicle writers did speak of unknown invaders from the East. In part this was invention, in part a misunderstanding on the part of modern historians. Fomenko points out, accurately, that in medieval Russian chronicles the Russian land is sometimes understood in a narrow sense as only applicable to Kiev, Chernigov and Pereayslavl'. Thus, he argues, anyone who came from beyond these lands was described as an attacker on the Russian land, even if the invading armies came from Smolensk, Novgorod, Vladimir-Suzdal or the Moscow region. Later, the Romanovs manufactured a myth of a historic confrontation between Mongols or Tatars and Russians in the medieval period, a myth that served their tactics of divide and rule. In so far as Russia did play host to peoples from Asia, these Asians were in fact Turks.

According to Fomenko, Russians of today mistakenly consider modern Tatars as the remnant populations of invaders from Asia. In fact, Turks, as well as other national minorities, always lived side by side with the Russians. The division into 'victorious' and 'defeated' sides was a latter-day myth produced by churchmen and German professors who preferred to write about the slave origins of the Russians humbled by the Mongol invasion rather than the true history of collaboration with non-Christian Turks.[171]

Here, Fomenko has set a difficult task, only slightly easier than the Eurasianist dream of having Russians embrace their Mongol heritage. In the nineteenth century, Turkishness was not a badge of honour for Russian nationalists. Kostomarov, the first historian to push strongly the idea that Russians and Ukrainians were separate peoples, argued that Russians were not sufficiently Slavic because the Mongol invasion affected Moscow much more than it did the southern and western borderlands where Ukraine is situated. Russian historians like Kliuchevskii and Soloviev responded that it

---

171 Nosovskii and Fomenko, *Novaia khronologiia Rusi*, 65-68.

was the Ukrainians who were insufficiently Slavic because of Turkic influence on the Cossacks who founded the Ukrainian state.[172]

For these historians, writing at a time when the Ottoman Empire was one of Russia's main rivals in the Slavic world, 'Turkic' was a pejorative term. The trend continued in Soviet historiography when, for example, the celebrated historian Artamanov was forced to conclude his history of the Khazars with the judgment that the Turkic Khazars contributed nothing of value to the history of Russia.[173] In predominantly Slavic Bulgaria, as late as the 1980s, Turks were under pressure to assimilate or to resettle in Turkey. Just as Russia has mostly looked upon the three hundred year Mongol era as a national calamity, Slavs in the Balkans have tended to look upon Ottoman rule as five hundred years of repression and humiliation. This perception has arisen despite the fact that a significant part of the Ottoman ruling elite in fact arose in the Balkans, the core and most prosperous part of this Islamic empire.[174]

On the other hand, Turkic empires, especially the Ottomans, are a useful ally to Fomenko given the expanse of Turkic influence and the proximity in space and time of Ottoman and Russian empire building. Linguists agree that the Mongol and Turkic languages belong to the same Altaic family and may have originally been western and eastern dialects of the same language. It was the Turkic language that spread most quickly so that in the sixth century, Christian claims that Turkic dialects were spoken 'from the Altai to the borders of Byzantium'.[175] The Ottoman Empire, like the Russian one, was a mixed host both at the leadership and popular level. Ottomans traced their lineage to Osman the First (1280-1324), a Turkic nomad from Anatolia whose successors displaced first the Seljuk Turks and then the Byzantine Empire in 1453. Ruling Constantinople and the Balkans, the Ottomans were clearly part of the same geo-political space as Russia and clearly interacted with the Russians. Fomenko's Ottomans are mostly imaginary Turks who resembled Slavs and spoke Slav and Turkic languages as required.

Explicit anti-Semitism takes a mild form in Fomenko or Abrashkin, as it

---

172   Tolz, *Russia*, 198.
173   See David Christian, *Russia, Central Asia and Mongolia* (Malden: Blackwell publishers, 1998), 298.
174   See, for example, Brian Silverstein, 'Islam and Modernity in Turkey: Power, Tradition and Historicity in the European Provinces of the Muslim World,' *Anthropological Quarterly* 76:3 (Summer 2003): 497-517.
175   Christian, *Russia, Central Asia and Mongolia*, 248.

does in Gumilëv. For Gumilëv the real yoke imposed upon Russia was not that of the Tatars but of the neighbouring Khazars. The Khazars were a steppe people whose leaders converted to Judaism and according to the Primary Chronicle extracted tribute from the tribes that formed Kiev Rus in the ninth and tenth centuries. Western historians have often praised the Khazars for having prevented what might have been an Arab and Islamic invasion of Eastern Europe. For Gumilëv and Abrashkin, the Khazars were the real medieval pestilence that burst upon the Russian land. For Fomenko, the Khazars were Slavs. As is the case with the Mongols, it turns out that Jews played a minimal role in Russia's medieval history, according to Fomenko.

II.2 Prester John, Columbus and the Russian Horde

Fomenko shows his contempt for conventional history by re-examining and endorsing myths and folk wisdom considered to be fairy tales since the eighteenth century – the derivation of the name 'Slav' from the Slavic word for glory, *slava*; Biblical stories about Gog and Magog and the prince of Rosh; Prester John and the Christian kingdoms of the East. Just because the Old Testament of the Bible was wrongly dated did not mean that its contents were of no historical value. Indeed the Biblical story of Gog and Magog is often found in early accounts of Russia's histories. It was a tradition that died out only in the eighteenth century when Tatishchev, regarded as Russia's first historian, began the search for more prosaic and secular origins to Russia's history. The image of Gog and Magog, the terrifying devils from the north, has long resonated with Russian readers, evidence, Fomenko believes, that the Russians were an ancient people.

For centuries, Russian patriots have found in the Book of Ezekiel, strong clues as to the history of Russia. This is because it makes reference to 'northern' peoples who are fierce warriors and to a Prince of Rosh, whose homeland sounds suspiciously like Russia.[176] Gog and Magog appear on several occasions in the Bible although it is not exactly clear if the reference is to individuals or places. According to Genesis, 10:2-4: Magog was one of the sons of Japheth. According to Ezekiel 38:1-4, Gog came from the land of Magog, was a chief prince of Meshech and Tubal and seems to have had an army of horses and 'horsemen, all of them clothed in full armour, a great

---

176 Nosovskii and Fomenko, *Bibleiskaia Rus'*, I, 144-146.

company...wielding swords'

Ezekiel 38:15-23 maintains that Gog was connected to 'the uttermost parts of the north', a land of 'many peoples', 'all of them riding on horses, a great host, a mighty army'. Revelations 20:6-10 suggests that Gog and Magog comprised innumerable hordes, Satan's armies who made war against the camp of the saints. It matters little to Russian patriots that Gog and Magog were in league with the devil so long as it can be suggested that Russia's ancestors were mighty warriors, a superpower of the ancient world. For modern anti-Semites it is especially appropriate that Gog and Magog seem to have been at war with the people of Israel.

Fomenko notes that medieval Byzantines seemed to think that the Prince of Rosh referred to in Ezekial was a Russian and wrote the Prince of Ross, not Rosh. Leo the Deacon, the Byzantine writer who lived in the second half of the tenth century, wrote in his *History* about the march of Grand Prince Sviatoslav from Kiev against Byzantium. According to Leo, 'Many know that this people are a mighty, warlike, brave and inconsiderate host. Divine Ezekiel told of the coming of people of Gog and Magog, the prince of Ross'.[177] For Fomenko, it is clear that the Biblical story is based in fact. It just needed to be interpreted correctly. The Prince of Rosh was Russia's Grand Prince. Gog, Magog in their different forms is a reference to the Russians, Tatars and Mongols, peoples who created the great empire of Magog. Meshekh is Mosokh, the legendary founder of Moscow according to medieval authors. Tubal is a reference to the river Tobol in Western Siberia, which remains one of the traditional centres of Russian Cossackdom.

The legends about Gog and Magog spread to the East, further evidence for Fomenko of how widespread the reach of the Russian Horde once was. In the Koran there is an account of how Alexander the Great built a wall to keep the fearsome Gog and Magog away. On a map of Palestine drawn by Matthew of Paris there are walls blocking the northern lands where Alexander had locked up the allegedly barbaric Gog and Magog. The commentary to the map states that this is the place from where the Tartars came from. Thus, Fomenko concludes medieval Europe identified Gog and Magog with the Tartars. Gog and Magog, were Tartars for the West and Russians for Byzantium. Further proof, Fomenko believes that Russians and Tatars were one and the same people in history.

Medieval artists portrayed ancient places and individuals in the settings

---

177   See Boris Grekov, *Kievskaia Rus* (Moscow, Leningrad: 1944), 622.

and dress of their own era. For most historians, this was simply a fantasy on the part of medieval art but for Fomenko these artists were painting what they saw. Fomenko notes that there are sixteenth century depictions of Jesus and Pontius Pilate that portray the trial as if it took place amid typically medieval surroundings. Pilate has even been painted wearing headgear that looks like a Turkic turban, sits on soft pillows, while his warriors wear medieval plate and chain armour. In the background there are two and three-story stone buildings with chimneys. Later in the nineteenth century, it was more likely that the scene of Jesus' trial would be depicted as we imagine it today with Pilate looking like a conventional Roman senator sitting on a hard stone chair. Is it not more likely, Fomenko argues, that earlier depictions closer to the real events in time, were more accurate? It might seem to a modern reader that drawings or paintings from the medieval period are obviously inaccurate or anachronistic. From Fomenko's perspective if ancient and early modern times were one and the same then these artists are eyewitnesses describing exactly what they saw.

Alternative writers have a common set of myths and heroes. They relate the mythology surrounding each and every lost or mysterious civilization to relate it to the history of Russia. Conventional historians consider that the Etruscans arrived in Italy from Asia Minor and used a version of Greek, evidence for Fomenko that Etruscan was part of the Slavonic language group and that these forerunners of the Romans were Slav-Turks. For Fomenko, the Etruscan link to the Slavonic language was further proof that the well-known ancient history of Greece and Rome has been deliberately elongated to hide the importance of proto-Slavs or proto-Russians to the story of world history. They claim that Rome, the basis of western civilization, was built upon a Slavonic-Etruscan heritage. How could Slavs have lived in ancient Italy prior to the Romans if traditional chronology dates the emergence of Slavs to the sixth, seventh, or eighth century AD? How indeed, respond conventional historians.

Russian nationalists, including the supporters of Fomenko venerate the famous excavations at Arkaim, in Siberia, which may have existed since the sixteenth or seventeenth century BCE. Some Russian archaeologists have claimed that the remains of twenty more cities are to be found in and around Arkaim. This leads to speculation of a pre-historic state, the Aryan 'Arkaim state'.[178] Fomenko is interested only in claiming Slav origins for Arkaim, just

---

178   See Viktor Mair and E. Kuzmina, *The Prehistory of the Silk Road* (University of

as Arkaim is claimed for and by Tatars and Bashkirs.

The myth of Prester John, the Christian ruler of the East, is a source of fascination to historians and pseudo-historians alike. Gumilëv devoted a study to explaining why Crusaders in the Holy Land considered they had an ally ruling this imaginary kingdom. He believed that he found the starting point of the myth in Kuchlug, the last Gur Khan and a Nestorian Christian.[179] The well-known letter from the mythical Prester John to the Byzantine Emperor Manuil is regarded as a forgery. For pseudo-history, it was unlikely to have been a forgery. There is no original of this letter, but there is a translation in Latin from the original Arabic. It starts with the following introduction – 'Prester John, by the might of our Lord Jesus Christ the Tsar of the Tsars, and the ruler of all rulers, wishes his friend, the prince of Constantinople Manuil good health and prosperity'.[180] About Prester John's address to Manuil, Gumilëv noted that Prester John addressed a sovereign ruler of Constantinople as a mere prince.[181] As Fomenko insists, this is not the only example of Russian rulers displaying staggering arrogance towards lesser rulers. One of the few documents we have from the reign of Ivan the Terrible was addressed to the English queen. In this letter, Ivan described himself respectfully as 'we', while Elizabeth the First is referred to with the Russian 'ty', you in the familiar form, as compared to the much more polite 'vy'.

The reach of the Russian Horde extended well beyond Russia. Fomenko combines the xenophobia and anti-Western sentiments to which Russian patriotism is prone with the tactic of inserting Russianness into the leading individuals and groups of the Eurasian world. Eurasia is at the centre of a world empire. The Slav-Turks were behind the alleged discovery of the Americas in 1492 by Catholic Europe. Christopher Columbus claimed the new world in the name of his imperial backers. These backers were not Ferdinand and Isabella of Spain but the Russian Horde. How does Fomenko justify this amazing claim?

Firstly, Fomenko alerts his readers to the fact that there is much that is not known about Christopher Columbus and his journeys. Fomenko notes that there are conflicting versions of Columbus's name – Colombo, Peter

---

Pensilvania Press, 2007); also Mikhail Demidenko, *Po Sledam SS v Tibete* (St-Petersburg: Olma-Press, 2003).
179 Lev Gumilev, *Searches for an imaginary kingdom: the legend of the kingdom of Prester John* translated by R.E.F. Smith (Cambridge: Cambridge University Press, 1987), 166-67.
180 Lev Gumilëv, *Poiski vymyshlennogo tsarstva* (Moscow: Tanais, 1994), 83.
181 *Ibid.*

Columbus, Christobal Colom, Xpoual de Colon, Xpo Ferens. Most likely his real name was nothing like Columbus and 'colon or 'column' merely designated 'a person who colonized in the name of God'. Not just his name but Columbus himself and the nature of his voyage are equally intriguing for Fomenko. Columbus's place of birth is unknown – Corsica, Majorca, Aragon, France, Portugal, Greece, Galicia and Poland are some of the suggestions that have been made. Even conventional accounts do not accept Columbus's own vague assertions of coming from Genoa or Italy. There is much speculation that Columbus was *a converso* given that Spanish Jews were the map-making specialists in early modern Spain.[182]

Most likely, Fomenko claims, Columbus was a Cossack. A miniature from the book *De Insulis inventis* published in Basel in 1493 depicts, at least to Fomenko's satisfaction, a bearded Columbus in a boat and typically Cossack or traditional Turkic dress as he approaches the native peoples of the New World.[183] This image is identical, Fomenko believes, to one that depicts the siege of Vienna by the Turks in 1529. Thus Columbus was most likely one of these Cossack Turks. Only later did Columbus come to be dressed as a noble Spanish knight in armour once the chronology of Scaliger tightened its grip on the writing of history in the seventeenth century. The original diary of Columbus's travels did not survive. Columbus's son Ferdinand published his first biography decades after Columbus' travels. While the details of Columbus's journey were suppressed, Fomenko has still succeeded in finding clues that hint at the truth.

Secondly, Fomenko relates world events to events in Russia. He notes that the date of Columbus's journey coincided with considerable political and military activity in Russia itself. Conventional historians have noted the coincidence that just as the Spanish were driving out Muslims towards the end of the fifteenth century, a similar process was happening in the east under Ivan the Third, whose victory at the Ugra River in 1480 over the Muslim Ahmad signalled Moscow's victory over the 'Tatar yoke'.[184] These simultaneous campaigns of Christian expansion could not have been a coincidence for Fomenko.

Thirdly, Fomenko cites authorities although these authorities are often pseudo-historians like he himself. Morozov's painstaking investigation of the

---

182 See, for example, Ralph De Toledano, 'The 'Mystery' of Christopher Columbus,' *Midstream* 47 (February 2001): 17.
183 Nosovskii and Fomenko, *Bibleiskaia Rus'* II, 156.
184 See Davies, *Europe*, 453-54.

Bible led him to the conclusion that the names Israel and Judea did not designate separate Biblical places or peoples but separate castes within the one state. Israelis were the 'fighters for God' or '*bogobortsy*', while Judeans were the 'glorifiers of God', or '*bogoslavtsy*'. Israelis fought for God on the battlefield as professional soldiers while Judeans were the monks and the bishops who glorified God through their prayers. This is a key finding for Fomenko, for it reflects a principal feature of Russian politics with its division into secular and church authority. The books of the Bible are reflections of the political and religious history of Russia from the tenth to the sixteenth centuries. In each case, the state was divided into political/military and religious/educational wings. The Jews living in Spain in the fifteenth century were not Jews in any religious sense but *bogobortsy* who served the Slav-Turk Tsar or Great Khan. The khans themselves were the generals or tsars (Caesars) of the Russian Horde, that is, its military wing. The civilian wing of the Russian Horde was under the sway of the princes led by a Grand Prince.

Fourthly, Fomenko finds parallels in other eras, easy to do because those who falsified history foolishly left clues as to how it is possible to link disparate stories into a coherent whole. According to Fomenko's reconstruction, in the fourteenth and fifteenth centuries, columns of the Russian Horde moved out across the globe. This same episode is retold differently in different lands. The Bible allegedly narrates this piece of history as the exodus of the Israeli tribes and the travels of Noah's Ark. It is no coincidence for Fomenko that at the beginning of August 1492, one day prior to the commencement of Columbus's first journey, tens of thousands of Jews were banished from their homes by the Spanish authorities. As Fomenko speculates, this was not anti-Semitism because the Spanish Jews were in reality the *bogobortsy* of the Russian Horde. They were not banished because of an Inquisition but were soldiers temporarily based in Spain as they prepared for a long and arduous military mission on behalf of the Russian tsar-khan.

Fifthly, Fomenko asks his readers to be persuaded by what he regards as the scientific logic of his argument and not to be swayed by the weight of conventional wisdom. As Fomenko describes it, the school textbooks are utterly illogical. Fomenko claims that in official documents relating to Columbus, there is not a word about a mission to look for an alternative route to India or China, the mission described in school textbooks. According to Scaliger's chronology, China was already under the suzerainty of the Great

Khan when Columbus undertook his journeys. Therefore Columbus, who was to assume the position of Viceroy of all newly discovered lands, was not heading for the East since he and everyone else knew that there were no new lands waiting to be discovered there. Departing on his travels, Columbus did not take with him any precious gifts for the Great Khan that might have been expected if he were intending merely to visit these established states. The might and power of the Great Khan were already well known worldwide. In reality, Columbus's task, which is stated at least nine different times in official documents signed by Columbus and the Spanish monarchs, was in discovery and exploration of the islands and continents still hidden in the western ocean.

Why then did Columbus carry letters from the Spanish monarchs addressed to the Great Khan? Columbus was a general of the Ottoman Cossacks and, like the Spanish monarchs, was ultimately a subject of the Great Khan, military ruler of the Russian Horde. Columbus knew that the lands ahead had not yet been settled. The letter from the Spanish monarchs was in effect Columbus's *iarlyk* or imprimatur, an official sign of Imperial recognition that Columbus was not a pirate but deserving of assistance from all the lands and governors of the Empire. Columbus was going to claim the New World, and the letter would guarantee his safe passage to the Great Khan to report about the new conquests.

Like a pseudo-scientist in search of evidence of alien visits to Earth, Fomenko has looked for evidence in maps and drawings for representations of the double-headed eagle, as confirmation that ambassadors of the Russian Horde visited the far-flung corners of the planet. Conventional historians are not sure of the origins of this eagle, a symbol used in ancient Rome that found its way into Habsburg and Russian heraldry. Khazanov believes that the symbol was borrowed from Byzantium in the fifteenth century. The double-headed eagle appeared as part of the coat of arms of Ivan the Third, whose wife Sophia, was a Byzantine princess. It has been speculated that the two heads symbolise Russia as the Third Rome, the inheritor and successor to Rome and Byzantium.[185] It has also been argued that Russia stole the symbol from the Habsburg Friedrich the Third as far back as 1442. For the alternative writers, there are no doubts on these matters. For Fomenko, it is very important that a crowned eagle is found on the so-called Cortez' map of

---

185 Anatolii Khazanov, 'Ethnic nationalism in the Russian Federation,' *Daedalus* 126:3 (Summer 1997).

ancient Tenochitlan, dated to 1524, further evidence of successful Russian colonisation.[186]

A map of the world of 1630 produced by Kepler has the entire world placed on the chest of a two-headed eagle. The same image can be found on the map of Hungary published in 1528 by the Hungarian cartographer Lazarus. The map of the German city Keln (Cologne) of 1633 has the two-headed eagle flying over the plan of the city while a medieval map of Vienna, 1561, has the entire map on the chest of the same two-headed beast. For Fomenko, the signs are unmistakable and the traces of the Russian horde are truly ubiquitous.

The eagle was not the only important symbol for the Russian Horde. When Russians and Turks were parts of one state, they preferred a single state symbol – an eight-pointed cross with a crescent moon under it designating the northern part of the Russian Horde. According to Fomenko, it can still be seen all over Russia, including on some of the Kremlin domes. For the Turks in the south, it was a crescent moon at the top and the Russian Orthodox cross below in the form of an eight-pointed star. After the Turkic conquest of Vienna was covered up by a humiliated West, Saint Stefan cathedral was purged of all signs that it was conquered, and the symbols of the Russian Horde consigned to the museums, ignored by the experts until Fomenko's expert eye rediscovered them. Just as importantly for Fomenko, the ancient drawings of the siege of Vienna of 1529 clearly show the presence of Christians among the Turkic troops –regiments march under banners depicting crosses. As is well known, Suleiman the Magnificent had a Greek general, Bulgarian miners and countless Christian soldiers in his army. For Fomenko, a perfect example of a successful combined Turkic and Orthodox war against the Catholic West.

As for the India that Columbus was seeking out, that too was, in a sense, already Russian.[187] As Fomenko argues, from the fourteenth to the sixteenth centuries, Western Europeans purchased exotic goods primarily from Russian merchants by order of the Russian Horde and its vassals. European merchants inquired of their Russian counterparts where the goods came from. The Russians responded that they came from India. However, the Russian merchants never meant to indicate modern India as a source of their goods. On the contrary, the ancient Russian word *ind'ia* meant 'somewhere

---

186   Nosovskii and Fomenko, *Bibleiskaia Rus* II, 161.
187   *Ibid.*, I, 140-142.

else' or 'there, not here', simply indicating a faraway country, or land.

The Russian traveller Afanasii Nikitin used this term in his famous travel account *Khozhdenie za tri moria* to indicate the distant lands he hoped to visit. Today the word has become archaic in Russian. But as Fomenko argues, it has been preserved in Latin in its original form where *inde* means 'from there, from that place'. This, it seems, is evidence that the Slavic language was the real imperial language and predecessor of Latin.

Russian power extended across the globe. Fomenko's evidence include his interpretation of a medieval drawing of an earthquake in Babylon where the tops of the roofs of the collapsing houses are adorned with Christian crosses, proof, according to Fomenko, that Babylon was not destroyed in ancient times as is usually thought but was a medieval and Christian city.[188] A drawing in the chronicle by the thirteenth-century English monk, Matthew of Paris, depicting European knights in the process of being taken away to the kingdom of the mysterious and evil Khorezmian Babylonians is evidence for Fomenko that the Babylonian captivity was a myth whose origins lay in the fate of Western crusaders captured by the Russians defending the lands of their horde. Babylon was, it turns out, a bastion of the Russian Horde of the fifteenth and sixteenth centuries.[189] Another illustration cited by Fomenko depicts the siege of Constantinople by the Ottomans in 1453: the picture is, according to Fomenko, stunningly accurate in geographic terms and military-architectural details portraying the Golden Horn bay, the shore of the sea, the fortress walls, bridges, cannons and siege engines. However, the temple of Saint Sophia is depicted as a typical medieval Gothic Catholic Church, reflecting the fact that Constantinople was the original home of Catholicism, a Rome on the Bosporus![190]

For Fomenko, it is intriguing that the troops depicted in this illustration sported a Russian high pointed *kalpak*, not the turbans that might have been expected in a Turkish army. The troops carried a banner with a dragon resting on two paws, identical to the official crest of Kazan – and using the colours of Russia. There is a silver shield with a black crowned dragon with a red tail and wings. His claws and beak are golden. According to Fomenko, the Ottomans who stormed Constantinople in 1453 were obviously Cossacks who used Kazan as their base. Another banner depicts the image of Saint

---

188   Nosovskii and Fomenko, *Bibleiskaia Rus'*, I , 419.
189   *Ibid.*, 420.
190   *Ibid.*, II, 48-53.

George the dragon-slayer, official protector of Russia and Moscow. The original Saint George was, in Fomenko's view, none other than Genghis Khan. Slavs and Turks were a single people with a common language and history. Whether Turks consider this to be a welcome or flattering development is a different matter.

II.3 The Competition for Ancestors and Alternative History

Why would anybody read what, on the surface, appears to be the preposterous nonsense that constitutes Fomenko's account of world history? Some of the reasons are general and not specific to Russia. Pseudo-history is a worldwide phenomenon. It is the form that the fantasy takes that relates to more specific issues of national identity.

Long before Frances Fukuyama proclaimed the end of history, J. H. Plumb declared the death of the past.[191] Plumb argued in the 1960s that history was losing its power over the imagination of those living in the second century of industrialized society. Modern communication, science and education were disenchanting the world, depriving the past of the secret meaning that priests and patriotic writers had once claimed to uncover for their armies of followers. Plumb wrote that it is important to distinguish between history and the past. History is a scientific investigation following procedures developed during the evolution of a discipline over hundreds of years. The past was something else, a malleable repository of useful facts to be used by priests or ideologues to win favour or loyalty among benighted subjects. The implication was that readers were increasingly adroit at knowing the difference between history and the past.

Plumb seems to have been wrong. In Russia, a century of industrialization and government-sponsored atheism failed to eradicate interest in an imaginary past. Nor is the search for amazing ancestors a purely Russian obsession. Sometimes, the claims are modest. Hugh Trevor Roper has demonstrated, for example, that most 'age-old' Scottish traditions were Irish imports, forgeries or recent inventions. Most famously, the kilt first appeared in the eighteenth century, invented by an Englishman and then rediscovered at the end of the nineteenth century by highland gentry who

---

191   John Harold Plumb, *The Death of the Past* (London: Macmillan, 1969), 11-17.

wished to show the importance and ancient lineage of their clan.[192].

Other claims are less modest. Elaine Showalter has pointed out that Western books which tell fantastic stories about the past often sell millions of copies. Graham Hancock has sold four million copies of books, complete with photographs, suggesting that all the wonders of the ancient world from Stonehenge to the Egyptian pyramids and Easter Island were the work of a single lost civilization.[193] Nor is it the case that it has become easier in the West to show why some views are deserving of being taken seriously and other views are not. Many writers have pointed out that science, for the non-expert, often seems to represent a leap of faith akin to belief in religions or the paranormal. That the universe began as a super-compressed incomprehensibly small and incredibly hot ball of gas that gave rise to quarks, protons, neutrons and then galaxies is a widely-accepted claim made by science but difficult for anybody outside of science to critically examine. It is easy to scoff at those who believe that the government has covered up evidence of visits by aliens to Earth but difficult to explain why this is absurd given that many scientists consider that there is likely to be life beyond Earth and many historians consider that governments systematically withhold information from the public.[194] Thomas Kuhn popularized the idea of paradigm shifts to show that normal science under the influence of revolutionary ideas has often shifted ground dramatically. Windschuttle found in this work the source of an insidious relativism common among Western academics.[195] On the other hand, it clearly is the case that accepted scientific ideas, from evolution to continental drift, were once ridiculed. As we will see, historians today often describe the Mongols as sophisticated state builders when once they were universally despised as barbaric bandits. Pseudo-historians rightly suspect that a modern audience is as susceptible to seemingly fantastic claims as earlier audiences.

The difference between healthy scepticism or revisionism and foolish pseudo-history becomes more apparent when specific claims made by pseudo-history are examined. But it is also easy to show those who grew up in Russia and the Soviet Union are entitled to more scepticism than most

---

192 Eric Hobsbawm and Terence Ranger (eds), *The Invention of Tradition*, 23-30.
193 Elaine Showalter, 'Why People Believe Weird Things,' (Review), *New Statesman* 127:4413 (November 27, 1998): 54.
194 Wayne R. Anderson, 'Why would people not believe weird things?,' *Skeptical Inquirer* 22:5 (September-October 1998), 42-47.
195 Windschuttle, *The Killing of History*, 187-90.

about the teachings of conventional history.

For good reason, Russian readers are deeply sceptical of much of what passed for history in the Soviet Union. Championing his policy of glasnost in the late 1980s, Mikhail Gorbachev boasted that there would no longer be 'blank pages' in Soviet history. History had been written and then rewritten so dramatically in the Lenin, Stalin and Khrushchev eras that a Soviet-era reader could have been forgiven for thinking that most of what they were told was history was in fact a fabrication written to serve whoever was in power. It did not take long for some Russian writers to conclude that Gorbachev and his successors, Boris Yeltsin and Vladimir Putin, were guilty of much the same abuse of history for political ends.[196]

The level of manipulation of history in the Stalin era was first revealed to the Soviet public from the time of Khrushchev's secret speech in 1956. In the 1980s and 90s a flood of reports in the popular press washed away the remaining certainties about Soviet history. Stalin's Soviet Union was literally a world where the present dictated the past, yesterday's heroes were today's villains and almost every image was retouched for the purpose of telling the desired story. For readers outside Russia, David King's account of Stalin's photography best conveyed the astonishing level of pictorial vandalism.[197] With airbrushes, scalpels and black ink, historical figures were excised or relocated from historic photographs while others were inserted to reinforce a political message. Logic suggested that evidence was routinely distorted and manipulated by authorities in earlier eras.

For readers, the situation improved after the death of Stalin but progress was slow. Between the 1960s and the Gorbachev era, readers were denied access to literature not approved by the authorities. According to Stelmakh, censorship in the Soviet Union was a complex social system with powerful control over information that bred distrust and a well-justified suspicion that information was withheld by and circulated only among the elite. In 1985 the *spetskhran* or specialist holding of the Lenin State Library of the U.S.S.R amounted to more than one million items for which there was only privileged access. Despite 'broadening readers' demands and new cultural contingents coming along', the number of published titles was almost

---

[196] See R. Davies, *Soviet History in the Yeltsin Era*, 96-114.
[197] David King, *The Commissar Vanishes: the falsification of photographs and art in Stalin's Russia* (New York: Henry Holt and Company, 1997).

the same in 1985 as it was in 1970.[198]

Amid the outpouring of writing about the past in the 1990s, there were many Soviet-era historians who succeeded in re-inventing themselves as Westernizers, making use of their knowledge and access to archives to shed new light on murky episodes of Communist history.[199] Many Soviet-era historians worked with Western academics to write new post-Soviet histories of the recent and distant past. Meanwhile, amateur historians inside Russia claimed that their strength lay in the fact that they were not tainted by official accounts of the past. While alternative writers mostly lacked professional training as historians, in the post-Soviet context, this could be viewed as a useful qualification and not an encumbrance.

Fomenko's history is not simply a fantasy that emerged from the imagination of this scientist and his collaborators. The Soviet system repressed Fomenko's history but it also provided him with all the tools he needed for his work as a pseudo-historian. Soviet history kept alive a Russian tradition of empire worship and sought to expose the many plots against Russia and its history. Fomenko was a child of the Soviet system to the point where his principal secondary sources are often Stalin-era histories and his usual way of dismissing an idea that he does not agree with is to label it as 'anti-scientific', as a Soviet Marxist might have done in the Stalin era. Thus, Fomenko described the German historian Bayer as the founder of the 'anti-scientific' Norman theory, just as his predecessors in the Stalin era did.[200]

Katerina Clark has described the socialist realist literature that emerged after 1930 as an allegory that focused upon the positive hero. The greatest hero was Stalin himself and the turning point episodes of his life – revolution, civil war, death of Lenin, became a 'canonised Great Time' where the boundary between the historical and the ideal was so blurred that historical reality was subordinated to legend. There was no gap between 'is' and 'ought to be'.[201] Such a blurring is of course true of all pseudo-history but rarely was conventional history so much a part of fantasy ritual as it was in the Stalin period. To a greater or lesser extent, even historians with a reputation in the

---

198 Valeriia Stelmakh, 'Reading in the Context of Censorship in the Soviet Union,' *Libraries & Culture* 36:1 (2001): 143-45.
199 The classic case here Dmitrii Volkogonov, a well-connected Soviet military historian who wrote exposes about Lenin and Stalin after the fall of Communism. See, for example, Dmitrii Volkogonov, *Stalin: Triumph and Tragedy*, edited and translated by Harold Shukman, (London: Weidenfeld and Nicolson, 1991).
200 Nosovskii and Fomenko, *Novaia khronologiia Rusi*, 27.
201 Clark, *The Soviet Novel: History as a Ritual*, 40-41.

Tsarist era had to write historical fantasy in the Soviet period just to get published.

Although more complex and diverse than simple propaganda, the novels, popular history and textbooks produced in the Soviet Union after 1930 were written to a formula. There was a market for literature in the Soviet Union in that some writers seemed to be able to connect the formula of socialist realism to the demands of a mass audience better than others. Some of this Soviet writing proved so successful than its hold upon the imagination of those who grew up with it lingers to this day. Fomenko would claim that his histories reject the lies of the Communist era but at the same time he seems to be a prisoner of exactly this type of writing. Instead of Stalin as the central antagonist in a timeless world, the hero now is Russia itself. Like Soviet heroes, Russia has overcome adversity and foreign plots, delivered great benefits to the world and shown no mercy to its enemies, and promises to safeguard the reader to a brighter future.

Vladimir Solonari has pointed out that Soviet historical narratives were 'powerful means of creating and manipulating the national identities of Soviet subjects, both Russians and non-Russians'. This was more than just a search for a pantheon of Sovietised Russian national heroes. For Solonari, formulaic texts and encoded cultural symbols acceptable to the Soviet elite and comprehensible to the Soviet public were woven into the history textbooks in much the same way that Socialist Realism provided a standard style for literary works. These textbooks shaped the Soviet worldview, and 'according to recent findings, exhibited remarkable resilience during the Soviet period and to a large extent survived the downfall of the Soviet Union'.[202]

As David Brandenberger has put it, the official ideology of 'national in form but socialist in content', soon gave way to 'national in form and nationalist in content' as a result of the party's unabashed trafficking in Russian heroes, myths and iconography'.[203] Fomenko has imbibed these attitudes, especially the heritage of World War Two. The pervasive and aggressive Russian patriotism of that era added colour to a previously drab orthodox Marxist approach.

On the surface, Fomenko's history seems to run counter to the

---

202 Vladimir Solonari, 'Creating a 'People': A Case Study in Post-Soviet History-Writing,' *Kritika: Explorations in Russian and Eurasian History* 4:2 (2003): 411-438.
203 David Brandenberger, *National Bolshevism, Stalinist Mass Culture and the Formation of Modern Russian national identity, 1931-1956* (Cambridge: Harvard University press, MA, 2002), 111.

Sovietised Marxist literature with which he grew up. Certainly, Fomenko does not deal with class struggle or peasant revolution. On the other hand, there was in the Stalin era a popular history genre and it dealt in a very patriotic way with great men, geopolitics and the destiny of Russia. The style and spirit of Eisenstein's film of Ivan the Terrible or Aleksei Tolstoi's account of Peter the Great has found its way into pseudo-history. Katherine Verdery has pointed out that Communism dealt in black and white dichotomies, distinguished 'us' from 'them', demonised the other as enemies and terrorists. Nationalism or patriotism are appropriate substitutes because they provide the comfort of the collective, identifies the 'us' and the 'them' and offers an opportunity to write history in a Soviet style but with a new message. With the collapse of the Soviet Union, the writing of Russian history entered a new phase. For professional historians, the importance of the freedom that began with glasnost was that archives could be consulted, mysterious blank pages in history filled in and a fuller and more complete history arrived at. For popular writers, the archives were less interesting than topics that were chained to a Marxist interpretation in the Soviet era. One such topic was the proud and ancient history of the Russian people.

Conveniently for Fomenko and his allies, a ready-made bridge already existed to cross the murky waters that separate conventional revisionism and pseudo-history. Among modern exponents of the new burst of patriotic history in Russia, Lev Gumilëv is probably the most famous and certainly the most important.[204] Until his death in 1992, Gumilëv maintained a foot in both camps with a reputation among conventional and alternative historians. He has won acceptance among conventional scholars to the point where he writes textbooks, has scholarly works translated into foreign languages and has a university named after him.[205] On the other hand he is highly regarded among the writers considered in this book, partly because he claims to have added a scientific dimension to nationalism with his theory of ethnies.

Victor Shnirelman has pointed out that in putting forward his concept of the ethnos, Gumilëv was unable or unwilling to escape the constraints of Soviet anthropology. The Soviet concept of the ethnos, championed by

---

204   Lev Gumilëv, *Drevniaia Rus i velikaia step'* (Moscow: Mysl', 1992); *Poiski vymyshlennogo tsarstva* (Moscow: Tanais, 1994); *Chernaia legenda* (Moscow: Ekopros, 1994); *Ot Rusi k Rossii* (Leningrad: 1989); *Etnogenez i biosfera zemli* (Leningrad: 1989); *Geografiia etnosa v istoricheskii period* (Leningrad: 1990); *Otkrytie Khazarii* (Moscow: AST, 2000); *Chtob svecha ne pogasla* (Moscow: AST, 2001); *Tysiacheletie vokrug Kaspia* II volumes (Moscow: AST, 2002).
205   Viktor Shnirelman and Sergei Panarin, 'Lev Gumilev,' 1-18.

Bromlei between the 1960s and 80s, held that 'a conscious or unconscious attachment to one's primary group is formed on the basis of blood relations, language, religion, cultural traits, and other characteristics that make for highly durable, if not permanent groups'.[206] In other words, the Soviet approach is 'primordialist'. Western anthropology, by contrast, tends to assume more fluid groups whose membership and character are subject to change. It is the Soviet version of durable ethnies that is evident in the thinking of Gumilëv and Fomenko.

Gumilëv's popularity partly lay in the fact that he found history's motor not in the official Soviet ideology of classes but in a quasi-scientific biology, a new element of the historical narrative for the Soviet imagination. Researchers have found it hard to pin down exactly what Gumilëv meant by ethnos.[207] Every known cultural, political and religious group from history seems to have had its own ethnos, although the categories of super-ethnos, sub-ethnos and ethnic chimeras suggest a hierarchy of collectivities striving to survive and flourish in the world. For some reason these ethnies survive for approximately twelve hundred to fifteen hundred years and spring to life because of a mysterious *passionarnost*, literally bursts of energy, caused by the arrival of a charismatic figure or external pressures like climate change or war. The ethnos exhausts its energy at some point and once vibrant ethnies decay and die.

Gumilëv had no time for the conventional story of Russian history. For Gumilëv, Kiev Rus is misunderstood and the Mongols are wrongly demonized. Russia was not a by-product of the European West but a symbiosis of many peoples who enjoyed a special relationship with the Russian land, a territory that extended over the vast area of Eurasia. Ancient Russia was not a handmaiden to Byzantium but grew together with its more celebrated twin.[208] Nestor, the chronicler responsible for the tale about Viking rulers of Kiev Rus was plainly mistaken.[209] The Westernizer tradition among Russian historians, fuelled by a fanatical Christianity and hostility to the non-Christian world, repressed the ancient and glorious history of the Russian Kaganate, the first state on Russian lands and the forerunner of Kiev Rus, Muscovy, the Russian Empire and the Soviet Union.[210]

---

206 Viktor Shnirelman, *Who Gets the Past?*, 8.
207 Shnirelman and Panarin, 'Lev Gumilev,' 6-7.
208 Gumilëv, *Drevniaia Rus' i velikaia step'*, 175.
209 *Ibid.*, 175.
210 *Ibid.*, 200; Here Gumilëv has a point. See Christian, *A History Russia, Central Asia*

For many Russian readers, Gumilëv represented a breath of fresh air and clarity in his withering attacks upon the Soviet and Romanov view of the past. At the same time, he rode the boundary between conventional and pseudo-history, speculating wildly but always trying to ground his work in accepted sources and paying close attention to the work of other experts in the field. For Fomenko, there are no such constraints.

As for why Fomenko has made such fantastic claims about Russia, it must be remembered that Russian pseudo-history is in competition with the pseudo-history of the other myriad national groups of the Russian Federation. There is a competition for ancestors and it is enlivening or afflicting, depending upon perspective, the entire space of the former Soviet Union. The Russian writers under consideration in this book have found themselves in a contest with their counterparts emerging among the Turkic nations of the Russian Federation. Popular, as distinct from state-inspired, chauvinism was frowned upon both in Tsarist and Soviet times. Only in the last decade has the debate reignited. For Russian players in this competition, it is only logical that Russia should make the most far-reaching claims as it is by far the largest and most powerful of the modern Eurasian states. For pseudo-historians, as for other Russian patriots, it is impossible to draw a border around Russia. Russian history is inevitably world history. Fomenko considers that he has offered the minority Turkic population of the Russian Federation an attractive proposition for joint ownership of the mythical Russian Horde. Fomenko's Turkic counterparts have rejected the offer.

Without Ukraine, Belarus and central Asia, Russia is much more Russian today than it was under the tsars of Communists. The largest minorities of the Russian Federation are Turkic nationalities, even though their numbers are dwarfed by their Russian neighbour. The nationalities within Russia comprise: Russian 81.5%, Tatar 3.8%, Ukrainian 3%, Chuvash 1.2%, Bashkir 0.9%, Belarusian 0.8%, Moldavian 0.7% and other 8.1%. It is no real comfort for Russian patriots to know that 75% of Tatars live outside of Tatarstan and that its leaders mostly deny that independence from the Russian Federations is an option. The fear is that on the basis of history, Tatars or Turks in general could lay claim to a historic homeland that stretches from Kazan to Astrakhan, Crimea and beyond. The writing of this type of history is already under way and political demands may follow. There is a competition within pseudo-history to make the most extravagant claims,

---

and Mongolia, 282-303.

to find the best ancestors and to deprive others of those ancestors.

In the 1930s, a group of Tatar historians attempted to link the history of their nation to the history of the Golden Horde, and thus, to the history of the Mongols. Their approach was doomed in Stalinist Russia, where the Golden Horde and the Mongols were demonised as much as the Vikings. Tatar historians were forced to trace their ancestry not from the Golden Horde, but from the ancient Bulgar state that was one of the first to fall victim to the Mongol onslaught. Just like the Russians, Turkic pseudo-historians now write much more fantastic tales about their ancestors.

In the 1990s, each Turkic nationality has produced its own 'pen and ink' warriors. Nationalistic historians emerging from among the Chuvash, Tatars and Bashkirs have tried to connect the history of their peoples to ancient ancestors such as the Sumerians, Scythians, Egyptians, and Etruscans.[211] According to these histories, the Turkic peoples were once the benevolent conquerors of the Russians and the latter owe the former a huge cultural debt. This debt not only includes the Russian words for paper, bathhouse, boots, money, and pencils, but the ancestors of Peter the Great, field-marshal Kutuzov, and the writer Dostoevskii who made such good use of the money, boots and pencils to assert Russia's greatness.

For all the nationalist movements among the Turkic peoples of the Volga, Russia was and remains the enemy. Happily for the Russians, the Turkic revival of the middle Volga looks to the past for unity but has generated considerable intra-Turkic conflict. Tatars tend to believe that the Volga Bulgars spoke a Turkic language and lent their language to the Chuvash. Chuvash tend to the opposite conclusion, that Volga Bulgars spoke a specifically Chuvash language and not a generic Turkic language. For the Chuvash, Tatars had nothing to do with the Volga Bulgars and arrived only as part of the Mongol invasion of the thirteenth century. Non-Tatar nationalist historians of the Middle Volga tend to insist that the term Tatars was simply a generic name for many different Turkic peoples who found their way into the Golden Horde after the thirteenth century. The very term Tatar emerged first as a nickname for wandering nomads and not for a specific ethnic group. The tsars then used the term Tatar, with its negative connotations, to justify their war of aggression against the Bulgars.[212]

In opposition to their Tatar and Chuvash counterparts, historians of the

---

211 Christian, *A History of Russia, Central Asia and Mongolia*, 5.
212 *Ibid.*, 45.

Bashkirs claim that their ancestors were the Bulgars. The Turkic-Iranian ancestors of the Bulgars lived in Bashkiria some 35,000 years ago, having created Idel-Ural, the world's first state. Bulgar migrations reached Central Asia, northern China, North and South Americas. Until the tenth century, Eastern Europe was ruled by the -Bulgars. It was brought to an end only in the thirteenth century under the dual pressures of the Golden Horde and then Russia.[213] Shnirelman has described the phenomenon of ethno-nationalism in the Volga region, the heartland of Russia's Turkic population:

> For people who believe they have been deprived of their cultural legacy, invention of the past becomes a powerful instrument – first, for the raising of self-esteem and the re-evaluation of their position among other peoples, and second, for demanding special rights and privileges with respect to others who lack their glorious past...[214]

If Fomenko's has a Turkic counterpart it is probably Murad Adzhi (formerly Adzhiev), an ethnic Tatar, who considers the word 'Tatar' as a form of a racial slur perpetuated by Russians and other European peoples. Rather, as the titles of his books suggest[215], he identifies himself as a Polovets, a descendant of the ancient state of Desht-i-Qipchaq. Adzhi was a professional Soviet economist who wrote his dissertation on the subject of the Baikal-Amur railroad, before turning his hand to popular history.

Adzhi, like Fomenko, is xenophobic in outlook and despises the West. While Fomenko concentrates on evil Germans, Adzhi demonises the evil Greeks.[216] In contrast to Fomenko, Adzhi considers the Russians or Slavs to be a 'Western' outpost in Eurasia, and laments the fact that Russian propagandists changed, stole and twisted the otherwise great Turkic historical and cultural inheritance. According to Adzhi, Huns, Alans, Goths, Burgundians, Saxons, Alemans, Angles, Langobards and many of the Russians were ethnic Turks.[217] The list of non-Turks is relatively short and seems to comprise only Jews, Chinese, Armenians, Greeks, Persians, and Scandinavians. Adzhi is obsessed with the idea that 200,000 years ago an

---

213   Shnirelman, *Who Gets the Past*, 42-44.
214   *Ibid.*, 2.
215   Adzhi, *My – iz roda Polovetskogo; Polyn' polovetskogo polia*; *Evropa, Turki, velikaia step.'*
216   Adzhi, *Evropa*, 152, 191.
217   *Ibid.*, 198.

advanced people of Turkic blood lived in the Altai Mountains, the forefathers of the future Turks. Surprisingly, they were tall and blonde people. The Turks built the so-called ancient Russian cities and produced the first plough.[218] According to Adzhi, Saint George was also a Turk, buried in the Caucasian mountains of Dagestan.

Adzhi has maintained that Turks, through the barbarian invasions, liberated Europe from its slavish dependence on Rome, built temples, hundreds of cities and roads, brought monotheistic religion to the Europeans, and invented Christianity. Europe lavishly borrowed from the Turks. It was the Turks who built Russia's monasteries and even invented Christmas trees, forks and spoons. Turkic was the language Europe used up to sixteenth century. According to Adzhi, while the majority of the Turkic peoples of Russia were Kipchaks and Khazars, Turkic Cossacks became the eastern Slavs. Prior to the nineteenth century Slavs were called Caucasian Tartars and they spoke the same language as the Turks. Adzhi notes that there are millions of Slavs with typically Turkic facial features who believe they are Russian. Given his description of ancient Turk features, their confusion seems unsurprising.

While Fomenko feigns inclusiveness by invoking a once mighty Slav-Turk Empire and by inviting the Turks to rule this imaginary kingdom together with the Slavs, there is no place for the Slavs in Adzhi's Turkic Empire. Even the light cavalry that defeated the German knights in the famous confrontation on the ice in 1242 were obviously Turkic Cossacks.[219] Adzhi's logic resembles Fomenko's but his conclusions necessarily contradict. The plot against Turkic civilization was hatched by an alliance of sedentary nations, including the evil Greeks, barbaric Romans and mean-spirited Slavs.

It would be true to say that conventional historians in Russia are deeply frustrated and feel themselves under threat because of the rise of pseudo-history. These sentiments are obvious in Shnirelman's comment that:

---

218 Adzhi, *Evropa*, 54-55.
219 *Ibid.*, 152, 237.

Today, anyone can do anything they want with history. They can turn over facts to suit their ethnic leanings. They can lean on dubious sources as if they were absolute proof. They can cite no facts at all. They can invent evidence where it does not exist, and even create whole chronicles on behalf of their ancestors, as if it were miraculously discovered in their granddad's shed.[220]

It is not clear precisely whom Shnirelman has in mind but it is likely that Fomenko would be caught in this net. As we shall see, historians in Russia have proved very industrious in coming up with explanations of the Fomenko phenomenon.[221] In what follows, I briefly list the principal suggestions that have been made. All have a degree of plausibility but lack a sufficient degree of self-criticism. I will argue that the way historians have told the story of Russia's identity is crucial to understanding the success of Fomenko.

A common theme is that Fomenko has misused his distinguished mathematical standing in order to lure trusting readers, when in reality his research has nothing to do with serious science or history. Some conventional historians explain what they regard as the temporary success of Fomenko in terms of the declining standards of the modern Russian state, where a lack of professionalism has permeated all aspects of society. Critics charge that the current secondary school education in Russia is spawning semi-educated intellectuals who attack official History Departments despite their obvious lack of expertise.[222] Meanwhile, the funding and resources of educational program in schools have declined and much of the ideological baggage from the Soviet era remains.

The mathematician Efremov was more saddened by the blow that has been dealt to Moscow University's reputation, where Fomenko remained a member of faculty. Efremov compared Fomenko to the infamous Stalinist academician Lysenko. He described Fomenko's research and its endorsement by some scientists as 'the greatest disgrace of Russia's science'.[223] Fomenko's supporters were those whose social status declined

---

220 Shnirelman and Panarin, 'Lev Gumilev,' 16.
221 Igor Nastenko (ed), *Istoriia i antiistoriia: Kritika 'novoi khronologii' akademika A. Fomenko* (Moscow: Yazyki russkoi kultury, 2000).
222 Valentin Yanin, 'Ziiaiushchie vysoty akademika Fomenko,' *Istoriia i antiistoriia*, 310-321.
223 Iurii Efremov, 'O tak nazyvaemoi 'novoi khronologii', 'Almagest i sindrom novoi khronologii', 'Zavershaia diskusiui', 'Konets novoi khronologii', *Istoriia i antiIstoriia*, 321, 348, 357, 361.

as a result of the collapse of Communism. This vulnerable audience included teachers at Russia's military academies, former officers and scientists who worked in the defence industries. Thus, there is a sadomasochistic streak among Fomenko's followers, who are attracted not to the essence of Fomenko's theory, which is incomprehensible, but to the novelty of its construction and its attack upon the conventional framework of history.

Other conventional historians view Fomenko not just as a symptom of Russia's decline but a cause of the falling level of Russian culture and its scientific and moral values. Milov, an expert in the early Russian chronicles, admitted to an emotional repugnance towards Fomenko, remarking that he hears satanic laughter whenever he reads New Chronology.[224] According to Milov, Fomenko and alternative historians in general do not seem to have read a single serious historical book in the past twenty years. A good mathematician is not enough to be a good historian. For Milov, New Chronology has no relation to science at all, and the conclusions made on the basis of these methods are insane.[225]

Fomenko's colleagues recalled that, in the 1970s, Fomenko suffered mild repression. A special meeting of the History Department of Russia's Academy of Sciences rebuked Fomenko, and turned his hypotheses into an object of derision. Fomenko was charged with creating a utopian past for Russia, for creating a mythological and pseudo-religious atmosphere. Thus, revenge upon his cowardly colleagues is a possible explanation of Fomenko's contempt for the sensitivities of his colleagues. Zalizniak argued that Fomenko's research attracted people who enjoy its radical approach and attack on a conventional history, despised because of its collaboration with official Soviet ideology. He noted that Fomenko was elevated to the status of a new Copernicus by his followers.[226] In the 1990s a desperate population embraced Fomenko's idea of Russia's past grandeur partly because of the authors' supposed scientific expertise. The claim that Russia once upon a time was a metropolis around which revolved the countries of Western Europe was an attractive one given the diminished status of the failed superpower. Others hasten to attach the label of fascists to Fomenko. Kharitonovich has argued that there are echoes of Fomenko's theories in the rhetoric of Zhirinovskii, the leader of the right-wing Liberal Democratic Party

---

224 Leonid Milov, 'K voprosu o podlinnosti Radzivillovskoi khroniki,' *Sbornik Russkogo Istoricheskogo Obshchestva* 3 (Moscow: Russkaia panorama, 2000), 31-47.
225 *Ibid.*
226 Andrey Zalizniak, 'Lingvistika po Fomenko,' *Istoriia i antiistoriia,* 18-76.

of Russia who once fantasized 'about Russian soldiers washing their boots in the waters of the Indian ocean', and in the pronouncements Russia ex-prime minister Valerii Primakov, famous for his suspicion of the West.[227]

Volodikhin, the chief editor of the journal *Russkoe Srednevekovie* characterized Fomenko's work as a negative phenomenon that has been enjoying a victory march in recent times. Volodikhin suggested considering Russia's alternative historians as a by-product of Russia's long tradition of folk-history.[228] There is a parallel between the rise of interest in pseudo-history and the rise of interest in occultism in Russia. There is a demand for both discourses everywhere in the world but in Russia the demand was repressed for seventy years. It is not surprising, therefore, that, freed from the Soviet straightjacket, Russian readers have taken their opportunity to explore forbidden topics and approaches. In the case of ethnogenesis, the topic itself was permitted but only if it were studied in an official Marxist way. Fomenko seemed like a breath of fresh air in comparison to the stale formulas of Soviet discussions of ethnic origins.[229]

Fomenko has antagonized not only historians who worked under the former atheistic Soviet system, but also the new religious historians of post-Communist Russia. Alexei Laushkin claims to have demonstrated the anti-Christian character of alternative history and their ties to the destructive ideas of postmodernism and occult neo-paganism.[230] Fomenko himself often delights in noting that religious sources take seriously the claim in the chronicles that the outcome of battles was determined by the intervention of heavenly creatures.

At one level, Fomenko's account of the past does indeed seem strange for a pillar of the Soviet scientific establishment. One striking feature of this professional scientist-turned amateur historian is that his notion of history is far removed from what might be expected of a careful and fact-driven scientist. Fomenko seeks to recover a fantastic past for Russia as a cradle of civilization and the birthplace of a mighty world empire. For Fomenko, ancient history was the product of a plot hatched in the West and designed to privilege the history of Western Europe over Russia. In reality, Russia was

---

227 Dmitrii Kharitonovich, 'Novaia khronologiia: mezhdu neizbezhnym i nevozmozhnym,' *Istoriia i antiistoriia*, 245-274.
228 Dmitrii Volodikhin, 'Fenomen Fomenko,' *Novyi Mir* (3): 165-188.
229 *Ibid.*
230 Aleksei Laushkin, *Lozh' novoi khronologii*; http://www.gumer.info/bibliotek_ Buks/History/laushkin/index.php (as of November 20, 2008)

central to the ancient world, and not a peripheral backwater as conventional ancient history described it.

At another level, this type of history is not so surprising. Here the key to Fomenko's approach is not just that he is a scientist and therefore lacking in professional training in history. The problem is the type of history that he has been exposed to. Fomenko was born in 1945 and moved through a Soviet school system that imbibed the patriotic propaganda of World War Two and vitriolic attacks upon foreign influences not just in Russian history itself but in the telling of Russian history. Communist history was a story of power and plots, of evil capitalists waging war against the Russian people. Fomenko recycled and embellished this plotline after the collapse of Communism to serve new but still patriotic ends. Fomenko and his future readers were shaped together in a Soviet educational system, whose origins can be traced back to the patriotic Stalinist catechisms of the 1930s and whose legacy lives on in the textbooks of present-day Russia. The explosion of pseudo-history points to the dissatisfaction of the Russian public not only with its political and economic circumstances, but with the inadequacy of historical knowledge produced in the Tsarist and Soviet eras.

History in the West is by definition a matter of interpretation. In Soviet Russia, history was taught as if it were objective truth. Those certainties collapsed in the Gorbachev era. For Russian readers of history, the primary sources of Russian history suddenly became even more problematic as new interpretations of Kiev Rus and the Mongols began to make their appearance. To make sense of Fomenko's popularity, we must examine the starting point of Russian historiography. The so-called Normanist controversy is the most enduring controversy in Russian history and, stale though the issue seems to historians in the West, it is alive and flourishing at a popular level in modern Russia.

III Russian History and Its Forgeries

III.1 Historians, Sources and Interpretations

Pseudo-history mimics and feeds upon conventional history. For more than two centuries a significant number of Russian historians have been fighting what they perceive to be a 'Western' version of Russian History that begins with the vexed question of Kiev Rus. It is impossible to understand the passion, arguments and credibility of pseudo-history without knowing the tortured story of the debate over the origins of Russia. For Fomenko, the scourge of 'Normanism' represented the first big lie invented by the Romanov academy. It was Stalin's Russia that fought hardest against this scourge and which provided Fomenko with an intellectual platform upon which he launched his own intervention in the oldest debate about Russian history.

Most accounts of Russian statehood commence in the mid ninth century. Vikings came to Russia in search of silver, established trade with Byzantium and the Arabs along the Russian rivers that connected 'the Varangians to the Greeks' and organised the first Russian state of Kiev Rus. The study of Russian history was born amid a debate about origins and many Russians consider that getting the story of the past right is crucial to a nation knowing who or what it is.

In the West, the tendency until recently was to view Russia as 'a backward, Asiatic, or medieval society until the reforms of Peter the Great' in the seventeenth and eighteenth century.[231] This view was not shared in Russia or the former Soviet Union. Kiev Rus was and remains a matter of great pride to Russians as well as Ukrainians and Byelorussians, a land of 'international commerce, flourishing cities, 'democratic' institutions and cultural achievements'.[232] Gumilëv thought that Kiev was the third richest city of the era after Constantinople and Cordoba.[233] Kiev Rus was certainly one of the largest medieval states, probably surpassed Carolingian France as a cultural centre and served as a bridge between Europe and Asia. For

---

[231] Michael C. Paul, 'The Military Revolution in Russia, *1550-1682,*' The *Journal of Military History* 68: 1 (January 2004): 9.
[232] Charles Halperin, *Russia and the Golden Horde: the Mongol impact on modern medieval history*, (Bloomington: Indiana University Press, 1985), 10.
[233] Gumilëv, *Drevniaia Rus' i velikaia step,'* 269.

Slavophiles, Kiev Rus was a cradle of East Slavic, and therefore, Russian civilization. For Eurasianists, Kiev Rus was an early example of the strength of the relationship between the early Slavs and their nomadic neighbours who lived along the southern steppe.

Outside of Russia, historians have been less impressed by Kiev Rus. According to Halperin, the golden age of Kiev was much exaggerated.[234] In reference to the reign of Iaroslav the Wise, a high point of Kievan civilization, a recent Western account concluded that Kiev Rus's:

> Literary culture – almost entirely borrowed – bears little comparison with the elite intellectual pursuits which might be found in the centres of Greek and Latin learning. Despite the triumphal image building, Kiev was not Constantinople.[235]

Norman Davies exceeded these polite rebuffs with his claim that this was the 'most downtrodden province of Christendom'.[236]

Kiev Rus in the ninth century was bordered by Turkic peoples to the east, notably the Khazar Kaganate on the Black Sea coast and the Bulgar khanate of the middle Volga. Further to the south was Byzantium and further to the southeast was the Abbasid caliphate. But it was the relationship between the East Slavs and their northern neighbours, the Varyags or Varangians, which proved most controversial for historians.

There remains heated controversy about the origins of Kiev Rus. For the protagonists in this debate, the question was whether Kiev Rus was a legacy of the early Slavs or a creation of Viking conquerors. The so-called Normanist viewpoint suggested that Vikings from Scandinavia gave Russia her name and established the first state in the lands that would become the Russian Empire. The Russian state came into existence as a military and trading outpost of the Viking world. Anti-Normanists rejected this account, arguing that a Russian state existed before the Vikings and that the Viking presence revolved around service as mercenaries to Slav princes. The controversy became a key element in the struggle between Slavophiles and Westerners, especially for the former who came to believe that knowledge of

---

234 Halperin, *Russia and the Golden Horde*, 10.
235 Simon Franklin and Jonathan Shepard, *The Emergence of Rus, 750-1200*, (London: Longman, 1996), 244.
236 Norman Davies, *Europe: a history* (Oxford: Oxford University Press, 1996), 457.

the past was the key to shaping Russia's future.[237]

The debate continued to flourish into the twentieth century. Western confidence that Normanism is correct is often cited in contemporary Russia as further proof that Normanism was a Western plot. This divergence of opinion reflects not just the complexity of the issues involved but different ways of conceiving answering the question of what Russia is. For anti-Normanists today as in the past, Normanism is insulting to Russia and equally insulting is the suggestion that anti-Normanists are motivated by a blind patriotic pride.

At the heart of the matter is the variety and complexity of the source material, comprising, as Davies put it, 'Slavic and Byzantine chronicles...Old Norse literature, comparative German and Turkic (Khazarian) mythology, runic inscriptions, Scandinavian and Friesian law codes, Danish and Icelandic annals, Arab geographies, Hebrew documents, even Turkic inscriptions from Mongolia'.[238] The basic source for the history of Kiev Rus is the *Povest vremennykh let*, or, as it is better known in English, the *Russian Primary Chronicle*. Allegedly written by the monks Nestor and Sylvester in the early twelfth century, the *Primary Chronicle* describes important events from the ninth to the twelfth centuries, most famously the invitation to the Varangians to come to rule over Russia.

As with most medieval documents, controversy surrounds the authenticity and reliability of the *Primary Chronicle*. The earliest copy we have is dated to 1377, three centuries later than the events described. In this earliest copy, the Laurentian version copied for the prince of Suzdal', the author appears to be Sylvester from St. Michael's Monastery near Kiev, but the full title of the *Primary Chronicle* recorded there suggests the body of the work was written at the Kievan Caves Monastery. The much later Khlebnikov copy of the Chronicle named the monk Nestor as the original compiler. For Gumilëv, Nestor was the first Westernizer in Russian history and the Norman theory he initiated would artificially locate Russia's history on the periphery of Europe instead of where it belonged in the heartland of Eurasia.[239]

A crucial passage in the *Primary Chronicle* recorded under the year 862 how:

---

237 Joseph Black, 'The State School Interpretation of Russian History: A reappraisal of its genetic origins,' *Jahrbucher for Geschichte Osteuropas* 2:173:511.
238 Davies, *History of Europe*, 656.
239 Gumilëv, *Drevniaia Rus i velikaia step,'* 200.

The four tribes who had been forced to pay tribute to the Varangians – Chud, Slavs, Merya and Krivichi drove the Varangians back beyond the sea, refused to pay them further tribute, and set out to govern them. But there was no law among them, and tribe rose against tribe. Discord thus ensued among them, and they began to war one against the other. They said to themselves, 'let us seek princes who may rule over us, and judge us according to custom. Thus they went overseas to the Varangians. These particular Varangians were known as Rus, just as some are called Swedes, and others Normans and Angles, and still others Gothlanders, for they were thus named. The Chud, the Slavs, the Krivichi and the Ves then said to the Rus 'our land is great and rich, but there is no order in it. Come reign as princes, rule over us.' Three brothers with their kinfolk were selected. They brought with them all the Rus and migrated. The oldest, Riurik, located himself in Novgorod; the second, Sineus, in Beloozero; and the third, Truvor, in Izborsk. From these Varangians the Russian land received its name. Thus those who live in Novgorod are descended from the Varangian tribe, but earlier they were Slavs. Within two years, Sineus and his brother Truvor died. Riurik gathered sole authority into his own hands, parcelling out cities to his own men, Polotsk to one, Rostov to another, and to another Beloozero. The Varangians in these cities were the colonists, while the first settlers in Novgorod were Slavs, in Polotsk Krivichi, in Beloozero Ves, in Rostov Mer, and in Murom Muromians. Riurik had dominion over all these folk.[240]

From this passage, it would seem that Russia obtained its name from a Varangian tribe, the Rus, whose kinfolk were Swedes, Normans, Angles and Gothlanders. It is stated just as clearly that Slavic peoples along with other presumably Finnic and Baltic peoples of the Novgorod region invited foreign intervention as a means of ending their civil war. Varangians were the active state-builders, warriors and colonists while Slavs needed to be saved from themselves.

From the early eighteenth century, historians pieced together evidence

---

240 The translation come from Samuel Hazzard Cross and Olgerd P. Sherbowitz-Wetzor (ed), *Russian Primary Chronicle: Laurentian text* (Cambridge: Medieval Academy of America, 1973), 144-45.

from Byzantine, west European, Arab and Persian sources to confirm that the Rus referred to in the *Primary Chronicle* were most likely from Scandinavia. This has long been the dominant view in the West. As Geoffrey Hosking has put it in his recent history:

> In the past there was a lively historical debate about the identity of the Rus, but today there does not seem to be much doubt that they were Scandinavian Vikings or 'Varangians' as the Slavs called them.[241]

Hosking is certainly correct to state that Normanists dominate the debate in the West. Hosking's suggestion that 'it is not unknown for relatively primitive peoples to accept a ruler from a higher culture' is unlikely to win over anti-Normanist writers inside Russia, who will not countenance the idea that the Slavs of that era were more backward than the notoriously brutish Vikings.[242] There has always been much less enthusiasm for this story of Viking hegemony in Russia itself. Starting with Lomonosov in the mid eighteenth century, there has been a consistent and virulent Anti-Normanism. The strength of alternative history reflects the strong view of many Russians not just that the Viking origins of Russia is a hopelessly inaccurate Western mythology but that their own pro-Romanov historians of the nineteenth century 'state school' betrayed Russia on this issue.

The obsession with identifying the Rus was confined to a handful of intellectuals until the Slavophile debates of the 1830s and 40s where the origins of Russia became an issue of national pride. In the Stalin era, Anti-Normanism, became the officially endorsed view of Russia's ancient history. On the other hand, Russia's best-known nineteenth century historians – Karamzin, Soloviev and Kliuchevskii – are all regarded as moderate Normanists.

Ironically, it was the educational reforms Peter the Great put in place that would elevate the Swedes, whom the founder of modern Russia vanquished on the battlefield, to place of pride in the story of Russia's origins. Peter the Great not only defeated Sweden in the war for control of the Baltic sea-lanes, but he established centres of learning, notably the Academy of Sciences in St. Petersburg in 1725, that would take charge of writing Russia's history.

---

241   Hosking, *Russia and the Russians,* 30.
242   *Ibid.*, 31.

The establishment of St. Petersburg's Academy of Sciences was entrusted to Laurentius Blumentrost, Peter the Great's physician. Born in Russia of German parents, Blumentrost presided over an academy dominated by scholars born outside of Russia. The first four presidents were Germans, a microcosm of the German-dominated political establishment of the mid eighteenth century. At that time, three-quarters of the fifty-seven individuals appointed to the Academy spoke German as their first language.[243] A similar pattern emerged after Moscow University was founded in 1755 with foreign-born scholars playing key roles. Lectures took place in Latin because none of the professors spoke proficient Russian, while Russian students did not speak German.[244] Despite the language problems, many Russian academics would subsequently praise the work of their German predecessors; others suspected a German plot against Russia.

For Fomenko, the German cultural invasion known as the Academy of Science was an especially significant development because now, for the first time, history would be written in the modern form that has reached us in the present day. The fabrication of Russian history, that is, the writing out of history of the Russian Horde and its replacement with the myth of first Viking and then Mongol conquerors of Russia, can be dated from this period.

The first of the German scholars to make a contribution to Russian history was S.H. Bayer (1694-1738), a philologist by training and one of the first appointments to the St.-Petersburg's Academy of Science.[245] Bayer had expertise in a great many languages. The striking exception was Russian. Even so, Bayer, in *De Varagis*, argued that the Varangians were clearly Vikings. Bayer found the answer to the rapid expansion of Kiev Rus in the political and military energy generated by the arrival of Scandinavian warriors in the area stretching from Novgorod to Kiev. Vikings, the only sea power of the era apart from the Byzantines and Arabs, established a powerful state in the shape of Kiev Rus.

Bayer not only deflated the pretensions of the Russians to have been a great medieval power. He also deprived the Slavs of the Scyths, describing them as people from Asia, and therefore not Slavs. Bayer's lack of expertise in Russian language later fuelled claims that foreigners were not competent

---

243 Edward Thaden, 'V. N. Tatishchev', German Historians and the St. Petersburg Academy of Sciences,' *Russian History* 13:4 (Winter 1986): 367-98, 371.
244 Beliavskii, *M. V. Lomonosov I osnovanie Moskovskogo Universiteta K 200 letiiu MGU* (Moscow: 1956), 77.
245 Guts, *Mnogovariantnaia istoriia Rossii*, 110.

to deal with Russian history. Critics derided Bayer for concluding that the Kievan Rus' princes Vsevolod, Olga, Vladimir and Svyatoslav were Scandinavian Vikings on the basis of their supposedly 'Germanic' names.[246] Kliuchevskii commented acidly:

> Foreign historians-academics had to deal with the Norman question, when the circumstances were against them. Knowing little or no Russian language at all, they nevertheless eagerly seized an opportunity to work with that (Norman) theory. Bayer did not even know that Sinopsis' was not a historian.[247]

Sinopsis was a popular history that first appeared in 1674 written by Innokentii Gizel who was then archimandrite of the Kievan Cave Monastery. It traced the Russians back to the Biblical flood. Bayer had a more secular approach and bolstered his case with strong evidence from non-Russian sources. The Byzantine document, *De administrando imperiia* was written by the Emperor Constantine VII Porhyrogenitus (913-959) to assist in the education of his son. On the basis of a source known to him but not to us, Constantine provided a bilingual list of the names of the seven Dnepr rapids in Slavic and in Rus, implying that the two languages and therefore the peoples who spoke them were distinct entities. Constantine's list of Rus names contained a majority of names that seem to have been Scandinavian in origin. For many subsequent commentators, this was decisive evidence in favour of the Norman theory.[248]

Gerard Fredrick Mueller (1705-1783) was the second of the German historians to work in Russia. Arriving in Russia in 1725, Mueller painstakingly learnt the Russian language and was, by most accounts, an excellent historian. Mueller noted the lack of sources in the Russian central archives. Between 1733 and 1743, Mueller travelled through Siberia, collecting and copying chronicles. He brought back with him thirty-eight copies of various chronicles, the famous Mueller portfolio.[249]

---

246 Mikhail Lomonosov, *Trudy po russkoi istorii, obshchestvenno-ekonomicheskim voprosam i geografii*, 1747-1765, vol. 6 (Leningrad: USSR Academy of Sciences, 1952), 30.
247 Vasilii Kliuchevski, *Neopublikovannye proizvedeniia* (Moscow, Nauka, 1983), 120.
248 See, for example, A D Stokes, 'Kievan Russia' in Robert Auty and Dimitrii Obolensky (eds), *An introduction to Russian History* (Cambridge: Cambridge University Press, 1976), 52.
249 Kliuchevskii, *Neopublikovannye proizvedeniia*, 191.

In 1748 Mueller received Russian citizenship, the title of Russia's historiographer, and an obligation to write Russian history.[250] The following year, Muller presented an oration to the Empress entitled *De origine gentis et nominis Russorum*. Mueller argued that Russia acquired its name from the Finnish word for Swedes, *ruotsi*. It is a claim that still has supporters.[251] Mueller also used the treaties signed in 911 and 945 between the Byzantine emperors and the princes of Kiev to show that the Rus, in Mueller's opinion, had names with obviously Scandinavian origins.[252]

The third of the German historians was August von Ludwig Schloezer (1735-1800). Schloezer was invited to Russia by Mueller and worked there between 1761 and 1767. He served as an honorary member of St.-Petersburg's Academy of Science after he returned to Germany in 1768. There is general agreement that it was Schloezer who undertook the first systematic study of the Russian chronicles. Schloezer's shining achievement was the preparation for publication of the *Russian Primary Chronicle*, the crucial source that has served as a foundation for the writing of the history of Kievan Rus. Schloezer also was involved in preparing for publication the Radzivill Chronicle, famous for its six hundred miniatures and dated to the fifteenth century. It was Schloezer who emphasised the importance of the *Primary Chronicle*, claimed that it was the work of the monk Nestor and argued most strongly that the Varangians must have been Scandinavians. Unlike Mueller, Schloezer did not think that the Varangians were Swedes specifically but instead saw them as being of mixed Scandinavian or Germanic origins.

While Nestor's authorship of the *Primary Chronicle* is often questioned, the *Primary Chronicle* itself remains the most widely used source for the history of Kiev Rus. The Soviet historian Priselkov, echoing Gumilëv, wryly remarked that Nestor was clearly an ultra-Normanist.[253] Schloezer, meanwhile, did not endear himself to future generations of Russian patriots when he commented famously in one of his later works published in Germany that:

---

250 Vernadsky, *Russkaia istoriografia*, 51
251 Franklin and Shephard, *The Emergence of Rus*, 28-30.
252 Walter Gleason, 'The course of Russian History According to an eighteenth Century layman," *Laurentian University Review* 10:1 (1977): 21.
253 Mikhail Priselkov, *Istoriia Russkogo letopisaniia XI-XV vekov* (Moscow: 1940), 39.

> Even if it is offensive for Russian patriots, their history... is not as ancient as Greek and Roman, and is even younger than that of Germans and Swedes...the wild, crude and dispersed Slavs became public people only with the help of the Germans, whose fate it was to spread the fruits of civilization in the North-Western and North-Eastern worlds.[254]

It has been pointed out that at other times Schloezer was generous to Russians and, for example, honored Tatishchev as the real father of Russian history. Nonetheless, it is fair to say that for the more extreme anti-Normanists, a category to which Fomenko and most of the alternative writers belong, Schloezer represented an instrument of German designs on Russia and his history was a way of destroying Russian morale.

Bayer, Mueller and Schloezer together established the basic features of what might be called 'strong' Normanism. The claims that the Varangians were Scandinavian, that the Rus were a sub-group of the Varangians and that it was Riurik and his offspring who established the Kiev Rus state lies at the heart of standard Western and, to a lesser extent, Russian accounts of Russia's origins. It is now clear that the claims of the early Normanists were overstated. By the twentieth century, it had become apparent that Viking influence upon Russian politics or culture was not as great as Schloezer imagined. Instead, modern Normanists tend to look upon the Varangians as a catalyst for a new and important phase in Russian history without insisting that this was the first example of statehood in Russian history or that Russian politics and language are deeply indebted to Scandinavians, the key claims of Schloezer.[255]

The eighteenth-century debate highlighted divergent ways of conceiving what Russia was. German historians tended to look upon the relationship between Scandinavia and Russia as if the two regions were distinct in the manner of modern states. Schloezer believed that here was a case of a more advanced Scandinavian or German culture lifting the backward Slavs out of their benighted and primitive pre-state existence, much as was happening thanks to German education of the culturally backward Russians at the imperial court.

---

254 Anti-Normanists invariably stress this statement as evidence of German bias. See Tolz, *Russia*, 52.
255 See, for example, David Christian, *A history of Russia, Central Asia, and Mongolia*, 334.

Despite or perhaps because of the ubiquitous signs of foreign culture in Russia, the eighteenth century Russian elite was, according to Hans Rogger, deeply patriotic.[256] Anti-Normanism's founding father was Lomonosov, the son of Russian peasants who studied chemistry and metallurgy in Germany and successfully turned his hand to poetry and history. Lomonosov was moved to write history when he reviewed the draft of the oration prepared by Mueller for the Empress in 1749.[257] Lomonosov's lengthy critique of Mueller's oration was committed to paper in *Ancient Russian History*, and *Short Russian Chronicle*. This was 'the initial declaration of the anti-Normanist interpretation of Kiev's founding'.[258] Lomonosov took issue with the idea that the Slavs were backward prior to Riurik and claimed that the Varangians as we call them today were actually people of Slavic ancestry.[259] More implausibly, Lomonosov traced the Russians deep into ancient history. Ancient Slavs or proto-Russians, Lomonosov insisted, participated in such great historic events as the defense of ancient Troy, and the destruction of Rome by the eastern hordes. Troy was certainly a popular starting point in the eighteenth century. Not long before, the scholar, Nicholas Freret, was imprisoned by the allegedly more enlightened French government for arguing against the theory that the Franks were descendants of Trojan warriors.[260]

Lomonosov's method was to compare the account of the *Primary Chronicle* with the ancient sources available to him. From Byzantine historians like Procopius, Zonaras and Jordanes Lomonosov concluded that statehood existed in Russia long before 862 when, according to the *Primary Chronicle*, Riurik arrived. The ancient Greeks noted many steppe peoples including Scyths and Sarmatians. Herodotus reported that the Sarmatians were the children of the Scythians and Amazons. According to Hippocrates, the female Sarmatians were themselves Amazons whose cauterised right breast was a small price to pay for strengthened arms and shoulders. The Sarmatians seem to have evolved into new and powerful tribes known as Aorsi, Roxolani, Alans, and Iazyges. Strabo claimed that in the second century BCE, the Roxolani had possession of the southern steppe and raided

---

256 Hans Rogger, *National Consciousness in Eighteenth Century Russia*, (Cambridge: Cambridge, 1960), 253-54.
257 Gleason, 'The Course of Russian History According to an Eighteenth Century Layman,' 17-18.
258 *Ibid.*, 20.
259 Mikhail Lomonosov, *Polnoe sobranie sochinenii*, S. I. Vavilov et al., eds., 10 volumes (Moscow, Leningrad: 1950-59), 6, 168-72.
260 Davies, *Europe*, 656.

as far as the Crimean peninsula. The Sarmatians later advanced south and west to threaten Rome.

Lomonosov thought that the term Rus derived from the Roxolani.[261] Not only were the Sarmatians Slavs according to Lomonosov but so too, in a sense, were the Germans. According to Lomonosov, in ancient times, Sarmatians migrated to the Baltic and mixed with Prussians and the Scandinavians there. Riurik was a Prussian Slav, according to Lomonosov, and the Prussians got their name from *po-russy* or *prussy*.[262] The Rus who signed treaties with Byzantium used Scandinavian soldiers as ambassadors, but the Rus princes were Slavs.

Lomonosov scorned the idea that Russia got its name from Scandinavia. According to Lomonosov, the settlement of Staraia Russa near Novgorod was known prior to the invocation of Varangians, yet there is a clear-cut nucleus of 'Rus' in this word. Lomonosov was in his own way a conventional historian, despite his obsessive patriotism and lack of training in the discipline of history. His work was written with a patriotic goal in mind but more or less anchored in the sources available to him.[263]

Lomonosov saw himself as an embattled scholar, besieged at the Academy by the attacks of the Germans whose intent was to exalt their own 'fatherland'. As Lomonosov would describe his goal in 1753, there was a need to write Russian history that 'would reveal to society the long and glorious history of the Russian people'.[264] Lomonosov used descriptors such as 'awesome', 'the most noble', 'magnificent' and 'splendid' when describing Russian/Slav history, wars and statehood. The term 'brave' and freedom-loving, (*khrabry, svobodoliubivy*) were used often but could not compete with 'glory and glorious' (*slava, slavnaia*) which appeared a dozen times in relation to Slav achievements in Lomonosov's notes on Mueller's dissertation.

Lomonosov should be credited not just with firing the first shots in the anti-Normanist campaign but also with inventing a justification for Russian Empire based on a reading of secular history. For Lomonosov, Russia was a mixed host but Russia's numbers and strength, its glory as Lomonosov put it, made Russia best suited to the task of leading this mixed host, something

---

261 Mikhail Lomonosov, *Trudy po russkoi istorii* 6, 198-199.
262 Joseph Black, *G.F. Mueller and the Imperial Russian Academy*, (Kingston and Montreal: McGill, 1986), 141.
263 Gleason, 'The Course of Russian History according to an Eighteenth-Century Layman,' 21-22.
264 *Ibid.*, 27.

that Russians had done since the beginning of recorded history. Those who played a subordinate role in this host needed only to be grateful to their Russian patrons to obtain the full benefits of empire. For Lomonosov, it was not just that Vikings did not conquer Russia but that German history was in the end an offshoot of Slavic history.

During the nineteenth century, Western writers usually dismissed anti-Normanists as the weaker side in this debate with little to recommend their views apart from naïve patriotism like that displayed by Lomonosov. One reason for that conclusion is that, on the surface, the major Russian historians, apart from dilettante renegades like Lomonosov and starry-eyed Slavophiles, were themselves mostly Normanists. In fact, these founding fathers – Tatishchev and Karamzin in particular - never did view the matter the way that Bayer, Mueller and Schloezer did. What this suggests is that there may be a default Russian way of looking at the question of the origins of Kiev Rus that relates to the nature of Russian imperial identity discussed in the previous chapter.

The first Russian critically to analyse the available sources was Tatishchev (1686-1750), a high-ranking bureaucrat who served Peter the Great and was, like Lomonosov, a self-taught historian. Tatishchev came to the conclusion that *Sinopsis* was full of lies and fables invented by the Poles.[265] In 1741-1745 Tatishchev was Astrakhan's governor and had access to the archive there. Tatishchev copied chronicles, read secondary works and wrote commentary. The sources available to Tatishchev amounted to native church chronicles as well as Greek, Roman and Byzantine writers, including Strabo, Ptolemey, Herodotus and Pliny.[266] According to Rogger, Tatishchev posed enduring questions; the ethnic origins of the Russian people; the foundation of the Russian state; the degree of enlightenment among the ancient Slavs; and the problem of whether there was, historically speaking, an ideal form of government for Russia, prescribed for her by history.[267] He set the agenda for ancient Russian history for the following two and a half centuries.

Western historians have not been able to decide whether, in answering these questions, Tatishchev was a Normanist or not. Rogger claimed that Tatishchev was a Normanist and Mazour thought that he rejected

---

265 Vasilii Tatishchev, *Istoriia Rossiiskaia* (Moscow-Leningrad: AN-SSSR, 1962), 68.
266 Rudolph Daniels, *V. N. Tatishchev: Guardian of the Petrine Revolution* (Philadelphia: Franklin Publishing Company, 1973), 92.
267 Rogger, *National Consciusness in Eighteenth Century Russia*, 197.

Normanism. Daniels discusses this issue and concluded that Tatishchev stood outside of the debate.[268] The confusion suggests that Tatishchev saw the issue differently to Bayer and Mueller. The Germans were precise and definitive in their claims about Rus ethnicity. For Tatishchev, the lands of Rus already had a monarchy and therefore a state before Riurik. Riurik's invitation resulted from his marriage to a daughter of the semi-legendary Slav prince Gostomysl of Novgorod. Gostomysl was the son of another Slav warrior prince Bravlin.

This seems not to have been an entirely fanciful theory. The most recent scholarship supports the idea that the Slavs of the eight and ninth centuries must have had political structures to defend themselves against steppe peoples and Vikings.[269] Gumilëv and Vernadsky endorsed Tatishchev's view that in 755 or 790, a strong and warlike prince Bravlin from Novgorod invaded Crimea.[270] Bravlin later suffered defeat at the hands of Varangian raiders. Gostomysl regained Novgorod from the Varangians and then consolidated an alliance with them through the marriage of his daughter to Riurik. Put this way, Riurik and his Varangians were a chapter in Russian history and not its source.

Tatishchev took the view that the steppe was a very mixed host. According to Tatishchev, 'Rus' was a Sarmatian word used to describe the earliest inhabitants of the Novgorod region.[271] Tatishchev concluded that the Rus and Varangians were descended from Finnish Sarmatians. Sarmatians were originally Slavs before dividing into different branches. Scythia was a very general name for steppe peoples and was home to Slavs, Turks, Mongols, and even Chinese. While Schloezer wrote about Varangians and Slavs as if the distinction between them could be clearly drawn and as if they interacted in the manner of modern states, Tatishchev assumed that the peoples of the ancient lands of Russia were as intermingled as the peoples of Peter the Great's empire. For Tatishchev, Russia was a land of migrants whose glue was the connection all of these peoples established to the land and their willingness to serve the rightful monarch. The German historians sought a neater map of old Russia, of the type that was developing in Europe

---

268 See Daniels, *V. N. Tatishchev, Guardian of the Petrine Revolution*, 93.
269 See Christian, *Russia, Central Asia and Mongolia*, 333, who cites Goehrke, Ruhrzeit,
270 Gumilëv, *Drevniaia Rus' i Velikaia Step'*, 124-125; George Vernadsky, *The Origins of Russia* (New Haven: Yale University Press, 1952), 80-183.
271 Daniels, *V. N. Tatishchev*, 68.

after the Treaty of Westphalia of 1648. For Tatishchev, Russia was not that kind of place.

Karamzin was Russia's first Imperial historiographer and is usually described as a Normanist. Yet Black has pointed out that Karamzin imposed strong qualifications on Schloezer's account of Russia's origins. The most widely read Russian historian of the early nineteenth century, Karamzin accepted the story of Riurik and the Varangians but noted that the Slavs had their own princes, politics and military organizations long before the decision was made to invite foreigners to help put an end to civil war. As Karamzin put it, Russia was:

> A mixture of old Eastern customs, brought by the Slavs to Europe and renewed, so to speak, by our long connection with the Mongols; Byzantine customs borrowed by the Russians along with the Christian religion, and some German customs imparted by the Varangians....[272]

Whereas Bayer, Mueller and Schloezer thought that everything important about Russian statehood was imported from Scandinavia, Karamzin saw only one influence among many.

Of course, Normanism was not simply a German perspective. The German background of Ewars, a contemporary of Karamzin, did not prevent him from arguing that Russia clearly had a state before the Varangians. The Russian, Soloviev, was a Normanist and thought that the Varangians had helped to rid Russia of its sluggish eastern backwardness and clan life through respect for the individual characteristic of the Germanic tribes. Pogodin and Miliuikov were adamant that there was a strong connection between early Slavs and Germanic peoples such as the Scandinavians. A story about Vikings had the advantage of rescuing Russia from any suggestion that its origins were entwined with Asian peoples such as Khazars or the Abbasid caliphate.

At the same time it is apparent that among a great many Russians who studied the issue before this century, clear-cut distinctions between the ethnic groups of Russia did not seem to match the reality of Russia's past or present. Anti-Normanism would reappear once Westernized elite created by Peter the Great began to give way first to Slavophiles. In the second half of

---

272 Black, *State School interpretation of Russian History*, 515.

the nineteenth century, there were renewed attacks on Normanism. These nineteenth century anti-Normanists made little impression in the West. More than a century ago, Donald Mackenzie Wallace expressed his profound weariness at what he regarded as excessive Russian pride. As Wallace put it, writing in 1877:

> Though I have myself devoted to the study of this question more time and labour than perhaps the subject deserves, I have no intention of inviting the reader to follow me through this tedious controversy. Suffice it to say that, after careful consideration, and with all due deference to recent historians, I am inclined to adopt the old theory, and to regard the Normans of Scandinavia as, in a certain sense, the founders of the Russian Empire.[273]

Tedium was the predominant mood for those late nineteenth century foreigners who dealt with the Normanist debate. As Thomsen described his anti-Normanist rivals in Russia:

> It would be wearisome to dwell longer on the details of this literature. It is really but a slight portion of it has any scientific value. By far the greatest part of the writings are...the vaguest and most arbitrary fancies, which appear to be inspired more by ill-judged national fanaticism than by any serious desire to discover the truth.[274]

This was wishful thinking. For his typically Russian fanatic, Thomsen had in mind Stepan Gedeonov (1818-78)[275], who along with Ilovaisky critiqued Normanism with mixed success. There are two well-known treaties with Byzantium from the first half of the tenth century. In the treaty of 911 almost all of the names of the Rus ambassadors seem to be Scandinavian, while in the treaty of 945 Scandinavian names clearly predominated. Gedeonov and Ilovaisky painstakingly attempted to establish a Slavic basis for the names of these ambassadors and even argued a Slavonic etymology for the name Riurik. To find Slavonic origins for such names as Karl, Farlaf or Vuefast

---

273 Donald Mackenzie Wallace, *Russia* (New York: AMS Press, 1970), 185.
274 Vilhelm Thomsen, *The relations between ancient Russia and Scandinavia and the origin of the Russian state* (New York: B. Franklin, 1877).
275 Stepan Gedeonov, *Otryvki iz issledovanii o variazhskom voprose* (Saint Petersburg: 1862); Stepan Gedeonov, *Variagy i Rus'* (Saint Petersburg: 1876), II volumes.

proved an impossible task. Tikhomirov would later prove more convincing when he argued that we should look not only at the names of the ambassadors but also at the names of the princes who sent the ambassadors. Among the princes – Igor, Sviatoslav, Peredslava, Vladislava, Olga, - at least three princely names out of five mentioned are probably Slavic while Igor and Olga are at least arguably Slavic.[276]

Ironically, Ilovaisky and Gedeonov today seem to stand up quite well in comparison to Thomsen himself. Writing in the 1970s Riasanovsky, the most able anti-Normanist among Western academics, pointed out that the Normanist case of his day was nowhere near as strident as it was when it was first formulated.[277] Few historians now argue, as Schloezer and Thomsen once did, that the politics, law and even the art and architecture of Kievan Rus were Scandinavian in origin.[278] Thomsen thought that the Vikings built the major institutions of Kievan Rus and even that *Yatviag* was a Varangian name when it is more likely to have been the name of a Baltic tribe.[279] Yet evidence of Norman institutions and customs is as difficult to find in modern Russia as it is to find traces of the Scandinavian language.[280]

The last and most famous Imperial investigator of the *Primary Chronicle* was Alexis Shakhmatov (1864-1920) whose work was, in a sense post-Slavophile and pre-Communist. Shakhmatov accepted Normanism with so many caveats and reservations that some anti-Normanists regarded him as a fellow traveller. Shakhmatov, better than anyone else, made readers aware that the early chronicles were not simply statements of fact but written in particular ways for political and dynastical reasons.

Shakhmatov analysed the many chronicles, comparing their differences and similarities.[281] His conclusion was that there were multiple additions to the texts made by successive generations of writers and copyists. Shakhmatov argued that the *Primary Chronicle* was a justification of the princely Riurikid line and so the chronicler's aim was to identify the Rus with

---

276 Mikhail Tikhomirov, 'Proiskhozhdenie nazvanii Rus' i Russkaia Zemlia,' *Russkii Narod* (Moscow: Kuchkovo pole, 2001): 240-241.
277 Alexander V. Riasonavsky, 'Pseudo-Varangian Origins of the Kievo-Pecherski Monastery: The 'Finger in the Pie' Hypothesis,' *Russian History/Histoire Russe* 7:3 (1980): 265-82.
278 See Vilhelm Thomsen, *The relations between ancient Russia and Scandinavia and the origin of the Russian state.*
279 *Ibid.*, 141.
280 Lomonosov, *Trudy po russkoi istorii*, VI, 35.
281 Alexander Shakhmatov, *Razyskaniia o russkikh letopisiakh, Akademicheskii proekt* (Moscow: Kuchkovo pole, 2001).

the Varangians to establish the genealogical connection between the Varangian Riurik and the Rus princes of Kiev who followed.[282] Shakhmatov praised the work of Schloezer but pointed to the inconsistencies in the text of the *Primary Chronicle*. According to Shakhmatov, there were obvious layers and additions to an original text, including the parts related to the alleged invitation to the Scandinavian warlords.[283] Shakhmatov pointed out that it was the *Primary Chronicle* that specifically described the invocation of the Varangians as we know it today and he noted that other chronicles such as the Novgorodian Chronicle were less specific on this matter.[284]

The Rus of the chronicles came to be associated with Kiev while Novgorod was home to Varangians and Slovenes. This seems strange given that, logically Vikings must have established themselves in the north, that is, Novgorod, before moving south to Kiev. The First Novgorodian Chronicle described Prince's Igor army and recorded that, 'he (Igor) had Varangians, men of Slovenes, that were called the Rus'. The *Primary Chronicle* relates this passage differently: 'he (Oleg) had Varangians, Slovenes, and others called the Rus'.[285] The version in the Novgorod Chronicle suggests that the Rus and Slovenes were one and the same.

Shakhmatov tried to separate what he described as 'northern' sources within the *Primary Chronicle* from the ones that were written in the south around Kiev.[286] According to Shakhmatov, in the ninth century, Scandinavian Vikings took over the middle Dnepr around Kiev and were called 'Rus' by their neighbours. The subjugated southerners, that is, the Slavs from the Kiev region, continued to refer to themselves using existing tribal names such as Polyane. Later, Scandinavians dominated the Slavic north, where they were known as Varangians. Thus, the name 'Rus' is southern and older than that of the Varangians. When the northern Varangians together with the subjugated Novgorodian Slavs returned under Oleg to capture Kiev, they adopted the older name of 'Rus'.[287]

For pseudo-history, Shakhmatov was academically expert but politically

---

282   Shakhmatov, *Razyskaniia o russkikh letopisiakh*, 234, 243, 244.
283   Shakhmatov, *Razyskaniia o russkikh letopisiakh*, 210-215 on the differences among the domestic Russian sources used to describe the invocation of Varangians and 217, 218, 220 on different descriptive approach of the *Primary Chronicle* to the issue of Varangian invocation compared to other Russian written sources
284   *Ibid.*, 218.
285   *Ibid.*, 217.
286   *Ibid.*, 219.
287   *Ibid.*, 243-244.

weak. Like so many of his contemporaries, Shakhmatov succumbed to governmental and peer pressure to conform to the West's preferred version of Russian history. Fomenko finds it incredible that Shakhmatov could seriously believe that Vikings would establish themselves first in the south and only later dominate Novgorod and the north. For Fomenko, the true scientist should stand up to the ignorance and brutality of political power, just as Lomonosov had done.

III.2 Normanists and Anti-Normanists

The Normanist thesis came under attack on at least three occasions. In 1749-50, it was Lomonosov. In the second half of the nineteenth century when Slavophilism and Pan-Slavism were strong currents among the Russian reading public, anti Normanism revived in the works of Dmitrii Ilovaisky (1832-1920), Stepan Gedeonov (1818-1878) and Mikhail Hrushevskii (1866-1934).[288] Finally in the Soviet era, and especially after the Great Patriotic War, it became standard practice to criticize Normanism. This was the literature with which Fomenko and many of the alternative writers grew up.

The Soviet political leadership, fanatically opposed to bourgeois nationalism in theory but pragmatically Russo-centric in practice, presided over a massive rewriting of Russian history from an anti-Normanist perspective. The chief exponents of Anti-Normanism in the Soviet era included Boris Grekov (1882-1953), Mikhail Tikhomirov (1893-1965), Boris Rybakov (1908-), Peter Tretiakov (1909-1976), Lev Cherepnin (1905-1977), Vasilii Mavrodin (1908-1987), Arsenii Nasonov (1898-1965), Alexander Udal'tsov (1883-1958) and M. Priselkov (1881-1941).[289] Backed by the

---

288 Dmitrii Ilovaisky, *Istoriia Rossii; Razyskania o nachale Rusi* (Moscow: 1882); Stepan Gedeonov, *Variagi i Rus* (St-Petersburg: 1876), and 'Otzvyki iz issledovanii o variazhskom voprose,' *Zapiski Akademii Nauk* 2 (1862); Mikhail Hrushevskii, *Kievskaia Rus* (St-P: 1911).

289 Boris Rybakov, *Obrazovanie drevnerusskogo gosudarstva* (Moscow: 1954), *Drevnie Russy* (Moscow: 1951); *Kievan Rus'* (Moscow: Progress, 1984); Boris Grekov, *Kievskaia Rus* (Moscow-Leningrad, 1944); Mikhail Tikhomirov, *Rossiiskoe gosudarstvo XV-XVII vekov* (Moscow: 1973), and *Russkaia kultura X-XVIII vekov* (Moscow: 1968); Peter Tretiakov, *Vostochoslavianskie plemena* (Moscow: 1953), and *U istokov drevnerusskoi narodnosti* (Leningrad: 1970); Lev Cherepnin, *Istoricheskie uslovia formirovania russkoi narodnosti do kontsa XV veka* (Moscow: 1957), and *Russkaia Istoriografia do XIX veka* (Moscow: 1957); Vasilii Mavrodin, *Proiskhozhdenie russkogo naroda* (Leningrad: 1978); Arsenii Nasonov, *Russkaia*

resources of the state, these historians presented a serious challenge to classic Normanist position represented by Schloezer and later by Thomsen.

The anti-Normanist strategy from the time of Lomonosov was to identify each element in the Normanist case and refute it piece by piece. The literature of the Soviet era after Stalin set about the task systematically of proving that the *Primary Chronicle* was contradictory, that foreign sources relied upon by Normanists were ambivalent, that advocates of Normanism were biased, that people called the Rus lived in Russia but not in Scandinavia long before 862, that Russia was civilised and agricultural with only isolated evidence of Scandinavian presence or a trade and plunder culture and that Slavs were as capable as Vikings of having achieved military feats such as raids on Byzantium or the Caspian ports.

The problem is that patriotically minded activists as well as historians want answers to questions for which the existing sources are simply not adequate. Even the staunchest supporter of Normanism would acknowledge that there is room for doubt about the claims made in the *Primary Chronicle*. For example, historians have pointed to the coincidence that the invitation sent to the Varangians, as recorded in the *Primary Chronicle*, resembles the history of other peoples, notably invitations sent to the Saxons by the Britons, and that the story of three brothers coming to a foreign land echoes many legendary texts. Historians mostly agree that the *Primary Chronicle* is a compilation of earlier chronicles, that at least some of the information presented there is not historically reliable[290], and that it is impossible to date with any precision the time of its writing.[291] Few Western historians think that Vikings first established a permanent presence in Russia as late as 862 as the *Primary Chronicle* suggests.

The *Primary Chronicle* suggests that a mere twenty years after Riurik arrived in the north, the Varangian warlord Oleg (Hilga/Helga) in 882 conquered Kiev from Askold and Dir, the mysterious Varangians who already ruled Kiev according to the *Primary Chronicle*. Recent Western accounts suggest that it is likely that the *Primary Chronicle* is simply wrong about these early dates and, on the basis of archaeological evidence, that Kiev did not

---

zemlia i obrazovanie territorii Drevnerusskogo gosudarstva (Moscow: 1951), and 'K voprosy ob obrazovanii drevnerusskoi narodnosti,' *Vestnik AN SSSR* 8 (1951); Mikhail Priselkov, *Istoriia Russkogo letopisaniia* XI-XV vekov (Moscow: 1940).

290 For examples see Franklin and Shepard, 106-07, which describes obvious latter-date interpolations that have found their way into the chronicle.

291 Henryk Paszkiewicz, *The Making of the Russian Nation* (Connecticut: Westport, 1963), 111.

even develop, let alone become the capital, until well into the tenth century.[292]

The detailed story of Russia's baptism, which took place over the years 985-89 according to the *Primary Chronicle*, seems to be an example of how chronicle writing served ends other than a purely factual record of events. At some point in the 980s the Kievan Prince Vladimir decided to reject his murderous, pagan and polygamist past and to become a Byzantine-style Christian. According to the *Primary Chronicle*, Vladimir received ambassadors from Catholics, Muslims, Orthodox Christians and Jews. After he had listened to their testimonies, Vladimir decided to send his own people to witness the different religions and then report to him. Eventually, Vladimir ruled out Islam because it prohibited alcohol and pork, chose Orthodox Christianity for the beauty of its service and married his sister to the Byzantine emperor at Korsun.

Critics have long argued that this was a strange undertaking given that Vladimir should have known very well the differences among the world's religions. He already knew of the Muslim Volga Bulgars, his eastern neighbours since the ninth century. The relationship with the Latin West had also been established long before Vladimir became the Prince of Kiev. In 959, Russian ambassadors visited Emperor Otto asking to send an archbishop and priests to Russia.[293] There were Byzantine churches in the south of Russia including Kiev whose remnants are still scattered along northwest Crimea. Kiev Rus had a long and complex relationship with the Khazar Khanate, whose elite practiced Judaism. As most historians would acknowledge, Kiev and Byzantium chose one another as the alliance of choice after Vladimir's father Sviatoslav obliterated the Khazar Empire in 965.[294]

It is not enough for anti-Normanists to show that the *Primary Chronicle* was fanciful about certain issues. There needed to be an alternative explanation of how Russia received its name, who the Rus and the Varangians were and why confusion about their identity flourished subsequently. The suggestions made by anti-Normanists as to who the Rus were if they were not Scandinavians seem almost endless. There are references to a people called Rus, or at least something like Rus long before 862 when according to the *Primary Chronicle*, Riurik and his Rus arrived. The

---

292   See Christian, *Russia, Central Asia and Mongolia*, 343.
293   Bushkov, *Rossiia I*, 49.
294   Christian, *Russia, Inner Asia and Mongolia*, 345-47.

Bavarian Geographer, an anonymous description of 'Cities and Lands North of Danube' dating to 850 mentions *Ruzzi* living next to Khazars and Hungarians. There is the testimony of Constantinople's patriarch Photius who in 867 described a people called 'Rhos' who surpassed all other nations in cruelty.[295] Such cruelty could as easily have been the calling card of Slavs as of Vikings, so the anti-Normanists claim.

Artamonov came to the same conclusion as Vernadsky, that the Rus from Novgorod were the descendants of the Rosomon tribes who fought against the Goths and allied with the Huns. They lived alongside the Slavs, but were different in language and customs until the tenth century when they merged completely. Earlier, the West knew these people as *Rugi*.[296] Novosel'tsev argued that the process of merger between the Rosomon (Rugi) and the Slavs began in the ninth century, a protracted and difficult process.[297] Kuz'min also identified Russes and Rugi: he claimed that Rugi were part of the Roman Empire in 307. For him these Rus or Rugi were not Germans but 'northern Illyrians' who originally hailed from the southern Baltic but were eventually pushed south toward the Balkans and northeast toward lake Ilmen' by the Goths.[298]

Rybakov and Nasonov came to the conclusion that neither the term Rus nor the Rus land represented a single tribe or area. Rybakov's hypothesis suggested that in the fifth or sixth centuries AD along the mid Dnepr the tribes that we know from the *Primary Chronicle* as Polyane, Severyane and Ulichi united to form a powerful entity known as Ros. These early Ros or Rus in the period before the ninth century resembled Turkic nomads because of their close association with the steppe. Ethnic differences between the Slavs and the Rus described by observers are so miniscule according to Rybakov, that they could not be distinguished.[299] Therefore, according to Rybakov, when the *Primary Chronicle* referred to the Rus land or Rus, it described the territory populated mostly by eastern Slavs.[300]

---

295 Paszkiewicz, *The Making of the Russian Nation*, 110.
296 Mikhail Artamonov, *Istoriia Khazar* (St-Petersburg: 2002), 366.
297 Anatolii Novosel'tsev, *Vostochnye istochniki o vostochnykh slavianakh i Rusi VI-IX vekov/Drevnerusskoe gosudarstvo i ego mezhdunarodnoe znachenie* (Moscow: 1965), 355-419.
298 Apollon Kuz'min, *Padenie Peruna. Stanovlenie Khristianstva na Rusi* (Moscow: 1988), 133-139.
299 Boris Rybakov, 'Problema obrazovaniia drevnerusskoi narodnosti,' *Voprosy Istorii* 9 (1952): 127.
300 Rybakov, *Obrazovanie drevnerusskogo gosudarstva*, 126 and *Drevnie Rusy*, 125.

Nasonov also argued for the existence of a tribal union called Rus, but for him the emergence of such a union occurred in the ninth century when Slavic tribes paid tribute to the Khazars; according to Nasonov, Polyane and Severyane were the ancestors of the Rus. Nasonov took the view that the term 'Rus land' has a more ancient history than Kiev Rus'.[301] Tretiakov argued that the nucleus of the future Russians formed before Christian times on the mid-Dnepr, later incorporating the tribes of Polyane, Severyane and Ulichi, while tribal formations bearing the name 'Ros' were known in northern Black Sea region as early as the times of the Gothic chieftain Germanarikh.[302]

Still other writers have sought answers to the origins of the term 'Rus' in the Iranian language where there are words such as rauka, ruk, that mean 'to shine', or 'the light'. The Ossetians have rux and roxs – whitish.[303] Padalka has argued that 'white' is not simply a colour but a symbol for leadership, the hegemony that the Rus enjoyed in the ancient Slavic world. As Padalka would have it, Scyths gave their name to a multitude of different tribes that had in common the same mode of living on the southern steppe, and who became known to the outside world as Sarmatians and Alans, then Anty and Venedy, and finally as Slavs.[304]

According to Grekov, Rus was the term for northern Slavs and Ros for the southern Slavs, and the socio-cultural collision between the north and the south provided the competing terms of Russia and Rossiia that still exist to this day.[305] While Normanists could cite evidence from the Arab traveller, Ibn Rusta, that the Rus 'have no landed property, nor villages nor cultivated lands', Grekov did his best to prove that the reverse was true.[306] Grekov devoted much of his research to proving that the ruling class of Kiev Rus was accustomed to taking tribute from a basically agricultural society that was

---

301 Arsenii Nasonov, *'Russkaia Zemlia' i obrazovanie territorii Drevnerusskogo gosudarstva* (Moscow: 1951), 97.
302 Peter Tretiakov, *Vostochnoslavianskie plemena* (Moscow: 1953), 162.
303 Oleg Trubachev, 'Rus, Rossiia; Ocherk etimologii nazvaniia,' *Russkaia Slovesnost'* 3 (Moscow: 1994): 67-70; Kaitiko Bzaev, *Proiskhozhdenie etnicheskogo termina 'Rus"* (Valdikavkaz: IR, 1995), 112; Valentin Krasnopevtsev, *Varvary-berbery i zagadochnaia Rus'* (Pskov: 2001), 150; Alexander Shakhmatov, 'Nazvanie Rus" Drevniaia Rus'* (Moscow: 2005), 31-38; N. Zharvin, *K voprosy o proiskhozhdenii etnonimov 'Rus" i 'Slaviane'* (Moscow: Noosfera, 2003), 183; G. Kovalev, 'K proiskhozhdeniiu imeni Rus': est' li alternativa?' *Nestor: Istoriko-kulturnye issledovaniia* 3 (Voronezh, 1995), 45-59; Mikhail Tikhomirov, 'Proiskhozhdenie nazvanii Rus' i Russkaia zemlia,' *Russkoe Letopisanie* (Moscow: 1979), 22-45.
304 L. Padalka, *O proiskhozhdenii slova 'Rus'* (Poltava: 1915), 103.
305 Boris Grekov, *Kievskaia Rus'* (Moscow: 1944), 47.
306 Quoted in Hosking, *Russia and the Russians*, 33.

quite different from the war and-trade-based society that early Normanists imagined.

For Tikhomirov, the Rus were included among the northern nations in the *Primary Chronicle* in error. The compiler of the *Primary Chronicle* found the name Rus in northern Scandinavian sagas written long after the foundation of Kiev. These sagas mention the Rus alongside Swedes and Normans, causing the chronicler to mistakenly identify the Rus as natives of Scandinavia. According to Tikhomirov, a twelfth-century Icelandic map placed Rus next to Sweden, Gothland and Norway, to the east of Scandinavia.[307] Therefore, the Rus and the Scandinavians could not have been the same people, but the Rus were identified as Varangians by the compiler of the *Primary Chronicle* because they were grouped in the same sentence with other northern nations.[308]

To reinforce his argument Tikhomirov cited passages from the *Primary Chronicle* that demonstrate the confusion of the chronicler about the connection of Rus to the foundation of Novgorod. Thus, one entry from the *Primary Chronicle* specifies that 'and Rus appeared from those Varangians, Novgorodians, that is people of Novgorod from the Varangian clan, although they were Slavs before'. At another point, the *Primary Chronicle* describes 'Polyane...whom we call Rus'. Since Polyane dwelled in the Kievan region, it is clear to Tikhomirov that Rus was the name of the Kievan domain, and that the Polyane adopted the name Rus in recognition of their homeland, while Novgorodian Slavs and Varangians came to be known as Rus only after they settled in Kiev.

Tikhomirov argued that other examples from the *Primary Chronicle* corroborate this view. According to the *Primary Chronicle*, Oleg, the founder of Kiev, was referred to as a Rus prince upon his ascension to the Kievan throne. When Oleg arrived in Kiev, he brought with him Varyags and Slovenes and others, who only then started to call themselves Rus. For Tikhomirov it is obvious that the Slav princes hired mercenaries, including Scandinavians, who later acted on behalf of their rulers and presented themselves as Rus as they went about their diplomatic and military tasks

For Udal'tsov there is no doubt as to the southern or Kievan origin of the word Rus. The nucleus Ros-Rus could be encountered in works of

---

[307] Mikhail Tikhomirov, 'Proiskhozhdenie nazvanii Rus i Russkaia Zemlia,' *Russkii Narod*, (Moscow: Kuchkovo pole, 2001), 236-237.
[308] *Ibid.*

Jordanes and Procopius, sixth-century writers connected to the Byzantine court.[309] Parkhomenko too believed that the term Rus originated in the south, around the Black and Azov seas. As for Scandinavians in the Russian north, the term 'Rus' is unequivocally encountered only in 1167, and, therefore, far too late to be connected to the origins of its use in the lands of Russia.[310] Other writers link the name of the Rus to geographic locations in the south. Vernadsky agreed with those who pointed to the river called Rus or Ros, a tributary of the Dnepr south of Kiev.[311]

For Fomenko, the chronicles have clearly been misinterpreted. Varangians refer not to the Vikings but to *vragi*, the Russian word for enemies just as the Mongol-Tatars was a generic reference to any horrifying invasion and did not designate a specific tribe. Riurik is most likely a corruption of Iurii and refers to Iurii Danilovich, the fourteenth-century prince of Moscow and Grand Prince of Vladimir.[312] More plausibly, Gumilëv has argued that it is obvious that Russia boasted a proud and ancient history long before we hear of Varangians. Gumilëv endorsed those who claimed identification between the Rus and Rugi. For all these mainly twentieth century writers, Russians got their name from ancestors called Rus or its equivalent but these ancestors were not Scandinavians. The early Russians were descended from an ancient ethnos known under many names – rogi, rugi, rutsi, ruyany, rosy, or ruthenians, long before the Varangians made their appearance. Their success in conquering a vast territory explains the instability in the spelling of their name.[313]

In the West, a moderate Normanism is adopted almost everywhere. In Russia, Normanism is under constant attack, as it has been since the Stalin era. For the consensus of scholarly opinion in the West, the point is not that the *Primary Chronicle* is infallible but that its general story fits with what is now known from non-Slav sources and from archaeological discoveries. The *Primary Chronicle*, a medieval source written by Orthodox Slavs and hailing the achievements of pagan Norsemen, represents one powerful argument for

---

309 Alexander Udal'tsov, 'Osnovnye voprosy etnogeneza Slavian,' *Sovetskaia etnografiia* VI-VII (1947): 168.
310 Vladimir Parkhomenko, *U istokov russkoi gosudarstvennosti* (Leningrad: 1924), 107.
311 George Vernadsky, *The Origins of Russia* (Oxford: Clarendon Press, 1959), 212; Paszkiewicz, *The Making of the Russian Nation*, 117; Stender-Petersen, *Varangica*, 16, 85-87, 243.
312 Nosovskii and Fomenko, *Novaia khronologiia Rusi*, 114.
313 Gumilëv, *Drevniaia Rus i velikaia step,'* 126.

the Normanist thesis. Other texts pointed to the Scandinavian presence in Russia and the association of Rus and Vikings. Arab sources reported the Rus burning their boats as part of funereal proceedings, as Vikings often did. Viking swords have been found in south Russia and Byzantine coins on the river Kama dating to the sixth century. From the Byzantine, Jordanes, it is known that Rus were travelling widely to trade in fur at this time. Given the scale of this sea-faring trade and military operation, these warriors seem to resemble closely the Vikings active in Western Europe.[314]

Nonetheless, a great many readers of Soviet literature about Kiev Rus have received the strong impression that there is no credible argument for Normanism whatsoever. As Rybakov put it, 'the sum total of the Normanist assumptions in the course of two centuries is insufficient not only to call Normanism 'a theory', but even a hypothesis, because it offers no analysis.'[315] Deeply frustrating to anti-Normanists is the fact that, seemingly, Westerners apparently knew that there was no basis for their claims. According to Rybakov, the 'leader' of the Normanists, Stender-Petersen, acknowledged in 1960 in speech to academics that Normanism as a scientific construction was dead because all of its basic pillars had been disproved. Nevertheless, this Danish scholar urged historians to create a neo-Normanism.[316] Pseudo-history is quick to repeat this apparent evidence of Western duplicity and dogmatism.

For anti-Normanists, the proposition that Vikings were state builders simply defies logic. Kiev Rus had many connections with its non-European neighbours to the south, including people from the Turkic steppe, the Byzantine Empire and Bulgaria. Anti-Normanists argue that in comparison to these advanced states, the Vikings were barbarians who failed to build cities even in their homeland or to leave any tangible legacy in Russia. Lomonosov's hypothesis that the Vikings who found their way to Kiev Rus were hired mercenaries of the Slavs flourishes in the popular literature today.

Anti-Normanists point out that no researcher has found reference to a tribe called the Rus living in Scandinavia at the time specified by the *Primary Chronicle*. Yet there are many references to Rus living in the lands of Kiev Rus' long before 862. The names of individuals seem fluid and it is impossible to know if two names have been attached to the one person. Khazar sources

---

314   Christian, *Russia, Central Asia and Mongolia*, 335.
315   Rybakov, *Kievan Rus*, 12.
316   *Ibid.*, 13.

suggest that in the 940s the Rus army of Helgi attacked Tmutorkan, the Black Sea base of the Khazars, and it seems possible that this Helgi was prince Oleg who captured Kiev.[317]

As for the ethnicity of the Rus princes, descriptions suggest natives of Russia and not Vikings. A Byzantine eyewitness described Sviatoslav, the Kievan prince and classic Rus warrior/adventurer of the tenth century as a medium-sized man who was snub-nosed, had blue eyes, thick shoulders, bushy eyebrows and a savage appearance. Sviatoslav described himself not just as Rus, but as a Tavridian Scythian, presumably a Scythian from the northern Crimean lands.[318] More importantly for Fomenko, Sviatoslav boasted a Cossack-style shaven head and forelock and a golden earring to distinguish his high birth. At his meeting with the Byzantines in 971, Sviatoslav crossed the river in a 'Scythian' boat dressed in a plain white garment and, like Cossack atamans, did not try to distinguish himself from the men he led. Alternative writers routinely quote this passage from Johan Tzimiskes, the Byzantine emperor, as evidence that the Rus Sviatoslav, far from resembling a Swede, seemed to have much more in common with steppe peoples in terms of appearance, and, in terms of horsemanship and attire, with the Cossacks of more recent times.[319]

It is the Vikings not the Slavs who have a reputation for boat building and piracy. But, as David Christian points out, the Rus depended upon the excellent canoes with the Greek name of *monoxyla* made by Slav craftsmen.[320] As for the seafaring of the Rus, there is no doubt as to the scale and effectiveness of maritime operations. As Gumilëv tells the story, around 790 the Rus stormed Sudak in Crimea, and then moved to the southern shore of the Black Sea. In 840, the Rus took Amastrida in Asia Minor and in 852 Kiev.[321] In 909, Rus boats launched attacks in the Caspian Sea and, in 913, a huge flotilla of five hundred ships with the permission of the Tsar of the Khazars entered the Caspian once more.[322] In 941 the Russians fought for four months against the Byzantine Emperor Constantine while three years later Igor led a land and sea army against Byzantium.[323]

---

317 See Christian, *Russia, Central Asia and Mongolia*, 343.
318 See Boris Grekov, *Kiev Rus*, trans. by Sdobnikov, (Moscow: Foreign Languages Publishing House, 1959), 620-21.
319 Vernadsky, *Origins of Russia*, 276-77.
320 Christian, *Russia, Central Asia and Mongolia*, 344.
321 Gumilëv, *Drevniaia Rus i velikaia step,'* 161.
322 *Ibid.*, 188.
323 *Ibid.*, 196.

If these were mainly Viking pirates, how could it be that these warriors rapidly disappeared from history, leaving virtually nothing to Russian politics, military organization or culture? The numbers of Rus sailors were impressive if ancient sources and the guesses of modern historians can be believed; in 913 there may have been five hundred Rus ships on the Caspian, with one hundred warriors on each ship. The Soviet historian V. Mavrodin considered that there were 20,000 warriors since according to the chronicles an average Russian boat could take forty warriors.[324] Gumilëv thinks that there were from 35,000 to 50,000 warriors.[325] Later, the Cossacks proved adept at seamanship, raiding the Turkish fort of Azov, the Turkic coast of the Black Sea and earning comparisons to Moroccan pirates of the Mediterranean.

Even the staunchest Normanists had to admit that the numbers of Varangians in Russia were probably limited. It follows logically that there was a significant number of experienced sailors among the Slavs who either learnt that trade from the Vikings or evolved largely without help from Scandinavia. In 965 the Russians under Prince Sviatoslav did not dare to attack the Khazars who dominated the steppe with their cavalry, and instead built boats in the land of Viatichi, set sail down the Volga, attacked Khazaria from the rear to destroy Itil, the Khazar capital. As Gumilëv stated, the power of the Rus of the tenth century was in the boats.[326] If Slavs built the boats and crewed them, it seems likely that they could also have been commanders and navigators.

For Normanists, it is irrelevant that the *Primary Chronicle* is almost certainly wrong about when the Rus first made their appearance in Russia. As Paszkiewicz put it:

> I have analysed many sources relating to this question, and have dealt separately with the Chronicle of Nestor. And it follows from this examination that even if the Povest' did not exist, we should still have to recognize Rus' as Norsemen.[327]

That there were stories about Rus in south Russia is hardly surprising given that Vikings were already active almost everywhere in Europe and the Middle East before this date. More important for the Normanists is that the *Primary*

---

324 Vasilii Mavrodin, *Ocherki po istorii feodalnoi Rusi* (Leningrad: 1949), 47.
325 Gumilëv, *Drevniaia Rus i velikaia step,'* 198.
326 *Ibid.*, 211.
327 Paszkiewicz, *The Making of the Russian Nation*, 114.

Chronicle in general terms corroborates sources from outside the Slav and Viking worlds.

De Adminstrando Imperio suggests Scandinavian origins for the names of the Russian ambassadors who signed treaties with the Byzantine Empire. In *Annales Bertinianne* there is an entry concerning ambassadors of the Byzantine Emperor Theophilus who arrived, in May 839 in Ingelheim, to the court of Louis the Pious. In a special letter Theophilus asked Louis to allow safe passage to the ambassadors of the people of the 'Rhos', who were in Constantinople to sign a friendly treaty, but who could not return home because the way was cut by hostile barbarians. Upon investigation Louis found out that the ambassadors were Swedes, and, out of fear that they were Norman spies ordered them detained. Nothing is known about their fate.

The fact that ambassadors calling themselves Rhos turned out to be ethnic Swedes gave Normanists reason to claim that this was proof that the Rus were in fact ethnic Swedes. However, for anti-Normanists, the fact that the ambassadors were detained should attract attention, not the fact that they were Swedes. Louis's logic seems to have been that if a person had called himself a Rus, how could he be a Swede?[328] If the Rus were known in Western Europe to be Vikings then Louis should not have been surprised. Baumgarten argued that the Byzantine Emperor had not realized that the Rhos were Swedes when he offered them safe passage. Anti-Normanists dismiss this argument as impossible to believe.[329]

For anti-Normanists, the Swedes who appeared at Ingelheim as ambassadors for the Rus had simply been hired by the Russians or were Vikings integrated into Kiev's army, who took upon themselves a Rus identity.[330] As Lomonosov had put it, the Varangians were 'northern soldiers' and not an ethnic group.[331] Normanists have dismissed such claims as highly unlikely. It would be the first example, Thomsen claimed, of Vikings offering their services as ambassadors to a foreign power. If there were a relationship between Vikings and Slavs in Kiev, it was more likely that the latter served the former, according to Thomsen. Normanists cite too the testimony of Liutprand of Cremona who described the Rus who attacked Constantinople as a people known to the Germans as *Nordmanni*.[332] Anti-Normanists counter

---

328   Sergei Lesnoi, *Istoriia Russov* (Paris: 1953), 43-44.
329   *Ibid.*
330   Vernadsky, *Origins of Russia*, 199-200.
331   Lomonosov, *Trudy po russkoi istorii*, 6, 203.
332   Hilda Davidson, *The Viking Road to Byzantium* (London: Allen and Unwin, 1976),

that the same Liutprand testified that his understanding was that the etymology of the term for the Rus referred to the blonde-reddish colour of the warriors' hair and so his testimony is at best contradictory.³³³

The anti-Normanists claim that Constantine, who listed the names of the Dnepr rapids in Slavic and Rus, was often wrong about names. For example, Constantine suggested an identical name in Russian and Slavic for the first Dnepr rapid, Essupi, which is unlikely to be the case if Slavonic and Rus were two very different languages. Secondly, the Byzantine Emperor suggested that the name Gelandri was of Slavonic origin, when Scandinavian etymology seemed a better explanation for it. On the other hand, the supposedly Scandinavian Strukun seems closer to Slavonic etymology. Meanwhile, other scholars have suggested not Scandinavian, but Iranian or even Greek etymology for the names of the Dnepr rapids mentioned by Constantine.³³⁴ It is not so much the argument but the strategy that is of interest here. The aim is to minimize or rule out Scandinavian influence. It does not matter that in the process, the purely Slavic element of the Rus is weakened because Russia was a mixed host where Slavs/Russians were first among equals. Iranian origins are much more acceptable to anti-Normanists whose thesis depends above all on combating the evidence for Scandinavians, close relations of the German founders of Normanism, in the history of Russia.

The descriptions of some Arab observers suggested that the Rus merchants who travelled to Arab lands were in fact Scandinavians, judging by their customs such as burying the dead in their ships.³³⁵ Not so, say the anti-Normanists who find their own Arab sources to paint a different picture. They point to the fact that Ibn-Khurdadhbih (d.912) claimed that Rus merchants, 'who belonged to the Slavonic people', and paid a tithe to Constantinople or the Khazar Kaganate³³⁶ used Slavonic eunuchs as interpreters. For anti-Normanists the fact that Slavonic eunuchs were used as interpreters is evidence that the merchants were themselves Slavs. This same writer, whose work describes the trade routes of his era, referred to Rus as a place of many towns, an unlikely home for the nomads of the sea. Another Arab writer of the

---

      59.
333 Lesnoi, *Istoriia Russov*, 37-38.
334 See Lesnoi, *Istoriia Russov*, 52-56 and Abrashkin, *Predki russkikh v etom mire*, 376-377.
335 Basil Dmytryshin, *Medieval Russia* (Holt, Rinehart and Winston, 1973), 11-17.
336 Boris Rybakov, 'Problema obrazovaniia drevnerusskoi narodnosti v svete trudov Stalina,' *Voprosy Istorii* 9 (1952): 44.

ninth century, Al-Jakhaini, wrote that Ruses lived in three clans. The first was adjacent to the Bulgars and had a ruler in Kiev. Thus, anti-Normanists respond, Kiev was known to the Arabs as the capital of the Rus long before the invitation to Riurik in 862.[337]

The proponents of Normanism argue that it was the quick absorption of the tiny Scandinavian ruling class by the mass of Slav underlings that caused a fairly rapid dying out of Scandinavian names. Anti-Normanists are sceptical and argue that history usually shows the reverse. Tikhomirov argued that in Bulgaria, Turkic princes managed to maintain their hereditary names, culture and language for at least two centuries despite living among a majority Slav population.[338]

In part, Tikhomirov's confidence comes from the comparative levels of civilization in Scandinavia and Russia. He has counted 271 towns in Russia at a time when Scandinavia was much less developed.[339] Lesnoi claimed that he found over two hundred more towns in the chronicles and evidence only of seven cities in total in Scandinavia.[340] Why the Vikings would have needed sophisticated settlements to achieve their political and military goals is not clear. Witnesses described them as expert in setting up temporary bases for their trading activities. At the same time the Vikings called medieval Russia *'Garda/Gardariki'*, the place of many cities/towns, a sign that Russia was older than Scandinavia in civilizational terms, the anti-normanists continue to argue.

Anti-Normanists note too that Byzantine texts suggest that the oaths that the Russian princes swore were to Perun, often associated with the Viking god Thor and Volos, a traditional Slavonic god. How could the Rus avoid distinctly Scandinavian god such as Odin, ask the anti-Normanists. The presence of a purely Slavonic god in Volos (Veles) suggests to them that the princes themselves were Slavs and not Scandinavian.

Anti-Normanists have argued that the names of Russian cities such as Novgorod, Smolensk, Kiev, Polotsk belong to the Slavonic language group, and appeared long before the Varangians were invited to cross the Baltic. The assumption here is that the city is the bearer of culture, and that the Varangians, even if they were of Scandinavian stock, appeared in Russia only after the cities were founded and named, producing little, or no impact on

---

337 Tikhomirov, 'Proiskhozhdenie nazvanii Rus' i Russkaia Zemlia,' *Russkii Narod*, 249.
338 *Ibid.*, 241.
339 Mikhail Tikhomirov, *Drevnorusskie goroda* (Moscow: 1956).
340 Lesnoi, *Istoriia Russov*, 689.

Russia. Anti-Normanists, starting with Lomonosov, emphasize that the Russian language is virtually free of Scandinavian borrowings as compared to heavy borrowings from the Tatar, Finnish or Polish languages, a conclusion that stands up well in the light of modern research.[341]

For anti-Normanists the sheer volume of alternative suggestions is proof not of the individual weaknesses of each of these arguments but of their collective strength in the war against the Norman myth. Nor do they regard as damaging to their case the fact that some foreigners seemed to know the Rus as Viking warriors. Kiev Rus like present-day Russia was a mixed horde. What anti-Normanists cannot accept is that Slavs/Russians played a subordinate role to a foreign band of conquerors and state builders. Thus, while Russians are happy to proclaim themselves free of any suggestion of racism or an obsession with biological races, the 'Russianness' of the original inhabitants of the lands that came to form Russia was a matter of furious debate that gained momentum in the Stalin era. When Lomonosov first attacked Mueller, the Normanist controversy had no name and was an elite parlour game fought out by duelling intellectuals. Even the Slavophile revival of anti-Normanism in the nineteenth century remained confined to a small group of interested readers in a largely illiterate peasant society. The Stalin era democratised reading, inflamed passions about history of a patriotic variety and gave its readers the impression that there was only a single historical truth. Those who argued against that truth were not engaging in scholarly debate but actively undermining Russian self-esteem. What is deeply frustrating to anti-Normanists is that they have failed to dislodge Normanism from the academy even in Russia.

To recapitulate, Anti-Normanism is an enduring obsession for many Russian historians and their readers. In the West, the war is declared over and a moderate and modified version of Normanism triumphant. This only infuriates anti-Normanists in Russia further and provokes claims that Normanists are not interested in scholarly debate. Of course, Normanists see little more than wounded pride in the more extreme statements of anti-Normanism.

The strategy adopted by anti-Normanists operates at different overlapping levels. The church chronicles are unreliable. The Vikings showed no sign of higher civilization naming no cities, imparting few customs or even words to the Slav underlings and seem to have bred into the basic Slav mass

---

341   Lomonosov, *Trudy po russkoi istorii* VI, 173.

within a generation or two. When the Scandinavian burial ground at Gnezdovo near Smolensk yielded the oldest Russian inscription (*goroushna* or mustard), Normanists claimed that this was evidence of just how quickly the Vikings were able to learn Slavonic. For anti-Normanists, this is too fantastic to be believed, and even if a Viking spoke and wrote Slavonic, he was not a Viking in terms of belonging, he was a Slav. If there were so few Normans, how then could the Rus have launched massive raids against the likes of Byzantium with as witnesses tell us tens of thousands of warriors. The Chronicle provides countless examples of Scandinavians hired by Rus princes to take part in military campaigns and civil wars so logically it would seem that the Rus spotted by the likes of Louis the Pious were simply armed ambassadors serving the more culturally advanced Slav rulers of Rus. As Hosking has put it, 'together, the 'Viking-Slavs' formed a kind of tribal super-alliance with its centre at Kiev'.[342] Anti-Normanists will not rest until the terms are reversed and this super-alliance is understood as one in which the Vikings served merely as the hired mercenaries of a Slav state.

III.3 Uncovering the Plot Against Russia

Anti-Normanists believe they have demolished the Normanist position point by point and have been persecuted for their trouble. Fomenko cites the exasperated criticism of the historian S. Stroev who argued that Normanism is simply the accumulation of falsehoods repeated so often by well-paid professors that they attained the status of conventional wisdom. Zagoskin, writing near the end of the nineteenth century expressed the same sentiment, that those 'who protested against the Norman theory were ridiculed and accused of vandalism: it was 'scientific terror', and it was extremely difficult to struggle against it'.[343] Conventional historians acknowledge that Normanism flourished outside of Russia after World War Two partly because of Cold War hostility to Russia.[344] Fomenko and his supporters take such statements as their starting point, arguing that it is pointless to battle such entrenched and obviously biased dogma and academic thuggery as Normanism in the usual manner.

---

342   Hosking, *Russia and the Russians*, 34.
343   Mikhail Zagoskin, *Istoriia prava russkogo naroda* I (Moscow: 1899), 336-337.
344   Christian, *Russia, Central Asia and Mongolia*, 334.

For many patriotic readers of Russian history, the debate had reached a dead end. The nuances, endless corrections and failure to prove the case definitively have indeed been deeply frustrating. The fact that anti-Normanists cannot see the truth is the clearest evidence of a conspiracy. How to escape from the impasse? To be a shining light alternative history, it is necessary to be bold in attacks upon enemies and ingenious in uncovering the details of plots against Russia. Fomenko has served as an excellent conduit for transmitting a Stalin-era version of the Lomonosov controversy to a new generation of Russian readers who will learn of a sinister German plot against Russian history.

While scholarly anti-Normanism dissects the Normanist position piece by piece in its efforts to refute it, Fomenko attempted a knockout blow by proving, he claims, that the very chronicles relied upon were forged as part of the German plot against Russian history. From Lomonosov to the Stalin era, anti-Normanists devoted themselves to meticulous source criticism. Fomenko claims that this was itself the source of the problem. If the *Primary Chronicle* can be discredited, the Normanist position, in Fomenko's view, would have collapsed centuries ago. To achieve this goal, Fomenko set himself the task of proving that we have no certain knowledge of the provenance of any chronicle earlier than the eighteenth century and that the real Ur-source of the chronicles we do have is the Radzivill chronicle that was fabricated by Schloezer and his allies in the middle of the eighteenth century.

Hostility towards Germany and its designs upon the Slav lands was a popular theme in Russia long before the emergence of Hitler. As the Slavophile Khomiakov put it:

> German scientists have investigated every little phenomenon or tribe on the face of this planet except for the Slavs. Whenever they deal with the Slavs, their mistakes are so obvious, blindness is so great, that there is no explanation to it. Nations also have emotions, exactly as individuals do, and sometimes these emotions and passions are far from being noble. Perhaps the Germanic instincts are based on a hostility that they do not admit to, a hostility that is found on fear of the future, or the remembrances of the past.[345]

---

345 Bocharov, Efimov, Chachukh, Chernyshev, *Zagovor Protiv Russkoi Istorii,* 17.

There are of course many conventional writers who note excessive Germanic influence in the political and cultural life of Russia in the eighteenth century. As one Western historian put it, Russian history following Peter the Great is usually described as a 'rapid succession of monarchs and the influence of foreigners and intriguers who used high government office for personal gain'.[346] The future American sociologist Pitirim Sorokin put it more dramatically when he complained that in the period between Peter the Great and Alexander the First, 'Teutons literally flooded into Russia, and in the end their presence was much more damaging to the country than even the Tatar wars'. For Sorokin, 'the otherwise great German civilization' with few exceptions exported only its social excrement to Russia.[347]

This is not the view that prevails in Western accounts of Bayer, Mueller and Schloezer in their efforts to establish a basis for Russian history. German scholars are heroes of scientific scholarship who had to work in difficult conditions with poor salaries, resentment from Russian colleagues and at the whim of the Romanov state. Mueller, for example, is praised for having made every effort to live up to his claim that the historian knew no 'fatherland, faith or ruler'.[348]

For Fomenko and his allies, the German scholars were brutal thugs in the pay of Western governments. Why, asks Fomenko, is Russian history in essence a product wholly of foreign writers who wrote its basic outline in the eighteenth century? The answer is that the Romanovs wanted it this way and not because of Russian cultural backwardness, as critics of Russia have sometimes suggested. Thus, Tatishchev is a shining example of a fine historian whose works mysteriously failed to find a publisher. Why? According to Fomenko, the reason was that Tatishchev, unlike his rivals, was a Russian.[349]

Conventional historians tell the story of foreign authorship of Russia's past rather differently. When Tatishchev died in 1750, his historical work was still in manuscript form.[350] He wrote an English colleague, Jonas Hanway, in the hope that the latter might arrange to have his work published through the Royal Society in London. Hanway found Tatishchev's request inconvenient

---

346   Daniels, *Tatishchev*, 3.
347   Pitirim Sorokin, *Teoriia natsional'nogo voprosa* (Moscow: 1994), 49.
348   For a positive account of Mueller see Edward C. Thaden, *The Rise of Historicism in Russia* (New York: Peter Land, 1999), 28-30.
349   Nosovskii and Fomenko, *Novaia khronologiia Rusi*, 20-22.
350   Elizabeth Koutaissoff, 'Tatishchev's 'Joachim Chronicle,'' *University of Birmingham Historical Journal* 3:1 (1951): 52-63.

and nothing came of Tatishchev's efforts to publish his work. The manuscript was left in the archives of the St. Petersburg Academy until 1768 when Mueller, starting with a copy of the manuscript provided by Tatishchev's son, began the task of editing what would appear in 1784 as *Istoriia rossiiskaia s samykh drevneishykh vremen*. Four volumes were produced with financial assistance provided by Catherine the Great herself. A fifth volume was uncovered and published by Pogodin in 1848.[351] Schloezer, meanwhile, praised Tatishchev, as 'the father of Russian history'. It was also Schloezer who would ensure that Lomonosov's work was published posthumously.

For Western writers, the German scholars continued their scientific work despite the fact that the Romanov government hindered them and favoured Russians. It was in fact the Germans who were the recipients of vicious academic attacks from Lomonosov. Lomonosov fell foul of the authorities in the Academy because of drunkenness, brawling and the threats and insults that he routinely hurled at those Academy members with whom he disagreed.[352] About Bayer, Lomonosov expressed the view that the German 'looks like an idolater priest who, having poisoned himself with henbane and altered his mind by spinning around on one foot, shouts vague, dark, wild and incomprehensible answers'.[353] Rather than a martyr, Lomonosov comes across in these accounts as an intelligent but unattractive figure whose vanity and prejudice often got the better of him. Lomonosov did his best to enlist the support of the government in his battle with Mueller and other foreign academics[354]. Karamzin and Kliuchevskii more or less apologized for Lomonosov's intemperate outburst against the scholarly and well-intentioned Mueller.[355]

Nonetheless, thanks in part to Fomenko, a new generation of Russian readers will learn of how the history of Russia was compromised from the outset by German historians. After World War Two when Stalinist historiography took a particularly patriotic and anti-German turn, the story of Lomonosov's battle against German influence was told in specifically dark terms. Fomenko utilizes this literature extensively. His chief source for the story of Russian intellectual life in the eighteenth century is a 1950s Soviet

---

351 Elizabeth Koutaissoff, 'Tatishchev's 'Joachim Chronicle,' *University of Birmingham Historical Journal* 3:1 (1951): 52-63.
352 Black, *Mueller*, 86.
353 Mikhail Beliavskii, *M.V. Lomonosov i osnovanie Moskovskogo Universiteta. K 200 letiiu MGU* (Moscow: 1956), 60.
354 Tolz, *Russia*, 47-50.
355 For an account see Black, *Mueller*, 203-05.

account by Beliavskii that is virulently anti-German.[356] Fomenko demonstrates his peculiar method of historical research by claiming that this Soviet era source is very rare, and thus full of suppressed and valuable knowledge.

How does Beliavskii tell the story? For the first thirty years of its existence (1726-1755), the Academy's gymnasium did not train a single student capable of entering the Academy of Sciences. The Academy's professorship came to the conclusion that 'the only way out of this situation is to draft students for the Russian Academy in Germany, because it is clearly impossible to train Russians'.[357] Rebelling against the alleged German dictatorship over the academy, some Russian students and teachers protested in Senate demanding reforms. The Senate appointed a commission to investigate, headed by Count Iusopov and it condemned the protests as a 'rebellion against authorities', and arrested Russian academicians. Vindicated, the German academics remained at the head of the departments and continued to draw their inflated salaries.

It seems that the conditions of academic life in the eighteenth century resembled those of Stalin's Russia. Beliavskii noted how one of the Russian members of Academy's staff, Gorlitskii, was sentenced to death after having spent two years chained in jail, for his stubbornness and disrespect toward the Iusupov commission. Others, such as Grekov, Polyakov, and Nosov were publicly whipped and sent to Siberia, while Popov, Shishkarev and others were kept under arrest till the future decision made by the next President of the Academy.[358] For Stalinist writers, the German-dominated government of the Romanovs favoured Bayer, Mueller and Schloezer. Despite Lomonosov's protests to Empress Catherine II, Mueller's intrigues resulted in the appointment of Schloezer, Lomonosov's rival, as professor of Russian history in the Academy of Science. Schloezer held a very low opinion of Lomonosov, stating that the Russian scientist 'was an ignoramus who did not know anything except for his chronicles'.[359]

These same German authorities were so infuriated by Lomonosov's defiant behaviour that they ordered him to be arrested him as well: members of the commission demanded the execution of Lomonosov on account of 'his disrespectful attitude toward the commission's members and the German land', or that at the very least he should be whipped, and his property and

---

356 Beliavskii, *Lomonosov*.
357 *Ibid.*, 77.
358 *Ibid.*, 82.
359 *Ibid.*, 64.

rights confiscated and cancelled. After having spent seven months in prison Lomonosov was released, but had to publicly read and sign an admission of guilt written by Mueller. In 1763, Empress Catherine the Great fired Lomonosov from the Academy on the basis of another report. Mueller and Schloezer were busily seeking out Lomonosov's historical archives to plunder it both to help their own careers and to distort what it was that Lomonosov had written.

Lomonosov's works were allegedly confiscated and disappeared after his death. None of his original works, including the documents and comments that Lomonosov intended to publish, nor the manuscripts of the second and third parts of *Drevniaia Rossiiskaia Istoriia* have reached us in their original form. Mueller and Schloezer edited the version we have today and it is therefore almost certainly only a pale reflection of the original.

Reading the accounts of the Stalin era and their repetition in Fomenko and comparing them to the more scholarly literature leaves the reader with the impression that completely different events are being described. Western accounts describe Lomonosov as a difficult personality and ungrateful towards those who tried to help him. Bayer remained on good terms with Tatishchev even after Tatishchev's fall from grace, and helped Tatishchev with his research.[360] Black records that Lomonosov received a pension and Gorlitsky was promoted, not sentenced to death. Those who wanted to help Lomonosov included Mueller.

Russian readers of Fomenko and other alternative historians are left with the impression that ill-intentioned foreigners wrote a history of Russia without collaborating with local Russian historians. Meanwhile, the openly pro-German court of the Romanovs rewarded its hand picked propagandists with good salaries, hereditary titles, and the prestige of pioneering historical studies in Russia.[361] It was therefore predictable that a 'pro-German' theory about the origins of the first Russian state, where 'incompetent' Russians invited Scandinavian-Germanic princes to rule over their lands, should have taken hold in the eighteenth century.

For Fomenko, Tatishchev and Lomonosov's conclusions are tamer than might have been expected of someone who took such a brave stand against foreign control of the Russian academy. Fomenko has embellished the story of the plot against Tatishchev who spent his last years in internal exile

---

360 Thaden, *The Rise of Historicism in Russia* (Peter Lang, 1999), 27-28.
361 Beliavskii, *Lomonosov*, 82-84.

towards the end of his life after he was found guilty of financial misbehaviour. In St.-Petersburg, the authorities were not really interested in corruption allegations against Tatishchev but instead warned the bureaucrat turned historian that he would be suspected of political freethinking if he pressed on with his publications. Tatishchev's history was not an original of his work and it was the German, Mueller, who readied the work of Tatishchev for publication. Mueller himself acknowledged that he edited the deceased Tatishchev's diaries and copies of his book in order to prepare them for publication.[362] For Fomenko, the original of Tatishchev's work, as well as the documents that Mueller had worked with, conveniently disappeared. Mueller's revision of Tatishchev's did not contain an account of the Slavs prior to the invitation to Riurik. What we know today as 'Tatishchev's information', the sources known only to Tatishchev and now lost to modern historians, was destroyed by the German clique. In this way, Mueller brought Tatishchev's conclusions sufficiently into line with his own, or at least rendered them so ambiguous that latter-day historians were in the end divided over whether Tatishchev was even anti-Normanist at all.[363]

The question for Fomenko then becomes; if it is so obvious that the Normanist position is hopeless, why did Normanism enjoy such success? Not all Russian academics were suppressed. How could Russian patriots such as Karamzin, Soloviev or Kliuchevskii have been fooled? The answer is that Schloezer's account of the *Primary Chronicle* has won them over. The fact that it was German historians who edited the *Primary Chronicle*, made the claim that the Varangians were Vikings and for nearly a century were in possession of some of the most important documents pertaining to early Russian history has led to the destruction of the true history of Russia. Schloezer all but succeeded in his attempt 'to destroy the Russian national history school with open support from the Russian court'.[364] Having suppressed the Russian version of Russia's ancient history, what did the plotters do next? They rewrote the Russian chronicles and then claimed the doctored versions as centuries-old originals.

Fomenko's biggest claim concerns the Radzivill Chronicle. To prove that important parts of the record of early Russian history were written by German academics in the eighteenth century, it is necessary to show that

---

362 Thaden, *The Rise of Historicism in Russia*, 31.
363 Nosovskii and Fomenko, *Novaia khronologiia Rusi*, 28-29.
364 Nosovskii and Fomenko, *Bibleiskaia Rus'* II, 319-23.

there were no extant chronicles that can be reliably traced back beyond the eighteenth century. This is not an easy task but Fomenko uses the works of established historians to attempt to prove that we have no direct proof of the existence of early Russian chronicles.

Kliuchevskii wrote that, in the seventeenth century, neither the Tsar's nor the Patriarch's libraries contained any information on the history of Russia.[365] According to the decree of Tsar Alexis of 1657, a church cleric named Kudriavtsev was charged with the task of seeking out chronicles in the central archives. After sixteen months of work he was unable to produce a single document. Kliuchevskii held a low opinion of Muscovite history writing and concluded that 'in old Muscovy neither the people nor their minds, nor the documents were ready for such an undertaking.' Fomenko embellishes Kliuchevskii's account by adding that Kudriavtsev's work was actively sabotaged. How else could the decree of Alexis be disobeyed? Fomenko concluded not just that this particular researcher failed in his mission but either few original chronicles existed in the seventeenth century or the chronicles were hidden by church and governmental authorities.

Fomenko next cites the opinion of Morozov, the imprisoned polymath who devoted years to his idiosyncratic reading of the major chronicles. In prison, Morozov had plenty of time to study and his passions included history. In his book *Khristos*, Morozov compared the styles and grammatical structures of the three earliest Russian Chronicles –Laurentian and Troitsko-Sergiev and Radzivill chronicles - each of which contains as its core the *Primary Chronicle*.[366] Morozov was surprised to discover that, apart from minor changes in style, their texts were absolutely identical.

This fact surprised Morozov because the conventional wisdom stipulated that the chronicles were discovered separately and in locations that were remote from each other – Suzdal, the Moscow region and Königsberg. If they were copies from a more ancient original, it is still unclear why they did not have more textual differences relating to important, local events. Fomenko built on this idea to conclude that the anonymous writer of the Troitsko-Sergiev as well as the Suzdal' monk Lavrentii used the 1767 Radzivill chronicle to create their own chronicles.[367] Thus the earliest Russian

---

365 Kliuchevskii, *Neopublikovannye proizvedeniia*, 188-191.
366 Nosovskii and Fomenko, *Novaia khronologiia Rusi*, 25; Nikolai Morozov, 'O russkoi istorii,' v. VIII, *Khristos* (Moscow-Leningrad: Russia's Academy of Sciences archive, Gosizdat, 1924-1932).
367 Nosovskii and Fomenko, *Novaia khronologiia Rusi*, 26.

chronicle first appeared six hundred years later than was originally thought.

For conventional historians, this is, to say the least, an astonishing claim. It was usually considered that the Radzivill Chronicle was a product of the fifteenth century, making it one of the oldest extant chronicles but certainly not the oldest chronicle.[368] Highly valued because it is a rare illustrated medieval chronicle with 617 miniatures and drawings, it contains most of the details found in the *Primary Chronicle*. According to Fomenko, all records of the *Primary Chronicle* are altered copies of the Radzivill chronicle.[369]

To build the case he reminds the reader of how little public access there has been to the Radzivill chronicle. The original may have been owned by the hetman of Vilnius, whose brother Boguslav transferred the chronicle to Königsberg's library. Although the conventional wisdom states that the Radzivill Chronicle was widely known and used as early as the middle of the sixteenth century, historians acknowledge that the proof is indirect.[370] In 1711, during his visit to Königsberg, Peter the Great saw what he assumed to be an original and ordered that a copy be made for his personal library. In 1758, Königsberg was overrun by Russian troops and the Radzivill Chronicle became a war trophy, delivered to the Library of Russian Academy of Sciences. Schloezer worked with the chronicle, which was reprinted in Germany in 1802-1809. A Russian edition perished in the fire of 1812. While the task of publishing a complete set of Russian chronicles got under way in 1841, it was only in 1902 that the Radzivill Chronicle was published and without the transcription of the text.[371] The complete Radzivill chronicle saw the light of day only in 1989.[372]

The Radzivill Chronicle provides ideal material for a conspiracy theory. Because of the presence of watermarks, historians believe that the chronicle's binding dates to the eighteenth century. The chronicle's page numbers follow the Arabic system that was normal for Russia in the eighteenth century. The first three pages have been marked with the letters a,

---

368 Leonid Milov, 'K voprosu o podlinnosti Radzivillovskoi khroniki', *Kritika Novoi Khronologii*, 8.
369 Nosovskii and Fomenko, *Imperiia: Rus', Turtsia, Kitai, Evropa, Egipet. Novaia matematicheskaia khronologiia drevnosti*, 18.
370 Nosovskii and Fomenko, *Novaia khronologiia Rusi*, 23-31.
371 Sovetskii Entsiklopedicheckii Slovar', *Sovetskaia entsiklopedia* (Moscow: 1984), 1028.
372 'Radzivillovskaia Letopis',' *Polnoe Sobranie Russkikh Letopisei* 38 (Leningrad-Moscow: Nauka, 1989), 3.

b, and c, while the remainder have Arabic numbers in the upper right hand corner.[373] Fomenko suggests to his readers that they should be deeply suspicious of an allegedly fifteenth-century manuscript that did not have the Church Slavonic numbering commonly in use before the seventeenth century. Conventional historians accept that the original markings were in Church Slavonic and that much later, in the eighteenth century Arabic numbers were added for the convenience of modern readers. More likely, claims Fomenko, that the chronicle we view today is an eighteenth-century creation.

Shakhmatov pointed out a major discrepancy in the text of the Radzivill Chronicle, where according to the text flow, page 236 should have been followed by pages 239-243, then 237, 238, and 244.[374] It seems that at some point the pages were mixed up. Shakhmatov speculated that at least two pages are missing altogether.[375] Since both Arabic and Church Slavonic page numbers ignore the obvious confusion of the pages, the conclusion that Fomenko has drawn is that the page numbers were added only after the binding of the chronicle. Having evaluated the quality of the paper and the presence of watermarks on the manuscript, Fomenko confidently asserted that the Arab page numbers were the originals, and the Church Slavonic numbers were added later in a clumsy attempt to establish the historical legitimacy of the text.

The plot thickened for Fomenko once he realized which topics are discussed in the pages that are in dispute. Fomenko claims that someone, most likely Schloezer himself, has omitted two pages, while adding one page under the Arab number 8 and Church Slavonic number 9 to the first book of the chronicle. The forger has changed the page numbers in order to create space for an extra page. These pages stand out from the rest of the book – one can clearly see the changes in numbers, while the corners of the inserted page are torn.

It is the allegedly inserted page that contains the story about the invitation to the Varangians. Thus Fomenko alleges that proof of the theory first put forward by Bayer finds its confirmation in an obviously doctored chronicle of the eighteenth century. Fomenko triumphantly noted that without the page detailing the Varangian invocation, Riurik appears in the chronicle

---

373 Nosovskii and Fomenko, *Novaia khronologiia Rusi*, 30-36.
374 See Alexander Shakhmatov, 'Opisaniie rukopisei. Radzovillovskaia ili Konigsbergskaia Letopis',' *Stat'i o texte i miniatiurakh letopisei* 2 (St. Petersburg: 1902).
375 Nosovskii and Fomenko, *Novaia khronologiia Rusi*, 32-34.

as an obviously Slavic prince.[376] Fomenko's forensic triumph is trumpeted everywhere in the literature of the alternative writers.[377] Without the doctored chronicle, anti-Normanism would have been able to show that either there were no important Vikings, or if there were Vikings, then they simply served the Russian princes and they left nothing of value to Russian history. For Fomenko, the find is so significant that if earlier generations had known about the forged chronicle, there would have been no Westerner/Slavophile divided in Russia.

Thus, according to Fomenko, the allegedly 'ancient' sources of Russian history, and Russian history as we know it today, were written during the era of Peter the Great and his successors – the most pro-western and anti-Russian monarchs. First Karamzin, then Soloviev, Kliuchevskii, Liubavski, Pogodin and others accepted the lie and Normanism became wide spread and accepted. Russian historians became weighed down under the voices of previous authority whose starting point, in the view of Fomenko, was as narrow and unconvincing as the histories that have appeared.

Milov is one conventional academic who has offered a point-by-point critique of Fomenko. Milov criticizes Fomenko for his amateurish approach to the problem. According to Milov, Fomenko should have thoroughly studied leading scholars in the field - Tatishchev, Shakhmatov, Priselkov, Bestushev-Riumin, Nasonov - before making wild claims about the *Primary Chronicle*'s validity.[378] For Milov, Fomenko has displayed breathtaking ignorance and arrogance in regard to the Russian chronicles. Russian historiography boasts at least ten generations of historians who have dealt systematically with the chronicles and ancient texts.[379] Those historians were professionals, Russians as well as Germans, and it is highly unlikely that they would have missed such a sensational discovery as the forging of the Radzivill chronicle in the eighteenth century.[380]

Milov noted that Fomenko claimed support from Kliuchevski but that Fomenko uses the famous historian out of context. Kliuchevskii noted the failed attempt of the priest, Kudriavtsev, to find and compile chronicles in the

---

376   Nosovskii and Fomenko, *Novaia khronologiia Rusi*, 35-36.
377   See, for example, Guts, *Mnogovariantnaia istoriia Rossii*, 73-83.
378   Leonid Milov, 'K voprosu o podlinnosti Radzivillovskoi khroniki,' *Sbornik Russkogo istoricheskogo obshchestva* (Moscow: Russkaia Panorama, 2000), 31-47.
379   *Ibid.*
380   *Ibid.*

middle of the seventeenth century.[381] Fomenko interprets Kudriavtsev's failure as evidence that no chronicles existed until the middle of the seventeenth century. Yet, Kliuchevski wrote elsewhere that Russian chronicle writing began in the eleventh century in such seats of princely power as Kiev, Chernigov, Novgorod, Smolensk, Polotsk, and Vladimir.[382] Milov points out that the mistake to which Fomenko is so attentive came to prominence at the beginning of the twentieth century. The young Shakhmatov, discovered the text discrepancy and suggested that Church Slavonic numbers were inserted after two pages were omitted, or lost. Milov insists that there was no justification for such a claim. Milov does not deny the page mix up that had been noticed practically by all the researchers in the field. However, according to Milov it was not a conspiracy, but a mistake made in an earlier version. Given the difficulties under which church chroniclers wrote, there should be no surprise about this sort of textual problem.

Milov argues that the unknown binder of the Radzivill chronicle was not very numerate in Slavonic. Therefore he had missed ten pages, indicating page number 200 after 189, instead of 190. In order to reinforce his claim, Milov invokes the opinion of other experts who also preferred the fact that the linear textual story of the chronicle was disturbed in the ancient past as compared to the plot or conspiracy theory favoured by Fomenko. Milov also points to the Troitsky Chronicle where the omissions in the text are identical to that of the Radzivill Chronicle. There are similar omissions and problems with many medieval documents. Therefore, for Milov, identical omissions discovered in different chronicles are a sign not only that they are historically accurate, but also that the mistake was made in the old proto-chronicle that does not exist today. In this respect Milov points out that the Radzivill chronicle was used to restore parts of the text of the Laurentian chronicle, while the events of 1206 that are fully preserved in the Laurentian chronicle are missing from the Radzivill chronicle.

It might be thought that wild claims would have discredited Fomenko. But it seems the reverse has occurred and Fomenko remains a folk hero to those inclined towards alternative history. Fomenko has suggested that a great deal remains hidden from the Russian public. Among the yet unpublished works of ancient Russian literature are for example the

---

381 Kliuchevskii, *Neopublikovannye proizvedeniia*, 188-190.
382 Kliuchevskii, *Sochineniia* I, 74-89.

Novgorodian Karamzin Chronicle[383] and the unpublished *Litsevoi Svod*, which is reputed to contain nine thousand pages of information and sixteen thousand miniatures describing history from the alleged creation of the world up to the year 1567.[384] Fomenko is sure that the latter work will turn out to be the oldest example of Russian literature.

Igor Nastenko head of the publishing house *Russkaia panorama*, noted in a forward to a collection of critiques of Fomenko that:

> In the 1990s there had been a high demand for the books of Fomenko. This newly baked guru, academic-mathematician, proclaimed a revolution in historical science. Professionals do not have the time and/or patience to answer this gibberish, while the general public has been fooled and confused. A decent answer had to be made. Fomenko and company are deceitful charlatans, and we are going to transfer the leftovers from our sales to school libraries free of charge as an injection against the disease of 'New Chronology'. A similar situation is taking place with the once buried, but now revitalized and very aggressive Normanism. In the nearest future we are planning to publish a series of anti-Normanist books.

Thus, this publishing house simultaneously announced a campaign against Fomenko and the Normanism Fomenko despises. Fomenko would almost certainly consider the decision of *Russkaia Panorama* to be a victory.

Pseudo-historians have pronounced themselves pleased that conventional history is, in their view, moving slowly in their direction. Alternative writers express some satisfaction that Russian textbooks are beginning to see the light. Instead of focusing upon the comings and goings of states, Russian pedagogy is making better use of archaeological evidence to take a longer view of Russian history. Sakharov and Buganov argue that the first ancestors of modern humans appeared on Russian territory 300,000-400,000 years ago.[385] The genealogy of these early people may in fact extend back millions of years. The roots of the Slavs are traced back to the Neolithic revolution and Indo-Europeans, at least six thousand years. This textbook gives information on the Scythians and their state, as well as

---

383 *Pamiatniki Literatury drevnei Rusi, XII vek* (Moscow: Khudozhestvennaia literatura, 1980), 540.
384 *Sovetskii Entsiklopedicheckii Slovar'*, 718.
385 A. Sakharov and V. Buganov, *Istoriia Rossii* (Moscow: Prosveshchenie, 1995).

detailed information about Scythian military feats as if these developments were part of the history of Russia. Other textbooks[386] suggest that Kiev was founded in the fifth or sixth centuries AD long before any Vikings. Yet another textbook dates the history of Russia one thousand years before the arrival of the Varangians. [387]

Finally, pseudo-history has extracted its revenge upon Scandinavia by reversing the terms of the Normanist debate. While Normanists considered that Russia owed its statehood to Scandinavia, a new generation of Russian readers are learning from Fomenko and other pseudo-historians that the reverse was apparently the case. The great deeds of Scandinavia were inspired by Russia.

There was, of course, a significant deal of involvement by Russia in the history of Scandinavia. During the reign of Vladimir the First, a Scandinavian Viking named Sigurd did outstanding service, according to Scandinavian sagas, in the defence of Kholmgard or Novgorod. Sigurd's nephew came under the protection of the Scandinavian wife of Vladimir the First who adopted the boy and this Olav was, according to the sagas, 'the most beautiful, powerful and strong' of all the Norwegians. Novgorod thus raised a prince for Norway. Later, Olav conquered Gothland and enjoyed immense popularity among his subjects for his honesty, martial prowess and generosity. Olav was king of Norway from 995 to 1000 and is credited with converting five separate areas to Christianity – Norway, Iceland, Shetland, Orkney, and the Faroe Islands. His turbulent life is described in Snorri Sturluson's *Heimscringla*, Old Snorrason's *King Olaf's saga*, and several other sources.[388]

Olav Tryggvasson was killed in the Battle of Three Kings in 1000 AD, betrayed by a jealous rival. Olav the Second was forced to flee to Russia after his defeat at the hands of the Danes in 1027. Novgorod helped him with money and soldiers. Iaroslav the Wise sent *druzhinas* to the Baltic provinces, defeated the Chud' tribes there and built the fortress of Uiriev to assist Olav in his endeavours. After Olav's death, a church was erected in Novgorod in his honour. Magnus, son of the deceased Olav II was brought up in Novgorod

---

386   Boris Rybakov, A. Sakharov, A. Preobrazhensky, B. Krasnobaev, *Istoriia otechestva* (Moscow: Prosveshchenie, 1993).

387   Alexander Novosel'tsev, *Istoriia Rossii s drevneishikh vremen* (Moscow: AST, 1996).

388   *Laxdaela saga*, translated by M. Magnusson and H. Palsson (Harmondsworth: Penguin books, 1969, 1972, 1975, 1976), 143; also see John Marsden, *Harald Hardrada* (Sutton: Oxbow books, 2007).

and served as Norwegian king. Harold, a future king of Norway, who served with the Byzantine guard, stored his plunder in Novgorod.[389]

The Scandinavians think that their raiders gave birth to the Russian state. For Fomenko and his supporters, it was obviously the Russians who were the source of the Scandinavian burst of *passionarnost* that led to the Viking era, and not the other way around.[390] It was the Russian princes who recruited Varangians for their military campaigns not Vikings who formed the first Russian state. The best of the Norwegian kings lived in and imbibed the spirit of Russia.[391]

Pseudo-historians, and their conventional rivals, claim that Normanism is a dead issue. But this is because each of the contestants believes that they have won, not because the issue is resolved. For pseudo-historians, the conventional story of Kiev Rus, like so much else in Russian history, is a hollow shell deeply encased in mythology. For pseudo-history as the Viking role in Russia's history was exaggerated by the West and its Romanov ciphers, the same was true of the Mongol era.

---

389 Snorri Sturluson, *Heimskringla*, translated with an introduction by Magnus Magnusson and Hermann Pálsson (Harmondsworth: Penguin, 1966), 46, 64.
390 Kandyba and Zolin, *Istoriia i ideologiia Russkogo naroda* II, 180-187.
391 Haakon Shetelig and Hjalmar Falk, translated by E. Gordon, *Scandinavian Archaeology* (Oxford: Clarendon Press, 1937), 303.

IV Farewell to the Mongols

IV.1 Mongol Rule in Russia – Vice and Virtue

For those who believe that the past is some sort of guide to the future, Kiev Rus was crucial to Russia's sense of identity. The Rus, whoever they were, gave Russia not just its name, but its first state and its Orthodox faith. After 1991, the heartland of Kiev Rus no longer fell within Russian or Soviet territory but instead came to rest in the territory of the independent states of Ukraine and Belarus. For many Russians, these developments have thrown into focus the period of Russian history that followed Kiev Rus, the Mongol era. Without Ukraine, the Mongols and other steppe peoples from the East seem much more important to the history of the lands that now comprise the Russian Federation. History and pseudo-history alike have engaged in a re-evaluation of the Mongols.

Attitudes towards the Mongols have changed in recent decades. Earlier accounts tended to adopt a hostile attitude vividly expressed by one Western writer who wrote that the Mongol invasion 'may be truly described as one of the most dreadful calamities which ever befell the human race'.[392] This view was reinforced during the Cold War when it was often assumed that Soviet totalitarianism occurred because Russia was located too far to the East. Harrison Salisbury, for example, wrote of Russia's struggle to overcome the 'legacy of backwardness, deceit, submissiveness and lies imposed by the Mongols'.[393] While more recent accounts still find in Russia a history of backwardness and lies, they are less inclined to blame it on the Mongols.

Instead of violent barbarians who bequeathed little to history apart from the tactics of ruthless terror, the Mongols have received more and more recognition as state-builders, traders and as a crucial conduit between the civilized East and the uncivilized medieval West.[394] David Christian, for example, has described the Mongols as the high water mark of pastoralism in the history of inner Eurasia, the rivet that held together the world system of

---

392 Edward Browne, *A History of Persian literature under Tartar Dominion* (Cambridge: Cambridge University Press, 1920), 4.
393 Harrison Salisbury, *War Between Russia and China* (New York: Norton, 1969), 31.
394 See, for example, Janet L. Abu-Lughod, *Before European hegemony: the world system A. D. 1250-1350* (Oxford: Oxford University Press, 1991), 3-4.

the thirteenth and fourteenth centuries.[395] His account placed Russia squarely within that history of Eurasia. In Russia, revisionist histories written by Gumilëv helped to improve the standing of the Mongols, a task undertaken earlier in the century by the Eurasianist, Trubetskoi. The pseudo-historians under consideration in this thesis believe that the truth is yet to be told about the Mongols. They have combined new information and interpretations with age-old prejudice to produce a popular fantasy about medieval Russia.

The story of the Mongol invasion of Russia is usually told this way. In the beginning of the thirteenth century, there emerged from the Mongolian steppes an energetic and talented warlord, Genghis Khan, who created a huge, disciplined and powerful army out of Mongolian nomads and neighbouring tribes, promising 'to conquer the entire world to the last sea'. David Morgan has argued that the Mongols were motivated by the search for booty and, on this occasion, channelled their warlike nature into external conflict rather than the debilitating internal wars typical of nomad history. The logic of sustaining long-distance war and rewarding allies necessitated more complex and systematic methods of extracting booty or tribute from the peoples they conquered.[396]

Christian has noted the increasing sophistication of nomadic confederations in the Mongolian steppes. By the time of the Hsiung-nu, in the second century BCE, states founded on the steppe were in a position to reshape the people they ruled. By the time of the Mongols, nomad political and military organization closely resembled the states established by sedentary peoples.[397] Having conquered their neighbours, including the powerful Chinese Empire, the invading hordes turned westward, and advanced more than five thousand kilometres. The Mongols destroyed the Central Asian kingdom of Khwarezm, the Christian kingdoms of Armenia and Georgia, the Muslim Bulgars on the river Volga and finally approached the southern borders of Kiev Rus' in 1223.

In the initial battle with the Russians on the river Kalka, the Mongols destroyed the armies of Kiev Rus and their allied Polovtsy. Lacking manpower or perhaps satisfied with the initial outcome, the Mongols headed back to Mongolia, only to return in 1237-40 with incredible force.[398] The

---

395   Christian, *Russia, Central Asia and Mongolia*, 426-27.
396   David Morgan, *The Mongols* (London: Basil Blackwell, 1986), 62-64.
397   Christian, *Russia, Central Asia and Mongolia*, 150.
398   George Vernadsky, *Kievan Russia* (New Haven and London: Yale University Press, 1973), 235-239.

Mongols sacked and burned the most important Russian cities, sparing only Novgorod. Unlike previous steppe nomads with whom the Russians were familiar, the Mongols made their presence permanent by establishing their base at Sarai on the Volga River.[399] Under Batu Khan, the Mongols founded a new state, the Kipchak khanate or Golden Horde, on the Volga and collected tribute from lands that stretched in an arc from the Middle East to western Russia.

In 1241 Batu Khan moved through Poland and the Czech lands to reach the Mediterranean and threaten Western Europe. Only the death of Genghis's successor, Ogedei, brought an end to this westward march and caused Mongol leaders to return to their homeland to settle the succession, saving Europe in the process. Meanwhile, the irruption of the Mongols set in motion other steppe peoples, including Seljuk and then Ottoman Turks who for centuries would dominate the eastern part of the Mediterranean.[400]

How did Genghis Khan establish such a powerful force? *The Secret History of the Mongols*, the main source for much of the detail of this early period, was written after Genghis Khan's death in 1240 and describes a rare combination of military and political talents.[401] The population was divided into military units, each with one thousand warriors, whose strength lay in horsemanship and mounted archers. Each commander was well known to Genghis Khan who expected all males from the age of fifteen to be ready for military duty.

Genghis Khan was far-sighted enough to recruit imperial administrators, tolerated different religions, established rules of commerce, and a code of laws known as the Great Yasa. Genghis Khan embraced the principles of standardisation and discipline so well that for hundreds of years thereafter the Mongols were masters not only of the steppe but of many neighbouring sedentary peoples as well.

The Golden Horde is the name that the Russians gave from the seventeenth century to the Kipchak Khanate, or Horde.[402] This entity formed

---

399   Morgan, *Mongols*, 138.
400   Davies, *Europe: a history*, 297.
401   See, for example, Francis Woodman Cleaves (ed), *The Secret History of the Mongols* (Cambridge: Harvard University Press, Mass, 1982); Rashid ad-Din, *Sbornik letopisei*, translated by Iu. Verkhovskii (Moscow-Leningrad: Academy of Sciences USSR, 1960); Boris Vladimirtsov, *Chingiz-Khan* (Moscow: 1922); Wilhelm Barthold, *Chingiz-Khan* (St-Petersburg: 1991), 856-862.
402   Donald Ostrowski, *Muscovy and the Mongols. Cross-cultural influences on the steppe frontier, 1304-1589* (Cambridge: Cambridge University Press, 1998), XIII.

after 1240 in the territory adjacent to the Volga River and incorporated areas once ruled by the Bulgars, Polovtsy/Kipchaks, Khwarezm and Kiev Rus. The Mongols appointed provincial and town governors, and taxed the population. Tax collectors known as *baskaki* were accompanied by armed detachments ready to deal with those brave or foolhardy enough not to accept the rule of the Mongols.

With Mongolian military help, the defeated Russian princes fought amongst each other, trying to outmanoeuvre competitors for the title of Grand Prince and Mongol favourite. Kiev was weakened by the Mongol onslaught and came under the influence of Lithuania, which remained independent of Mongols. For much of the Mongol period, Vladimir was the centre of Russian affairs. In 1380, a stronger Russia, with a newly emerged political centre in Moscow under the leadership of Dmitrii Donskoi, defeated Mamai and his Tatar troops. The contest continued for another hundred years until, in 1480, Ahmad retreated from Russian lands having been stared down by the troops of the Moscow Grand Prince, Ivan the Third.[403]

The largest continental empire in the history of mankind stretched from Beijing in the East, westwards along the Central Asian trade routes to the Volga and into Europe itself, overshadowing the Russian lands. From Sarai, Mongol khans plundered Russia, levying taxes in the form of a tithe, ten percent of everything, including the population. While formally governed by Russian princes, the local population had to endure the burden of double taxation, supporting their Russian and Mongol overlords. The Mongols appointed Grand Princes of Russia who received the *iarlyk* enabling the holder to extract tribute. Moscow grew more influential and became the principal successor state of the Golden Horde because it voluntarily acted as the conqueror's surrogate.

For critics of Russia in the West, Moscow and the Tartars (sic) were inseparable. Davies described Ivan the Third, the Moscow Grand Prince who threw off the Tatar yoke as 'an exponent of Tartar financial, military and political method who used the shifting alliances of khans and princes to replace the Tartar yoke with a Muscovite one'.[404] Eurasianists, like Trubetskoi or Gumilëv, responded to this sort of barb by proudly acknowledging Russia's Mongol inheritance. The pseudo-history of Fomenko, Bushkov or Guts takes

---

403 George Vernadsky, *History of Russia* III (New Haven: Yale University Press, 1952), 258-263.
404 Davies, *Europe*, 461.

the next step, arguing that there never was a Mongol invasion, that Russian and Mongol rule appeared similar to outsiders because they were in fact a single phenomenon. For Fomenko, there may have been Mongols in Mongolia but there were none who reached the territory of modern-day Russia. The non-Slavs who sometimes rose to become tsar-khans were Turks who had always lived along the Volga River and were partners of the Russians who presided over the Russian Horde.

IV.2 Russia's Pastoralists: Pechenegs, Qipchaqs, Mongols, Tatars

The history of a nomadic people is never straightforward and difficulties and unsolved problems abound in the conventional literature. Pseudo-history preys upon the imperfect knowledge and bitter debates within conventional history. Even the name of the Mongols is a matter of confusion. The Russian chroniclers knew the Mongols as Tatars and applied that name not just to Mongols, but to all the steppe peoples with whom they came into contact.[405] The Tatars were originally a neighbouring Mongolian tribe defeated or absorbed by the Mongols. Europeans confused matters further by adding 'r' to this inaccurate name so that the nomadic invaders were *Tartars* to readers in the West.[406] Later, the Russians referred to the Tatar Empire based at Sarai as the Golden Horde. Earlier, it was known as the Kipchak khanate, the Kipchaks and Cumans forming two parts of the Polovtsy, the nomadic Turkic people who occupied the southern Volga before the arrival of the Mongols.

Fluidity was a feature not just of names but the people to whom they referred. Like the Vikings among the Slavs, Mongols were elite warriors in the initial invasion but were soon assimilated by the subjugated Turkic peoples that formed the vast majority of their horde. There may have been as few as four thousand authentic Mongols from Mongolia who actually reached the lands of Kiev Rus.[407] Almost immediately, Turkic was the written and spoken language of the Golden Horde. As Halperin put it, Genghis Khan's "Mongols' were actually a tribal confederation of various Uralo-Altaic peoples, many of them Turkic, led by Chinghis and his Mongol tribe'.[408]

---

405 Ostrowski, *Muscovy and the Mongols*, XIII.
406 *Ibid.*
407 *Ibid.*, 32.
408 Charles Halperin, *Russia and the Golden Horde* (Bloomington: Indiana University Press, 1985), 23.

Representatives of all the conquered peoples, including Slavs, soon found their way into Mongol employment. The Golden Horde seems not to have paid taxes to the Mongol capital of Karakorum after the 1260s. The focus of the Mongols was almost certainly not Russia itself, which was looked upon as a source of tribute that could be used to finance the Golden Horde's core empire to the south.[409] On the other hand, we cannot be certain about Mongols aims as the conquerors themselves left us little primary evidence of their deliberations.

To make their case, pseudo-historians usually point out that conventional accounts are interpretations and that these have fluctuated over the years according to political and cultural fashions. Latter-day church writers did not like nomads and Muslims so invaders from the steppe were treated less than favourably in their accounts. The Romanovs waged continuous war against the Ottomans and so Russian propagandists wrote out of history any evidence of cooperation between Russians and Turks. As Richard Pipes described this process, Russians at least until nearing the end of the Soviet period, tended to take offence at any suggestion that their society was part of the East.[410]

It is clear that Western historians have engaged in a much more wide-ranging and open-ended debate about the Mongol era than was the case in Soviet Russia. Nonetheless, Western historiography is much more divided over the Mongols than it is over Kiev Rus. A brief survey of the historiography concerning the Mongols and Russia shows that this era has undergone an almost complete rewriting in recent decades. That process has only just begun in Russia itself. Pseudo-history is most likely to flourish in conditions where patriotic issues are at stake, evidence is unavailable or ambiguous and interpretations of an era are undergoing change.

Ostrowski has identified five principal views or models that historians, Russian and non-Russian, have used to explain the relationship between Moscow and the Mongols. The first contends that Moscow, and by extension, Russia, was *sui generis* and developed for indigenous reasons with little outside influence. This was the predominant view of much Russian and Soviet history. For most Imperial and Soviet historians, the Mongols were a curse and the Russians victims of an unprovoked attack. Uncivilized in

---

409   For a summary of the debate on this issue, see Janet Martin, *Medieval Russia, 980-1584* (Cambridhe: Cambridge University Press, 1995), 153-57.
410   Pipes, *Russia under the Old Regime*, 74.

comparison to the Slavs, Mongols came out of nowhere and made little positive impact upon Russia even if they caused its development to fall behind that of Western Europe. Soloviev considered the Mongols to be barbarians who bequeathed nothing of value to Russia.[411] The Soviet-era historians, Grekov and Iakubovsky argued that:

> The Russian state with Moscow at its head was created not with the assistance of Tatars, but in the process of a hard struggle of the Russian people against the yoke of the Golden Horde.[412]

Soviet historiography mostly considered that the Mongol Empire worked to the detriment of the Mongol people as well as the Russians. Their ruling dynasties were parasitical, and their conquests had a negative effect on the development of the various sedentary peoples subjugated by the Mongol war machine.[413] In 1944, Stalin's Central Committee even passed a decree declaring that the Golden Horde was both 'reactionary' and 'parasitic'.[414] Ostrowski groups with these writers the best-known Western historian of medieval Russia, Edward Keenan, who argued that Byzantine influence upon Russia was a mythology for which there is no contemporary evidence.[415] Keenan's argument that Byzantine influence in Muscovy was a latter-day invention is an indication of the suspicions that serious scholars of Russian history harbour about the sources for Russian history prior to the era of Peter the Great. Fomenko in his own amateurish way echoed this type of argument to show that the Mongol invasion in its entirety was a latter-day invention.

Many scholars have rejected the indigenous model but in different ways. The second and third models identified by Ostrowski comprise those writers, Russian and Western, who think that Moscow/Russia is entirely derivative of other cultures. Obolensky, for example, saw Moscow as having borrowed its beliefs and values from Byzantium. Other writers underscored the importance of the Mongols. Karamzin, the most popular of Russia's

---

411 Soloviev, *Istoriia Rossii s drevneishikh vremen* volume II, 489, volume IV, 179.
412 Boris Grekov and Alexander Iakubovsky, *Zolotaia Orda i ee padenie* (Moscow-Leningrad, 1950), 256; also Arsenii Nasonov, *Mongoly i Rus* (Moscow: 1940).
413 Nikolai Merpert, Lev Cherepnin, Vladimir Pashuto, 'Chingiz khan i ego nasledie,' *Istoriia SSSR* 5 (1962): 91-110; I. Maiskii, 'Chingiz khan,' *Voprosy Istorii* 5 (1962): 74-83; Vadim Kargalov, *Mongolo-tatarskoe nashestvie na Rusi XIII vek* (Moscow: 1966), *Narod-bogatyr'* (Moscow: 1971), *Sverzhenie Tataro-Mongolskogo iga* (Moscow: 1973), and *Konets ordynskogo iga* (Moscow: Nauka, 1980).
414 Viktor Shnirelman, *Who Gets the Past? Competition for Ancestors among Non-Russian Intellectuals in Russia*, 7.
415 See Ostowski, *Mongols and Muscovy*, 4-6.

nineteenth century historians, admitted that without the Mongols, Kiev Rus was likely to have perished because of internecine princely feuds.[416] Karamzin considered that Moscow, which grew in strength as a Mongol surrogate, 'owed its greatness to the khans'.[417] Kostomarov emphasized the role of the khans' decrees in strengthening the authority of the Muscovite duke within his realm.[418]

Trubetskoi firmly rejected the notion that the term 'yoke' was applicable to Russian-Mongol relations.[419] For Trubetskoi, 'the Russian state was an inheritor, the successor, the continuation of the historical work and legacy of Genghis Khan'.[420] The Muscovite dukes became genuine Russian rulers only after they gathered the Tatar lands.[421] Writing in the West, Vernadsky tried to show that the Mongols left an important legacy in Russia in terms of politics and law even if their overall impact represented a heavy burden.[422]

A fourth model identified by Ostrowski tried to combine Byzantine and Mongol influence. Thus, Russia's attachment to Byzantium could be explained in terms of its need to find something Russian about Russia following centuries of Mongol domination. The fifth model comprises those who, from Karl Marx to Alexander Yanov, see Russia as undergoing stages of development similar to those of Britain, France or Germany. These writers emphasise economic developments rather than superficial changes in the elites of the emerging Russian state. It would be fair to say that the first three models presently attract the greatest interest from scholars.

One trend that is clear in both Western and Russian scholarship is that the relationship between Russia and the Mongols was more of a partnership, symbiosis or interrelationship than was previously thought. Fennell, Vernadsky and most Soviet historians represented an older view when they argued that Moscow was instinctively hostile to the Tatar khanates, allying with the Crimean Khans, for example, only in times of need in the face of a common enemy like the Lithuanians. More recently, Western writers like

---

416 Nikolai Karamzin, *Istoriia gosudarstva rossiiskogo* vol. V (St-Petersburg: 1851-1853), 223.
417 *Ibid.*, 365-384.
418 Nikolai Kostomarov, 'Nachalo edinoderzhavia v drevnei Rusi,' *Sobranie sochinenii* V (St-Petersburg: 1905), 41-47.
419 Nikolai Trubetskoi, *The Legacy of Chengiz-Khan and Other Essays on Russia's Identity*, 182, 185, 189.
420 *Ibid.*, 163, 167, 175, 180.
421 *Ibid.*, 185.
422 *Ibid.*, 344.

Halperin, Ostrowski and Christian have noted the links between not just Moscow but Kiev Rus and their nomadic neighbours. Halperin noted that the term Kagan or emperor was used by the Turks and applied not just to the leader of the Khazars but to the prince of Kiev as well. According to Halperin this seems to be the only case of the application of this title to a non-nomadic people. Russians dealt with Turkic peoples without the aid of interpreters and Turkic of some sort must have been the *lingua franca* of the steppe[423] The Mongols and their empire connected Russia to the outside world.[424] It was only in the reign of Ivan the Terrible in the middle of the sixteenth century that Moscow's policy toward the East became one of conquest.

For Halperin the medieval world was one of 'mixed Christian and Islamic societies'. Russia's church chroniclers misled future generations of historians because they were silent about the fact that Russians and Tatars intermarried, shared institutions and together launched military campaigns.[425] According to Halperin, a similar process of forgetting about an earlier relationship would take place among the Turks. Thus, the 'widespread use of Christian soldiers, farmers, artisans, and bureaucrats in the early Ottoman empire' were passed over in silence not just by Russian chroniclers but by Ottoman writers as well.

Ostrowski emphasized a strong Mongol influence on Muscovy in terms of administration and military organization.[426] He has argued that medieval Russia was an amalgam of Byzantine theoretical and philosophical concepts, legal concepts derived from Kiev Rus, and Mongol/Islamic governmental structure and administration.[427] The church chroniclers gave the impression that the leaders of Russia had thought in negative terms about the Tatars since time immemorial or at least since the initial invasion of the mid thirteenth century. Ostrowski has pointed out that in reality there is not much evidence of official hostility towards the Tatars before the Orthodox Church in Moscow finally broke with its elder brother, the Byzantine Church in the fifteenth century. Byzantium treated the Tatars as a 'valuable ally and trading partner'.[428] An anti-Tatar ideology came to suit the rulers of Moscow thereafter and evidence of cooperation with the Tatars was written out of

---

423 Charles Halperin, *Tatar Yoke* (Slavica Pub, 1986), 24.
424 Halperin, *Russia and the Golden Horde*, 5-28.
425 *Ibid.*, 7.
426 Ostrowski, *Muscovy and the Mongols*, 35.
427 *Ibid.*, 15.
428 *Ibid.*, 164.

history.

In Russia, it was Gumilëv who brought to the Russian reading public the clearest picture of cooperation between Russia and its nomadic neighbours. Gumilëv pointed out that Western Europeans of the early modern period took a dim view of steppe nomads, the enemies of civilisation since Roman times.[429] Thus, Catholic Europe was the source of a 'black legend' about the Tatars. Gumilëv equated stories about the terror tactics of the steppe nomads to the Black Death in terms of its damage to the reputation of the Tatars. As Gumilëv and his Eurasian predecessors would have it, it was not the Tatars who cut Russia off from civilization for two hundred and fifty years, but the Tatars who saved Russia from becoming a colony of the Teutonic knights, Poles, Lithuanians and other Europeans who in general were far less civilized than the Eurasian world.

Gumilëv contended that church chroniclers misrepresented this relationship with the steppe. Long before the Mongols, Kiev Rus dealt with a succession of eastern neighbours – semi-nomadic Khazars, sedentary Volga Bulgars, nomadic Pechenegs, and pastoral Polovtsy.[430] The Christian bias against nomads was accentuated after the Mongols, the most powerful of the nomads, adopted Islam.[431] Instead, Gumilëv has argued, the relationship between the agrarian Slavs and semi-nomadic Turks at the time of Kiev Rus' and the Khazar Khanate was more complicated.[432] Like their nomadic neighbours, the Russians often struck into the steppe, stole animals and enslaved women and children.[433] Some years Rus and Polovtsy combined to attack a mutual enemy and other years there was trade and inter-marriage.

From Gumilëv Russian readers learned that Russian princes actively cooperated with the Mongols, that the national hero, Alexander Nevsky was the Mongols' staunchest ally in wars against fellow Russians, that the Orthodox Church seemed to flourish under Mongol rule, that Mongol trade routes were a source of international commerce, that Russians experienced an improved bureaucracy, that postal roads were built, that Cossacks most likely intermingled with the Mongols and did not simply replace them on the

---

429 Lev Gumilëv, *Chernaia legenda* (Moscow: AST, 2002).
430 *Ibid.*, 11.
431 Thomas Haining, 'The Vicissitudes of Mongolian Historiography,' *The Mongol Empire and its Legacy*, 334.
432 Lev Gumilëv, *Drevnie Turki* (Moscow: 1999), *Drevniaia Rus' i velikaia step'* (Moscow: 1989).
433 Halperin, *Russia and the Golden Horde*, 15.

steppe.⁴³⁴

In fostering a more positive image of the Mongols, Gumilëv followed in the footsteps of Trubetskoi and the Eurasianists. The task has never been an easy one because this positive view of the Mongols in history was at odds with popular prejudice against Asia. According to Halperin, studies of the Mongol invasion did not flourish in Tsarist or Soviet times because Russia's wars against the Ottoman Turks, Central Asian separatists and the Japanese meant that Asians, nomads and Muslims were the great scourge of Russian history in popular legends, epics and folk tales and for the majority of academic studies.⁴³⁵ It was a mark of inferiority to appear Asiatic in ethnicity or Islamic in religion. Asia represented an enticing but dangerous frontier. Christian chroniclers, Russian Imperial historians and Stalin-era propagandists all found a reason to fear and hate the East.

Neither Russian historians nor the reading public have embraced the Mongols the way that Trubetskoi or Gumilëv would have liked.⁴³⁶ In 1997, *Rodina*, the most successful of a new breed of popular history journals, made use of glossy illustrations and commentary from leading historians to bring up to date a Russian reading public struggling to come to grips with what was credible and what was not in the new historical literature about the Mongols. The survey of academic opinion provided by *Rodina* showed that academic historians remain divided about the Mongols but that, just as in earlier times, the overall consensus was still negative. Darkevich was typical when he wrote that the Mongol invasion of Russia was catastrophic, leaving Russia one hundred and fifty years behind the West. In his opinion, the current trend of viewing the Mongols in more positive terms is the result of a growing national consciousness among the non-Russian subjects of the Russian Federation and nothing to do with historical accuracy. Golman also described the role of the Mongol invasion of Russia in negative terms, although he, following the example of Soviet historians, pointed out that ultimately the Mongols paid a high price for their victory given that their descendants are

---

434 For confirmation that these were important revelations for the non-specialist reader see the series of articles dedicated to the Mongols in Vernadsky, 'Chto dali Rossii Mongoly?', 'A bylo li igo?', Irina Konovalova, 'Stepnoi biznes,' *Rodina* 3-4 (1997): 96, 85, 36.
435 Halperin, *Russia and the Golden Horde*, vii.
436 For example, *Rodina*, the popular journal devoted to history with impressive print runs of 90,000 (Robert W. Davies, *Soviet History in the Yeltsin Era*, 126) claimed that it was introducing Vernadsky to the Soviet public for the first time, fifty years after his work appeared in the West.

dominated by neighbours who once lived under Mongol rule.[437]

Not only are Mongols still unpopular in Russia but there remains the vexing question of explaining Russia's humiliation in the face of the Mongol invasions of the thirteenth century. Many Russians view their country as unconquered in war. There were temporary setbacks and strategic retreats. Napoleon occupied Moscow in 1812 but Cossack horsemen rode through Paris in 1814. The signing of the Treaty of Brest-Litovsk in 1918 was followed by a complete victory over Germany in 1945. Only the Mongols broke this pattern, ruling Russia for more than two centuries. Not only had the Mongols successfully subdued the Russian lands, but they overthrew the flower of early Slavic civilisation, Kiev Rus.

Fomenko would neatly resolve these problems by claiming that Russian history was in fact uncontaminated by Mongols. The price to be paid was that Russians would have to accept that they were closely related to the Turks and that ancestors of the Russians and Turks had long shared a common homeland and ruled a mighty world empire together. Using the information that was made available in the specialist historical literature and armed with the certainty that conventional history was mainly lies, Fomenko and other pseudo-historians have attempted to write the Mongols out of Russia's history. If the conventional historians were unsure how many Mongols there were and were divided about their legacy, was it not likely that the Mongol invasion was another Romanov fable, just like the myth of the Vikings?

IV.3 Sources

While plainly aware of the debates of the professional historians, Fomenko and many of his readers were convinced that conventional history lacked all credibility on the issue of the Mongols after years of lies, silences and gaps in official histories. While his conclusions were speculative, Fomenko's premise, that there was something wrong with Russian history, struck a chord with the Russian public. For Fomenko, the Mongol/Tatar invasion was a poorly named and deliberately twisted episode in the civil wars that broke out occasionally within the Russian Horde, this great Slav-Turk Empire.

Fomenko's ideal type of an invasion and conquest seems to be the Nazi

---

437 Polemika, 'A bylo li igo?', *Rodina* 3-4 (1997): 86.

blitzkrieg of 1941-45 when the German invaders made a systematic effort to destroy the Soviet state, eradicate all political or cultural independence and reduce the population to slave labour. Soviet writers certainly gave their readers the impression that the Mongols operated in much the same way as modern conquerors. This picture was simply wrong. It is now clear to historians that the Mongols chose not to impose an occupation of this kind and left Russia, so long as it paid tribute, semi-independent. Pseudo-historians argue that the story of the Tatar yoke is yet to be exposed as another of the lies told by official history.

Fomenko and his allies follow their usual pattern of argument, pointing to the paucity of reliable sources from the medieval period, the obvious inaccuracies and forgeries that abound in the sources that do exist, the plot on the part of Church and State in Romanov Russia aimed at extirpating all traces of a Russian alliance with Turks or Moslems and the strange resemblances among the array of characters described in conventional accounts of this period. Pseudo-history cites indiscriminately the works of Russian and Western historians to highlight problems in the conventional account. It then offers its own reconstructions as if they are at least as plausible as anything that the flawed conventional wisdom can offer.

As ever, the sources really do present a challenge to conventional history. Many latter-day writers chose to view the first Russian state as a golden age or paradise that fell victim to its own pride and was then punished by demonic invaders in the shape of the Mongols. The Orthodox Church, the Romanovs and Slavophiles all had reason to celebrate the East Slavic successes story and medieval power of Kiev Rus. Russian historians idealized Kiev Rus as a centre of Christianity, as a civilized place where commerce and popular institutions flourished only to be destroyed by warlike and unchristian Mongols. The problem is that the evidence of the Tatar yoke is not as strong as earlier readers were led to believe. According to Halperin, the church chroniclers were so stunned by Russia's ill fortune that they adopted an 'ideology of science', pretending that the conquest had not occurred.[438] For Fomenko, their silence about the conquest is comprehensible in terms of fact and not discourse. The conquest never happened.

As Abu-Loghod has put it, 'the Mongols left only a modest primary record that is focused largely on campaigns, dynastic successions and

---

438 Halperin, *Russia and the Golden Horde*, 8.

conquests'.[439] It seems likely that Russia was a peripheral issue to the original Mongols even though the Mongol era endured longer in Russia than most other places. According to Fennell, the basic sources for the Russian reaction to the Mongols comprise what he describes as four 'princely' chronicles (Lavrent'evskyi, Novgorod First, Ipat'evskyi and Sofyskyi First) that conveniently provide information, albeit in latter-day editions, from all the affected areas, Kiev, Chernigov, Galicia, Smolensk, Rostov and Vladimir.[440] On the other hand, there is much that is not known about the Golden Horde, in part because Tamerlane's fourteenth-century raiding party destroyed the archive at Sarai.[441] Ostrowski, pace Fennell, recommends that we do not distinguish between princely and church chronicles in Russia for in reality they were all church chronicles.[442]

Initially, the chroniclers portrayed the Mongols as ruthless and barbaric nomads from the eastern steppe, strangers to the lands of Kievan Rus, who established their rule suddenly and with great force. As not only Russian but also Georgian and Armenian chronicles put it, following the 'clouds of Tatars not an eye was left to weep'.[443] According to the Russian chroniclers, 'in those times there came upon us for our sins, unknown nations. No one could tell their origin, whence they came, what religion they professed. God alone knew who they were.' It seems powerful evidence that the Mongols did indeed come from far away if the Russians, who knew so many steppe peoples, regarded them as complete strangers.

Not so, counters Fomenko. The chronicles are the mouthpieces of the church and are mostly latter-day inventions intended to demonise non-Christians whenever possible as horrible and strange. All the evidence we have, claim the alternative writers, points to familiarity to the point of contempt among those who fought in Russia during the so-called Mongol era. The chroniclers even called these people Tatars, the name they bestowed upon other steppe peoples.

Historians outside of Russia have long acknowledged the difficulty in

---

439   Janet L. Abu-Lughod, *Before European hegemony: the world system A. D. 1250-1350* (London: Oxford University Press), 25-26.
440   John Fennell, *The Crisis of Medieval Russia, 1200-1304* (London: Longman, 1983), 65.
441   Halperin, *Russia and the Golden Horde*, 44.
442   Ostrowski, *Muscovy and the Mongoly*, 166.
443   Haining, 'The Vicissitudes of Mongolian Historiography,' *The Mongol Empire and its Legacy*, 334. Alfred Rambaud, *History of Russia, from the earliest times to 1800*, trans. by L.B. Lang, H.A. Bolles (Boston: 1882).

using church chronicles for an account of the Mongols. Ostrowski identified three distinct periods of chronicle writing and in each case the attitude towards the Mongols appears to have been determined mostly by political considerations. From 1223 to 1252, the chroniclers were plainly hostile to the Tatars, the 'godless Moabites' from the East. In 1252, the Mongol surrogate, Alexander Nevsky became Grand Prince of Vladimir and, for the next two hundred years, barely a harsh word is to be heard from the chroniclers about the Tatars. It was as if there were no invaders. The Tatars who do appear in the chronicles are occasional interlopers and not occupiers.[444]

Finally, from the middle of the fifteenth century as the power of the Golden Horde waned and the Moscow church stood alone as the last outpost of Orthodox Christianity, the modern view of the Mongols as horrible heathens rapidly gained ascendancy. For Ostrowski, it is clear that, for two hundred years, Russians and Tatars were joint administrators of the 'Tatar' yoke. Only nearing the end of the Mongol period was the 'Church concocted virtual past of Rus' princes trying to free the Rus' lands from the Tatars' invented.[445]

Halperin argued that the chroniclers could not bring themselves to describe the Mongol occupation or the Russian defeat. Ostrowski preferred to call it a conspiracy of silence, involving the deliberate falsification of sources, with the aim of smoothing the trading and diplomatic relationship between the Mongols on the one hand, and the Rus and Byzantium on the other.[446] Gumilëv claimed that Mongols, Polovtsy, Slavs and Turks coexisted and intermingled for centuries before and after 1223. In this context it is not so fantastic a leap for Fomenko to claim that Russia seemed little changed by the allegedly catastrophic and unprecedented Mongol invasion.

Fomenko makes the reasonable claim that chronicle sources are obviously written to a formula, are full of obvious errors and fantastic detail, and were mostly likely composed or altered after the Tatars came to be associated with Islam in the fifteenth century. Certainly, the reader needs to be armed with considerable scepticism when reading the chronicle accounts of the Mongols. The Novgorod chronicler, for example, seemed confused about who the Mongols were or at least found it convenient to use stock phrases to describe them. The chronicler quoted the Revelation of Methodius

---

444 Ostrowski, *Muscovy and the Mongols*, 147-50
445 *Ibid.*, 163.
446 *Ibid.*, 145.

of Patara that described the sudden appearance of a strange people put to flight by Gideon, but had used exactly these Biblical words to describe the Polovtsy in years past.[447] The chroniclers are amazingly unforthcoming about why, once the ferocious Mongols left in 1223, no precautions were taken against their return a decade later. That the war affected different areas differently is attested to by the Vladimir chronicler who amid the apparent carnage of the era reported that between March 1238 and February 1239, 'there was peace'.[448]

Riazan fell in December 1237 after resisting for a mere five days. Fennell notes that the principal source we have is the fragmentary *Povest o razorenii Riazani Batuem* or 'Tale of the Destruction of Riazan by Batu'. As a Russian historian has put it: 'for a description of the Mongol invasion of Russia, researchers, teachers and artists rely upon the *Povest*'.[449] Yet it is not clear when this document was written and how reliable it is. *Povest* resembles other chronicle accounts and, in place of credible information, simply lists the usual litany of princes murdered, nuns raped and all manner of barbaric acts perpetrated by the Mongols.[450] We are asked to believe that Batu Khan was possessed by lust and beheaded the city's prince for refusing to present his wife. The servant of the prince, who lived to tell the tale, not only saw the execution, but succeeded in smuggling the beheaded prince's body out of Batu Khan's tent to bury it nearby.

According to the chroniclers, Vladimir was taken in just four days in February 1238 after the use of siege guns to breach the walls. Here the unfortunate inhabitants were, it seems, burned to death after they took refuge in the Cathedral of the Assumption. This story of Christian martyrdom is for Fomenko just another staged piece of latter-day chronicle writing. Fomenko notes that the much smaller town of Kozelsk took two months to subdue, no siege guns were used and the siege cost thousands of Tatar lives, if the chronicles are to be believed. It is not only Fomenko who is puzzled as to why and how Kozelsk resisted, why casualties were so high and why the Mongols even bothered with this seemingly unimportant town when they chose not to ride to Novgorod.[451] Whereas the professionally trained historian might accept as typical the puzzling nature of these events, the lack of logic is, Fomenko

---

447 Fennell, *The Crisis of Medieval Russia*, 68.
448 *Ibid.*, 81.
449 Andrei Amel'kin, 'Kogda rodilsia Evpatii Kolovrat,' *Rodina* 3-4 (1997): 48
450 *Ibid.*, 79.
451 Fennell, *The Crisis of Medieval Russia*, 81.

claims, damning evidence that the chronicles in the form that they have reached us cannot be taken literally.

Much of our knowledge about the Mongols comes from Western travellers, papal envoys and merchants, who visited the Mongol heartland. They reported seeing fantastic things. According to the testimony of William of Rubruck, the Franciscan monk who claimed to have travelled to Khan Mongke's headquarters in Karakorum in 1253-55, there was even a Parisian goldsmith named Buchier who created a magnificent mechanical silver fountain, which spurted different alcoholic beverages from each pipe.[452] Plano Carpini, whose travels among the Mongols preceded William of Rubruck, commented that the Mongols exterminated everyone in the conquered Russian lands except for the artisans and that this explains the wonders of Karakorum.[453] According to the testimony of Carpini, in Karakorum the supreme khan sat upon an ivory throne that was carved for him by the Russian master Kozma.[454]

Yet Plano Carpini contradicted himself when he wrote that Kiev, which had just been ravaged by Batu Khan, was under the control of the Kievan commander, Vladimir Eikovich, who continued to carry out his duties as he did prior to the Mongol attack.[455] According to Rubruck, 'the Russians lived with the Tatars...they mixed with them...borrowed Tatar customs, traditions, clothes...all the river crossing are manned by Russians, all the transportation systems are served by Russians.'[456] Fomenko comments ironically that it took only twenty years for the Tatars and the Russians to blend into a homogenous ethnic entity.[457] Fomenko insists that Rubruck and Carpini saw the riches of the cities of the Volga River, the capital of the Golden Horde, where archaeologists have discovered numerous and ornate eastern Slavonic artefacts, enamel and amber Orthodox crosses. Carpini wrote that

---

452 Peter Jackson, 'From Ulus to Khanate,' *The Mongol Empire and its Legacy*, 20.
453 Marina Poluboiarinova, 'Russkie v Zolotoi Orde,' *Rodina* 3-4 (1997): 53.
454 Vernadsky, *A History of Russia*, III, 63; Poluboiarinova, 'Russkie v Zolotoi Orde,' 54.
455 Christopher Dawson (ed), *The Mission to Asia: narratives and letters of the Franciscan missionaries in Mongolia and China in the thirteenth and fourteenth centuries*, translated by a Nun of Stanbrook Abbey, ed. by Sheed and Ward (London: 1955); Dawson, Plano Carpini, *Istoriia Mongalov/Rubruck, Puteshestvia v vostochnye strany/kniga Marko Polo* (Moscow: Mysl', 1997); The analysis of his journeys is in Nosovskii and Fomenko, *Bibleiskaia Rus'* II, 287-295; Poliakovskii, *Tatary-Mongoly, Evraziia, Mnogovariatnost'*, 83; Bushkov, *Rossiia kotoroi ne bylo* I, 178-190.
456 Nosovskii and Fomenko, *Novaia khronologiia Rusi*, 71.
457 Ibid.

Russian clergy lived 'in the horde with the emperor', evidence for Fomenko that Carpini had visited the court of a Russian tsar-khan on the Volga.

Fomenko is especially interested in Carpini's geography. Fomenko asks how it could be that Carpini does not describe in detail the countries lying to the east of the Volga.'[458] Geographically, Carpini indicated that China was to the east of the Mongol lands, whereas Fomenko points out that it is to the east only from the Volga, and that it has to be south of the real Mongolia. Carpini instead has the Saracens located to the south of Mongolia. Fomenko points to the fact that the medieval Saracens lived to the south of the Volga and Caspian, whereas south of Mongolia there is present day China. Carpini wrote that to the west of Karakorum there were tribes of Naiman. Most probably, Fomenko concludes, implausibly, the Naiman was a reference to the Normans who lived to the west of Russia. Carpini wrote that to the north of the lands of the Tatars there are oceans and seas, while Fomenko points out that it is common knowledge that there are thousands of kilometres of dense forests and tundra to the north of present-day Mongolia. On the other hand, north-eastern Russia is indeed located very close to the Arctic Ocean, having cities and villages running almost all the way up to the northern coast.[459]

Fomenko is certainly correct when he claims that there is widespread scepticism among experts about much of this travel literature. The historian, Denis Sinor has pointed out that Carpini was often wrong in factual matters. Carpini claimed to have come across peoples called *parossites* with 'small stomachs and tiny mouths' that feed simply by smelling their cooked meat. Later he met peoples who had a human shape in every respect except for their ox-like hooves and dog-like heads, who barked after every two or three words.[460] It seems unlikely that Carpini was an eyewitness to all that he reported. In the West, there has long been a debate over whether Marco Polo reached the Far East. Frances Wood, for example, has argued that Marco Polo never reached China, in part, because Polo did not describe the Great Wall, tea drinking, or foot binding. On the other hand, Marco Polo did report witnessing banquets for forty thousand people. Whether Polo simply reflected 'the Western cultural imaginary with its Orientalist phantasms and its fascination with the marvels of foreign worlds' or was indeed a remarkable

---

458   Nosovskii and Fomenko, *Bibleiskaia Rus'* II, 288-89.
459   *Ibid.*, 289-290.
460   See Dawson (ed), *The Mission to Asia,* 30-31.

traveller, remains in dispute, although the consensus of expert opinion seems to be that he did see China.[461] Fomenko insists that observers like Polo, were more likely to witness such marvels along the Volga River, an area that was certainly more accessible to travellers from Western Europe than Beijing.

What can Fomenko and his allies offer in place of the existing selection of allegedly biased and unreliable sources? It is not enough simply to claim that all evidence for a hypothesis was destroyed by the new authorities, a ploy that Fomenko criticises in rival popular writers.[462] Pseudo history has its own pseudo evidence. Firstly, there are arguments from silence. *Slovo o pogibeli Russkoi zemli* is a famous medieval document less than a page in length that describes how successful Kiev Rus was before misfortune came upon it. Conventional historians believe that its gloomy prognosis was simply a reflection of the level of disintegration in Kiev Rus on the eve of its wars against the Mongols.[463] For alternative writers, Slovo is clearly a reference to the Mongol invasion. The reason it is so brief is that Romanov historians edited it in order to hide the truth about the Russian nature of the Mongols. For pseudo-history, the reason that we have only fragmentary information about pagan priests in Novgorod, medieval maps displaying the conquests of the Russian horde and clear proof that Vikings and Mongols served Russian princes and tsar/khans and not the other way round is that this inconvenient information has been excised from the historical record by Romanov propagandists.

Secondly, pseudo-historians claim that there are brief glimpses of the truth in the sources used by conventional historians. Pseudo-history has made a great deal of the fact that Rashid Ad Din, the Persian writer who knew the Mongols best, seemed to suggest that the first people to suffer from the Mongol invasion were Christian Bulgars, neighbours of the Franks.[464] For Morozov it was obvious that the Mongol invasion was in fact an invasion of Western Europeans who attacked the Bulgarian lands north of Greece. Reading the remainder of Rashid Ad Din's account it becomes obvious that this first observation was simply an error. Elsewhere, Rashid Ad Din discusses Bulgars whose neighbours are the Bashkirs, in other words, clearly

---

461 Gabriele Schwab, 'Traveling literature, traveling theory: literature and cultural contrast between East and West,' *Studies in the Humanities* 29:1 (June 2002): 5.
462 Nosovskii and Fomenko, *Novaia khronologiia Rusi*, 10.
463 Gumilëv, *Drevniaia Rus' i velikaia step,'* 376.
464 I have used Rashid Ad Din, *Sbornik letopisei*, translated from Persian by Iurii P. Verkhovskii, (Moscow: Izdatel'stvo akademii nauk SSSR, 1960), 37.

the Bulgars who live on the middle Volga who were indeed attacked and overrun by Batu Khan's horde before the invasion of Russia. Nonetheless, alternative writers, including Fomenko, Bushkov and Poliakovsky, invariably mention this initial mistake by Rashid Ad Din as confirmation that the early writers were at best confused about what happened at the time of the Mongol invasion.

Fomenko lays great importance upon the testimony of ibn-Hawqal who wrote that:

> Rus consisted of three tribes, one is the closest to the kingdom of Bulgar. The tsar of this tribe lives in Kuiaba [an Arabic name for Kiev]... the second tribe is located above the first and is called Slaviia...the third tribe is called Artaniia, and its tsar lives in Arta.[465]

For Fomenko, earlier writers knew that ancient Russia was divided into three parts. One part of Russia was based around Kiev and a second was found farther north and known as *Slaviia* (Novogorod or Iaroslavl). The third tribe of Slavs lived in *Arta* (thus *Orda* or Horde in Russian), obviously (for Fomenko) a reference to a horde present on the Volga river hundreds of years before the Mongols.[466] For conventional scholars like Pritsak, there are far too many possible translations for the Arabic word Fomenko wants to translate as Arta to make any conclusion at all.[467] For Fomenko, this perceptive ancient source has made reference to the three constituent territorial pieces of ancient Russia whose modern footprints confront us to this day. Kuiaba, Slaviia and Artaniia became the White, Blue and Golden Horde of the medieval period, White Rus, Russia Minor and Great Russia of the Imperial period, and Ukraine, Belarus and Russia of the twentieth and twenty first centuries.[468]

---

465 Nosovskii and Fomenko, *Novaia khronologiia Rusi*, 13-14.
466 *Ibid.* Conventional Russian historians disagree, arguing that this Arta is a reference to a southern Russian principality situated at the Azov Sea that was cut off from the rest of Russia by the nomadic raids – famous Tmutorakan' princedom. See Alexander Novosel'tsev, 'Vostochnye istochniki o vostochnykh slavianakh i Rusi VI-IX vekov,' *Drevnerusskoe Gosudarstvo i ego mezhdunarodnoe znachenie* (Moscow: Nauka, 1965), 355-420, and Mishin, *Sakaliba (slaviane) v islamskom mire v rannee srednevekov'e* (Moscow: In-t Vostokovedeniia RAN, Kraft+, 2002).
467 Omeljan Pritsak, 'The Name of the Third Kind of Rus and their City,' *Studies in medieval Eurasian history* XII (London: Variorum Reprints, 1981), 2-9.
468 Pritsak, points out that there are many views on this issue. He examined the works of Ibn Hawqal and Al-Istakhri and notes that it is possible to find affinities with many semi-legendary places including Arkona, Biarma, and Varton. See Pritsak, 'The

Thirdly, pseudo-history is not opposed to fudging the truth. Fomenko extensively cites Herberstein, the Holy Roman Empire's ambassador to Russia in 1517 and 1526 who is generally regarded as an acute observer of Russian life and meticulous recorder of Russian words and pronunciations. As Khoroshkevich has pointed out, Fomenko claims that Herberstein noted that Muscovites were very proud of Attilla the Hun, boasting that he, a Russian Muscovite, devastated Europe. However, in the Latin edition of Herberstein's work published in 1549 and cited by Fomenko, Attilla is referred to as a Hungarian chieftain, a detail that Fomenko preferred not to share with his Russian readers.[469]

Fourthly, Fomenko claims to have discovered sources uncontaminated by the lies of the chroniclers and Romanov historians. Fomenko's favourite source is Andrei Lyzlov's *Skifiiskaia Istoriia*.[470] Before his death in 1697, Lyzlov wrote accounts of Russia's war against the Mongols, translated Polish historical works and studied the Turkish court. For Lyzlov, the peoples of Eurasia – Slav and Turk alike - were descendants of the Scyths, the invincible warriors memorably described in Herodotus. Whatever its merits, Lyzlov's book was not reprinted for more than two hundred years in Russia after printings in 1776 and 1787. For Fomenko, Lyzlov's account was suppressed because it told the inconvenient truth about the origins of Russia. Lyzlov identified the Tatar-Mongols and the Scyths, who fought in Mongol fashion to overcome such famous Persian rulers as Cyrus and Darius. For Lyzlov, the Tatars lived on the territory of modern Russia but were divided into European and Asian Tatars.[471] For Fomenko, this is evidence that Russians and Turks were respectively European and Asian Tatars. Unlike the Arab writer cited above, Lyzlov seemed to consider that Russia was divided into two and not three parts. This is not a difficulty for Fomenko who claims that Russia was ethnically two halves (Slav and Turk) but geographically located in three different strongholds.

Thus the nomadic invaders of Russia whom the West called the

Name of the Third Kind of Rus and their City,' 12, pp. 2-9; also see Alexander Novosel'tsev, 'Vostochnye istochniki o vostochnykh slavianakh i Rusi VI-IX vekov,' *Drevnerusskoe Gosudarstvo i ego mezhdunarodnoe znachenie* (Moscow: Nauka, 1965), 355-420.

469 See Anna Khoroshkevich, 'Novoe neizdannoe poslanie 'Sigizmuda Gerbershteina,'' *Istoriia i antiistoriia: Kritika 'novoi khronologii' akademika Fomenko* (Moscow: Iazyki russkoi kultury, 2000), 274-290.
470 Andrei Lyzlov, *Istoriia skifiiskaia* (Moscow: Nauka, 1990).
471 Lyzlov, *Istoriia skifiiskaia*, 9.

Mongols came not from far-away Mongolia, but, like the Scyths, emerged from the northern Black Sea steppe and the Caucasus.[472] Lyzlov guessed about the origins of other peoples of the steppe in ways that appeal to Fomenko. The Pechenegs and Polovtsy according to Lyzlov were the descendants of the Goths, Lithuanians and old Prussians. That their language was a peculiar mixture of Russian and Polish, according to Lyzlov, is further evidence for Fomenko that the Pechenegs, Polovtsy and the Goths were all Slavs.[473]

Fomenko finds further support for his theory in the relatively obscure account of the medieval religious cleric Koniskii, an archbishop of Byelorussia, entitled *Istoriia Russov ili maloi Rossii*.[474] The archbishop, commenting on the wars between the Slavs, Pechenegs, Polovtsy and Khazars, came to the conclusion that their wars were nothing but transient disputes between otherwise fraternal tribes. Koniskii wrote that the eastern Slavs were the Scyths. The southern ones were Sarmatians. Northern Slavs living along the Baltic were Varangians. In the middle between the three lived Roxolans, or Russes, named after the Biblical prince Rus, and Muscovites, who named themselves after their prince Meshekh who used to migrate along the Moscow River with his tribe, and thus gave the future Russian capital its current name. Ultimately, all Slavic warriors came to be called Khazars or Cossacks who were chosen from the general population for permanent war service. They supplied their own ammunition and armour, and migrated with entire families, if necessary. During times of war the civilian population was obliged to help these troops with the tax that was called with indignation 'the Khazar tax'. Koniski was convinced that these warriors were renamed by the Byzanine Tsar Constantine Monomachus as Cossacks, and since then kept this name.[475]

This is a statement of a huge significance for Fomenko. First of all, Khazars are clearly not simply steppe people whose ruling class mysteriously adopted Judaism as conventional history alleged, but Cossacks. The alleged massacre of the Khazars by the Russians is an invention of the Romanovs whose aim was to separate Russia from its eastern steppe heritage.[476]

---

472   Lyzlov, *Istoriia skifiiskaia*, 14, 18-19.
473   *Ibid.*, 20, 21.
474   George Koniskii, *Istoriia Russov ili maloi Rusi* (Moscow: Universiteskaia tipografia, 1846).
475   Koniskii, *Istoriia Russov ili maloi Rusi*, 2.
476   Nosovskii and Fomenko, *Bibleiskaia Rus'* I, 149-150.

Khazars, Pechenegs and Polovtsy were all ethnic Slavs in this account. Koniskii also described the ancient Russian state exactly as Fomenko does – the separation of the society into two distinct parts, one purely military, the Cossack Hordes, and the second purely civilian, which had to pay a tithe in order to guarantee its protection. The infamous Tatar yoke was in fact nothing more dramatic than the continuation of tithe payments to the Cossacks.

IV.4 Eurasianism

The initial picture that the chroniclers paint of Russia does seem to be of a land under foreign domination. They describe the subservience of Russian princes called to visit the Horde, raids and occupations, the increasingly large numbers of Tatars involved in military operations and Tatar involvement in inter-princely wars among the Russians.[477] At the same time, this was a very different invasion to the experience of the Napoleonic or Nazi invaders of later centuries.

Modern readers often take the 'Tatar yoke' to imply a system of extortion carried out over nearly three hundred years by the Mongol overlords of Kievan Rus', a model that has parallels with the experience of the Nazis in World War Two.[478] Russian folklore suggests this type of analogy when it proclaims: 'if there is no money, the Tatar will take your property, if there is no property, the Tatar will take your wife, if there is no wife, the Tatar will take you as a slave'.[479]

None of this makes sense, according to Fomenko. The cooperation between the Russian Orthodox Church and supposedly brutal foreign invaders is difficult to explain, pseudo-history claims, if it really were a foreign conquest. Batu Khan issued an order according to which the plunder of Orthodox churches was to be punished by court martial, and the church itself was granted the right to prosecute Tatar soldiers and civilians for crimes against church property. The Churches and monasteries were declared exempt of any form of taxation in 1257.[480] In 1261, Khan Berke established

---

477 Fennell, *The Crisis of Medieval Russia*, 140.
478 *Rasskazy Russkikh Letopisei XII-XIV vekov*, 75-76, 78-79.
479 Bushkov, *Rossiia I*, 200.
480 Halperin, *Russia and the Golden Horde*, 9; Rambaud, *The History of Russia*, 172-173.

an Episcopal See in Sarai.[481] The Church did not split into regional centres under the Mongol conquerors but remained united, powerful and wealthy.

On the surface at least, the Mongols appear to be among the most reasonable tax collectors in Russian history, taking as their booty a mere ten per cent of everything - crops, goods and people, just like the ethnic Russians princes did before them. While Soloviev compared the Mongols to petty bandits, more recent historians describe the Golden Horde as embracing the sophisticated bureaucratic practices of sedentary populations. Halperin described the Mongol taxation system as complex suggesting that the Mongols must have made excellent use of captive sedentary peoples to act as bureaucrats.[482] Halperin has found it strange that the devastated and allegedly subsistence-level Russian villages paid tribute to the Mongols in silver, and concludes that if Russia were able to sustain such taxation then the resilience of the medieval Russian economy has been so far underestimated.[483] It is certainly likely that the degree of plundering of Kiev Rus has been exaggerated by church accounts with a vested interest in demonising the Mongols.[484]

Besieging Riazan' in 1238 the Mongols asked only for a tithe and the city would be spared.[485] As Halperin has put it, the tithe was 'improbable'.[486] Why would ruthless invaders make this very reasonable offer to defenceless foreigners who were now at their mercy? To Fomenko, it seems too great a coincidence that ten per cent was the size of the tax levied on the subjugated peoples first by the Khazar Kagan, then by the princes of Kiev, and later by the Grand Prince of Vladimir. Thus, for Fomenko, the tithe of the Khans was simply the existing method of taxation well known to the citizens of Kiev Rus.

Fomenko finds the establishment of the tribute system in Russia difficult to reconcile with a genuine invasion. There is no evidence that Tatar tax collectors appeared in Russia before 1257. Why did the Tatar/Mongols wait more than a decade in order to impose taxation, failing to act when the population was first brought to heel? A break from taxation should have provided the Russians with a splendid opportunity to recuperate and to raise

---

481 Ostrowski, *Muscovy and the Mongols*, 18.
482 Halperin, *Russia and the Golden Horde*, 26-27.
483 *Ibid.*, 84.
484 Ostrowski, *Muscovy and the Mongols*, 123.
485 *Povest' o razorenii Riazani Batyem,' Drevnerusskaia literatura* (Moscow: Prosveshchenie, 1973), 153; Vernadsky, *A History of Russia* III, 216; Hosking, *Russia and the Russians*, 52.
486 Halperin, *Tatar Yoke*, 38.

armies against the Mongols. Conventional historians suggest that there was no need as Russia had been terrorised into submission and a census would take time to organize. Fomenko noted that during Novgorod's rebellion against the tax collectors in 1262, the Russian princes openly expressed their approval. A wave of repression might have been anticipated but none occurred. The rebellious provinces even declared the abolition of conscription for the Tatar army. The Tatars did not retaliate. In the case of Novgorod, prince Alexander Nevsky (1220-63) did not take stern action against his subjects when they rejected Tatar tax collectors. Vernadsky explains the benevolence of the khans toward the Russians by reference to the direct involvement of the Russian princes who begged the Khan not to punish the population.[487] For Fomenko, begging is not something that comes easily to Russian princes. It is more likely, he claims that this was routine politics. Russians taxed fellow Russians and only occasionally employed Tatars as hired thugs much as their predecessors hired Vikings for raiding parties. These were punitive and tax-collecting operations carried out periodically by warrior bands against co-ethnics, not a sudden and spectacular invasion by unknown hordes from the Far East.

Such a benign and reasonable attitude suggests that this was not an issue of invasion and resistance but more likely the bungled introduction of a new tax, different to custom, and it was this, not its foreign origins, that provoked the citizens of Novgorod to rebellion. Thus, the pragmatic Alexander Nevsky and his Tatar entourage backed down and chose not to punish the citizens too severely.[488]

Fomenko is also attracted to the identity of Mongol tax collectors. In the Iaroslavl' region in 1261, the Mongol tax collector was a Russian Orthodox monk named Izosim, and in the city of Ustuyg, a Russian Christian named Ioann.[489] These Russian tax collectors were clearly unpopular among some of their countrymen, and identified as 'vicious Muslims'.[490] One chronicler recalls with obvious relish how 'Izosim was killed in Iaroslavl, his body was eaten by the crows while his legs, (that) were so quick to do evil, were dragged by dogs through the streets to the amazement of the citizenry'.[491] Vernadsky suggests that the hostility of the local population was caused by the

---

487 Vernadsky, *History of Russia* 3, 161.
488 Bushkov, *Rossiia*, 204-07.
489 Vernadsky, *A History of Russia* III, 158-60.
490 *Ibid.*, 159.
491 *Rasskazy Russkikh Letopisei XII-XVI vekov*, 98.

conversion of the monk to Islam.[492] But for Fomenko, it is simpler to envisage a war of Russian and Turk against Russian and Turk, with Orthodox and Muslim to be found on both sides. There were Christian Turks and Islamic Russians in an era when religious differences were less important than they were in the era of religious wars that was to follow. The more advanced Russians of course dominated these partnerships with the Turks but it was a partnership of peoples already living on Russian land and not a war against foreign invaders.

Could the Mongols really have been that exploitative, asks Fomenko? Where are the gold, silver, diamonds and priceless artefacts that the invaders supposedly extracted from the conquered Russian territories? If the Mongols did extract massive treasures from the enslaved lands, why are these treasures yet to be found in Mongolia? Somewhere in the mysterious Mongolian capital, Karakorum, mountains of gold and silver are waiting to be found. So far the location of the Mongol capital remains a matter of dispute while the treasures remain unaccounted for.[493]

According to Vernadsky, the tribute paid by eastern Russia to the Mongols only in 1384, without Novgorod, amounted to 145,000 silver roubles.[494] This tribute, conventional and pseudo historians agree, certainly found its way to the Volga, where archaeological digs have yielded evidence of substantial cities. Lyzlov, writing in the seventeenth century, has described the splendid homes, towns and structures erected by Russian builders and masters along the Volga and Ural rivers where the regional centres of the Golden Horde were situated. It was because of the riches of the Volga region that, according to Lyzlov, the Russians gave this area its golden name.[495]

In modern-day European Russia, many objects of eastern origin, presumably created in or acquired by the Golden Horde, have been uncovered.[496] Alternative historians argue that this is proof that the so-called Mongol invasion began from the shores of the Volga, not farther east, and that the alleged treasures of the khans in fact circulated mainly within the present-day bounds of European Russia.

The Mongols certainly seem to treat the Volga as home from a very early date. Following the invasion of Europe in 1241-42, Batu Khan was

---

492 Vernadsky, *History of Russia* 3, 159.
493 Nosovskii and Fomenko, *Bibleiskaia Rus'* II, 289.
494 Vernadsky, *History of Russia* III, 231.
495 Lyzlov, *Istoriia skifiiskaia*, 29.
496 Poluboiarinova, 'Russkie v Zolotoi Orde,' *Rodina* 3-4 (1997): 56-57.

expected to return to Karakorum to settle a succession crisis but he did not do so. According to Sinor, the Mongol troops who had ridden as far west as Hungary now happily made a new home in the Russian steppes.[497] Conventional accounts suggest that no tribute was paid to the Great Khan in Karakorum after the 1260s.

The Russian prince who dealt with the Mongol invasion best was Alexander Nevsky, a controversial figure in Russian historiography.[498] For many Russian patriots, Alexander Nevsky seems an ambiguous figure, a patriot who saved Novgorod from German invaders to the West but at the same time did more than anyone else to ensure Russian servitude to the Tatar yoke. For Eurasianists, Alexander Nevsky is the embodiment of Russian virtues, an enemy of the west and friend of the east, a warrior elected by the people and a successful unifier of Russian territory.

Later acclaimed a saint of the Orthodox Church, Alexander Nevsky was the son of the Grand Prince of Vladimir, the most powerful individual in Russia at this time, and was elected prince of Novgorod, the Russian principality where the democratic traditions of the *veche* or popular assembly were strongest, in 1236. In 1240 Alexander Nevsky won a victory over the Swedes on the Neva River and in 1242 he defeated the Teutonic Knights at Lake Peipus. At the same time, Alexander Nevsky actively collaborated with the Mongols, who made him Grand Prince.

Alexander Nevsky was, according to Gumilëv, the adopted son of Batu Khan.[499] This is a surprising relationship between conquerors and the defeated peoples, in the opinion of Fomenko. Alexander Nevsky not only ensured that Suzdal became an obedient subject of the Tatars and put up with repeated raids and incursions, but visited the Great Khan in Karakorum and clearly profited from his cooperation with the Mongols even when his own family made efforts to defy the invaders.[500] Fomenko and his allies speculate that Alexander Nevsky was in fact a so-called Mongol khan. Rather than Batu Khan's adopted son, it was more likely that Alexander Nevsky was Batu Khan himself.

Alexander Nevsky was not alone in adapting quickly to the new reality of the Mongol invasion. In 1249, the soldiers of Danill of Galich astounded the

---

497   Denis Sinor, 'Horse and Pasture in inner Asian history,' *Oriens Extremis* 19 (1972): 181.
498   See Fennell, *The Crisis of Medieval Russia 1200-1304*, 120-21.
499   Gumilëv, *Drevniaia Rus' i velikaia step,'* 534.
500   Fennell, *The Crisis of Medieval Russia*, 141.

Poles and Hungarians with their oriental style of dress and equipment - short stirrups, very high saddles, long caftans, turbans surmounted by an *aigret*, sabres and poniards in the belt.[501] Daniil's adoption of Mongol customs came barely a dozen years after the initial Mongolian onslaught. Conventional historians argue that it would have been surprising if Kiev Rus' did not borrow from the superior strategies, tactics, and weaponry of the Mongols.[502] Fomenko insists that Daniil of Galich was not adopting, spontaneously and remarkably adroitly, the tactics of his enemy but expressing the military customs long typical of the Russian Horde.

There is much continuity between Kiev Rus and the Mongol era. The Mongols prided themselves on their military organization. There were units of one thousand that broke down into hundreds and then to tens. All of this was surprisingly familiar to pre-Mongol Kiev Rus, claims Fomenko. It is well known that the basic unit of the *opolchenie* or city militia of Kiev Rus was the hundred or *sotnia*, and in the cities, there were thousands commanded by a *tysiatskii*, often an elected warlord.[503]

European travellers thought that Muscovite soldiers fought in the style of Ottoman Turks. Halperin writes that pictures show them in a Mongol saddle with Mongols stirrups, helmet and compound bow and quiver.[504] At the same time, the khan was often depicted in medieval pictures in the robes of a Byzantine emperor. Genghis khan was known in Russia as Genghis Tsar.[505]

The Russians still enjoyed great power as elite soldiers in the so-called Mongol army.[506] Russians often took command and led Tatar troops into battle. Thus we have descriptions of punitive expeditions led by *voevoda* Fedorchuk.[507] Fedorchuk is clearly a Slavic name and *voevoda* (rather than *murza*) a Russian term that the chronicler has found appropriate. Alexander Nevsky's son, Andrei Gorodetskii and Ivan Kalita, are other examples of Russians at the head of Tatar/Mongol troops. Various sources show a significant degree of participation of Russian troops in the feudal squabbles among Tatar nobility, while the same degree of participation of Tatar troops on behalf of Russian princes fighting each other is just as evident.[508]

---

501   Rambaud, *History of Russia*, 169-170.
502   Ostrowski, *Muscovy and the Mongols*, 7.
503   Hosking, *Russia and the Russians*, 36.
504   Halperin, *Russia and the Golden Horde*, 91.
505   *Ibid.*, 98.
506   Vernadsky, *A History of Russia* III, VI, 88-89.
507   Halperin, *The Tatar Yoke*, 86; Guts, *Mnogovariantnaia istoriia Rossii*, 242.
508   Nikolai Polevoi, *Istoriia Russkogo naroda* II, (Moscow: Veche, 2006), 293; Bushkov,

World history, Fomenko claims, offers few examples where the representatives of the defeated side, supposedly totally different in language, appearance, culture and religion from the victors, have found themselves in charge of running the victorious invading army in a short space of time after the initial bloody encounter. Moreover, the victors, Tatar nobles who became subordinate to the defeated opponents, seemed surprisingly content with that position.

IV.5 The Blonde Genghis Khan

Proud of the multi-racial composition of Russia, Russian patriots emphasise that racism is foreign to the Russian character. Nonetheless, race figures prominently in the discourse of alternative writers. The lineage of Genghis Khan is not surprisingly a murky matter even for conventional historians. We have no precise date for the birth of Temuchin, who later became Genghis Khan. The Mongols lived among other tribes including Tartars, Keraits, Naiman and Uighurs and incorporated into their armies the peoples that they conquered. Fomenko draws upon Gumilëv to argue that Genghis Khan did not in appearance resemble modern Mongols. Genghis Khan, suggested Gumilëv, was most likely a tall, blue-eyed individual with a long white beard given that ancient Mongols, judging by the statements of the chroniclers, and the image depicted in frescoes found in Manchuria. Gumilëv explains the appearance of modern Mongols as the result of mixed marriage with a variety of neighbouring indigenous peoples.[509]

There were contemporaries who saw stereotypic Asiatic features in the Mongols. According to the striking description of the Persian Amir Khuzru:

> Their eyes so narrow and piecing that they might have bored a hole in a brazen vessel. Their stench was more horrible than their colour. Their heads were set on their bodies as if they had no necks, and their cheeks resembled leather bottles, full of wrinkles and knots. Their noses extended from cheekbone to cheekbone. Their nostrils are rotting graves, and from them the hair descended as far as the lips. Their chests were covered with lice, which looked like sesame

---

Rossiia I, 142; Guts, *Mnogovariantnaia istoriia Rossii*, 174, 180.
509   Gumilëv, *Drevniaia Rus' i velikaia step,'* 389, 395.

growing in bad soil.[510]

Fomenko argues that the only ethnic group of European Russia that might meet this type of description was the Kalmyk host that reached the Volga-Don steppe only after the Mongol period. Otherwise, in Fomenko's view, European Russia is remarkably free of Asiatic physical features.

This last claim seems absurd. On the other hand, conventional historians do not doubt that at least part of the Golden Horde's population was ethnically Russian.[511] The tax collectors, who worked as *baskaki* for the Mongols, boasted names with Slavic, Armenian and Turkic origins.[512] Mongol aristocrats made use of the imperial post or *yam* to as *posoly* or envoys but the chronicles make no mention of their need for interpreters.[513]

Vernadsky noted that there was a wide variety of tribes and clans involved in the Mongol conquests and suggests an admixture of Alanic, that is, Ossetian, blood in the clan of Genghis Khan.[514] Alternative writers look hard for evidence of Mongols who had blue eyes on the grounds that they were obviously related to their nearest blue-eyed neighbours, the Russians. Fennell records how the Mongols tricked the Polovtsy into abandoning their Ossetian allies with the claim that Mongols and Polovtsy were of the same blood.[515] For Fomenko, this was no trick and the Polovtsy did indeed recognize their kin.

Fomenko notes that the Arab historian Abdu-l-Fida in his 'Geography of the Lands' claimed that the Russians were of Turkic blood, and lived next to the Oghuz (Torki of the Russian chronicles).[516] Polish and Belarus historians including Martin Stryikovskii and George Koniskii, the archbishop of medieval Bielorussia, considered the semi-nomadic tribes of Polovtsi-Qipchaq and Pechenegs as ethnic Slavs, related to Muscovite Russians, an opinion that was shared by Lyzlov.[517]

Vernadsky has pointed out that most of the Mongols of the Golden Horde were descendants of the four thousand troops assigned to Juchi by

---

510 Francis Carr, *Ivan the Terrible* (Totowa, New Jersey: Barnes and Nobles Books, 1981), 32.
511 Poluboiarinova, 'Russkie v Zolotoi Orde,' 53.
512 Halperin, *Russia and the Golden Horde*, 37.
513 *Ibid.*, 40.
514 Vernadsky, *History of Russia* III, 17.
515 Fennell, *The Crisis of Medieval Russia*, 63.
516 Nosovskii and Fomenko, *Novaia khronologiia Rusi*, 15.
517 See Lyzlov, *Skifiiskaia istoriia*, 10-13, George Konisskii, *Istoriia Russov, ili Maloi Rossii* (Moscow: Universitetskaia tipographia, 1846).

Chingiz-khan,[518] a number too small to produce a visible and lasting effect on the European population of Russia. The Mongols migrated primarily toward southern China, southern Central Asia and Middle East, while few Mongol warriors stayed with the ulus on the mid Volga River. The local Turkic population rapidly assimilated this relatively small reservoir of Mongol warriors.[519]

Following Gumilëv, Fomenko maintains that a mixed Turkic and Slavonic speaking semi-sedentary host populated medieval Russia. It echoes observations made by Western historians, who accept the hypothesis of an ethnically mixed Russia, created under successive waves of nomadic invaders. The only difference is that the Russian element, for Fomenko, was predominant.

IV.6 Asiatic Russia: Myth and Reality

According to Halperin, 'it is one of the ironies of the Mongol period that Russian culture flourished under infidel domination'.[520] The relationship between Russians and the steppe was certainly diverse and pragmatic. Culturally Muscovite rulers had always resembled Eastern, rather than Western rulers until the time of Peter the Great. The eastern aspect in Russian culture and polity was very strong partly due to the proximity of the Byzantine Empire. Although geographically Constantinople lay further west than Moscow, or Kiev, nevertheless it was firmly considered as the East by Western historians who drew lines of division along religious, rather than geographical boundaries.

Western travellers who visited Muscovite Russia pointed to the Asiatic luxuries, wealth, military organization that surrounded the Muscovite ruler and the upper class.[521] Russia had always traded in eastern goods. Halperin explains the eastern customs of the Russian princes partly in terms of their background, since by the late twelfth century some Russian princes were

---

518 Vernadsky, *History of Russia* III, 208-09.
519 *Ibid.*
520 Halperin, *Tatar Yoke*, 25.
521 Marshall Poe, *A People Born to Slavery, Russia in early modern European ethnography, 1476-1748* (Cornell University Press, 2000); Basil Dmytryshin, *Medieval Russia, a source book 900-1700* (Holt, Rinehart and Winston, 1973); *Moskovskoe Gosudarstvo XV-XVII vekov po skazaniiam sovremennikov-inostrantsev* (Moscow: Kraft +, 2000).

seven-eighths Turkic by blood and could hardly have been unaware of their heritage.[522]

This steppe influence was evident long before the Mongols. Archaeological digs have revealed a society that accumulated eastern style glass beads, shells and boxwood combs.[523] Historians have emphasized the 'Asiatic cast' of Kievan politics, arguing that competing princes employed rival contingents of Turkic nomads, where steppe ornaments, dress, and modes of fashion prevailed.[524] In general, Muscovy was described as 'a rude and barbarous' kingdom by the European visitors of the sixteenth and seventeenth centuries, and it was omitted from the published register of Christian powers maintained by Vatican.[525] European dress and behaviour codes were rejected and despised.

In the case of the Normanist debate, anti-Normanists argued that if the Vikings left virtually no traces in terms of language or political institutions, then it stands to reason that Vikings were not important to the history of Kiev Rus. In the case of the Mongols, there is ample evidence of a substantial 'eastern' legacy. The alternative writers find no difficulty here because what Western Europeans called an Asiatic mode of dress or Eastern despotism was simply Russia in its pure form. Nomads, like the Tatars, cross-fertilised Russia and its customs but emerged far more changed than the Russians themselves. Underlying the flexibility of the alternative logic is that Russia is a vast sponge soaking up peoples, ideas and institutions but somehow clinging to a core identity. This identity is expressed in its greatness and the respect that other peoples felt obliged to show Russia. Therefore, alternative writers are happy to admit the connectedness of the peoples of Eurasia and then advance arguments as to why it was clearly the Russians who were first among equals.

Halperin acknowledges that looking at names is suggestive but that we cannot infer ethnicity from names with any assurance.[526] Concerning the Tatar-Mongol issue, proper names of peoples and persons are often a matter of dispute. The names of Polovtsy listed by the Kievan Prince Monomakh

---

522 Halperin, *Russia and the Golden Horde*, 18.
523 *Ibid.*, 81.
524 D. Rasovskii, 'O roli Chernykh Klobukov v istorii drevnei Rusi,' *Seminarum Kondakovianum* I (1927): 93-109; also D. Rasovskii, 'Polovtsy,' *Seminarium Kondakovianum* 7:11 (Prague: 1935-40); K. Kudriashov, *Polovetskaia step'* (Moscow 1948).
525 Hosking, *Russia and the Russians*, 5.
526 Halperin, *Russia and the Golden Horde*, 37.

contain what are for, the modern Russian ear, apparently Russian and Turkic names.[527] According to Keenan, out of almost three thousand names in the Muscovite court rolls of the sixteenth century there are no persons with Kievan names such as Igor, Sviatoslav, or Mstislav and relatively few Vladimirs and Glebs; a Muscovite courtier of Ivan's time was more likely to be called Bulgak, or Temir.[528] Ostrowski, on the other hand, warns against the narrow use of the names of sixteenth century courtiers as reflecting a break with Kiev and its past.[529]

Nicknames were given to children but the same could apply to adults as well.[530] Alternative writers claim that in medieval Russia the inhabitants went by more than one legitimate name. In the *Razriadnaia Kniga* where the names of all Muscovite military commanders were stored for 150 years, the Russian voevoda Pronski is also identified under a Turkic name as 'Turuntai'. The celebrated Tamerlane was also known as Timur, Temir-Aksak, Temir-Kutlu, and Timurleng. The Russian military commander of the pre-Petrine era, Nogavitsa-Pestry, was known as Zasekin-Sosun, Solntsev and Cherny-Sovka. The Turkic armies knew the Russian field marshal Suvorov as Topal-pasha.[531]

Fomenko cites the work of Karnovich, where the author argued that Tatar-sounding nicknames such as Bulat, Akhmat, Murat were used by ethnic Russians so often that they eventually acquired the status of proper names.[532] Morozov claimed that in the medieval archival Russian law acts there were not a single Greek name, only one Slavonic name (Iaroslav), but many names of animals, numbers and rivers (Volga, Danube, Pechora). Among the remaining names, 'Tatar' etymology predominates in names such as Tatarinko, Saltyr', Saltanko, Sunbul, Shaban, Tenbiak, Tursulok, Sumgur.[533]

Fomenko's favourite example is the story of the Tatar noble Solokhmir Miroslavov, who was invited to Riazan in 1371 by its prince, Oleg. Solokhmir adopted Christianity, became Ivan Miroslavovich, married the daughter of the

---

527 Halperin, *Russia and the Golden Horde*, 16.
528 Edward Keenan, 'On Certain Mythical Beliefs and Russian Behaviors,' in *The Legacy of History in Russia and the New States of Eurasia*, ed. S. Frederick Starr (New York: Armonk, M.E. Sharpe, 1994): 23.
529 Ostrowski, *Muscovy and the Mongols*, 170.
530 Halperin, *Russia and the Golden Horde*, 111.
531 Bushkov, *Rossiia I*, 105-107.
532 Nosovskii and Fomenko, *Novaia khronologiia Rusi*, 78.
533 *Ibid*.

Grand Prince and thus seeded the famous boyar clan of Verderevskikh in Russia. His son was named Grigorii, his grandsons Mikhail, nicknamed Abumailo, Ivan, nicknamed Kanchei, and Konstantin nicknamed Divnoi. As Fomenko describes it, this was a typical of medieval Russia. Thus, a pagan Tatar bearing a Slavic name Solokhmir was baptised with Christian names. His children and grandchildren bore Christian names, but Tatar-sounding nicknames.[534]

Bogdan Khitrovo, an arms master under Tsar Alexis had the Christian name Iov that became known only after his death. The medieval Russian law acts contain personal names that seem to be numbers or animals such as Pervyi, Vtoroi, Volk, Zaiats; or, they bear Tatar etymology - such as Mansur, Bulat, Uriupa, Urzan, Suleisha, Temir, Murza, Ermak, Kudiar, Khazarin, Bakhmet, Tork, Mamai.[535]

It is often noted that there were well-connected Mongol families in Russian history, including at least one hundred and thirty Mongol families that became Christian and served the Russian state.[536] Among them were the Turgenevs, Glinskiis, Naryshkins and Yusupovs, and even the kingmaker and tsar, Boris Godunov.[537] Fomenko is happy to describe Godunov as a Tatar, a Tsar/Khan descended from Juchi's ulus.[538] Natalia Naryshkin, Peter the Great's mother, is described as descended from Mongols. Yet contemporary drawings suggest the face of a Slavic woman.[539] Fomenko argues that the misunderstanding originated due to the fact that ethnic Russians were very often described as Tatars in Western Europe.[540] Some Europeans made a distinction between the 'white' or European Tatars and 'yellow' or Asiatic Tatars,[541] a point that according to Fomenko reinforces his reconstruction about a Slavic/Turkic union where the two halves were sometimes recognisable and sometimes obscured.

---

[534] Nosovskii and Fomenko, *Novaia khronologiia Rusi*, 80.
[535] Ibid., 16.
[536] Carr, *Ivan the Terrible*, 38.
[537] Ibid.
[538] Nosovskii and Fomenko, *Bibleiskaia Rus'* I, 1232-23.
[539] Robert Massie, *Peter the Great* (London: Victor Gollancz, Ltd, 1981), 211.
[540] Nosovskii and Fomenko, *Novaia khronologiia Rusi*, 12-16.
[541] Poluboiarinova, 'Russkie v zolotoi orde,' 55.

IV.7 Foreign Conquest or Civil War

Fomenko would not be surprised to learn that Halperin has described the Mongol conquest of Russia as 'unique',[542] and that, for Hosking, the Mongol capacity for war was decidedly unusual for a nomadic society.[543] It is not enough, however, for pseudo-history to cast doubt upon the conventional wisdom and call for new histories. This is what standard revisionist works attempt to do. Pseudo-history invariably offers a replacement for the allegedly discredited conventional wisdom. Fomenko has applied Ockham's razor and cut Mongols, the unnecessary part of the existing accounts of medieval Russia out of the equation altogether. In their place, emerges the Russian Horde.

The term 'horde' is another matter of great interest to pseudo-history. Mongols sources seem to have used the word 'horde' before Russian and European sources. Mongol sources speak of 'great ordas' in the valleys of the Onon and Kerulen rivers as having been inherited by the Mongol ruling hierarchy.[544] There was also Orda, Batu-Khan's brother, whose domain comprised the eastern territories of the Golden Horde[545]

This does not prevent Fomenko and his allies from speculating that the word itself. Which, they claim, later found its way to the West in the form of the German *Ordnung* and English 'order'.[546] For Fomenko it is most probably an old Slavic word referring not to the Mongols specifically, but to any large army.[547] Thus, Herberstein, one of the most observant travellers to Russia, wrote about various 'hordes' on its territory. The Russian chroniclers used terms such as 'the Swedish horde', or 'the German horde' in relation to any large foreign army.[548]

For Fomenko, it is no wonder that military historians are amazed at Mongol military achievements. Most likely, they never occurred and certainly could not have occurred the way that they were described in the chronicles. Pseudo-history devotes considerable space to the complex military history of this period.

---

542 Halperin, *Russia and the Golden Horde*, 8.
543 Hosking, *Russia and the Russians*, 49.
544 Peter Jackson, 'From Ulus to Khanate,' *The Mongol Empire and its Legacy*, 26.
545 *Ibid.*, 16.
546 Bushkov, *Rossiia I*, 130; Guts, *Mnogovariantnaia Istoriia Rosii*, 192.
547 Nosovskii and Fomenko, *Novaia khronologiia Rusi*, 11.
548 Bushkov, *Rossiia I*, 129.

The famous introduction of the Russians to the Mongols took place in 1223 on the river Kalka, which, it is thought, was somewhere on the Don steppe near the Sea of Azov.[549] Russian historical documents, including the Novgorod Chronicle, suggest that the invaders and their religion, language, indeed virtually everything about them was foreign to the Russian side.[550] The Novgorod Chronicle labels the Tatar side as *poganye*, a term that later became a pejorative name for Muslims. Regardless of linguistic intricacies, alternative writers insist that the events at Kalka demonstrate an obvious discrepancy between the conventional account and reality.

According to the chronicles, the military clash between the Russians and the Tatars was preceded by a visit made by Tatar ambassadors to the Russian princes.[551] The presence of ambassadors also raises the issue of the seemingly absent interpreters, unless the allegedly unfamiliar warriors knew each other's language. The Tatar ambassador's task was to warn the Russian leadership not to become involved in an unfolding war between the Tatars and the Polovtsy. The Polovtsy had already asked the Russians for military assistance.

The fact that the Tatars began with diplomacy might suggest that they had significant knowledge about Russia and assumed that they would receive a fair hearing. On this occasion, the Tatars were mistaken. The Russian princes from the southwest principalities of Kiev, Galicia and Chernigov, who saw the Polovtsy as an important ally, killed the Tatar ambassadors,[552] and immediately called for mobilization of their respective military units. Altogether there were three senior southern princedoms with their junior princes, who mobilized for war.[553] As for north-eastern Russia, the prince of Suzdal, Iuri Vsevolodovich, not only did not send troops, but also failed to arrive to the war summit held by the southern princes,[554] clearly dissociating himself from the war against the Mongols. In the ensuing battle, it seems that the Polovtsy fled from the battlefield, while the besieged south Russians desperately fought the enemy for three days. There was no help from the Russian princes in the north, a fact that suggests to Fomenko that these princes were in alliance with the Tatars.

---

549 Nosovskii and Fomenko, *Novaia khronologiia Rusi*, 123.
550 *Rasskazy Russkikh Letopisei XII-XIV vekov* (Moscow: Detskaia literatura, 1973), 69.
551 Ibid., 71.
552 Fennell, *The Crisis of Medieval Russia*, 65.
553 *Rasskazy Russkikh Letopisei XII-XIV vekov*, 71.
554 Ibid.

The enraged Tatars murdered the south Russian survivors after their surrender. The manner in which the surrender happened demonstrated a peculiar relationship between the hostile sides: the Russian princes agreed to surrender only after a Tatar ambassador swore on his Christian Orthodox cross promising not to kill the besieged Russian troops.[555] Surely, the besieged Russian soldiers would not have trusted the promise of a foreigner, prisoner, or pagan after the cowardly murder of the Tatar ambassadors, Fomenko has claimed. The Russians would have never agreed to surrender to an unknown, allegedly heathen people, especially after three days of fierce battle and the murder of ambassadors.[556]

The chronicle identified the person who swore on the cross as a Russian named Plaskinia. He played a treacherous role in the battle, joining the Tatars, then offering to rescue the defeated Russians and then handing over the defeated Russian princes to the Mongols.[557] Soviet writers viewed Plaskinia, the leader of the mysterious *brodniki* as an archetypal traitor to the Russian cause.[558] For Fomenko, the term traitor makes no sense. Plaskinia was not a traitor but one of many Russians engaged on both sides of the battle at the Kalka. Pseudo-history suggests that not only Plaskinia, but also his *brodniki* were Christian Slavs who populated the steppe between the Volga and the Don.

This conclusion finds some support in Gumilëv who regarded *brodniki* as Orthodox Christian forefathers of the Cossacks and descendants of Orthodox Khazars.[559] The nineteenth-century conventional historian, Nikolai Polevoi (1796-1846), also considered that *brodniki* and Cossacks were one and the same.[560] The chronicler is insistent that there were many *brodniki* and that it was they who personally handed the Russian princes to the Tatars, and then persuaded the Tatar khans to execute the hostages.[561]

For Fomenko and his allies this was obviously a civil war. Tatar/Turks, like the Varangians before them, fought on both sides as hired warriors serving the Russian and Turkic speaking tsar khans. Historians note that in the thirteenth century, all communication seems to have ceased between northern and southern Russia as the respective chroniclers minded their own

---

555 *Rasskazy Russkikh Letopisei XII-XIV vekov*, 71.
556 Bushkov, *Rossiia I*, 120-121.
557 *Rasskazy Russkikh Letopisei XII-XIV vekov*, 74.
558 See Gumilëv, *Drevniaia Rus' i velikaia step,'* 501.
559 *Ibid.*, 500.
560 Nikolai Polevoi, *Istoriia Russkogo naroda* I (Moscow: Veche, 1997), 630.
561 *Rasskazy Russkikh Letopisei XII-XIV vekov*, 75.

business and kept silent about more distant neighbours. It is usually thought that this was simply a result of dislocation brought about by Tatar incursions. Not so, according to the alternative writers who see in thirteenth century Russia a kind of forerunner to the American (1861-65) and Russian (1918-20) Civil Wars when the contest became one of north versus south. In Russia's case, Tatars tended to favour the northern princedoms but could be found on all sides of this debilitating conflict.

IV.8 The Myth of Mongol Terror

The opponents of the conventional story of the Tatar-Mongol invasion claim that nomads would have had great difficulty in establishing an empire of any sort. Pseudo-historians argue that sedentary peoples were more likely to accumulate sufficient wealth to wage prolonged wars of conquest than a nomadic people, whose scarce resources would limit military capacity, as much they would provide a motive for aggression.[562]

For pseudo-historians, their conventional rivals do not have a clue about why barbarian invasions get under way in the first place. Khazanov has written the best-known recent account of nomads and their periodic irruptions into the histories of sedentary societies. His explanation entailed cycles of power and weakness that depended upon such factors as climate or the relative strength of sedentary neighbours. A number of writers cite changing weather patterns as important to the sudden irruptions of nomad societies. Toynbee emphasized desertification[563] while Gumilëv argued that increased precipitation prompted nomadic restlessness.[564] Some historians suggest that the nomads were naturally aggressive and were perhaps motivated by periodic overpopulation. Marxists fought to find evidence of class struggle between nomadic and sedentary societies or an economic contest driven by nomads who attack sedentary populations in order to replenish their livestock. Nomads may have resented the rejection of their goods for trade or have been inspired by a charismatic leader.

Gumilëv was sufficiently disappointed in existing explanations that he

---

562 See, for example, Poliakovskii, *Tatary-Mongoly, Evraziia, Mnogovariatnost'* (Moscow: 2002), 122.
563 Arnold Toynbee, *A Study of History* (Oxford: Oxford University Press, 1934; 1935; 1945), 3, 393, 395, 399-402, 431.
564 Gumilëv, *Drevniaia Rus' i velikaia step,'* 514-15.

offered the suggestion that it was the *passionarnost* or vibrant exuberance of a new conquering people.[565] But this seems one of the weaker arguments put forward by Gumilëv, not endorsed by either professional or amateur historians of Russia. For Fomenko, the fact that conventional historians drastically disagree about why nomadic invasions take place is not evidence of a healthy scholarly debate but the futility of present explanations.

The conventional account claims that in the short space of a few years Ghengiz Khan created the strongest army in the world out of dispersed nomadic clans. The distance from Mongolia to European Russia is approximately 5000 kilometres. If the distance covered by the Mongols in their European expedition is added, the Mongols travelled 6500 kilometres. They defeated and secured not just cities but entire civilisations along the way. Meanwhile, the Mongols tried to assail Japan twice and fought in Korea, Vietnam, Indonesia and Burma.

Impossible, claim the pseudo-historians. Russian and American pioneers took approximately thirty to forty years in order to reach the eastern and western shores of the Pacific respectively. Russian and American forces enjoyed the backing of government finances and military institutions with sophisticated weapons in their possession. They fought against enemies that were technologically inferior and geographically dispersed. In both cases the expansion was accompanied by the gradual erection of forts and towns used as protection against the indigenous population.[566]

Russian explorers in their march eastwards, travelling across the Urals in the sixteenth century, found no staging posts of the once glorious Mongolian Empire. There were only technologically primitive tribes living in small numbers in the wilderness. The Mongols left behind no military, or civilian, infrastructure to remind future generations of their deeds. Not surprisingly, alternative writers ignore the reverse of this argument that if, as they claim, there were Russians who acted as powerful political and military figures at the court of the khans in Beijing, how did they cover these mighty distances and do so without leaving a trace of their presence? Nor does pseudo-history wish to take into account the fact that the Mongols, unlike colonial settlers, were often able to move along established trade routes on their way to Russia, replenishing their strength as they moved westwards.

The Tatar-Mongols displayed outstanding military capabilities fighting in

---

565   Gumilëv, *Konets i vnov' nachalo* (Moscow: 1992).
566   Bushkov, *Rossiia I*, 170-73.

unexpected conditions and ambushing, encircling and fully eradicating Russian military expeditions at Kalka and returned, a decade later, to defeat Grand Prince Iurii of Vladimir on the river Sit'. The second battle took place on unknown land for the Mongols, in wintertime.[567]

How did the nomadic Mongols live and travel, let alone fight, in the Russian winter? Although the first military encounter between the Russians and Mongols occurred in summer at the river Kalka, the subsequent invasions took place in winter. It is true that the Kazan Tatars were known to conduct their raids against Muscovy throughout all seasons, including winter. But Kazan is much closer to Moscow than Mongolia and its Turkic inhabitants were intimately familiar with the geography of what would later be known as European Russia.[568] The more distant Crimean Tatars preferred to attack Moscow in early spring, summer, or late autumn, but not winter.

Vernadsky explained the fact that 'general winter' did not work for the Russians because of the Mongols' toughness. They, like their Russian opponent, were used to extreme weather conditions in Mongolia, wore well-insulated fur coats and knew how to use the frozen rivers as roads.[569] Halperin points out that Kiev Rus' was too close to the steppe for its own good, so that even the most remote Russian cities were within easy striking distance of mobile punitive expeditions, while armies of horses could feed on the vast pastures in the land bridge between the Volga and Don, and on the Caspian steppe.[570]

Fomenko is unimpressed with this type of argument, claiming that even the sturdy and compact Mongolian horse, born in an area of continental climate similar to Russia, would not have been able to find sufficient sustenance in an unknown land covered with thick snow cover, deeper than that usually encountered in Mongolia. It seems likely that the invaders also had to supplement their cavalry with non-Mongolian horse breeds, which are likely to have been even more sensitive to subzero temperatures.[571]

Many historians, dealing with the reasons why Russia was defeated so easily and swiftly, claimed that the Russians were not inferior to the Mongols

---

567 Bushkov, *Rossiia I*, 116.
568 William Pokhlebkin, *Tatary i Rus', 360 let otnoshenii 1238-1598* (Moscow: Mezhdunarodnye otnosheniia, 2001), 179-180; Pokhlebkin notes that on the frequent occasions when the winters were harsh, entire military expeditions launched by the Kazan Tatars against Moscow froze to death.
569 Vernadsky, *A History of Russia* III, 50.
570 Halperin, *Russia and the Golden Horde*, 31.
571 Vernadsky, *A History of Russia* III, 112; Bushkov, *Rossiia I*, 115.

from a military point of view but were simply inferior in numbers. Contemporaries and early histories described a huge invasion force. It has been claimed that there may have been one million Mongols on the march, about as many as could have been found in Mongolia itself.[572] Chronicles estimated that Mongol forces comprised 300-400 thousand horsemen for the invasion of Russia alone,[573] while Lyzlov estimated the force of Batu Khan as 600,000 strong.[574] According to Carpini, Batu's army consisted of six hundred thousand men, one hundred and fifty thousand of whom were Tatars, alongside four hundred and fifty thousand foreigners, Christians and infidels.[575] Rashid Ad Din thought that the Mongols had a surprisingly exact 129,000 troops at the time of Genghis Khan's death in 1227. Among nineteenth-century Western historians Rambaud, for example, repeats the legend that Batu Khan probably had with him five hundred thousand warriors.[576] Other sources tell us how in 1256, reinforcements increased the Mongol presence in the Middle East to 150,000 troops, accompanied by half a million women and children and fifteen million animals. Yet we are told that simultaneously an even larger Mongol contingent attacked southern China.[577] Fennell endorses the figure arrived at by the Soviet historian Kargalov who estimated the invasion force at 120,000-140,000 troops when Batu Khan's scouts first approached Russia in 1237.[578] Soloviev too considered that when the Mongols struck in the thirteenth century, the Russian princes had a potential army of one hundred thousand fighters. Fennell has pointed out that this figure assumes that the fifteen or so large Russian cities provided between three thousand and five thousand soldiers. The Polovtsy, then in alliance with the Kievan princes, may have numbered around forty thousand soldiers.[579] This, however, was only a potential figure if all the princedoms united. This was not the case at any of the battles in which Russian princes

---

572 Udo Barkmann, 'Decline of the Mongol Empire,' *The Mongol Empire and its Legacy*, ed. by Morgan and Amitai-Preiss, 275.
573 *Drevnerusskaia Literatura*, 170.
574 Lyzlov, *Skifiiskaia Istoriia*, 22.
575 In Carpini's testimony, he mentions that he had his letters of introduction translated into 'Ruthenian' or Russian as well as 'Saracen'. See Dawson, *Mission to Asia*, 56.
576 Rambaud, *History of Russia*, 156.
577 John Masson Smith Jr., 'Nomads on Ponies vs. Slavs on Horses,' *The Journal of the American Oriental Society* 118:1 (January-March 1998): 54; 'Mongol Nomadism and Middle Eastern Geography,' *The Mongol Empire and its Legacy*, ed. by Morgan and Amitai-Preiss, 39-40.
578 Fennell, *The Crisis of Medieval Russia*, 84.
579 *Ibid.*, 85.

fought the Mongols.

Alternative writers doubt that such extraordinary movements of people happened at all. In the case of Russia they like to point out that the invading Mongols travelled with three horses, thus hundreds of thousands of warriors required an implausibly large herd of horses. Eyewitnesses confirm that each Mongol brought three or four horses with him. The Western historian, Denis Sinor used data collected from nineteenth century Chinese Turkestan to argue that 100,000 horses meant 1,500 camel loads of fodder per day, a figure Sinor regarded as staggeringly large.[580] The invasions of 1237-38 and 1239-1240 took place in winter, allowing the Mongols to use the rivers as roads but making it extremely difficult for them to secure food and pasture. According to Rubruck and Carpini, Mongols relied upon mare's milk and were understandably reluctant to slaughter the animals needed for war and transportation. The conditions were obviously difficult even for the best of soldiers. Moreover, a frequent complaint from the alternative writers is that Russia's hardy steppe mares do not give milk in winter.

Morozov could not imagine how nomads could obtain sufficient mass to defeat much larger sedentary empires. The essence of a nomadic existence amounted to living in separate patriarchal groups scattered over a vast territory requiring plentiful food for herds of cows, sheep and horses. If the tribes united, they would have had to join their livestock together. The greatly increased number of cattle would force the entire nomadic population to relocate constantly in search of new pastures. A prolonged and successful conquest conducted by a combination of nomadic tribes feeding off their livestock was impossible, claimed Morozov.[581] For Morozov, it was clear that the Mongol invasion must have come from the West, that is, the Hungarian plain.

It is often thought that the Mongols sent raiding parties into the forests of Russia, using the steppe as a base. On the other hand, the Russian chronicles reported how at the siege of Kiev 'the grinding of the wooden chariots, the bellowing of the buffaloes, the cries of the camels, the neighing of the horses, the howling of the Tatars rendered it impossible to hear your own voice in the town.'[582] The depiction of this huge supply train creates an

---

580 See Greg S. Rogers, 'An examination of historians' explanations for the Mongol withdrawal from East Central Europe,' *East European Quarterly* 30:1 (Spring 1996): 3.
581 Bushkov, *Rossiia I*, 123.
582 *Rasskazy Russkikh Letopisei XII-XIV vekov*, 84.

impression that apart from warriors, many civilian Mongols travelled with the army.

If the Mongols did take their families, as the above-mentioned passages might suggest, then how are we to accept the thesis that the Mongols' lightning speed was integral to their victory? Some sources suggest that because of the huge size of the migration, Mongol troops were capable of covering only three to four miles a day.[583] Thus, there is no, or little academic agreement the field of Russian history on the numbers of the invading Mongol armies, on their policies of drafting alien nations in their military units, or on whether the Mongols travelled alone or together with their families, cattle and belongings.

The major striking forces in the Tatar army comprised mobile groups of cavalry archers. Each warrior carried two types of bow. The first was light and designed to be fired rapidly from horseback, while its heavier companion was for dismounted action. Vernadsky has claimed that the heavy bow's average draw weight of 166 pounds was more powerful than the British longbow.[584] Each rider used a sharpening stone for keeping the arrows in good shape. Gumilëv described how the Mongols allegedly made use of poisoned arrows.[585] But how, Fomenko asks, and where could the Mongols have replenished their supplies of ammunition, especially arrows, under the stress of continuous warfare and severe cold in a hostile foreign country?

Not all conventional historians have taken the view that Mongols rode all the way from Mongolia. Tatishchev thought that the invaders came from the steppe beyond the Volga and the Caucasus, a view shared by his contemporary, Lyzlov. Morozov thought that the invasion came from the West, from Hungary. Pseudo-historians often prefer homelands closer to Russia. Fomenko believes that the so-called Mongol invasion got under way within Russia itself.

---

583   John Masson Smith Jr, 'Mongol Nomadism and Middle Eastern geography,' *The Mongol Empire and its Legacy*, 40.
584   Vernadsky, *History of Russia* III, 112, 125.
585   Gumilëv, *Searches for an Imaginary Kingdom*, 294-296.

IV.9 Steppe Warriors

The Russian chronicles described medieval Russia as an era of war and violence. Sometimes the violence was inflicted upon Russia by waves of barbarian nomads but just as often seemed to revolve around internal feuds and civil wars. Gumilëv noted that relations between the forest farmers and the steppe nomads appear peaceful compared to the brutal civil wars that the Russian princes constantly waged with one another. From the fall of the Khazar Kaganate in 965 to the founding of the Golden Horde in 1241, there was no unity among the people of the steppe, and therefore no danger to the Russian land from the east.[586] Kiev Rus was however a place of great internal strife. For Fomenko, this tradition of civil war continued into the period known erroneously to history as the Mongol era.

As conventional history describes the medieval period, there was constant war and successive waves of barbarian invasions. The chronicles claimed that the Rus destroyed the Khazar kingdom in consecutive blows that began with Sviatoslav's raid on Itel in 965. Meanwhile, the Polovtsy, who were also known as Kipchak in Turkic and Cuman in Latin, swept the Pechenegs from the steppe. The same fate awaited the Kipchak when the Mongols arrived. The image of waves of invaders – Pechenegs overrun by Polovtsy who are then overrun by Mongols strikes the alternative writers as a key fantasy of conventional history. Pritsak for example has estimated the Pecheneg population at 800,000 in 1048 yet the conventional literature gives the reader the impression that they were washed away or exterminated by a wave of Kipchak/Polovtsy who in turn fell victim to the Mongols.[587]

Gumilëv argued that the Pechenegs and Polovtsy resembled each other so closely that they were in fact part of a single entity that together made up the semi-nomadic populations of the Caucasian, Caspian and Black Sea territories. According to Kluichevski, the Pechenegi lived along the lower Dnepr in eight clans, each of which was further divided into five tribes. Such a substantial host could not have vanished overnight giving way to newcomers, the Polovtsy. These peoples were not purely nomadic or insignificant in number. The Polovtsy were a settled agricultural people; the Primary Chronicle provides details about the villages and towns of Polovtsy that were

---

586 Gumilëv, *Searches for an Imaginary Kingdom*, 292.
587 Pritsak, 'The Pechenegs: A case of Social and Economic Transformation,' *Studies in Medieval Eurasian history* 10 (Variorum reprints, 1981), 25.

burned by the Tatars.[588] For some Soviet writers, Polovtsy were in a sense the 'Russian' steppe peoples while the Mongols, more Asian in appearance, were clearly foreign invaders. Because of their continuous presence and familiarity with the geography, language and culture of the Rus, the Polovtsy became in effect a part of the social fabric of Kiev Rus'.[589] For Fomenko, this seems to have been true of all the steppe peoples.

In any case, having described the demise of the Pechenegs, the chronicles continued to invoke their name hundreds of years after they should have left the historical stage. The Pechenegs made their final appearance in the Battle of Kulikovo Field in 1380, when the Tatar champion, reportedly a Pecheneg, challenged the army of Moscow to single combat. The chronicler, describing the aftermath of this duel when both combatants suffered mortal wounds, referred to the 'infidel Pecheneg, the evil Tatar, lying like a mountain' on the battlefield.[590] For alternative historians, this is clear evidence that if the Pechenegs were an ethnic group, then Tatar refers to something else, such as the cavalryman status of this Pecheneg soldier.[591]

The Soviet writers, Iakubovskii and Parkhomenko, were happy to accept that trade and not war was the dominant mode of intercourse in relations between Russians and Polovtsy.[592] Recent accounts published in the West tend to agree, arguing that trade was the dominant form of interaction on the steppe frontier, that there were special trading posts and markets along the border with the steppe where Russian merchants exchanged goods with their nomadic counterparts.[593]

There is evidence too not just of continuity among nomadic tribes but also of familiarity between nomads and Kievan Rus. The Primary Chronicle records under the year 968 the story of a Kievan escapee who deceived his Pecheneg captors by waving a bridle as he ran through the camp, calling for his missing horse. Halperin points out that the story shows that readers of the

---

588 Ostrowski, *Muscovy and the Mongols*, 63, 91.
589 Halperin, *Russia and the Golden Horde*, 16.
590 See *Kulikovskaia bitva v literature i iskusstve* (Moscow: Nauka, 1980), 46-48.
591 Guts, *Mnogovariantnaia istoriia Rossii*, 203.
592 Alexander Iakubovskii, 'Feodal'noe obshchestvo Srednei Azii i ee torgovlia s vostochnoi evropoi v X-XV', in *Materialy po istorii Uzbekskoi, Tadzhikskoi i Turkmenskoi SSR*, III and I (Leningrad: 1932), 24; Vasilii Parkhomenko, 'Sledy polovetskogo etnosa v letopisiakh,' *Problemy istochnikovedeniia* III (Moscow-Leningrad: 1940): 39. For further evidence of this view, see Irina Konovalova, 'Stepnoi biznes,' *Rodina* 3:4 (1997): 36-37.
593 T. Noonan, 'Rus', 'Pechenegs and Polovtsi: Economic Interaction along the Steppe Frontier in the pre-Mongol Era,' *Russian History* 19 (1992, 1-4): 313-314.

Primary Chronicle were evidently unsurprised to learn that a Kievan knew the Pecheneg language and that his appearance was not especially strange to the enemy.[594] Other stories in the Primary Chronicle seem to confirm that Russians, Pechenegi, Polovtsy, and Tatars did not need interpreters to communicate with one another.[595] Several Russian princes were executed at Sarai but often it was Russians and not Mongols who carried out these murderous deeds. Thus, we are told that Prince Mikhail of Chernigov was tried in Sarai, and then was stabbed to death by ex-Christians.[596]

For the alternative writers, the Mongol domination of a mixed host in Asia was no more than a reflection of Russia as it was at the time of Kiev Rus' with the Slavs interacting freely with neighbouring khanates. This was a military society where membership depended not upon blood or citizenship but loyalty to the horde, host, or state. Its modern remnant is the Cossack model of a warrior society geared permanently to war and accepting warriors from any region or ethnicity so long as they were prepared to serve the ataman, the elected chief of the host.

Fomenko transformed Gumilёv's concept of two halves of the one whole, a settled agricultural Russia living alongside a semi-nomadic deeply multiethnic steppe stretching from the Volga across the Don to the Dnepr into a single Slav-Turk ethnos. For Bushkov, instead of a foreign conquest, the Tatar invasion was part of a Russian civil war, a final episode in a feudal squabble among the Russian princes, while the 'fairy tales' about evil Tatars were introduced into Russian history during later periods of Romanov rule. For Fomenko, this invasion was the process of internal unification as Slav-Turkic Russia transformed itself during the period between the disintegration of the Kievan state and the rise of Moscow.

---

[594] Halperin, *Russia and the Golden Horde*, 13.
[595] Ellen Hurwitz, *Prince Andrey Bogoliubsky: the man and the myth* (Firenze: Licosa editrice, 1980), 44.
[596] *Rasskazy Russkikh Letopisei XII-XIV vekov*, 85-89.

V   Russia's Medieval Near Abroad

V.1   From Confrontation to Cooperation

If the chronicles are accurate, the battlefield history of the Mongol presence in Russia seems to have consisted of four battles, all of which took place on various rivers. The battle at the river Kalka was the first encounter in 1223; the battle of the river Sit' came in 1238; there is a gap of one hundred and fifty years until 1380 when the battle at Kulikovo Field near the river Don took place, and in 1480 the 'Tatar-Mongol yoke' ended with a final confrontation at the river Ugra.

We have already examined Kalka in the previous chapter where Fomenko rejected the idea that Russian princes fought unknown barbarian invaders from the East. For Fomenko, the battle at Kalka was a 'phantom event', a duplicate of the battle between troops of the Hungarian King Bela, whose son briefly occupied the throne of Galicia, and the Tatars.[597] It was duplicated due to the errors, mistakes and deliberate forgery on behalf of later day historians and then used as evidence of a great battle fought against Tatar invaders. According to Fomenko, one of the features linking chronicle accounts of the battle at the river Kalka and the battle involving King Bela was the presence of *brodniki* who fought against the Russians at Kalka and who fought against King Bela. For conventional historians, the Mongols arrived, fought at Kalka and then retreated for fourteen years. Preposterous, Fomenko claims. The mysterious disappearance of the Mongols from Russia was just another strange interpolation of the chroniclers desperate to string together known facts to tell a politically motivated story.

Pseudo-history, as ever, looks for holes in the standard story and finds no difficulty in casting doubt upon the primary sources. When the Mongols returned in 1237 in full force, the stage, according to conventional accounts, was now set for the major battle against the invaders, about which we know almost nothing. The Mongols stormed Riazan in December 1237 and Vladimir in February 1238. On 4 March 1238, on the banks of the Sit' river, Grand Prince Iurii of Vladimir suffered a crushing defeat at the hands of Batu Khan's

---

597   Nosovskii and Fomenko, *Novaia khronologiia Rusi*, 122-123.

horde. In this defeat, only two Russian princes seem to have lost their lives.[598] Iurii, we learn from his own Lavrent'evskyi chronicle, was decapitated at some point during the fighting. Novgorod's chronicle seems less than certain on the matter as it noted that 'God knows how he died, for there are many different opinions about him'. Fennell, a leading expert on the sources for the Mongol invasion, concluded that it may have been that the details were too horrific to relate. On the other hand, the severed head suggested to Fennell treachery on the part of Yuri's own men.[599] It is equally plausible that the chronicler lacked knowledge or was simply evasive about a more complicated relationship between conquerors and conquered.[600] It is little wonder that the pseudo-historians claim that there is no certain knowledge about this battle, who fought there or why.

Halperin noted that the behaviour of the fallen Yuri's troops after the Sit' battle seemed inappropriate. According to the chronicler, the Russians enjoyed their post-battle festivities despite or perhaps because of the decapitation of their Grand Prince.[601] Fomenko find absurd the fact that the chronicler devoted several pages to the description of Yuri's funeral at the very time that the alleged foreign army was at the city's gates. For Fomenko, the chain of events is illogical. The Russians were supposed to have been defeated, but they were able to bury the body of their Grand Prince according to their customs in a city that was overrun by Tatars. Meanwhile, the city continued to be ruled by Yuri's brother, Iaroslav.[602]

According to Fomenko, the events of 1223-1238 should be read not as a foreign invasion but as a civil war and most likely it is a case of Russians hiring mercenaries on occasions to do their dirty work. The chronicles mention the Tatars very often, but few Tatar warlords as if Russian princes continued to hold sway.[603] According to the Vladimir chronicle, 1238 was a year of peace, suggesting that, at the very least, this source was pleased with the outcome of the fighting, whatever it was, in that year. If for Halperin this is the ideology of silence, then for Fomenko, it is a reflection of the way it really was. As a good pseudo-historian, Fomenko could not resist making at least one implausible suggestion at this point, and claims that the deceased Iurii

---

598   Fennell, *Crisis of Medieval Russia*, 80.
599   *Ibid.*
600   *Ibid.*, 81.
601   Halperin, *Tatar Yoke*, 38.
602   Nosovskii and Fomenko, *Novaia khronologiia Rusi,* 124.
603   Fennell, *Crisis of Medieval Russia*, 81.

was confused with the deceased Genghis Khan, as the mythology of both leaders subsequently became entwined with that other celebrated horsed warrior, St. George the dragon-slayer.

The route of the Mongol invasion of 1237-1238 seems peculiar to conventional and alternative writers alike. The Mongols seem to have chosen their targets with great care[604] but did not see fit to attack Novgorod, allegedly the richest of the Russian cities.[605] Conventional accounts suggest that the thawing swamps put off the rampaging Mongols. Russian chronicles recorded that a miracle saved Novgorod, and there were reports of an image of a holy cross in the sky. Alternative writer dismiss both explanations as equally fanciful. An early thaw in the beginning of March is a rare sight in northern Russia even today. In April 1242 Alexander Nevsky defeated the Livonian knights on the ice of the Peipus Lake. It is true that the knights' heavy cavalry broke through the ice and drowned. But the lightly armoured Russian cavalry, that is, the Mongol style of horseman, crossed the ice easily.

Bushkov offers the explanation that Novgorod, and Smolensk as well, were spared because they comprised the German trading outposts of the region and were of value to Batu Khan.[606] While the Russian Horde did not object to the slaughter of Germans, at this moment Batu Khan needed to conserve resources to consolidate his hold over newly-conquered lands to the east and south of Novgorod. In any case, Novgorod became a regular tribute payer and so a reliable servant of the empire.

Fennell acknowledges that the Mongols' decision not to storm Novgorod in 1238 is puzzling.[607] Instead of concentrating upon Novgorod, the richest trading city of the Russian north, the Mongol force moved south and devoted seven long weeks to the storming of the obscure town of Kozelsk, paying a high price of four thousand lives according to the chronicles. Why would an army of mobile horsemen whose major goal was profit and plunder storm the walls of a minor city like Kozelsk? Why did the Mongols prefer to take Kozelsk in the old fashioned way, storming the walls, instead of using their famous catapults, which they did indeed use with great success against neighbouring Chernigov? Western historians often emphasize the Mongol capacity to eradicate strong and technically more developed states. As Halperin described it, the Mongol military machine was capable of conquering

---

604 Fennell, *Crisis of Medieval Russia*, 77.
605 Martin, *Medieval Russia*, 184.
606 Bushkov, *Rossiia I*, 156.
607 Fennell, *Crisis of Medieval Russia*, 81.

China, Turkestan, and Persia, all areas with immense population and gargantuan walled cities.[608] Why did this experience fail them at Kozelsk? Upon the fall of Kozelsk the exasperated Mongols took their revenge and all the survivors including the children were executed. Yet Kozelsk, this 'wicked town' according to the Mongols, was neither wealthy nor important strategically or to the invaders.

If indeed Kozelsk were strategically unimportant, it would not be the first time in military history that a huge battle has been fought over a place of disputed military value. For the alternative writers, few mistakes are made in history and almost nothing happens by accident. Thus alternative writers alert the reader to what they consider to be Kozelsk's importance in the dynastical struggles that fuelled the civil war of which the Mongols conquests were just one part. The prince of Chernigov, one of the possible contenders for the title of Grand Prince, ruled Kozelsk.[609]

According to the reconstruction favoured by Fomenko, the unification of the Russian lands spread out from the Volga region, the source of the 'northern' faction of the Russian Horde. Chernigov was a loser in this process as the political centre of Russia shifted to the northeast. Kozelsk was taken as part of the north's war against the south amid fierce fighting and bloodshed. The chronicles tell us that the twelve-year old prince of Chernigov was drowned in blood.[610] It put up stout resistance precisely because its insignificance and relative poverty compared to Vladimir, Suzdal, and Novgorod in the northeast or Kiev, Chernigov and Pereyaslavl in the southwest meant that it had been spared sackings in the past.[611] Thus, another mystery is solved in the minds of the alternative writers.

For pseudo-historians, the greatest prize awaits the solution of perhaps the biggest question. The Tatar-Mongol invasion of Europe is, to say the least, an enigma. As Rogers has noted, 'the Mongol military campaign into East Central Europe in 1241 is noteworthy for two important and intriguing features: the ferocity of the attacks, which appeared to signal doom for the rest of Europe; and the sudden and unexpected withdrawal of Mongol forces in the following year, thereby 'saving' Europe'.[612] The Mongols seemed to

---

608 Halperin, *Russia and the Golden Horde*, 48.
609 Bushkov, *Rossiia I*, 155.
610 Martin Dimnik, *The Dynasty of Chernigov 1146-1246* (Cambridge: Cambridge University Press, 2003), 346.
611 See Bushkov, *Rossiia I*, 158.
612 Greg S. Rogers, 'An examination of historians' explanations for the Mongol

have Catholic Europe at its mercy, having already subdued the Islamic and Orthodox worlds. The Mongols desired the goal but then abandoned it with the prize seemingly at their mercy.

Halperin points out that the puzzling withdrawal of the Mongols has attracted various explanations.[613] It is possible, as most accounts state, that the demise of the Great Khan in Karakorum caused the Mongols to return home to settle the succession. This is the most popular explanation proffered by Vernadsky and others but suffers from the fact that it is not clear that Batu Khan knew about the death of Ogedei. In any case, when Batu Khan withdrew from Europe he chose to remain at Sarai and did not return for the *kuriltai* at Karakorum. Pleading ill health, Batu Khan sent to Mongolia the late Yurii's brother, Iaroslav, father of Alexander Nevsky.[614] Yet, simultaneously, an important military campaign was unfolding in the Middle East where the troops were left behind at Aleppo and the khan returned to attend the *kuriltai*.

Sinor thought that the retreat was a logistical matter and that the Hungarian plain would not have been able to feed such a large number of horses.[615] It is possible too that the Mongols lacked sufficient siege weapons. On the other hand, the Mongols were often reckless in their initial invasions, attacking tropical south-east Asia, insular Japan and frozen Russia with equal impetuosity as if assuming their élan would overcome most obstacles.[616] If the Mongols guessed that the northern route was insufficient for their needs, it seems strange that the Tatars instead decided to move to the south of Europe, the mountainous Balkans, where there was relatively little to plunder, and where the pastures, except those of Hungary, were even poorer than those of northern Russia.

Soviet writers of the Stalin era emphasised the exhaustion of the Mongols thanks in part to heroic Russian resistance in the rear. As many writers have pointed out, Russians, Poles and Hungarians each believe that, even though their armies were defeated, they did their neighbours a favour by slowing the Mongols down. More plausibly, it has been argued that the invasion was a first terror stage after which the Mongols intended to return to collect taxes in the style of their invasion of Russia. More recently, Rogers

---

withdrawal from East Central Europe,' *East European Quarterly* 30:1 (Spring 1996), 3.
613 Halperin, *Russia and the Golden Horde*, 47
614 Vernadsky, *A History of Russia* III, 61.
615 Denis Sinor, 'Horse and Pasture in Inner Asian History,' *Oriens Extremis*, 19 (1972): 171-83.
616 Halperin, *Russia and the Golden Horde*, 47-48.

has suggested that the pursuit of the Kipchak/Cuman who took refuge with the Hungarian King Bela led the Mongols first to the Adriatic but then back to Bulgaria where the fleeing Kipchak/Cuman eventually came to rest.[617] Clearly, conventional historians have not agreed and are unlikely ever to agree about Mongol motives and behaviour.

After the Tatar-Mongols defeated Henry the Second, the Duke of Silesia, at Liegnitz in 1241, the Mongols moved in a southerly direction fighting their way through Hungary and south across the northern tip of the Balkans in order to reach the Mediterranean. A strange choice of route, Fomenko thinks. It is puzzling as to why the Tatars did not continue their movement along the north European plain, into the heart of Europe where rich merchant German cities along the Rhine River were waiting to be sacked. Germany's cities were located in the European lowlands, easy to reach on horseback. It was the route favoured by barbarians since Roman times. Western sources describe the sacking of Polish cities and churches. These acts were at odds with the Mongols' often-praised religious tolerance toward the Russians and Orthodox Christianity. The alternative writers insist that the Tatar-Mongols committed systematic atrocities against the Catholic West, the most important clue as to the nature of the Mongol incursion.[618]

For conventional historians, there is nothing strange in the Mongols laying waste the towns and monasteries of Eastern Europe. The Mongols in Russia initially destroyed Church buildings and killed orthodox clergy if it were suspected that they were part of the resistance to the invaders. Only later, the Mongols developed a more sophisticated method of control that partly relied upon allowing relative freedom to the Orthodox Church. In the case of Poland, there was no prolonged occupation and therefore no way of knowing how the Mongols would have ruled Poland once the initial requirement of terror tactics has passed. Most likely, the Mongols would have chosen similar tactics to those employed in Russia, dividing and ruling by making concessions to a docile Church. This is much too simple for pseudo-history. For alternative writers, the savagery of this attack Poland reflected the typical Russian hatred of the Pope.

Fomenko points out that Western European sources contain conflicting evidence of who invaded Europe. For example, the Hungarian king Bela

---

617 Greg S. Rogers, 'An examination of historians' explanations for the Mongol withdrawal from East Central Europe,' *East European Quarterly* 30:1 (Spring 1996): 3.
618 Bushkov, *Rossiia I*, 163-64.

wrote the Pope, describing the ethnic composition of the Tatar army. According to Bela, the kingdom of Hungary was devastated by the Mongols whose forces were accompanied by 'eastern tribes of Russians, *brodniki*, and other infidels from the South'. Why, asks Fomenko, did the Hungarian king mention Russians first if they were not among the leaders of the so-called Mongol invasion of Europe?[619] For Fomenko and his like-minded 'alternative' historians, the most treasured illustration is found in the tomb of Henry the Second who led the Polish resistance and heroically fell at the Battle of Liegnitz. This drawing shows Henry stomping the body of a fallen foe representing a vile Mongol. This Mongol, however, has European features, including a long beard, and seems, to Fomenko, to be dressed in Cossack attire.[620]

Of course, Liegnitz is, like almost everything else in the Mongol invasion of Europe, a matter of conjecture. Conventional historians are not sure who fought for Henry; his army seems to have comprised, Poles, Czechs, Teutonic knights and a host of other peoples. For readers of Western literature about the Mongols, it would come as no surprise to learn that an array of ethnic groups fought in the army of the Mongol invaders. This fact is more surprising to students of history who grew up during Soviet times where the war against the Mongols was represented in clear-cut national terms as a battle for survival where every patriotic Russian fought against the Tatars.

Although the invading Mongols burned and sacked European cities occasionally, little attempt was made to levy taxes on the population of any of the conquered territories, or create the administrative units that would be needed to impose law and order. The Mongols seemed to want to move quickly towards the Mediterranean. When they reached the shores of the Adriatic, they promptly turned their cavalry back towards the Eurasian heartland. Here, Fomenko and Bushkov invite their readers to consider the geopolitics of the era, a subject closely studied by conventional historians, in its allegedly true light.

Bushkov is more inventive than Fomenko in this instance and has argued that the Tatars and their Russian allies launched their European raid in order to help Holy Roman Emperor Frederick the Second in his struggle against the Pope.[621] This was typical of Russian hostility towards the Catholic

---
619   Nosovskii and Fomenko, *Novaia khronologiia Rusi*, 69.
620   See Bushkov, *Rossiia I*, 166.
621   *Ibid.*, 169.

faith, present, it seems, in the medieval and modern periods. In this instance, the Russian Horde was in alliance with the Holy Roman Empire. It is true that the Holy Roman Emperor was himself Catholic and German but the Pope was an even more 'natural' enemy for the Orthodox-Islamic Russian Horde. The surprising end to the Mongol invasion reflected a falling out between the invaders and their temporary ally, Frederick the Second.

It is well known that mid-thirteenth century Europe was a time of hostility between the Roman Pope and Holy Roman Emperor.[622] The two powers of central Europe fought over territory in Italy so much that while most of Europe panicked as Mongols sacked Hungary, Slovakia, the Czech lands and Croatia, Frederick focused his attention on gaining territory at the expense of the Pope and even engaged in secret correspondence with Batu Khan. Frederick offered to become Master of the Khan's Falcons in what Gumilëv and conventional historians regard as an attempt at friendly or obsequious banter on the part of Frederick.[623] Fomenko takes this offer very seriously as evidence of the awe and respect that Western leaders of this time had for the tsar/khans and their Russian Horde. When Pope Innocent the Fourth fled to Lyon in 1243 he anathematised both Frederick the Second and Batu Khan, further evidence, for Fomenko, that 1241 was an Orthodox/Islamic or Slav/Turk war against Catholicism.

To explain the defeat at the hands of the Mongols, Soviet historians have described a pincer attack where Russia, while parrying the Mongols in the east, was attacked by the encroaching Swedes, Germans and Lithuanians in the west. In 1202, the Orders of the Brothers of the Sword launched a crusade against Livonia. The neighbouring Teutonic Knights converted the Prussian tribes in Poland to Catholicism in 1230 and then moved east to take Pskov in 1240. At the same time, the enemy of the knights, Lithuania under Mindovg, expanded westwards to take Polotsk.[624] After 1237, the Teutonic and Livonian knights joined forces for operations that would take them into Russian territory. This was the same year that the Mongols returned to devastate northern Russia.

In 1242, the knights invaded the territories of northern Russia directly threatening Novgorod. Conventional accounts suggest that the knights launched an opportunistic attack, seeking to plunder the Russian land, now

---

622 Verndasky, *History of Russia* III, 53.
623 Gumilëv, *Drevniaia Rus i velikaia step,'* 512.
624 Martin, *Medieval Russia*, 162-64.

unable to mount an organized resistance because of the devastation caused by Mongol raids.[625] Although the Mongols did not storm Novgorod, the city paid tribute, and Novgorod's *druzhina* alone could not match the heavy cavalry of these Catholic crusaders. Only thanks to the outstanding military skill of the Mongol-supported Russian warlord Alexander Nevsky did the Russian troops achieve a famous victory on the battlefield.

According to the alternative writers under consideration here, this was no opportunistic attack but a crusade and the knights struck the Russians as if the latter were Saracens like those fighting the Catholics in Palestine.[626] The Pope had blessed the knights and so the war between the knights and Novgorod, divided by ethnos and religion, was cruel and pitiless.[627] Invading Russia, the knights imposed tribute upon the vassals of the Russians, constructed fortresses in north-western Russia, captured towns, pillaged the merchants of Novgorod, enslaved peasants and stole crops and cattle.[628] Fomenko and his allies claim that, if viewed as a response to the Mongol (read Russian Horde's) invasion of Europe, then the crusade of the Livonian knights in 1242 makes more sense. It was a failed counterattack where the Catholic knights attempted to repay the Russian Horde invaders in kind.

V.2 Four Battles

After the battles at the rivers Kalka and Sit', the next substantial military encounter between Russians and Tatars seems not to have occurred until one hundred fifty years later, in 1380. We learn from the chronicles of occasional rebellions but no large-scale resistance to the invader.[629] For Fomenko, this is what you would expect given that civil wars eventually lose momentum and require time before the warring sides were ready to resume conflict. It is not what you would expect if Russia really were under foreign occupation for centuries.

The second half of the fourteenth century was a troubled time for the Golden Horde. Three waves of Black Death carried off about one quarter of

---

625 Rambaud, *History of Russia*, 160-161.
626 Bushkov, *Rossiia I*, 170.
627 Martin, *Medieval Russia*, 162-164.
628 Rambaud, *History of Russia*, 160-161.
629 Fennell, *The Crisis of Medieval Russia*, 97.

the population.[630] The crucial trading route of the Great Silk Road came under pressure because Ottoman Turks gained control of the entrance to the Black Sea and in the east the Mongol dynasty known as the Yuans were overthrown in 1368 by the Chinese Ming dynasty. The Horde itself was split among rival contenders for power, including Mamai, the non-Chingisid who dominated the western lands, and Tokhtamysh, the Chingisid who dominated the eastern lands and who seized control of Sarai in 1378.

For centuries, Russian and Soviet historians hailed Kulikovo Field as a crushing victory of Russia over the Tatar occupiers, the first blow in a national war of liberation that would eventually leave Russia in possession of the lands of the Golden Horde.[631] Victory at Kulikovo Field represented the entry of the previously obscure principality of Moscow onto the Eurasian stage. Its valiant prince was thereafter known as Dmitrii Donskoi in honour of this famous battle that took place near the Don River.

Imperial and Soviet historians hailed Dmitrii Donskoi as a national hero who refused to pay tribute to the rapacious Tatars, rallied support from fellow Russians and defeated the Tatars. This is still a popular image in Russia. Western historians have always been more inclined to view Dmitrii Donskoi as a surrogate in a battle between Tatars for control of the Golden Horde.[632] Precocious though Moscow was, it was still a relatively junior partner in the politics of the Golden Horde. Only much later did Kulikovo Field become a symbol of Russian resistance and Moscow's destiny to become the centre of a great empire. For Fomenko, this account of a battle between Russians and Tatars was yet another modern invention of Romanov propagandists. Fomenko's scepticism about Kulikovo Field, but not his solution, is shared by Western historians.

Western accounts do not portray fourteenth-century Moscow in the heroic light shone by Soviet historians. Dmitrii Donskoi was a secondary figure in a war between Tatar khans, according to Western accounts. Mamai, under threat from his great rival, Tokhtamysh, needed tribute urgently to prepare for war against his fellow Tatar. At Kulikovo Field, Dmitrii Donskoi showed that he was capable of resisting Mamai's demand for tribute and in effect assisted Tokhtamysh who decisively crushed Mamai the next year. Kulikovo Field was a Pyrrhic victory for Moscow because, having lost so

---

630 Martin, *Medieval Russia*, 202-03.
631 Halperin, *Russia and the Golden Horde*, 32.
632 Martin, *Medieval Russia*, 215.

many soldiers, it was harried by Lithuanian forces as it returned to Moscow and was unable to resist Tokhtamysh who, in 1382, occupied Moscow and took Dimitri Donskoi's son as hostage. Dmitrii Donskoi fled in the face of Tokhtamysh's advance, showing little heroism in leaving Moscow to a terrible fate. The Golden Horde lived on and Moscow's rulers, including Dmitrii Donskoi, continued to pay tribute. It was Tokhtamysh who confirmed Dmitrii Donskoi as Grand Prince of Vladimir.[633] At best, Dmitrii Donskoi won a temporary victory at Kulikovo Field. Moscow's prince died as he was born, a vassal of the Tatars.

For alternative historians, the Western account is only moderately more acceptable than the Romanov version. Romanovs describe a war of Russians against Tatars and Western historians believe it was a war of Tatars against Tatars. Pseudo-history insists that this was a war of Russians against Russians. Fomenko proposes that Tokhtamysh and Dmitrii Donskoi must have been one and the same individual. Kulikovo Field took place not near the Don but in Moscow itself and became confused in latter-day accounts with a mythical occupation of Moscow by Tokhtamysh in 1382. It is worth examining Fomenko's reconstruction of Kulikovo Field because it is a good example of the scientist's cavalier approach to puzzling aspects of Russian history.

It bears repeating that the sources for Kulikovo Field are not of the quantity or quality that conventional historians would prefer. The main source for the fighting at Kulikovo Field is the popular epic *Zadonschina* although the dating and authorship of this work are in dispute. Even less reliable sources include *Skazanie o Poboishche na Donu* and *Povest' o Kulikovskoi bitve* but their provenance is even more suspect. *Zadonshchina* has reached us in six different versions, and the oldest of 1470 is only a partial copy.[634] Soviet historians tended to accept that a citizen of Riazan named Sofonii wrote *Zadonshchina* soon after the battle of Kulikovo Field took place. For Soviet writers, the fact that a citizen of Riazan took pride in the achievements of Moscow, a rival princedom, was evidence that all of Russia hated the Tatars and were now prepared to work together for their expulsion. A more likely explanation is that the accounts we have of Kulikovo were written much later to justify Moscow's pretensions to leadership of the Russian princedoms.

---

633 See Robert O. Crummey, *The Formation of Muscovy, 1304-1613* (London: Longman, 1987), 56-59.
634 *Khrestomatiia po drevnei Russkoi literature*, 172.

Ostrowski suggests that the sources for Kulikovo Field must be dated no earlier than the 1440s,[635] eighty years after the battle. Zimin dated *Zadonshchina* to the 1520s.[636] There are insertions in *Zadonshchina* from another Russian medieval source, *Slovo polku Igoreve*.[637] Both works are a matter of great pride for Russian historians, the latter because it appeals for Russian unity, and the former because it is a glorification of a great victory in battle.[638] As for historical substance, most historians would concede that there is little that is agreed.

Fomenko acknowledges that *Zadonshchina* is the earliest source that has reached us, since *Skazanie* has facts taken from it. At the same time, Fomenko argues that *Zadonshchina* is flawed because it is not an eyewitness account and shows the influence of later generations of historians who corrected the medieval chronicler.[639] For his analysis, Fomenko relies mostly upon *Skazanie*. Fomenko's logic seems to be that if all sources are in dispute, the historian is entitled to choose the one he prefers and imagine the rest.

Conventional historians believe that the Battle of Kulikovo Field occurred near the river Don three hundred kilometres south of Moscow, in September 1380. According to Fomenko, meticulous archaeological excavation conducted since 1982 has produced convincing evidence only of a handful of arrowheads and parts of a warrior's belt. In any case, the size of the alleged battlefield is too small for a battle of such epic proportions.[640] *Zadonshchina* suggested that Russian losses alone reached 250,000 dead,[641] and although such a figure seems preposterous even to Fomenko, he claims that it is likely that the battle claimed many thousands of lives.

Fomenko has reproduced his own photograph of chain mail, allegedly discovered at Kulikovo. It is an obvious forgery, Fomenko claims, because the chain mail seems surprisingly unblemished after enduring more than six hundred years in the damp earth. In 1380, Moscow comprised no more than scattered villages and monasteries.[642] For Fomenko, the Battle of Kulikovo Field was not a struggle between Russians and Tatars but a border dispute

---

635 Ostrowski, *Muscovy and the Mongols*, 158.
636 *Ibid.*, 160.
637 *Rasskazy Russkikh Letopisei XII-XIV vekov*, 212.
638 *Ibid.*
639 Nosovskii and Fomenko, *Novaia khronologiia Rusi*, 134.
640 *Ibid.*, 132.
641 *Khrestomatiia po drevnei Russkoi literature*, 179.
642 Nosovskii and Fomenko, *Kakoi seichas vek?*, 369-372.

between Moscow and Lithuania over the towns of Moscow, Kolomna, Vladimir and Murom.[643] Tatars were of course involved in the fighting, closely connected as they were to all political and military aspects of the Russian Horde. Lithuania courted Mamai, considered a tsar or khan by some Russian sources and chronicles,[644] but identified by other sources as emir Mamai, to carry out war against Moscow.[645] Thus, while historians consider that Moscow was a cipher of Tokhtamysh in the war against Mamai, pseudo-history turns Mamai into a cipher of Lithuania in the war against Moscow. Moscow, therefore, is the true focus of this battle. Elsewhere, Fomenko attempts to show that Lithuania was never Lithuanian but was in fact western Russia, an ally of the south in the civil war against the north.

Fomenko used the chronicle's text to trace the route of Dmitrii Donskoi and his armies.[646] Fomenko claims that Dmitrii Donskoi never left Moscow and its surrounding region and that the alleged Don location offered by the chroniclers is replete with geographic names found today in the Moscow region. Although we are told that the Battle of Kulikovo Field took place at the river Don, Fomenko points out that in earliest times the Don was known as the Tanais. It is not clear when this river found its modern name, the Don. Fomenko is struck by the repetitions of sound patterns in the names of many rivers flowing through lands in which Slavs lived. According to Fomenko, names like Don, Dniestr, Dnepr and even Danube are obviously similar and their common consonants mostly likely simply denoted a river or deep stream in early Slavic. Thus, any river could have been called Don in the Russian chronicles. Most likely, Fomenko claims, the Don in question at the Battle of Kulikovo Field was in fact the River Moskva.

For Fomenko, *Zadonshchina* indirectly confirms this intuition when it describes how 'Mikula's wife Maria cried at the shores of the Moskva-river, addressing it and weeping 'Don, Don, quick river.'[647] The 'red hill' from where Mamai observed the battle was, of course, Moscow, already expressing its preference for the colours of the Kremlin. Fomenko has promoted his expertise in forensic science when he claims to have discovered the remains of the fallen warriors from this battle, not at Kulikovo Field where archaeological digs have proved disappointing, but in the Simonov monastery

---

643 Nosovskii and Fomenko, *Novaia khronologiia Rusi*, 131.
644 Nosovskii and Fomenko, *Bibleiskaia Rus'* II, 545.
645 Halperin, *Russia and the Golden Horde*, 54.
646 Nosovskii and Fomenko, *Novaia khronologiia Rusi*, 132-154.
647 *Khrestomatiia po drevnei Russkoi literature*, 177.

in Moscow where thousands of skulls, allegedly from the fourteenth century have been unearthed.

Conventional historians confirm that Kulikovo Field pitted 'a mixed Tatar and Rus army led by Grand Prince Dmitrii Ivanovich Donskoi against a mixed Rus and Tatar army led by the emir of the Qipchaq khanate Mamai'.[648] Fomenko cites chronicle writers to show that Dmitrii Donskoi's retinue consisted of ethnic Russians but that his cavalry comprised 'baptised Tatars, Lithuanians and Russians who fought in the Tatar manner, alongside Siberian and Volga Tatars'. Mamai's force comprised Crimean Tatars, Poles, and even Genoan mercenaries, but only a few Volga Tatars; such was the unpopularity of Mamai among his own people.[649] It was a typical medieval battle for Fomenko where Russians and Tatars fought not against one another but on both sides.

How, asks Fomenko could the Golden Horde's military leader have been defeated by his own Horde? According to *Skazanie*, the defeated Mamai learned that the Zalesskaia Orda' bested him, that is, the Horde from beyond the forest.[650] 'Beyond the forest' often is taken to mean the Caspian steppe but for Fomenko it could equally apply to lands north of the Volga, that is Vladimir-Suzdal.[651] For Fomenko, it is far more likely that this Horde from 'beyond the forest' was a reference to another faction of the Russian Horde.

It is true that historians have puzzled over Mamai's remarkable ability to fight major battles in consecutive years. Ostrowski points out that it seems unlikely that Mamai raised another army at short notice to face Tokhtamysh the year after his overwhelming defeat at Kulikovo.[652] Fomenko's reconstruction offers an explanation to that inconsistency, arguing that in fact there was only one battle, the battle of Kulikovo Field where Dmitrii Donskoi/Tokhtamysh decisively defeated Mamai. This would explain too the otherwise puzzling account in the chronicles of the Lithuanians failing to make a serious effort to finish off the exhausted Russians as they retreated to Moscow. Dmitrii Donskoi did not need to retreat to Moscow as he never left it.

Russian historians would these days agree that the conventional account of Kulikovo Field is problematic but understandably are less than impressed with Fomenko's reconstruction. Kuchkin points out that Fomenko's

---

648 Ostrowski, *Muscovy and the Mongols*, 155.
649 Nosovskii and Fomenko, *Novaia khronologiia Rusi*, 142.
650 'Zadonshchina', *Drevnerusskaia literatura*, 170.
651 *Khrestomatiia po drevnei Russkoi literature*, 179.
652 Ostrowski, *Muscovy and the Mongols*, 155.

new revelation is the fact that no material objects have been discovered at Kulikovo Field.[653] He notes that even at Prokhorovka, where the biggest tank battle in the history of the world took place, there are few material objects left behind. In fact the great battles of the thirteenth, fourteenth and fifteenth centuries mostly do not boast artefacts. Fomenko does not mention that since the eighteenth century Kulikovo field has in fact yielded many human bones, ancient armour and weapons, although evidently not enough to satisfy the mathematician's intuition as to what should have been found there.

The only source that Fomenko has used is the fragmentary 'Skazanie o Mamaevom Poboishche', written more than a century after the described events. Its validity has been criticized many times by different historians, and the results of these evaluations are well known, but ignored by Fomenko. The Cathedral of all Saints is known to have existed in 1365, fifteen years before the battle took place, and therefore could not have been built to commemorate the victory, as Fomenko claims. Dmitrii Donskoi is unlikely to have been Tokhtamysh because Dmitrii Donskoi died in 1389, while it is well known that Tamerlane defeated Tokhtamysh in 1395. The Kolomna of the chronicles could not be the village of Kolomenskoe in Moscow, as Fomenko insists, because the Kolomna archbishop met the Russian army at the city's gates. It is unlikely that Moscow, then little more than a village would have had city gates and an Episcopal see. The piles of skulls[654] discovered by Fomenko at the Simonov monastery could belong to the victims of the 1382 Tatar raid, 1654 plague victims, or the victims of 1812. For Kuchkin, Fomenko's past is an 'Alice in Wonderland world' that lacks Lewis Carroll's sense of humour.

Petrov is just as critical, writing that he responded to Fomenko because, unbelievably, 'everyone is listening to the mathematician turned historian, while the real historians are being ignored'.[655] For Petrov, the only thing that Fomenko has got right is that for once he at least agrees that the date of 1380 for Kulikovo Field is accurate. Petrov points out that it is irrelevant that Kulikovo Field is too small for the numbers mentioned in the chronicles – 200,000 or more on either side. Knowing the passions of the medieval

---

653 Vladimir A. Kuchkin, 'Novootkrytaia bitva Tokhtamysha Ivanovicha Donskogo c Mamaem na Mosckovskikh Kulizhkakh,' *Otechestvennaia istoriia* 4 (2000): 9-16.
654 Nosovskii and Fomenko, *Novaia khronologiia Rusi*, 152.
655 A. Petrov, 'Progulka po frontovoi Moskve s Mamaem, Tokhtamyshem i Fomenko,' *Istoriia i antiistoriia: Kritika 'novoi khronologii' akademika Fomenko* (Moscow: Iazyki russkoi kultury, 2000): 131-91.

authors combined with their poor mathematical proficiency most historians consider the size of the fighting armies as more likely to have been 50,000-60,000 men on each side, but no one apart from Fomenko has drawn the conclusion that the battle did not take place. Fomenko seems to have relied upon only one source for these events when he might have used several chronicles, each of which seem more reliable than *Skazanie*. The identification of Dmitrii Donskoi and Tokhtamysh is ridiculous: The chronicler responsible for *Rogozhskii letopisets* tells us how 'in summer 6891 Dmitrii sent his elder son Vasilii to Tokhtamysh and the Horde'. Did Dmitrii Donskoi send his own son to himself, according to Fomenko? The same source described the victory of Tokhtamysh over Mamai. The victorious khan sent messages to all corners of the Russian land, including Dmitrii Donskoi. For Petrov, it is unlikely that Tokhtamysh would have forgotten that he himself was Dmitrii.

There is strong evidence that the Battle of Kulikovo Field really did take place near the Don River. There are treaties between Moscow and Riazan, at that time part of the alliance against Moscow, that stipulate that Riazan destroyed the bridges across the Don so that the Muscovites could not cross back, that the people of Riazan took some of the wounded soldiers as slaves, and stole war booty from the Muscovite army. The famous red hill from where Mamai was watching the battle was not mentioned in any of the early sources. This is a poetic expression introduced in the eighteenth or nineteenth century and, according to Petrov, the careless Fomenko stumbled across these new sources and declared them genuine. On the one hand, according to Fomenko, the word 'Don' meant simply river, and in this meaning it has entered the names of many rivers – Danube, Dnepr, Dniestr. Elsewhere, Fomenko contends, that it is possible that 'don' stands for *dno* in Russian, meaning bottom. Thus, Dmitrii was the ancestor of the '*nizovykh*' or lower Cossacks of the nineteenth century, (niz=dno in Russian), as opposed to '*verkhovykh*' (upper) Cossacks, mostly Tatars, who lived on the mid Volga. The presence of two conflicting theories does not embarrass the mathematician in this case even if it probably disconcerts his more careful readers.

There is no doubt that Kulikovo Field was told in the version we have it today to glorify Moscow's struggle against the Tatars. If conventional history hails the triumph of the Muscovite ruler Dmitrii Donskoi over the Tatar emir

Mamai in 1380 as 'the triumph of Europe over Asia',[656] according to Fomenko it was nothing more than a civil war involving Slavs and Turks who sometimes fought alongside one another against a common enemy and sometimes fought each other. Fomenko's account reminded conventional historians in Russia that the primary sources for Mongol military history are, to say the least, frustratingly vague or absent. It has not yet convinced any of them to change their allegiance to the new pseudo-history. For Russian readers, it is a different matter. Soviet history worked on the basis of certainty, or at least near certainty and doubt was rarely admitted to. Any fair-minded reader of medieval history would acknowledge that there is a great deal of doubt concerning most of the sources. This was a shock to Russian readers and an invitation to the writers of historical fantasy.

The Golden Horde did finally enter a phase of terminal decline in the early fifteenth century but the catalyst was the Turkic warlord Tamerlane and the beneficiary was the rising power of Lithuania and not the still subservient Moscow. According to Halperin, it was not Dmitrii Donskoi's victory, but Tamerlane's spectacular conquests that finally led to the Golden Horde's downfall by cutting the Horde from the Asian caravan groups.[657] Between 1370 and 1405, Tamerlane built one of the world's greatest empires. His army comprised Turks, peoples from Central Asia, the Caucasus and Russians. It combined nomads and sedentary peoples, Christians and Muslims. Fomenko has declared Tamerlane a Turkic Cossack on the basis of the famous reconstruction of his appearance by the archaeologist Gerasimov.[658] Gerasimov depicted Tamerlane in Eastern headdress to try to give the impression that he was from the East, but could not, it seems, conceal his Turkic, almost Russian, features from Fomenko's keen eye.

V.3 The Romanov Falsification of History

What is usually looked upon as the final military confrontation between the Russians and the Mongols took place at the River Ugra in 1480. Today this battle signifies the end of the Tatar-Mongol yoke over Russia. Because of Tamerlane's raids, the Kipchak Khanate or Golden Horde was in effect dead

---

656 Florinsky, *Russia*, 70.
657 Halperin, *Russia and the Golden Horde*, 57.
658 Nosovskii and Fomenko, *Novaia khronologiia Rusi*, 207, 230-234.

by the middle of the fifteenth century and the Volga belonged to the poorly named Great Horde whose most important leader was Ahmad, a descendant of Genghis Khan who tried to restore the Golden Horde with the aid of Lithuania and the Turkish Sultan. Ahmad had to eliminate the rising power of Moscow and force it to pay tribute if he were to achieve his goals and, to this end, led a large force into Moscow territory in 1480.

Moscow stopped paying tribute to the khans in 1452 and when, the following year, Constantinople fell to the Ottoman Turks, it could justifiably claim to be the only independent Orthodox power still standing. The reign of Ivan the Third (1462-1505) is usually looked upon as a turning point for Moscow in military terms with the conquest of Novgorod in 1477-78 and in diplomatic terms with Ivan the Third's marriage in 1472 to Zoe Palaelogos, niece of the deposed Byzantine Emperor. Ugra was, for many tsarist and Soviet historians, Ivan the Third's crowning achievement.

Ivan the Third formed an alliance in 1480 with Mengli-Ghirey, a descendant of Tokhtamysh and khan of the Crimean khanate.[659] The task of the Crimeans was to tie down Moscow's enemy to the West, Lithuania. Casimir, grand duke of Lithuania and king of Poland was stung into action by Moscow's capture of Novgorod and was anxious to prevent Moscow's westward expansion.[660] While Casimir attacked Pskov, his ally, Ahmad advanced to the Ugra where the army of Ivan the Third confronted him. Predictably, the sources seemed confused about whether there was any fighting at Ugra or not. Once the armies confronted one another, they seemed reluctant to fight. Indeed, it seems that Ivan the Third only committed himself to a military campaign after the Orthodox archbishop Vassian shamed the prince with his sermons and letters, literally forcing Ivan the Third to go to war. Even so, the fighting was sporadic and confused, the details are sketchy and what seems to have been a relatively minor military encounter became a symbol of Russian military valour for subsequent generations.

Just as in the Battle at Kulikovo Field, the Russian princes offered little support to Moscow and, as at Kulikovo, the Lithuanians failed to appear to assist their Tatar allies. Some accounts suggest that the Tatars were exhausted after a lengthy standoff, others that the Russians overwhelmed the Tatar troops with their firearms, and still others that Ahmad was afraid to commit to a decisive battle. Ahmad retreated without offering any substantial

---

659 Martin, *Medieval Russia*, 319.
660 *Ibid.*, 304.

resistance and was murdered the next year. The Great Horde never again threatened Moscow and was partitioned in 1502 between the khanates of Crimea and Astrakhan.

Fomenko claims to have solved the puzzle of why Ahmad retreated. He relies upon the account of Lyzlov writing in the seventeenth century. According to Lyzlov, Tsar Ahmad in 1480 gathered a huge army and with his princes and nobles, then moved too quickly towards Moscow foolishly leaving in his rear only the civilian part of the Great Horde. Ivan the Third met the Tatars at the river Ugra with the aim of preventing their crossing. Here Ivan the Third learned that Tsar Ahmad had left his rear unprotected and shrewdly dispatched a sizeable army to the Great Horde under the command of his generals, referred to by Lyzlov as Tsar Urodovlet and voevoda Gvozdev.

Urodovlet and Gvozdev sailed southwards along the Volga to outflank Ahmad. Upon arriving at the Great Horde, they found only women, children and elderly, some of whom they slaughtered or took captive while burning the camp. The massacre might have been worse had not one of the commanders or *murzas* who was called Oblyaz the Strong, whispered to Tsar Urodovlet: 'Oh Tsar! It is wrong to destroy this great Tsardom, because it is our ancestral home, and all of us, including you have come from here. We have done enough: let us leave before God will become angry with us.'[661]

Fomenko finds in Lyzlov's account confirmation that a part of the Russian army still considered the Volga as their ancestral home. Tsar Urodovlet was probably a Chingizid prince since they alone had the right be called tsar. Fomenko makes much of the evidence that there were Turkic tsars and a *murza* leading the Russian raiding party. A more prosaic explanation emerges in the conventional history where Ivan the Third's raiding party is described as having been under the command of Nur-daulet (obviously Lyzlov's Urodovlet), the estranged brother of Mengli-Ghirey, the Crimean khan.[662] It would be unsurprising if Nur-daulet or his retinue regarded the Great Horde as an ancestral home, or that official Russian historiography was silent about the fact of a cowardly raid upon the women and children of the Great Horde. Fomenko's detective work, as ever, seems badly flawed. No more convincing is his contention that because Ahmad died the next year at the hands of the Nogai, the Nogai Khan and Ivan the Third were almost certainly one and the same individual. Lyzlov seems to have led

---

661 Lyzlov, *Skifiiskaia istoriia*, 43.
662 Martin, *Medieval Russia*, 318.

Fomenko astray here. Lyzlov wrote that Khan Ivan killed Mamai but elsewhere the leader of the Nogai Horde is known as Khan Ibak.

Until the late fifteenth century, coins circulated by the Russian princes often had Arabic inscriptions and only after Ugra did Cyrillic inscriptions come to dominate.[663] To commemorate the Russian victory at Ugra in 1480, a famous coin was minted depicting St. George on one side and the victorious Ivan the Third on the other with his name written in Arabic.[664] Proof, according to Fomenko, of the fluidity of this tsar's identity and his attachment to the Islamic world. Fomenko cites also the evidence of Chertkov who claims the existence of coins minted in the fourteenth century depicting on one side Dmitrii Donskoi and on the other Tokhtamysh with the inscription 'Long live Sultan Tokhtamysh Khan'. For Fomenko, there is no doubt that the coin has imitated life, commemorating the two faces of the one individual.[665]

It is difficult to know exactly how a modern Russian audience reads Fomenko's military history. It may be that Fomenko's apparent command of detail is superficially impressive. More likely readers are impressed by the abundant evidence that the military history of this era was much more complicated than the patriotic but anti-Tatar history written by churchmen and Communists. Russians fighting on both sides is not a revelation to Western historians who have long emphasised this obscured part of Russia's heritage. For Russian readers, the ubiquitous evidence of Russian and Tatar collaboration, hidden or at least marginalised until the popular history of Gumilëv and now Fomenko and Bushkov, came as a surprise that makes alternative writers more credible on this issue.

Western historians uniformly look upon Moscow, as most contemporary travellers did, as a place of despotism. While Mongols and Muscovites were two very different peoples, their way of government was the same. Fomenko and his allies are in complete agreement that Moscow was the destroyer of older and more democratic traditions within Russia associated with Novgorod and Pskov. But for pseudo-historians, the despotism of Moscow was an evolution that took place within the Russian Horde. Ivan the Third neither learned from, nor threw off, nor inherited the practices or mindset of the Golden Horde. He was simply its latest manifestation, the faction that came to power at the end of the fifteenth century. For at least part of a generation of

---

663 Ostrowski, *Muscovy and the Mongols*, 166.
664 Halperin, *Russia and the Golden Horde*, 100.
665 Alexander Chertkov, *Opisaniie drevnikh russkikh monet* (Moscow: 1834), 6.

readers struggling to come to grips with the collapse of the myths peddled by Communists and the Church, alternative history seems no less fanciful than what went before.

Fomenko claims to have found all sorts of evidence of cooperation between Slavs and Turks in the military sphere, proving the existence of his Slav-Turkic Cossacks and the khan-tsars. The chief master of the Muscovite Armory Nikita Davydov adorned this helmet with golden letters, diamonds and other precious stones in 1621. The helmet has the image of the Tsar's crown on it, the Orthodox cross and an inscription in Arabic – 'make the faithful cheer'.[666] Fomenko claims that it is revealing that the helmet is adorned with a well-known verse from the Koran, and is not written in Russian. Fomenko is just as impressed by the sword of prince Andrei Staritskii, which bears an engraving in Russian stating that the sword 'belongs to prince Andrei Ivanovich, year 7021', but also boasts an Arabic insignia. The sword of prince Mstislavskii, Ivan the Terrible's *voevoda*, has an inscription in Russian certifying that the prince is the rightful owner of the blade, but there is also an Arabic engraving 'Let the defense be strong in battle'; Gregory Viatkin, one of the best arms masters of Russia of the second half of the seventeenth century made the glass armour and a helmet for Tsar Alexis Mikhailovich in 1670. The helmet bears Arabic insignia and citations from Koran, proclaiming that 'there is no God except for Allah; Mohammed is a messenger of Allah'. Moreover, the bottom rim of the helmet displays an entire passage from the Koran. Heroes of Russian history, including Minin and Pozharsky also wore Russian swords with Arabic engravings.[667] Fomenko uses the evidence of a battle helmet to prove the proficiency in language and links to the Islamic world of medieval Russians.

It is certainly true that evidence of Eastern influence in Russia was ignored or denied for centuries for political reasons. This silence has come at a price in that it now fuels the emerging pseudo-history. For Fomenko, Cossacks were the most obvious point of connection between Slavs and Turks. The term Cossack is itself usually described as a Turkic word for brigand and the original Cossack as a mixed host of Tatar renegades and runaway Slav serfs. The Central Asian writer Olzhas Suleimenov claimed to have identified many Turkic nucleuses and words among what we believe to be the traditional Russian vocabulary. He believes, for example, that the

---

666 Nosovskii and Fomenko, *Bibleiskaia Rus'* II, 128.
667 *Ibid.*, 285-287.

Russian word Cossack means the 'white swan' in Turkic (kaz-ak), corroborating the theory that the Cossack was a Turkic free man, swan being the sign of the freedom loving.[668] Albert Seaton has pointed out that from the 1400s, the term Cossack was used to describe any light horsemen, whether they were Tatars or not.[669] Fomenko would prefer Seaton's account of the Cossacks to that provided by a majority of his own countrymen. In early Russian literary works such as the *Azov Tales*, Cossacks were defenders of Christianity, the light cavalry of European knighthood in the never-ending war against the Saracen/Tatars. In Tsarist and Soviet historiography, the word Cossack was associated exclusively with Orthodox warriors. Fomenko's generic application of the term Cossack brings him closer to Western interpretations on this point.

Fomenko and his allies do not claim that any of their speculations is definitive history or convincing in itself. They invite the reader to consider the sum of the evidence that shows, at least to the satisfaction of pseudo-history, that the traditional account of a war between Russians and Mongol/Tatar invaders was a figment of the Romanov/Christian imagination. Even at the first Battle of Kalka, there was evidence of cooperation between Slavs and the alleged Mongol invaders with *brodniki* brokering the peace. Gumilëv points to the closeness of Russian leaders and their Mongol counterparts so much so that Alexander Nevsky became an adopted son of Batu Khan. The Mongols always showed great tolerance of the Orthodox Church. There are coins that have Russian portraits or inscriptions on one side and Islamic equivalents on the other. Russian, and Turkic names were often applied to the same person, no interpreters were needed suggesting identical language and linguistic expertise, Tatars served the Russian princes and Russian princes served at the head of Mongol/ Tatar armies.[670]

The Eastern customs of the Russian princes suggests to Fomenko not conquest but an alliance.[671] There was occasional war in Russia but this was civil war and not an invasion. The Russian Horde was divided into military and civilian parts.[672] Civilian leaders, the princes, ruled the civilian population

---

668 Nosovskii and Fomenko, *Novaia khronologiia Rusi*, 77.
669 Albert Seaton, *The Horsemen of the steppes* (Bath: Pitman Press, 1985), 27.
670 Vernadsky, *A History of Russia* III, 383; Halperin, *Russia and the Golden Horde*, 13, 16; Keenan, 'On Certain Mythical Beliefs and Russian Behaviors,' in *The Legacy of History in Russia and the New States of Eurasia*, ed. S. Frederick Starr (New York: Armonk, M.E. Sharpe, 1994), 23;
671 Halperin, *Russia and the Golden Horde*, 18.
672 Nosovskii and Fomenko, *Novaia khronologiia Rusi*, 65-68.

while the Tsar-Khans operated the military side. The civilian population paid a traditional tax in the form of a tithe to the military administration, including each tenth boy aged ten years who was drafted permanently into the army. Occasionally, this internal violence became a major conflict especially in the thirteenth century when the northern Russian princedoms and their allies along the Volga wrestled control of Russia from Kiev and the south-west. What should have been described as the process of reunifying the Russian Horde became, in the hands of the Romanovs and their priestly lackeys the Mongol/Tatar invasion.

As Fomenko puts it, the Romanov dynasty made skilful use of propaganda as a tool to manufacture the myth of a historic confrontation between ethnic Tatars and Russians in the medieval period, a myth that served their tactics of 'divide and rule'. Although ethnic Tatars, as well as other national minorities always lived side by side with the Russians, the division into 'victorious' and 'defeated' sides was a latter-day myth produced by Romanov historiography. According to Fomenko, churchmen and German professors developed the story of the slave origins of the Russians who were first humbled by and then schooled in the Mongol invasion.[673] This was the Romanov pedagogic technique. Russians were helpless and hopeless, defeated and crushed by Vikings and Mongols, until the Romanovs. It was a justification for the massive changes that took place under the Romanovs, and especially under Peter the Great. It served the interests of the Romanov and their Western backers but not the interests of Russia or historical truth.

---

673 Nosovskii and Fomenko, *Novaia khronologiia Rusi*, 65.

VI The Four Ivan the Terribles

The 'Time of Troubles' (1598-1613) is the third of the turning points that is the main focus of the pseudo history investigated in this book. It is a relatively obscure moment in the West but is well known to every Russian student in Soviet schools. It was a time of great weakness and change when Russia, just as it would in 1917, literally collapsed, suffered foreign invasion and remerged under the Romanov dynasty. In conventional history it was a tragic period made good by its legacy of brilliant Romanov triumphs culminating in Peter the Great.

Fomenko believes that he has identified the moment in Russian history when the West began to get the upper hand in its struggle with Russia. It was the era of Ivan the Terrible. Fomenko pursues the dual aim of pinpointing the wrong turn in Russia's history and to restoring the good reputation of Ivan the Terrible, a loyal servant of the Slav-Turk Empire. The alleged atrocities that took place in that era were not the deeds of the 'real' Ivan the Terrible but of a pretender to the Russian throne put forward by the pro-Western faction among the restless and competing nobility. The bloodbath of the boyars known to history as the *oprichnina* actually took place after the death of Ivan the Terrible.

In reality, Ivan the Terrible has not experienced a particularly bad press in Russia, except among the liberal minority who saw continuity between this tsar and Stalin. State school historians like Soloviev in the nineteenth century tended to exonerate Ivan the Terrible for his bloodthirsty deeds on the grounds that his war against the nobles was essential for the task of building a Russian state in an era when the state was vital to the survival of a people. In the Stalin era, Vipper's book and Eisenstein's film idealised this people's tsar who accumulated power only because ordinary people wanted it to be so. The real issue for Fomenko is that Ivan the Terrible's significance as a representative of the leadership of the Russian Horde has been overlooked, having fallen victim, like so much else in Russian history, to the Romanov conspiracy against history that got under way in the eighteenth century.

The period when Ivan the Terrible ruled Russia is well studied but poorly documented.[674] The Russian historian cited in all studies of Ivan the Terrible is Skrynnikov and he is often referred to in this chapter either by name or as the source of the conventional wisdom. Historians tend to agree that the second half of the sixteenth century is one of the most interesting periods of Russian history, separating old, medieval Russia and its Golden Horde heritage from the early modern period when the Romanov dynasty transformed and Westernized Russia. Fomenko sees parallels between the Time of Troubles, 1917 and 1991. In the twentieth century, Lenin and the Communists published documents from the Tsarist archives that seemed to prove the imperialistic and generally evil nature of Tsarist government. Later, in the era of Glasnost a flood of documents appeared that claimed to tell the truth about the first socialist revolution, concealed and twisted by Lenin and his propagandists. In history when there is a drastic change of power, the newcomers try to portray themselves as the progressive and rightful claimants, while the losers are usually depicted as darkly as possible. Given that the Tsarist past was declared as a totally negative experience by the Bolsheviks, it is likely, argues Fomenko, that the same, or similar processes took place at the beginning of the seventeenth century when the Romanov clan came to power after the Times of Troubles.

Ivan the Terrible reached the throne as a child in 1533. Grand Prince Ivan Vassilievich the Fourth was crowned as tsar on January 16, 1547 and in the same year married Anastasia Romanovna. By giving himself the title 'tsar', Ivan was supposed to have asserted Russia's independence from the Golden Horde and its rightful claim to be the latter's successor. Popular accounts describe Ivan the Terrible as a forceful ruler but a deranged personality who as a child threw animals off roofs and who would eventually murder his own son.[675] On the other hand, conventional accounts insist, Ivan the Terrible fought religious or territorial wars both against the West in the name of recovering the lost Orthodox lands of Ukraine and Belarus from Polish and Lithuanian Catholic oppressors, and against the East, conducting a crusade against Islamic Kazan on the Volga river in 1552-1553. Ivan the Terrible personally took part in the campaign against Kazan. Upon the

---

674 The early testaments of Ivan the Terrible (1553 and 1554) have not been preserved and the same is true of a testament written in 1582. We do have a copy of the testament of 1572 copied inexpertly in the early nineteenth century. Robert Howes, *The testaments of the Grand Princes of Moscow*, Translated and edited with commentary by Robert Craig Howes (Ithaca: Cornell University Press, 1967), 306.

675 See, for example, Andrei Yurganov 'The father of Tsarism,' *Russian Life* 40:1 (January 1997): 12.

completion of his crusade, Ivan ordered an impressive Orthodox cathedral to be erected in Red Square, to symbolize the religious significance of his victory. By 1560, the army of the Catholic Livonian order was completely routed, and the Order itself ceased to exist. Thereafter, Ivan the Terrible's military record was more mixed. From 1565, Russia was racked by civil war, the era of the *oprichnina*. The Crimean Khan sacked Moscow in 1571 and defeats at the hands of the Poles and Swedes would follow. When Ivan the Terrible died in 1584 the so-called Livonian War had only just come to an end and Russia's ambitions in the West had not been realized. After the death by poisoning of, Anastasia, Ivan the Terrible seemed to lose both humanity and his mind until he eventually found solace in a religious rebirth that culminated in his burial in the robes of a monk.

Ivan's family life was, to say the least, complicated. After a bride show of fifteen hundred eligible women, Ivan the Terrible chose Anastasia Romanovna whose father Roman Iurevich-Zakharin was head of the hitherto undistinguished clan that would be known to history as the Romanovs. Anastasia gave birth to three sons. The first, Dmitrii, drowned while still an infant. The second, Ivan Ivanovich lived from 1554 until 1581 when his father murdered him. The third son, Fedor, became tsar in 1584 upon the death of Ivan the Terrible but ruled under the influence of Boris Godunov. When Fedor died childless in 1598, the Riurikid dynasty was extinct and the Time of Troubles ensued.

Ivan fell out with almost all of his close associates during his long reign. Prince Andrei Kurbskii for example had to flee abroad in 1564 to save his life. By 1565 Ivan had brought into existence the *oprichnina*, the collective term for several areas of Russia put under his direct rule. The rest of the Muscovite state was placed under the control of Boyar Duma. The *oprichnina* was a bloody prison house famous for the torture and murder of at least four thousand victims.[676]

Predictably, Fomenko has dismissed as open to doubt and speculation, the documents that are left to us from the times of Ivan the Terrible. The most authoritative specialist in Russia on the era of Ivan the Terrible, Skrynnikov, wrote a number of works on this subject. According to Skrynnikov, the major problem that any student of that era will encounter is the lack of sources for 'the state of the Russian archives and libraries in the

---

676 Martin, *Medieval Russia*, 349.

sixteenth century was the worst in Europe'.[677] Moreover, even those documents that have reached us are clearly edited.[678] Historians have noted that the paucity of documents from the era of Ivan the Terrible is surprising given that testaments from other Muscovite princes have survived in their original form. Prince Vasilii I (1389-1425) wrote three different testaments at different periods of time, and they have survived although Vasilii lived 150 years earlier than Ivan.[679] Even the original of Ivan Kalita's will has survived although it is 250 years older than Ivan the Terrible's documents.[680] Ivan the Terrible's will has reached us only in the form of a damaged copy with no exact date on it.[681] Even when historians hope to rely upon the original, as is the case with the letter of Ivan the Terrible to Queen Elizabeth received in London in 1570, parts of this letter were scratched and damaged.[682] How could there be almost forty original decrees dated to the times of Ivan the Third, but none from Ivan the Fourth, Fomenko asks rhetorically. Destroyed as part of a plot against the reputation of Ivan the Terrible and the Tatars, is his answer. The era of Ivan the Terrible has reached us in the descriptions, documents and forgeries of the seventeenth and eighteenth centuries.[683]

Since there are few original documents available, historians analyse Ivan the Terrible's reign using the questionable sources that have survived. Skrynnikov's books on Ivan the Terrible and Boris Godunov provide the most comprehensive and exhaustive account of the events that took place in the era of Ivan the Terrible. Analyzing Skrynnikov's works Fomenko has come across glaring inconsistencies. Thus, according to Skrynnikov, in 1553 Ivan the Terrible instituted Council of Trustees to look after his young son Dmitrii since Ivan himself was very sick and his supporters feared an early death. The Tsar recovered from illness, but the Council of Trustees continued its work. As Fomenko exclaims, why would this awesome and almighty tsar need an obsolete council after he was restored to health?[684]

Ivan's subjects had to take numerous oaths of loyalty to the Tsar,

---

677 Ruslan Skrynnikov, *Ivan Groznyi* (Moscow: Nauka, 1975), 23.
678 Skrynnikov, *Ivan Groznyi*, 81.
679 Nadezhda Soboleva, *Russkie pechati* (Moscow: Nauka, 1991), 149-150; also see Soboleva, *Ocherki istorii rossiiskoi simvoliki: Ot tamgi do simvolov gosudarstvennogo suvereniteta* (Moscow: Iazyki slavianskikh kul´tur, 2006).
680 *Ibid.*, 149-150.
681 Ruslan Skrynnikov, *Tsarstvo Terrora* (St-Petersburg: Nauka, 1992), 51.
682 *Pamiatniki literatury drevnei Rusi, vtoraia polovina 16 veka*, 115, 587.
683 Nosovskii and Fomenko, *Bibleiskaia Rus'*, I, 107.
684 *Ibid.*

even though according to a regular practice it should have needed to be done only once. Moreover, a second coronation took place in 1572, repeating the procedure of 1547. Why did Ivan the Terrible need a second coronation after twenty-five years in power?[685] The explanation usually given is that Ivan the Terrible was so deranged that he needed constant reassurance as to his status. This seems to be the only example in Russian history when a monarch was crowned twice and received an oath on more than one occasion.[686]

In 1575 Ivan the Terrible decided to abdicate in favour of the former khan of the Kasimov Khanate, Semen Bekbulatovich, who became the Tsar of all Russia.[687] Bekbulatovich boasted royal blood and traced his ancestry to Genghis Khan. Conventional accounts explain this once more in terms of the erratic Tsar's behaviour, or that it was some shrewd calculated manoeuvre in order to rule the Boyar Duma more efficiently.[688] Ivan the Terrible sacked and burned Novgorod, and then allegedly moved there with his entire court and treasury.[689] Why had the Russian monarch moved from Moscow to a smouldering and devastated hotbed of his enemies?

Ivan the Terrible's behaviour and motives are so difficult to explain that generations of researchers found it easier to find answers in psychology and found echoes of his behaviour in the twentieth century in Stalin. Kovalevski's diagnosis insisted that Ivan the Terrible was a neurotic, and his paranoiac psychology combined with the complex of megalomania were the foundation for the creation of his repressive state, the *oprichnina*.[690] Shcherbatov noted that Ivan the Terrible was represented in so many different ways that he 'does not appear to be one person' while Billington considered the schizophrenia of Ivan the Terrible to so acute that he was in effect 'two people'.[691]

Fomenko tackles the puzzling events of Ivan's reign in typical fashion when he suggests that the above-mentioned events are parts of the biographies of several tsars, not one, and that Ivan the Terrible in the singular is a latter-day composite created by the propagandists of the Romanovs.[692]

---

685 Nosovskii and Fomenko, *Bibleiskaia Rus'*, I, 107.
686 *Ibid.*
687 Halperin, *Russia and the Golden Horde*, 101.
688 *Ibid.*
689 Skrynnikov, *Tsarstvo Terrora*, 498.
690 *Ibid.*, 500-501.
691 Ostrowski, *Muscovy and the Mongols*, 88-89.
692 Nosovskii and Fomenko, *Bibleiskaia Rus'*, I, 107.

Ivan the Terrible literally was several people.

According to Fomenko's reconstruction, the period from 1547 to 1584, the reign of Ivan the Terrible, breaks naturally into four consecutive parts, and correspondingly into the reigns of four different tsars. The Romanovs subsequently created the composite Ivan the Terrible in the seventeenth century in order to justify their claims and the legitimacy of Mikhail, the first Romanov to the Russian throne. Simultaneously they achieved the equally important goal or reorienting the Russian state towards the West and away from its Turkic/Tatar associations. According to Fomenko, the history of the Times of Troubles, troubles brought about by the Romanovs themselves, was in fact substantially longer, and began in the second half of the sixteenth century. The Romanovs won what was in fact a civil war and having achieved a military takeover of power, blamed the bloodshed of the terror period known as the *oprichnina* upon the invented personality of Ivan the Terrible.

In order to disguise the beneficial character of Slavonic-Turkic friendship and cooperation during the time of the Russian Horde, Romanov historians presented this part of a Russia's history as a bitter struggle for survival between Slavic and Turkic-nomadic ethnic groups. The Romanovs presented themselves as the true Russian dynasty, which had consolidated Russian rule over the lands that would become the Russian Empire. Boris Godunov, the last legitimate Slav/Turk Tsar-Khan was declared an evil impostor, a usurper, and his descendants' rights to the Russian throne were denied. As Fomenko imagines it, the justification for Mikhail Romanov as the only rightful contender for the Russian throne was one of the primary reasons behind the merging of the reigns of several Tsars into one.

The Romanovs presented the eight wives of four different tsars as the wives of a single depraved ruler.[693] According to Fomenko, this could not have been so. The strict church rules in Russia stipulated that the third marriage must be the last legal one. All other marriages were considered as illegal and children born from these marriages were illegitimate. According to Romanov history Tsar Fedor Ivanovich, the last son of Ivan the Terrible, was childless. According to Fomenko, he did have a son, Boris Fedorovich Godunov whom the Romanovs later declared a usurper of the throne.[694]

According to the hypothesis put forward by Fomenko, in 1547 Ivan the Terrible, then 16 years old, was crowned as a Tsar; he was married only

---

693 Nosovskii and Fomenko, *Bibleiskaia Rus'*, I, 107.
694 *Ibid.*, 109.

IMAGININGS OF THE RUSSIAN PAST   219

once, and his first and last wife was Anastasia Romanov.[695] Her father was Roman Zahar'in, the patriarch of the future Romanov clan.[696] Ivan the Terrible ruled until 1553 and his most outstanding accomplishment was the siege and capture of Kazan in 1552.[697] In 1553 tsar Ivan IV became seriously ill. By that time he already had a son Dmitrii, and soon a second son, Ivan, was born.[698]

Conventional historians believe that Dmitrii died soon after Ivan's illness, but there is confusion surrounding Dmitrii's death in Russian historiography. One version of his death suggests that he died in 1553 from drowning; his nanny was crossing an unstable bridge and because of her carelessness the infant heir fell into the river.[699] Fomenko has described events differently. In the early 1550s, it was Ivan the Terrible who was dying. Ivan failed to recognize people he knew and was consumed by fever to the point where his death was anticipated. On 11 March 1553 the boyars swore an oath of loyalty to little Dmitrii.[700] As Fomenko described it, Ivan's illness was nearly terminal, and although he did not die, he nevertheless abandoned his royal duties. As Skrynnikov pointed out, the premature oath of loyalty of 1553 is clear proof that there was a widespread belief that the Tsar was on the brink of death.[701]

Before his death, Ivan became increasingly pious, greatly influenced by the preaching of Sylvester, the tsar's priest. According to Skrynnikov, it was Sylvester who inspired the religious fanaticism in the Tsar. According to the testimonies of his English visitors, the Tsar no longer liked hunting and rude jokes but instead found solace in religious services. In 1552, Ivan saw his first visions.[702] This was an era of holy fools or *iurodivye*, whose strange actions included wearing chains, renouncing comforts and working miracles.[703] The most famous was Vasili*i* Blazhenny, the holy fool who, despite or perhaps because he roamed Moscow naked even in winter, was especially respected and revered. Vasilii, was, it seems, so beloved by Ivan the Terrible, that when he died in 1552, he was accorded the unusual honour

---

695   Skrynnikov, *Ivan Groznyi*, 23.
696   Skrynnikov, *Tsarstvo Terrora*, 94.
697   Nosovskii and Fomenko, *Bibleiskaia Rus'*, I, 109.
698   Skrynnikov, *Tsarstvo Terrora*, 109.
699   *Ibid.*, 117.
700   Skrynnikov, *Ivan Groznyi*, 48.
701   Skrynnikov, *Tsarstvo Terrora*, 114.
702   *Ibid.*, 125.
703   Geoffrey Hosking, *Russia and the Russians* (Cambridge, MA: Harvard University Press, 2001), 25.

of having his death registered in official papers and was buried in the Troitse-Sergiev Monastery on Red Square.[704] Crowds of people attended the funeral.[705]

Fomenko's reconstruction suggests that Vasilii the Holy Fool and Ivan the Terrible were one person.[706] In 1553 Ivan the Terrible, recovered in body but not in mind from his illness, abandoned the throne and became a holy fool; his early piety and religiously-inspired visions only contributed to his new spiritual awareness, or alternatively, mental breakdown. For Fomenko, this is the only possible explanation of Vasilii the Holy Fool and his enormous popularity in Moscow. That his funeral was well attended is not surprising given that he was an ex-Tsar.[707] The name 'Vasilii', Greek in origin, means 'tsar' in Russian. Therefore 'Vasilii Blazhennyi' should be read in Russian as 'tsar - holy fool'. Another indirect evidence that Fomenko believes identifies these two personalities is the fact that the Cathedral of the Deposition of the Robe on the Moat in Red Square, which was built in order to commemorate the victory of Ivan the Terrible over the Kazan khanate, is still popularly known as the Cathedral of Vasilii the Holy Fool, or *Sobor Vasiliia Blazhennogo*.[708]

Finally, according to Fomenko, the earliest and most reliable picture of Ivan the Terrible is the so-called Copenhagen portrait, preserved in the Danish royal archive. This portrait resembles, for Fomenko, a typical Russian icon, and was clearly painted with the idea in mind that the conqueror of Kazan had died a holy fool.[709] Ivan the Terrible, who was dressed in a monk's robe after his death to emulate the model of taking holy orders set by his father, was, according to Fomenko, an object of religious veneration. Portraits are of course often a matter of opinion. Payne saw in the Copenhagen portrait not a saintly, iconic image, but a rakish warrior with sensual lips and brooding countenance weighed down by the troubles of the world.[710]

According to Fomenko, when Ivan the Terrible believed that he was dying, he established Council of Trustees or *Izbrannaia Rada* so that it would be responsible for watching over young Dmitrii, his first son whose mother

---

704 See, for example, Robert Payne and Nikita Romanoff, *Ivan the Terrible* (New York: Cooper Square Press, 2002), 177-78.
705 Skrynnikov, *Tsarstvo Terrora*, 126.
706 *Ibid.,* 126.
707 Nosovskii and Fomenko, *Bibleiskaia Rus'*, I, 110-11.
708 *Ibid.*
709 *Ibid.*
710 Payne, *Ivan the Terrible*, 331.

was his beloved Anastasia. This council functioned till 1563. Conventional history maintains that little Dmitrii died in 1553 after the oath of loyalty to him was taken by the boyars.[711] Ivan the Terrible, having miraculously recovered, continued his rule, but still shared his power with the Council of Trustees. It is not entirely clear why the recovered Tsar Ivan the Terrible needed such a Council, Fomenko notes. The presence of such a Council makes more sense according to Fomenko if it is admitted that little Dmitrii did not die in 1553 but continued to rule as a child sovereign, while Ivan the Terrible degenerated into his holy dementia.[712] Representatives from the future Romanov clan were appointed as Trustees.[713] However, their influence at court soon came under pressure from rival nobles who resented the Romanov regency over the infant Tsar.[714] Conventional history offers another explanation, whereby Ivan was still a somewhat progressive state ruler, who wanted to rule the country benefiting from the close advice of his associates. Only later, after Anastasia's death did he lapse into his famed hatred of the world, and his former allies and friends.

Janet Martin has described this era as one of competing clans, although whether it represented a battle between established and newly elevated families is unclear.[715] The Glinskii family, of Lithuanian descent and relatives of Ivan the Terrible's mother replaced the Romanov clan as the principal guardian. There was a long-standing history of hostilities between the Glinskii and Romanov clans. According to Skrynnikov, when Russian troops marched into Livonia under the leadership of Glinskii, his soldiers treated the Romanov's north-western estates as enemy's lands.[716]

In 1563 Dmitrii died, probably as a result of accidental drowning. Now the Romanovs seized their opportunity, according to Fomenko. Ivan Ivanovich, the second son of Ivan the Terrible became tsar, and again the court and the boyars had to take an oath of loyalty. What evidence is there of a change of tsar at this time? The same year, according to Skrynnikov, 'fifteen years after the Tsar's coronation, messengers from Constantinople's patriarch arrived to Moscow bringing confirmation of the Muscovite (Ivan's) rights to Tsar's title...the splendid services were designed to strengthen his

---

711   Skrynnikov, *Tsarstvo Terrora*, 109.
712   Nosovskii and Fomenko, *Bibleiskaia Rus'*, I, 111.
713   Skrynnikov, *Tsarstvo Terrora*, 111.
714   *Ibid.*, 111, 115.
715   Martin, *Medieval Russia*, 331.
716   Skrynnikov, *Tsarstvo Terrora*, 147.

power'.[717] There is a problem here, Fomenko claims, since it is doubtful that such an endorsement would have occurred fifteen years after the original coronation of Ivan the Terrible. Instead this event signified the coming to power of young Ivan, now recognized in Constantinople.[718] According to Skrynnikov, this year saw the third oath given to the same sovereign Ivan the Terrible.[719] Since the Romanov family brought up the ten-year old Tsar Ivan, they were effectively now in power. They disbanded the Council of Trustees, prevented Adashev, the trusted advisor of the deceased Ivan the Terrible, from entering the capital, and began the terror of the *oprichnina* that the reign of Ivan the Terrible is famous for.

Having abandoned Adashev and Sylvester, young Ivan Ivanovich started to rule with the help of his family and at the same time abolished century old traditions, offending ordinary people in the process. The traditional nobility's anger was directed at the Romanov clan whom they held responsible for Adashev's untimely death and the style of rule of the new tsar.[720] The *oprichnina*, which conventional history attributes to Ivan the Terrible should therefore be attributed to the actions of Romanov clan, the future Romanovs, who acted violently against their political opponents.[721] These opponents were the rightful rulers of Russia, friends and family of the first Ivan the Terrible and representatives of the old Tatar dynasties. This is how the civil war known as the Times of Troubles began. It was not simply a matter of clans but of political and geographic orientation.[722] According to Fomenko, the Romanovs oriented themselves toward the West, hoping for assistance in their royal ambitions. Ivan the Terrible had been a typical Russian tsar-khan.

Ivan Ivanovich ruled from 1562 to 1571. Fomenko quotes Skrynnikov to the effect that; 'The Tsar was alarmed at the discovery of boyar traitors and set out to fix the history of his rule in 1563-1564.'[723] Fomenko is especially proud of his apparent discovery that government orders from this period were printed on paper bought in Europe.[724] For Fomenko, this connection to

---

717 See Ruslan Skrynnikov, *Ivan the Terrible*, edited and translated by Hugh F. Graham (Gulf Breeze, FL: Academic International Press, 1981), 55.
718 Nosovskii and Fomenko, *Bibleiskaia Rus'*, I, 112.
719 *Ibid.*, 171.
720 Skrynnikov, *Tsarstvo Terrora*, 171.
721 Nosovskii and Fomenko, *Bibleiskaia Rus'*, I, 112.
722 *Ibid.*, 113.
723 Skrynnikov, *Tsarstvo Terrora*, 172.
724 *Ibid.*, 20.

Western printers was added proof that the Romanovs were in league with the West. Skrynnikov noted that: 'The rise in the book printing in the end of 1550s and beginning of 1560s and its sudden termination in 1568 came about because of the tragic fate of those people who were in charge of chronicle-writing.'[725] As Fomenko would have it, the chronicle writers fulfilled their duties by presenting the history of this civil war in a pro-Romanov and were then dispatched by the ruling group to hide the evidence of this forging of the historical record.[726]

The destruction of Novgorod in 1569-1570 is considered as the culmination of the terror of the *oprichnina*. Prince Vladimir Staritsky, a famous victim of Ivan the Terrible's rage according to the conventional story, was, in the opinion of Fomenko, executed by the Romanovs. As a result, opposition forces to the *oprichnina*, and therefore to the Romanovs, started a rebellion. In the conventional accounts this military episode is presented as an invasion of Moscow by the Crimean khan, when, 'in 1571, the Tatars burned Moscow while Ivan, having abandoned his troops, escaped to Rostov.'[727] Not long before, in 1569, Ivan the Terrible negotiated with English ambassadors, asking for political asylum in Britain, perhaps fearing that his party might lose the war. For Fomenko, this was the cowardly young Ivan negotiating with Elizabeth the First, one of the Western backers of the Romanov clan.

As a result of the Crimean Khan's invasion, the Romanov party suffered heavy losses in men and their power declined. According to the conventional accounts, Maliuta Skuratov then weeded out the ranks of the old *oprichnina* executing its members on behalf of Ivan the Terrible.[728] Skuratov made his dramatic appearance only after the siege of Novgorod,[729] so he did not participate in the first wave of terror. According to Fomenko, Skuratov was part of the opposition to the Romanov clan.[730] In conventional accounts, Skuratov is always portrayed as a bloodthirsty executioner. For Fomenko, Skuratov is portrayed in such negative terms because the nucleus of the prosecuted *oprichnina* boyars belonged to the temporarily defeated Romanov clan.

With the end of *oprichnina*, sweeping changes took place in

---

725   Skrynnikov, *Tsarstvo Terrora*, 22.
726   Nosovskii and Fomenko, *Bibleiskaia Rus'*, I, 113.
727   Skrynnikov, *Ivan Groznyi*, 162.
728   *Ibid.*, 175.
729   *Ibid.*, 169.
730   Nosovskii and Fomenko, *Bibleiskaia Rus'*, I, 114.

governmental institutions. Representatives of the oldest families, that had formerly been victims of the *oprichnina*, formed a new Boyar Duma.[731] The English ambassador was notified that political asylum for a Russian Tsar was unnecessary.[732] In 1572, the Tsar prohibited the very use of the word *oprichnina* on pain of death.[733] For Fomenko, the tsar's behaviour was very strange if the conventional accounts are to be believed. Strangest of all, in 1572 the Tsar even moved to Novgorod, which he had recently destroyed,[734] with his court and treasury.[735]

The conventional account continues in its strange way when it describes Ivan the Terrible as having abdicated the throne once more in 1575 in order to allow the Tatar khan Semen Bekbulatovich to rule Russia.[736] Semen Bekbulatovich moved to the Tsar's chambers while Ivan the Terrible resided in the Arbat district of Moscow. The Khan gave orders while Ivan the Terrible, now adopting the name of Ivan Vasilievich Moskovskii or Ivan of Moscow, listened obediently.[737] Historians have struggled to explain the actions of Ivan the Terrible, blaming it on schizophrenia, or arguing that his actions were political ploys aimed at giving him a better chance to rule his restive nobles. Ostrowski has endorsed the view that Ivan the Terrible was acting out a parody of steppe custom according to which 'powerful non-Chingizid emirs (beks), such as Nogai, Tamerlane, Edige, and Mamai... set up Chingizid puppet khans on the throne.'[738] Because Ivan the Terrible was hailed by Church chroniclers as a descendant of the brother of Rome's Augustus Caesar and was therefore non-Chingizid, he may have suddenly felt the need to appoint the Chingizid Bekbulatovich as his puppet. Ivan the Terrible told the English ambassador that Semen Bekbulatovich reigned only at his pleasure and that the situation could quickly change.[739] The next year,

---

731 Skrynnikov, *Ivan Groznyi*, 174-175.
732 *Ibid.*, 189.
733 *Ibid.*, 190.
734 According to Nosovskii and Fomenko, old Novgorod was the name of modern Yaroslavl' that used to be the capital of the northeastern Russia. The Romanovs later renamed the city leaving only one Novgorod in the northwest in order to tie their dynasty regionally to Riurik, since originally Romanovs were from Pskov. Therefore it was Iaroslavl that was burned by Ivan; according to his orders Novgorod's walls were erased, and Yarsolavl today is the only city with powerful towers surrounding the city and no walls.
735 Skrynnikov, *Ivan Groznyi*, 181.
736 *Ibid.*, 195.
737 *Ibid.*, 195.
738 Ostrowski, Muscovy and the Mongols, 188.
739 Payne, *Ivan the Terrible*, 360.

1576, Ivan the Terrible resumed his title of Grand Prince and appointed Semen Bekbulatovich Grand Prince of Tver.[740] History would never hear from Semen Bekbulatovich again. Ostrowski acknowledges that, however the matter is examined, it can only be described as 'bizarre'.[741]

For Fomenko, the whole episode makes more sense if it is assumed that Semen Bekbulatovich really was in control from 1575 and that it was he who ordered the young Ivan Ivanovich, the Romanov favourite, into exile. The strange events of 1576 were not a case of Ivan the Terrible taking up the reins once more but of Semen Bekbulatovich officially consolidating his position as tsar. As a result of the civil war of 1571-1572 the 'Muscovite' party of Romanovs was defeated and its leaders executed.[742] A new *oprichnina* was created headed by representatives of the old dynastical families who were the victims of the original *oprichnina*. As Skrynnikov put it, 'the *oprichnina* achieved its greatest increase in size when five hundred Novgorodian nobles joined.[743] The Novgorodians under Skuratov were the means by which Semen Bekbulatovich achieved his victory over Ivan Ivanovich.

Semen Bekbulatovich was probably the youngest son of Ivan the Third, Fomenko speculates, and uncle of the deceased Ivan the Terrible. In 1575, young Ivan Ivanovich was forced to abdicate but Semen Bekbulatovich could not yet seal his victory by taking the title of tsar. In 1576 Semen Bekbulatovich was crowned as Tsar of Russia, after adopting the name Ivan and ruling until 1584. As Fomenko tells the story, the change of a royal name was common practice in medieval Russia. Otherwise it is difficult to explain why for one hundred and fifty years there were no names other than Ivan or Vasilii among Russia's rulers.[744] Vasilii the Third was known as Gavril before he became tsar. The custom of changing female royal names survived until the early seventeenth century when Mikhail Romanov's future wife Maria was renamed Anastasia.[745]

For Fomenko, the conventional account indirectly supports the claim that a Tatar khan did become Russian tsar. Skrynnikov wrote, 'in the following years (after 1575), the Tsar, who had always enjoyed excellent health, started

---

740   Payne, *Ivan the Terrible*, 362.
741   Ostrowski, Muscovy and the Mongols, 188.
742   Skrynnikov, *Tsarstvo Terrora*, 163.
743   Skrynnikov, *Ivan Groznyi*, 169.
744   Nosovskii and Fomenko, *Bibleiskaia Rus'*, I, 116.
745   Ivan Zabelin, *Domashnii byt Russkikh Tsarits v 16-17 stoletiiakh* (Novosibirsk: Nauka, 1992), 114.

to look for expert doctors abroad and overseas.'⁷⁴⁶ The Tsar seemed to have become fifty years older, his decline attributed to his poor mental and health state.⁷⁴⁷ The 'original' Ivan the Terrible was only forty-four years old when he allegedly resumed the throne in 1576 and should not have appeared old and in poor health in the years that followed. Semen Bekbulatovich was about eighty years old and therefore a more likely candidate for poor health.

Thus, for Fomenko, it was not Ivan the Terrible who mysteriously relocated to Novgorod but Semen Bekbulatovich who abandoned Moscow, the nest of the Romanov- conspiracy against him. Semen Bekbulatovich first settled in ancient Novgorod where he began the construction of a powerful fortress, and then moved to Tver where he took the title of Grand Prince.⁷⁴⁸ The young ex-tsar, Ivan Ivanovich, following his abdication, escaped punishment for the crimes committed during the *oprichnina*. For Fomenko the Tatar Semen Bekbulatovich proved an excellent ruler because there is no record of terror or domestic disturbances in Russia in the period of 1572-1584, only foreign wars.

Conventional accounts suggest that Ivan the Terrible had five, six, seven or eight wives, the single example in Christian Russia of a tsar who married so often. In Fomenko's reconstruction, while none of these four tsars had more than three wives as prescribed by Church laws, the person of Ivan the Terrible created by Romanov history was saddled with them all.⁷⁴⁹ Russian sources do not contain evidence of a conflict between the Tsar and the church on the issue of Ivan the Terrible's marriages. Therefore, it seems probable to Fomenko that Ivan the Terrible's only wife was Anastasia Romanov. The son Ivan Ivanovich had three wives and Tsar Fedor one. There were one or two wives for Semen Bekbulatovich.⁷⁵⁰ The third and last wife of Ivan Ivanovich, Maria Nagaya, was the mother of Dmitrii, the future False Pretender from the Time of Troubles. He was crucial to the next phase of Russia's history.

According to the conventional accounts, Ivan the Terrible died in 1584. According to Fomenko it was Semen Bekbulatovich who died in this year. Conventional accounts suggest that Ivan the Terrible's son Fedor Ivanovich became Tsar in that year. For Fomenko, Fedor was Semen

---

746 Skrynnikov, *Ivan Groznyi*, 178.
747 Payne, Romanoff, *Ivan the Terrible*, 227.
748 Skrynnikov, *Ivan Groznyi*, 169, 205.
749 Nosovskii and Fomenko, *Bibleiskaia Rus'*, I, 118.
750 *Ibid.*

Bekbulatovich's son. In the last years of his rule, the boyar Boris Godunov suddenly became very influential if the conventional accounts are to be believed. Although conventional history stipulates that Tsar Fedor died childless, Fomenko insists that he had a son, named Boris, who is known to us under his mother's last name Godunov.[751] Meanwhile, Ivan Ivanovich's son Dmitrii, known to history as False Dmitrii, represented a second dynastical branch and a rival for Boris Godunov.[752]

According to Fomenko, there are a number of sources that confirm the royal lineage of Boris Godunov. In 1591 during the rule of Tsar Fedor Ivanovich, the Crimean khan Gazi-Girey sent a letter to Moscow to Boris Godunov.[753] Although the message is entitled 'Crimean Khan's letter to Muscovite Boyar Boris Godunov' the reverse side bears an inscription from the Tsar's chancellery: 'Translated in summer 7099...that which is written to Tsar Boris Fedorovich by the Crimean Tsar's confidante.' Fomenko notes that in 1591, Boris Godunov was referred to as 'a Tsar', that is, seven years before the conventional date for the death of Tsar Fedor and the crowning as tsar of Boris Godunov. They assert further that Godunov's infant son Fedor was also referred to as a Tsar in certain unspecified official papers.[754]

The Crimean khan's letter is not the only evidence that has reached us confirming Boris Godunov's affiliation with the tsars of Russia. When Fedor was still alive, Boris attended a meeting with the Austrian ambassador. The protocol, according to Skrynnikov, was arranged and handled as if Boris Godunov were a Tsar.[755] It was usual practice that an elder son would deputize for his father and received full royal honours. With their fondness for historical parallels, Fomenko point out that this honour was bestowed upon Ivan the Third when his father Vasilii the Second was still alive.[756] Skrynnikov confirmed that Boris Godunov used many titles, dealing not only with the Russian court but also with foreign countries and ambassadors long before conventional history recognized him as tsar.[757] His messages to the English Queen were signed, 'Boris, by God's will the sovereign of all Russia.'[758] In her replies the English queen referred to Boris as 'cousin', another proof,

---

751 Nosovskii and Fomenko, *Bibleiskaia Rus'*, I, 119.
752 *Ibid.*
753 *Ibid.*, 120.
754 Nosovskii and Fomenko, *Bibleiskaia Rus'*, I, 120.
755 Ruslan Skrynnikov, *Boris Godunov* (Moscow: Nauka, 1983), 38.
756 Nosovskii and Fomenko, *Bibleiskaia Rus'*, I, 120.
757 Skrynnikov, *Boris Godunov*, 85.
758 *Ibid.*, 86.

Fomenko argues, that Boris Godunov was a legitimate tsar.[759]

Boris Godunov became 'the hated usurper' only after the Romanovs came to power, because, under Boris Godunov, the family of Romanovs was the most persecuted. Boris Godunov exiled Fedor Romanov to a remote northern monastery and destroyed the Romanov party in the Boyar Duma. After the Romanovs came to power, the chroniclers painted Boris Godunov as darkly as possible while the Romanov clan was depicted as comprising holy martyrs.[760]

According to conventional accounts, Boris was born in 1552, and became a sovereign at the age of forty-seven years, in 1599.[761] Yet portraits portray him as a young person according to Fomenko. Because of his youth, he encountered opposition in the Duma from powerful boyar clans, especially the Shuisky clan. According to Skrynnikov, the tensions in the Duma ran so high that Boris had to abandon his Kremlin residence and move to a well-protected *Novodevichii* monastery.[762] The conventional account insists that as an experienced and cunning populist Boris Godunov left Moscow's Kremlin for a monastery in order to force his rule upon the Russian populace in a manner reminiscent of Ivan the Terrible's abdication and departure for Aleksandrovskaya sloboda. After a period of turmoil Boris Godunov won this struggle for power, and his supporters came to the monastery in order to transport Boris back from exile.[763]

When Boris Godunov died in 1605 he was 53 years old, yet his heir was still an infant. Fomenko claims that this is further proof that Boris Godunov was in reality the son of Fedor Ivanovich and only 20-25 years old when he inherited the throne in 1599. Thus it was not surprising that his only son was still an infant when Boris died.[764]

Boris Godunov's death ushered in the era known to conventional history as the Times of Troubles. The Times of Troubles revolves in part around False Dmitrii who was according to popular legend Ivan the Terrible's son. The mystery surrounding Prince Dmitrii, the False Pretender, has not yet been resolved. As some historians have put it, how could Prince Dmitrii challenge Boris Godunov, a clever, energetic, charismatic powerful supreme

---

759 Nosovskii and Fomenko, *Bibleiskaia Rus'*, I, 121.
760 Skrynnikov, *Boris Godunov*, 134-136.
761 *Ibid.*, 5.
762 *Ibid.*, 110-111.
763 *Ibid.*, 112-120.
764 Nosovskii and Fomenko, *Bibleiskaia Rus'*, I, 124.

ruler?'⁷⁶⁵ Fomenko argues that the reconstructed version of events logically explains what happened. False Dmitrii was in fact a prince, but his father was Ivan Ivanovich who ruled in 1563-1572, not Ivan the Terrible. The Romanov family not only brought up Ivan Ivanovich but also his young son Dmitrii. He was initially sent to a monastery in order to avoid any dispute between the young Dmitrii and his father's conqueror, Semen Bekbulatovich or his descendant, Boris Godunov. According to Russian law, a person of royal descent who became a monk or a cleric could not be crowned as tsar.⁷⁶⁶

We have differing accounts of the deaths of two princely children during the reign of Ivan the Terrible, both named Dmitrii Ivanovich. Fomenko insists that there was most likely only one death, in 1563, when young Tsar Dmitrii Ivanovich, son of Ivan the Terrible, died at the age of ten or twelve. Fomenko believes that Prince Shuisky who fought against Godunov invented the story about the second Dmitrii's death in 1591 to undermine the rival to his preferred candidate as Tsar.⁷⁶⁷ According to conventional accounts, after Ivan the Terrible's death, the new Tsar Fedor exiled Dmitrii and his mother to Uglich. Dmitrii had his throat cut in 1591. The investigation by Shuisky first found that the death was the result of a lack of supervision and youthful exuberance playing with knives. Later Shuisky changed his story, allowing suspicion to fall on Boris Godunov. Skrynnikov noted that there has been a long-standing suspicion in academic circles that the so-called Uglich affair was falsified. Skrynnikov points out that even a superficial analysis of the documents demonstrates traces of censorship given that the lists are in the wrong order. It seems certain that the originals of the Uglich interrogation have disappeared.⁷⁶⁸ To Fomenko it is obvious that when Prince Dmitrii became the False Pretender, a story about the Uglich tragedy was invented. The grave of the first Dmitrii, the first son of Ivan the Terrible who died, seemingly by drowning, in 1563, was declared to be the grave of Dmitrii, son of Ivan Ivanovich.⁷⁶⁹

Conventional accounts claim that the False Dmitrii was really the vagabond Gregory Otrep'ev. This seems incredible to Fomenko given that False Dmitrii received considerable acknowledgement as the genuine heir. Indeed, from the very beginning of Dmitrii's struggle for the throne,

---

765 A. Gordeev, *Istoriia Kazakov* II (Moscow: Strastnoi bul'var), 97.
766 Nosovskii and Fomenko, *Bibleiskaia Rus'*, I, 125.
767 *Ibid.*, 126.
768 Skrynnikov, *Boris Godunov*, 70-72.
769 Nosovskii and Fomenko, *Bibleiskaia Rus'*, I, 126.

eyewitnesses asserted their confidence that he was a prince. The Polish king and nobility, Russian boyars, crowds of ordinary people in Putivl' and other cities, and even his own mother, Maria Nagaya, recognized Dmitrii.[770] In Putivl', Dmitrii displayed the real Gregory Otrep'ev to the crowd.[771] Meanwhile, events in Moscow developed rapidly. On 13 April 1605 tsar Boris Godunov died not of old age as the conventional account implies but poisoned by the rival boyars clans of Shuisky, Romanov and Golitsyn.[772]

Fomenko acknowledges that there is at least one major problem with his theory. What motive did the Romanovs have for portraying Dmitrii as a False Pretender when he was brought up in their family? False Dmitrii was also an enemy of Boris Godunov who was enemy number one for the Romanovs. Fomenko answers his own question by claiming that Dmitrii was simply a tool for the Romanovs to achieve power. Dmitrii was still a Riurikid, although related to the Romanovs through his grandmother Anastasia Romanov.

When Dmitrii became tsar in 1605, he too had a son. Consequently the election of Mikhail Romanov as tsar in 1613 was not legitimate since there was a child of the royal line still alive. The Romanovs unsurprisingly declared Dmitrii to be a False Pretender, and Dmitrii's son was slandered as the 'little thief'. The problem of an unwanted heir was solved very rapidly and efficiently, as the 'little thief' was soon dispatched on the Spassky gates of the Kremlin. Thus the Romanovs and the Shuisky clan supported one another in the struggle against Dmitrii for their own self-interested reasons.[773]

As Fomenko tells it, neither the Russian people, nor Russia's neighbours, readily accepted the lies perpetrated by the Romanovs. In seventeenth century Poland, Mikhail Fedorovich Romanov was not recognized as the rightful ruler of Russia. The second Romanov, Tsar Alexis Mikhailovich sent an envoy to Poland in 1650 who demanded that 'all dishonest books be confiscated and burnt in the presence of ambassadors, while their authors, as well as the printers, owners of print houses, and landlords on whose territories the print houses were situated, were to be executed.' According to Fomenko, this process had already taken place in Russia.

For conventional historians, the Golden Horde passed out of history in

---

770 Skrynnikov, *Boris Godunov*, 49.
771 Gordeev, *Istoriia Kazakov*, II, 113.
772 Nosovskii and Fomenko, *Bibleiskaia Rus'*, I, 126.
773 *Ibid.*, 128.

the fifteenth century. For the alternative writers it lived on through Ivan the Third, Ivan the Terrible and Boris Godunov. It survives to this day in the shape of the Cossacks. For Fomenko and other alternative historians, the Cossacks of the Don and Volga are much older than conventional historians think and date back to the twelfth century. This, of course, contradicts the conventional axiom of Russian history, that the Cossacks were runaway serfs of the seventeenth century.[774]

The alternative historians dismiss as fantasy the contention that a runaway serf, whose life revolved around his plough, was miraculously transformed into a merciless warrior trained in the art of mounted combat. According to Fomenko, Cossack troops were living on the steppe at the time of the Mongols, and they were an integral part of the Russian Horde's army.[775] Fomenko notes that Cossack troops assisted Dmitrii Donskoi at Kulikovo Field and Ivan the Terrible at the siege of Kazan', at a time when serfdom was only in the process of formation. Only in 1649 under the Romanovs did serfdom take its final, repressive form. Fomenko points out that Russian textbooks tended to date the Cossacks only from the seventeenth century.[776]

Fomenko notes that Cossack communities are presently scattered all over Russia's territory. There are Don, Volga, Yaik (Urals), Dnepr, Terek, Pskov, Riazan', Zaporozhie, Meschera, Nogai and Azov Cossacks, as well as the 'town' Cossacks situated in regional strongholds.[777] Fomenko cites the usual array of modern and ancient sources, including the *Dictionary of the Cossacks*, which notes that the first of the conventionally recognised Cossack Hosts, the Zaporozhie, based in Ukraine, were known as 'Horde Cossacks'. For Fomenko, the geographic dispersion of the Cossacks suspiciously resembles the geography of the former Golden Horde.[778] According to Fomenko, Cossack troops were living on the steppe at the time of the Mongols, and they were an integral part of the so-called Tatar-Mongol

---

774 Here Fomenko skillfully utilizes the intentional gaps of Imperial/Soviet historiographies that treated the Cossacks with either hatred or suspicion. See Gerasim Vdovenko and Alexei Gryzov et al, *Kazachestvo* (Moscow: Sobranie, 2007), 19, 135.
775 Nosovskii and Fomenko, *Novaia khronologiia Rusi*, 11.
776 *Ibid.*, 14.
777 Skrylov and Gubarenko, *Kazachii slovar'-spravochnik* (Cleveland: Ohio, USA, 1966), 254; also *Kazachii slovar'-spravochnik* II volumes (San Anselmo: California, USA, 1968).
778 Nosovskii and Fomenko, *Novaia khronologiia Rusi*, 14.

army.[779] In the first half of the twelfth century, Cossack hordes populated all eastern and Central Asia.[780] Romanov historians later disguised and twisted the Cossack heritage. Romanov propagandists claimed that the Cossacks were runaway serfs. Cossacks were elite warriors, not runaway peasants.

Sixty years after the Romanov's ascension to power the most serious Cossack revolt occurred in Russia, the uprising of Stepan Timofeevich Razin in 1667-71. Conventional accounts portray Stenka Razin's Cossacks as rebellious peasants who wanted to sail to Moscow to reveal to their 'little father', the Tsar of Russia, the wrongdoings of his boyars. Fomenko argues that there is no evidence that the Cossacks wanted to side with the Tsar against his own advisers. Moreover, the extant copies of documents put out by the rebels ask the peasants to rise up and fight 'for the house of the Holy Mother (Russia), for the Great Sovereign, for our little father Stepan Timofeevich and all the Orthodox Christian faith'.[781]

Fomenko claims that the Romanovs at that time only controlled one part of Russia, that is, its central princedoms and the northeast. Meanwhile, the middle and lower Volga remained independent. There were other tsars there, including those who belonged to the Tatar dynasties. This is why the Cossacks constantly repeated that they were fighting for the Tsar against the boyars. They were opposed to the Romanov-boyars and supported their own Russian Horde Tsar, not Alexis Romanov. Fomenko notes that the war lasted four years, a long war by any standards. In Europe it was looked upon as a fight for the throne. Razin's uprising became known as the 'Tatar rebellion'. The Romanovs won the war with the aid of foreign mercenaries, having failed to find reliable troops inside Russia.[782] The era of the Slav-Turks was over, its energy spent and the Romanovs triumphant. Fomenko's hope is that once Russians learn the truth about the greatness of the Russian Horde, this victory of the West will be reversed.

---

779 Albert Seaton, *The Horsemen of the Steppes: The Story of the Cossacks* (New York: Hippocrene books, 1985).
780 Nosovskii and Fomenko, *Novaia khronologiia Rusi*, 14.
781 Nosovskii and Fomenko, *Bibleiskaia Rus'*, I, 131.
782 *Ibid.*, 133.

Conclusions

Khazanov concluded his recent account of Russian nationalism with the judgement that 'the struggle against nationalism, whether under the banners of Marxism, classical liberalism, economic integration-ism, or any other -ism has so far proved to be futile. The only hope that remains for the foreseeable future is not to eradicate nationalism but to curb its excesses, in other words, to make it civil'.[783] Fomenko's writings indicate just what a difficult task this will be.

Some of Fomenko's supporters argue that the concept of the Russian Horde is a relatively benign and harmless channel for Russian nationalism to move towards. Fomenko's history is so fantastic that it can safely be ignored by the majority of Russia's population whose task revolves around the more mundane goal of earning a living. Other commentators view the underlying message of Fomenko's version of the past is serving to stir up passions about the inseparable unity of the lands stretching from Ukraine to the Pacific and the historical role of Russia in those regions.

Fomenko believes that his history offers the Turks in Russia a new understanding of their past that will prepare them for a new partnership in the Russian Federation. If they do not accept the Russian state, they will be turning their backs not just on Russia but their history. Not to accept that offer will be catastrophic for both sides. Fortunately for Russia, it turns out that the Tatars of the medieval period were not modern ethnic Tatars. Tatars were simply the light cavalry formations of Russia, part of a unity that existed when Russia's ancestors ruled all of Eurasia.

By proposing the existence of the mixed, mingled, brotherly ethnic Russian-Turkic host in the past Fomenko seems to believe that he might counteract ethnic tensions among the Russians, Tatars, Bashkirs, Chechens and others. By stressing the fact that the Slavic-Turkic empire occupied approximately the same territories as the former Soviet Union Fomenko indirectly lays claim to the former Soviet colonies, not in the name of the Great Russian nation as it had been done before, but rather on behalf of a multi-cultural, bilingual mixed-ethnic empire. Upon closer investigation, it turns out that, according to Fomenko, the majority of ancient tribes living on

---

783 Anatolii Khazanov, *After the USSR*, 242.

the territory of the former Soviet Union were Russians. Khazars Pechenegs, Polovtsy, and Genghis Khan were, in the end, Slavs. In the patriotic Russian imagination, it does not get much better than this.

It is not difficult to see why some commentators regard the view of Fomenko as fascistic even though he denies that bloodlines have anything to do with Russia's sense of identity. Davies has pointed out that the Nazis embraced a restrictive internationalism and were happy enough to acknowledge that Anglo-Saxons or Scandinavians were their partners even though Germans retained their overall leadership of this mixed horde.[784] In designating chosen peoples who occupied important places in the Russian Horde, Fomenko shows the hostility towards West and East that remains one of the elements competing for Russian identity.

At another level, Fomenko's pseudo-history is an unsurprising outcome in the climate of post-Communist Russia. McDaniel has pointed out that one of the great continuities of Russian history is the fact of discontinuity.[785] There have been several obvious breaks with the past in Russia's history –the coming of Christianity, Peter the Great, the Communist revolution, Stalin's revolution from above, the collapse of the Soviet Union. At each point, those who came to power obliterated the past from the historical record and invented a new history. According to the early Russian chronicles, Vladimir the First converted Kiev Rus *en masse* to Christianity in 985-88 and literally destroyed all trace of the pagan gods. Peter the Great attacked almost everything old from the existing church hierarchy to the beards of his subjects and then set up an Academy of Sciences in St. Petersburg in 1725 whose mission included the writing of Russian history. After 1917, Lenin and Stalin destroyed the pillars of the former establishment, tsar, nobility, church and peasantry and then destroyed any information that could be viewed as positive concerning their imperial predecessors. There is widespread agreement that Russian history was misrepresented and misinterpreted by generations of Soviet historians whose task was to prove the inevitable and progressive evolution of socio-economic formations as stipulated in the Marxist-Leninist doctrine. The pattern continued after the fall of Communism in 1991 when Russian reformers declared an end to the Communist *Sonderweg* as if Russia was a land with a future but no past.

Fomenko reads this pattern of history as suggesting that at every crisis

---

784 See Davies, *Europe,* 1017.
785 McDaniel, *The Agony of the Russian idea*, 16-17.

in Russia's history, a new idea is needed to account for the crisis and to enable Russia to move forward. Because there is a point to history, it is too important to be left to purely academic research. The Marxist historian Pokrovsky put this idea most cynically when he described history as politics projected into the past. When pseudo-historians like Fomenko are told that the past they have invented is full of lies and distortion, they invariably reply that the history written by conventional historians suffers from the same defects. Their aim is to unsettle the consensus built upon the lies and distortions of a previous rewriting of history that in their view has paralysed not just Russia's historians but the revival of Russia as a state. Fomenko and his allies consider that history determines the future, that the sudden collapses to which Russia has been prone in the twentieth century are evidence of how far Russia has strayed from its true historical roots.

The enemy for Fomenko is always the West, and their corrupt Russian minions, most notably the Romanovs and the Yeltsin-era reformers. For Fomenko, there can be no reconciliation with Germans who constantly involve themselves in Russia's affairs, who corrupted and rewrote the Russian chronicles, who launched military and cultural attacks against Russia. Not that other western Europeans are much better. Italians composed false chronicles from the antiquity in order to make the Romans appear older and wiser than the rest of Europe, the French sent their mercenaries along with other European powers to protect the first Romanovs, the English always acted against Russia out of envy that it was in reality Russia who once ruled the greatest empire the world has ever seen.

For Fomenko, the Russians need Asia if they are to maintain their existence in the face of the challenge posed by the West. This challenge has not just come in the form of invasions such as that of Napoleon or Hitler. Russia shares its longest land frontier with China, which has five times its population and is rapidly overhauling it and other parts of the world in terms of indices of economic growth. Russia's relationship with China must inevitably impact upon the newly independent countries of Central Asia who live in the shadow of their gigantic neighbours. Meanwhile illegal Chinese immigration and illegal trade in the Russian Far East has the potential to establish a case for a Chinese Siberia at some point in the future. Only six million Russians live east of the Ural Mountains. This turnaround in the population mix provokes occasional bouts of panic among Russians that the potential is there for a modern version of the Mongol invasions in the shape of Chinese economic and subsequent political domination.

Russia is more fractured than it has been since the medieval period. For present day Russians, much of the steppe lies in foreign countries, that is, Ukraine and Kazakhstan. Gumilëv's image of Russia as a symbiosis seems to carry within it the possibility that the two components, Russia and Asia, might at some point cease to interact. Within the Russian Federation, Chechen separatists confront the Russian state militarily while Turkic peoples have attempted to reclaim an ancestry that, on the surface seems more ancient and more impressive than that of their Russian hosts. The post-Communist Russian elite has tried its best to be integrated into the West, not least because the stability of Russia is still dependent upon Western trade.[786] On the other hand, the rapid falling out of Russia and the United States during the second half of the presidencies of Putin and Bush, the disputes over American weapons systems in Eastern Europe, instability in Ukraine, and Russia's war with Georgia in 2008 suggest to many commentators that Russia is repositioning itself as a hostile rival of the West. It is still not clear what the orientation or identity of Russia will be. The contest about the future has to an extent taken the form of a contest for the past. For many Russian readers, the muscular approach of pseudo-history tackles the important questions of national identity in a more satisfying way than more cautious academics.

Fomenkoism is an amalgam of disillusionment with and rediscovery of Soviet ideals, mixed with feelings of lost grandeur, hope, vengeance and envy. For Fomenko, the story of Russian greatness has to be told a different way to the version favoured by Romanovs and Communists. The latter ignored the greatness of the Russian Horde. All those who lived on the steppe and forests of Eurasia once owed their allegiance to Russia. The Russian Horde was, and remains, entitled to demand their loyalty in a new time of troubles.

---

786 Dmitrii Shlapentokh, 'Russian nationalism today: the views of Alexander Dugin,' *Contemporary Review* 279 (July 2001): 1626.

Bibliography

Selected Works of Fomenko and Related Pseudo History:

Abrashkin, A, *Predki russkikh v drevnem mire*, Veche, Moscow, 2001.
Abrashkin, A, *Drevnie Rossy. Mifologicheskie paralleli i puti migratsii*, NNGU, Nizhny Novgorod, 1999.
Abrashkin, A, Chudo-Uydo: *Istoriia odnogo perevoplashchenia*, NNGU, Nizhny Novgorod, 1999.
Abrashkin, A, *Avesta v Russkikh perevodakh*, NNGU, Nizhny Novgorod, 1997.
Abrashkin, A, *Rus' sredizemnomorskaia i zagadki Biblii*, Veche, Moscow, 2003.
Abrashkin, A, *Tainy troianskoi voiny i sredizemnomorskaia Rus'*, Veche, Moscow, 2006.
Abrashkin, A, *Sredizemnomorskaia Rus': velikaia derzhava drevnosti*, Veche, Moscow, 2006.
Abrashkin, A, *Skifskaia Rus'. Ot Troi do Kieva*, Veche, Moscow, 2008.
Adzhi, M, *My – iz roda Polovetskogo*, Moscow, Rybinsk, 1992.
Adzhi, M, *Polyn' polovetskogo polia*, Pik-Kontekst, Moscow, 1994.
Adzhi, M, *Evropa, Turki, velikaia step'*, Mysl', Moscow, 1998.
Adzhi, M, *Kipchaki*, Novosti, Moscow, 1999.
Adzhi, M, *Tiurki i mir: sokrovennaia istoriia*, AST, Moscow, 2004.
Adzhi, M, *Aziatskaia Evropa*, AST, Moscow, 2006.
Adzhi, M, *Dykhanie Armagedona*, AST, Moscow, 2006.
Bushkov, A, *Rossiia kotori ne bylo*, vol. I, 'OLMA-Press', Moscow, 1997.
Bushkov, A, Burovskii, A, *Rossiia kotoroi ne bylo, Russkaia Atlantida*, vol. II, 'OLMA-Press', Moscow, 2001.
Bushkov, A, *Rossiia kotori ne bylo, mirazhi i prizraki*, vol. III, 'OLMA-press', Moscow, 2004.
Bushkov, A, *Rossiia kotori ne bylo. Blesk i krov' gvardeiskogo stoletiia*, vol. IV, 'OLMA-press', Moscow, 2005.
Bushkov, A, *Zemlia. Planeta prizrakov*, 'OLMA-press', Moscow, 2008.
Bushkov, A, *Ivan Groznyi. Krovavyi poet*, 'OLMA-press', Moscow, 2007.
Bushkov, A, *Chingiz-khan. Neizvestnaia Aziia*, 'OLMA-press', Moscow, 2008.
Bushkov, A, *Rasputin. Vystrely iz proshlogo*, 'OLMA-press', Moscow, 2008.
Bushkov, A, *Stalin: Krasnyi monarch*, 'OLMA-press', Moscow, 2008.
Bushkov, A, *Stalin: Ledianoi tron*, 'OLMA-press', Moscow, 2008.
Burovskii, A, *Nesbyvshaiasia Rossiia*, Eksmo, Moscow, 2007.
Burovskii, A, *Ariiskaia Rus': lozh' i Pravda o vysshei rase*, Eksmo, Moscow, 2007.
Bocharov, L, Efimov, N, Chachukh, I, Chernyshev, I, *Zagovor protiv russkoi istorii*, ANVIK, Moscow, 2001.
Valianskii, S, Kaliuzhnyi, D, *Put' na vostok ili bez vesti propavshie vo vremeni*, Kraft+Lean, Moscow, 1997.
Demin, V, *Otkyda ty, russkoe plemia?* Veche, Moscow, 1996.

Demin, V, *Tainy Russkogo naroda*, Moscow, 1997.
Demin, V, *Giperboreia – kolybel' tsivilizatsii*, Veche, Moscow, 1997.
Demin, V, *Zagadki Russkogo severa*, Veche, 1999.
Demin, V, *Tainy zemli Russkoi*, Veche, Moscow, 2000.
Demin, V, *Giperboreia: istoricheskie korni russkogo naroda*, Veche, Moscow, 2000.
Demidenko, M, *Po Sledam SS v Tibete*, Olma-Press, St-Petersburg, 2003.
Fomenko, A, Nosovskii, G, Kalashnikov, V, *Datirovka zvezdnogo kataloga 'Almagest', geometricheskii i statisticheskii analiz*, Faktorial, Moscow, 1995.
Fomenko, A, Nosovskii, G, Kalashnikov, V, *Astronomicheskii analiz khronologii: Almagest. Zodiaki*, Delovoi ekspress, Moscow, 2000.
Fomenko, A, Nosovskii, G, *Novaia khronologiia i kontseptsiia drevnei Rusi, Anglii, Rima. Fakty, statistikia, gipotesy*, II volumes, State University press (MGU), Moscow, 1995, 1996.
Fomenko, A, *Novaia khronologiia Gretsii. Antichnost' i srednevekov'e*, II volumes, MGU, Moscow, 1996.
Fomenko, A, Nosovskii, G, *Imperiia: Rus', Turtsia, Kitai, Evropa, Egipet. Novaia matematicheskaia khronologiia drevnosti*, 'Faktorial press', Moscow, 1996, 1997, 1998, 1999.
Nosovskii, G, Fomenko, A, *Rus' i Rim. Pravil'no li my poinimaem istoriiu Evropy i Azii?* II volumes, 'Olimp', 'ACT ', Moscow, 1997.
Fomenko, A, Nosovskii, G, *Novaia khronologiia Rusi*, Faktorial press, Moscow, 1997.
Fomenko, A, Nosovskii, G, *Matematicheskaia khronologia bibleiskikh sobytii*, Nauka, Moscow, 1997.
Fomenko, A, 'Smysl russkogo dela v sokhranenii imperii,' *Nezavisimaia Gazeta*, 1996, November 21.
Fomenko, A, 'Global'naia khronologicheskaia karta', *Khimia i Zhizn'*, 9, 1983, pp. 85-92.
Fomenko, A, *Metody matematicheskogo analiza istoricheskikh tekstov: prilozhenie k khronologii*, Nauka, Moscow, 1996.
Fomenko, A, Nosovskii, G, *Bibleiskaia Rus'*, II volumes, 'Faktorial press', Moscow, 1998, 2000.
Fomenko, A, Nosovskii, G, *Rus'-Orda na stranitsakh bibleiskikh knig*, 'Anvik', Moscow, 1998.
Fomenko, A, Nosovskii, G, *Vvedenie v novuiu khronologiiu, kakoi seichas vek?* 'Kraft+Lean', Moscow, 1999.
Fomenko, A, Nosovskii, G, *Rekonstruktsia vseobshchei istorii. Issledovaniia 1999-2000*, 'Delovoi ekspress', Moscow, 1999.
Fomenko, A, Nosovskii, G, *Kakoi seichas vek?* Aif-Print, Moscow, 2002.
Fomenko, A, Nosovskii, G, *Khronologiia*, 2002-, seven volumes.
Fomenko, A, *History: Fiction or Science*, vol. 1, Delamere, London, 2003.
Guts, A, *Mnogovariantnaia Istoriia Rossii*, ACT, 2000, 'Poligon', Moscow, 2001.
Guts, A, Mif o vosstanovlenii istoricheskoi pravdy, *Matematicheskie struktury i modelirovanie*, 6, OMGU, Omsk, 1998.
Guts, A, *Podlinnaia Istoriia Rossii*, OMGU, Omsk, 1999.
Guts, A, Modeli mnogovariantnoi istorii, *Matematicheskie struktiru i modelirovanie*, 4,

OMGU, Omsk, 1999.
Kandyba, V, *Istoriia ruskogo naroda*, Lan', St-Petersburg, 1996.
Kandyba, V, Zolin, P, *Real'naia Istoriia Rossii*, Lan', St-Petersburg, 1997.
Kandyba, V, Zolin, P, *Istoriia i ideologia ruskkogo naroda*, Lan', St-Petersburg, 1997, II volumes.
Kesler, Ia, *Russkaia tsivilizatsia*, Eko-press, Moscow, 2000, 2002.
Kesler, Ia, *Kniga tsivilazatsii*, 'Eko-press', Moscow, 2001.
Lesnoi, S, *Peresmotr osnov istorii slavian*, Omega-Press, Melbourne, 1956.
Lesnoi, S, *Istoriia Russov v neizvrashchennom vide*, pts. 1-7, Paris, 1953-1958.
Morozov, N, Khristos, *Istoriia chelovecheskoi kul'tury v estestvennonauchnom osveshchenii*, 7 volumes, Gosizdat, Moscow, Leningrad, 1924-1932.
Petukhov, Iu, *Kolybel' Zevsa: Istoriia Russov ot antichnosti do nashikh dnei*, Moscow, 1998.
Petukhov, Iu, *Gibel' Rossii*, Mysl' Moscow, 1999.
Petukhov, Iu, *Istoriia Russov: 40000 let do nashei ery*, vol. I, Mysl', Moscow, 2000.
Petukhov, Iu, *Russkaia Khazaria*, Mysl', Moscow, 2001.
Petukhov, Iu, *Tainy drevnikh russov*, Veche, Moscow, 2001, 2002, 2003.
Petukhov, Iu, *Russy drevnego Vostoka*, Veche, Moscow, 2003.
Poliakovskii, V, *Tataro-Mongoly, Evraziia, Mnogovariantnost'*, Moscow, 2002.
Storozhev, A, Storozhev, V, *Rossiia vo vremeni*, book 1, ANVIK, Veche, Moscow, 1997.
Shcherbakov, V, *Gde zhili geroi eddicheskikh mifof*, Moscow, 1989.
Shcherbakov, V, *Gde iskat' Atlantidu*, Moscow, 1990.
Shcherbakov, V, *Asgard –gorod Bogov*, Moscow, 1991.
Khamtsiev, V, Balaev, A, *David Soslan, Friedrich Barbarossa, Alaniia ot Palestiny to Britanii*, Vladikavkaz, 1992.

Selected Criticisms of Fomenko:

Antifomenkovskaia mozaika, 5 books, (ed.) Nastenko, I, Gorodetskii, A, Russkaia panorama, Moscow, 2000, 2001, 2002, 2003.
Astrologiia protiv 'novoi khronologii', (ed.) Nastenko, I, Russkaia panorama, Moscow, 2001.
Astronomiia protiv 'novoi khronologii', Ruskaia panorama, Moscow, 2001.
Azhgikhina, N, 'Terminator mirovoi istorii', *NG-Nauka*, January 19, 2000.
Baranov, V, 'Logika ne fakty', *Tekhnika i nauka*, 8, 1983, pp. 28-30.
Begunov, Iu, *Tainye sily v istorii Rossii*, St-Petersburg, 1998, pp. 418-420.
Begunov, Iu, *Russkaia Istoriia protiv novoi khronologii*, Russkaia panorama, Moscow, 2001.
Borisenok, Iu, 'Fomenkiada, konets istorii?' *Izvestia*, December 24, 1999.
Broshten, V, 'Velikii perebor,' *Zemlia i vselennaia*, 3, 1997, pp. 87-95.
Bialko, A, 'My ves', my drevnii mir razrushim?' *Priroda*, 2, 1997, pp. 75-76.
Vinskaia, L, 'Narkotik po imeni Bushkov', *Argumenty i Fakty*, 44(889), 1997, p. 19.
Volodikhin, D, Oleinikov, D, Eliseeva, O, *Istoriia Rossii v melkii goroshek*, Manufactura-

Edinstvo, Moscow, 1998.
Volodokhin, D, 'Uchil li Khristos na Altae?' *Knizhnoe obozrenie*, 9, 1999.
Volodokhin, D, 'Fenomen folk-istorii,' *Otechestvennaia Istoriia*, 4, 2000, pp. 16-24.
Golubtsova, E, Koshelenko, G, 'Istoriia drevnego mira i novye metodiki', *Voprosy istorii*, 8, 1982, pp. 70-82.
Gorbachev, N, 'Mify novoi khronologii ili raskrutka na temnoi volne', *Moskovskii literator*, 5(731), 2000, pp. 4-5.
Danilevskii, I, 'Sindrom narodnogo akademika', *Znanie-Sila*, 4, 1998, pp. 120-125.
Dragunskii, D, 'Massovaia kul'tura dlia izbrannykh', *Itogi*, March 10, 1998, pp. 50-53.
Eliseev, G, Stankova, I, 'Pod znamenem folk-istorii', *Chitaiushchaia Rossiia*, 2, 1998.
Zlobin, E, 'Mashinochitaemye dokumenty v svete novoi khronologii', *Informatsionnyi biulletin Assotsiatsii 'Istoriia i Komputer'*, 16, 1996.
Istoriia i antiistoriia: Kritika 'novoi khronologii' akademika A. Fomenko, (ed.), Nastenko, I, Yazyki russkoi kultury, Moscow, 2000.
Kapitsa, S, 'Prognoz – Istoriia, obraschennaia v budushchee', *Izvestia*, November 19, 1983.
Klimishin, I, *Kalendar' i khronologia*, Nauka, Moscow, 1990, pp. 409-415.
Laushkin, A, *Lozh' novoi khronologii*, Palomnik, Moscow, 2002.
Leskov, S, 'Po raschetam vyshlo: sluzhil Iisus Khristos rimskim papoi', *Izvestia*, January 29, 1997.
MGU History Department (ed.), *Kritika novoi khronologii*, Anvik, Moscow, 2001.
Mikhailov, N, 'Zagadka Kulikova Polia', *Literaturnaia Rossiia*, November 22, 47, 1996.
Manfred, A, 'Nekotorye tendentsii v zarubezhnoi istoriografii', *Kommunist*, 10, 1977, pp. 106-114.
Novikov, S, 'Matematika i Istoriia', *Priroda*, 2, 1997, pp. 70-74.
Oleinikov, D, 'Globalnyi rozygrysh', *Rodina*, 6, 1997.
Pashaeva, N, 'A byla li bitva na Kulikovom pole?' *Slaviane i ikh sosedi*, 10, Moscow, 2001, pp. 228-235.
Ponomarev, A, 'O chem svidetelstvuiut novye datirovki Ptolemeia', *Istoriia i komputer*, 22, 1998, pp. 258-267.
Portnov, A, 'Iaroslav Mudryi byl khanom Batuem?' *Trud*, September 11, 1998.
Rich, V, 'Byl li temnyi period?' *Khimia i Zhizn'*, 9, 1983, p. 84.
Russkaia istoriia protiv 'novoi khronologii', Russkaia panorama, Moscow, 2001).
Sbornik Russkogo istoricheskogo obshchestva, vol. 3, (ed.) Nastenko, Russkaia panorama, Moscow, 2000.
Smirnov, A, 'Globalnyi sdvig', *Rodina*, 6, 1997.
Sviridenko, Iu, Neborskii, M, *Rossiskoe mnogonatsionalnoe gosudarstvo: puti soglasiia narodov*, Moscow, 1997, pp. 138-139.
Soloviev, N, 'Roman s istoriei', *Literaturnaia Rossiia*, 8, 1998, p. 10.
Tak ono i okazalos': kritika 'novoi khronologii', (ed.) Chacschikhin, U, ANVIK, Moscow, 2001.
Uliankin, N, *Antinauchnaia sensatsia (o gipotezakh Fomenko)*, Moscow, 1999.
Shreider, Iu, 'Ot Kolumba – k Niutonu', *Znanie-sila*, 4, 1983, pp. 26-28.
Shubin, A, *Garmoniia istorii (vvedenie v teoriui istoricheskikh analogii)*, Palomnik, Moscow,

1992, pp. 163-164.
Kharitonovich, D, 'Fenomen Fomenko', *Novyi Mir*, 3, 1998, pp. 165-188.
Yakovenko, I, 'Replika', *Znanie-sila*, 4, 1998, pp. 125-127.
Yanin, V, 'Byl li Novgorod Iaroslavlem, a Batyi – Ivanom Kalitoi', *Izvestiia*, June 11, 1998.
Yanin, V, 'Ziiauishchie vysoty akademika Fomenko', *Rodina*, 4, 2000, pp. 12-15.

Secondary Sources in Russian:

Anninskii, L, *Russkie plius*, Algoritm, Moscow, 2001.
Artamonov, M, *Istoriia Khazar*, St-Petersburg, 2002.
Bakunin, M, *Narodnoe delo, Romanov, Pugachev ili Pestel'*, Moscow, 1917.
Beliavskii, M, *M. Lomonosov i osnovanie Moskovskogo universiteta. K 200 letiiu Moskovskogo universiteta 1755-1955*, ed. by Tikhomirov, MGU, Moscow, 1955.
Berdiaev, N, *Sud'ba Rossii, Opyty po Psikhologii Voiny i Natsionalnosti*, Moscow, 1990; St Petersburg, 1918.
Berdiaev, N, *Novoe srednevekovie*, Berlin, 1924.
Borisov, N, 'Otechestvennaia istoriografia o vliianii tataro-mongolskogo nashestvia na russkuiu kulturu,' *Problemy Istorii SSSR*, 5.
Brodsky, N, (ed.), *Rannie slavianofily*, Moscow, 1910.
Burlakov, V, *Mirovaia i otechestvennaia Istoriia*, Kultura, St-Petersburg, 2002.
Vladimirtsov, B, *Chingiz-khan*, Berlin-St-Petersburg-Moscow, 1922.
Vigasin, A, Goder, G, Sventsiskaia, I, *Istoriia drevnego mira*, Prosveshchenie, Moscow, 1993.
Vol'fkovich, S, 'Nikolai Aleksandrovich Morozov, ego zhizn' i trudy po khimii', *Priroda*, 1947, no. 11.
Herzen, A, *Byloe i dumy*, Leningrad, 1947.
Gedeonov, S, *Variagi i Rus'*, St-Petersburg, 1876.
Gedeonov, S, *Otryvki iz issledovanii o variazhskom voprose*, Saint Petersburg, 1862.
Gordeev, A, *Istoriia kazakov*, Strastnoi bulvar, Moscow, 1992.
Grekov, B, *Kievskaia Rus'*, Moscow, Leningrad, 1944.
Grekov, B, Iakubovsky, A, *Zolotaia Orda i ee padenie*, Moscow, Leningrad, 1950.
Hrushevskii, M, *Kievskaia Rus*, St-Petersburg, 1911.
Gumilëv, L, *Drevniaia Rus i velikaia step'*, Mysl', Moscow, 1992.
Gumilëv, L, *Drevnie Turki*, Moscow, 1999.
Gumilëv, L, *Poiski vymyshlennogo tsarstva*, Tanais, Moscow, 1994.
Gumilëv, L, *Chernaia legenda*, Ekopros, Moscow, 1994; AST, 2002.
Gumilëv, L, *Ot Rusi k Rossii*, Leningrad, 1989.
Gumilëv, L, *Etnogenez i biosfera zemli*, Leningrad, 1989.
Gumilëv, L, *Geografiia etnosa v istoricheskii period*, Leningrad, 1990.
Gumilëv, L, 'Biografiia nauchnoi teorii ili avtonekrolog', *Znamia*, 1988
Danilov, S, Nikitin, V, *Ocherki istorii otechestva*, Dashkov dom, Moscow, 2000.
Danilevsky, N, *Rossiia i Evropa*, 5th edition, St Petersburg, 1895.
Drevnerusskaia literatura, Shkola-press, Moscow, 1993.

Dostoevskii, F, *Dnevnik pisatelia*, Berlin, 1922.
Dugin, A, *Osnovy geopolitiki*, Moscow, 1997.
Dugin, A, 'Ot imeni Evrazii,' *Moskovskie Novosti*, 1998, 7.
Istoriia otechestva: *Drevniaia Rus'*, *IX-XIII vekov*; *Moskovskaia Rus'*, *XIII-XVI vekov*; *Moskovskoe Tsarstvo, XVI-XVII vekov*, Norint, St-Petersburg, 2000.
Zabelin, I, *Domashnii byt Russkikh Tsarits v 16-17 stoletiiakh*, Nauka, Novosibirsk, 1992.
Zagoskin, N, *Istoriia prava russkogo naroda*, I, Moscow, 1899.
Zlatkin, 'Ne sintez a eklektika,' *Narody Azii i Afriki*, 1970, 3.
Ilovaiskii, D, *Rozyskaniia o nachale Rusi*, Moscow, 1882.
Ilin, I, *O Rossii*, Sofia, 1934, quoted in Russkii vestnik: Izdanie Leningradskogo otdeleniia Vserossiiskogo fonda kul'tury, no. 1, Leningrad, 1990.
Iskhakov, D, 'Istoriia naroda' in *Tatary, Tatarstan: Spravochnik* ed. Mukhametshin, R, Tatknigizdat, Kazan, 1993.
Ed. by Sandulov, Iu, *Istoriia Rossii, narod i vlast'*, St-Petersburg, 1997
Kazachii Slovar'-Spravochnik, by Skrylov and Gubarenko Cleveland, Ohio, USA, 1966.
Kazachii Slovar'-Spravochnik, II volumes, San-Anselmo, CA, USA, 1968.
Karamzin, N, *Istoriia gosudarstva rossiiskogo*, St-Petersburg, 1851-1853), 12 volumes.
Kargalov, V, *Mongolo-tatarskoe nashestvie na Rusi XIII vek*, Moscow, 1966.
Kargalov, V, *Narod-bogatyr'*, Moscow, 1971.
Kargalov, V, *Sverzhenie Tataro-Mongolskogo iga*, Moscow, 1973.
Kazachestvo, Sobranie, Moscow, 2007.
Kovalev, G, *Istoriia russkikh etnicheskikh nazvanii*, Voronezh, 1982.
Kozhinov, V, *Istoriia Rusi*, Charli, Moscow, 1997.
Kostomarov, N, 'Nachalo edinodershavia v drevnei Rusi', *Sobranie sochinenii*, St-Petersburg, 1905, 5.
Koniskii, G, *Istoriia Russov ili maloi Rusi*, Universiteskaia tipografia, Moscow, 1846.
Klassen, E, *Novye material dlia drevneishei istorii Slavian voobshche i Slaviano-Russov do Riurikovskogo vremeni v osobennosti s legkim ocherkom istorii Russov do Rozhdestva Khristova*, ed. 1-3, with addition *Opisanie pamiatnikov ob'iasniaiushchimi slaviano-russkuiu istoriiu, sostavlennogo Volanskim i perevedennogo Klassenom*, Universitetskaia tipografia, Moscow, 1854, reprint 1995.
Kliuchevskii, V, *Neopublikovannye proizvedeniia*, Nauka, Moscow, 1983.
Kliuchevskii, V, *Kurs russkoi istorii*, Moscow, 5 volumes.
Kulikovskaia bitva v literature i iskusstve, Nauka, Moscow, 1980.
Kuz'min, A, *Padenie Peruna. Stanovlenie Khristianstva na Rusi*, Moscow, 1988.
Lomonosov, M, *Trudy po russkoi istorii, obshchestvenno-ekonomicheskim voprosam i geografii 1747-1765*, Moscow, Leningrad, 1952, vol. 6.
Lomonosov, M, *Polnoe sobranie sochinenii*, ed. Vavilov, S, 10 volumes, Moscow-Leningrad, 1950-59.
Liubavskii, M, *Lektsii po drevnei russkoi istorii do kontsa XVI veka*, St-Petersburg, 2000.
Lyzlov, A, *Istoriia Skifiiskaia*, Nauka, Moscow, 1990.
Maiskii, I, 'Chingiz khan,' *Voprosy Istorii*, 1962, 5.
Mavrodin, V, *Proiskhozhdenie russkogo naroda*, Leningrad, 1978.
Mavrodin, V, *Ocherki po istorii feodalnoi Rusi*, Leningrad, 1949.

Matuzova, V, *Angliiskie srednevekovye istochniki*, Nauka, Moscow, 1979.
Merpert, N, Cherepnin, L, Pashuto, V, 'Chingiz khan i ego nasledie,' *Istoriia SSSR*, 1962.
Mirovaia khudozhestvennaia kultura: Rossiia, IX-XX vekov, 'MKHK', Moscow, 2000.
Mishin, D, *Sakaliba (slaviane) v islamskom mire v rannee srednevekov'e*, Moscow, In-t Vostokovedeniia RAN, Kraft+, 2002.
Moskovskoe gosudarstvo XV-XVII vekov, Kraft+Lean, Moscow, 2000.
Morozov, S, *Zagovor protiv narodov Rossii segodnia*, Algoritm, Moscow, 1999.
Nasonov, A, 'K voprosy ob obrazovanii drevnerusskoi narodnosti,' *Vestnik AN SSSR*, 1951, 8.
Nasonov, A, *Russkaia zemlia' i obrazovanie territorii drevnerusskogo gosudarstva*, Moscow, 1951.
Nasonov, A, *Mongoly i Rus*, Moscow, L, 1940.
Nesterov, F, *Sviaz' Vremen, Opyt Istoricheskoi Publitsistiki*, Moscow, 1980.
Nikolai Aleksandrovich Morozov 1854-1946, Moscow, Nauka, 1981.
Novosel'tsev, A, *Vostochnye istochniki o vostochnykh slavianakh i Rusi VI-IX vekov/Drevnerusskoe gosudarstvo i ego mezhdunarodnoe znachenie*, Moscow, 1965.
Novosel'tsev, A, *Istoriia Rossii s drevneishikh vremen*, AST, Moscow, 1996.
Padalka, L, *O proiskhozhdenii slova Rus'*, Poltava, 1915.
Pamiatniki literatury drevnei Rusi, vtoraia polovina 16 veka, Khudozhesvennaia literatura, Moscow, 1986.
Parkhomenko, V, Sledy polovetskogo etnosa v letopisiakh, *Problemy istochnikovedeniia*, 3, Moscow-Leningrad, 1940.
Parkhomenko, V, *U istokov russkoi gosudarstvennosti*, Leningrad, 1924.
Pogodin, M, *Kniaz Andrei Iurievich Bogoliubsky*, Moscow, 1850.
Pokhlebkin, W, *Tatary i Rus'*, Mezhdunarodnye otnosheniia, Moscow, 2001.
Polevoi, *Istoriia Russkogo naroda*, Veche, Moscow, 1997, v.1.
Poliakov, Iu, *Istoricheskaia nauka: liudi i problemy*, Rosspen, Moscow, 1999.
Popov, I, *Rossiia i Kitai: 300 let na grani voiny*, Moscow, Ast, Astrel', Ermak, 2004.
Plano Carpini, *Istoriia Mongalov/Rubruck, Puteshestvia v vostochnye strany/kniga Marko Polo*, Mysl', Moscow, 1997.
Platonov, O, *Russkaia tsivilizatsia*, Rada, Moscow, 1992.
Priselkov, M, *Istoriia Russkogo letopisaniia XI-XV vekov*, Moscow, 1940.
Radzivillovskaia letopis', Isskustvo, M, Glagol, St-Petersburg, 1995.
Rasovskii, D, 'O roli Chernykh Klobukov v istorii drevnei Rusi,' *Seminarum Kondakovianum* I, 1927.
Rasskazy russkikh letopisei, Detskaia literatura, Moscow, 1973.
Rashid ad-Din, *Sbornik letopisei*, translated by Iu. Verkhovskii, Academy of Sciences USSR, Moscow-Leningrad, 1960.
Rodina, Collection of articles on the Mongols, 3-4, 1997.
Rozanov, V, *O Sebe i Zhizni Svoei*, Moscow, 1990.
Rybakov, B, Sakharov, A, Preobrazhensky, A, Krasnobaev, B, *Istoriia otechestva*, Prosveshchenie, Moscow, 1993.
Rybakov, B, *Drevnie Russy*, Moscow, 1951.
Rybakov, B, 'Problema obrazovaniia drevnerusskoi narodnosti,' *Voprosy Istorii*, 1952, 9.

Rybakov, B, *Kievskaia Rus'*, Progress, Moscow, 1984.
Rybakov, B, *Remeslo drevnei Rusi*, Moscow, 1948.
Rybakov, B, 'O preodolenii samoobmana,' *Voprosy istorii*, 1971, 3.
Sakharov, A, and Buganov, V, *Istoriia Rossii*, Prosveshchenie, Moscow, 1995.
Sedov, V, *U istokov vostochnoslavianskoi gosudarstvennosti*, 'URSS', Moscow, 1999.
Soboleva, N, *Russkie pechati*, Nauka, Moscow, 1991.
Soboleva, N, *Ocherki istorii rossiiskoi simvoliki: Ot tamgi do simvolov gosudarstvennogo suvereniteta*, Iazyki slavianskikh kul'tur, Moscow, 2006.
Sovetskii Entsiklopedicheckii Slovar', *Sovetskaia entsiklopedia*, Moscow, 1984.
Sorokin, P, *O Russkoi natsii: Rossiia i Amerika, teoriia natsionalnogo voprosa*, Moscow, 1994.
Soloviev, S, *Istoriia Rossii s drevneishikh vremen*, volumes 1-6.
Soloviev, V, *Sochinenia*, 2 volumes, Moscow, 1989.
Soloviev, V, *Smysl liubvi*, Moscow, 1991.
Soloviev, V, *Natsional'nyi vopros v Rossii*, St Petersburg, 1888.
Skrynnikov, R, *Boris Godunov*, Academic International Press, 1982.
Skrynnikov, R, *Tsarstvo terrora*, Nauka, St-Petersburg, 1992.
Skrynnikov, R, *Ivan Groznyi*, Nauka, Moscow, 1975.
Skrynnikov, R, *Tragediia Novgoroda*, Sabashnikovykh, Moscow, 1994.
Sukhorukov, *Istoriia Voiska Donskogo*, Don, 1989.
Tikhomirov, M, 'Proiskhozhdenie nazvanii Rus i Russkaia Zemlia', *Russkii Narod*, Kuchkovo pole, Moscow, 2001.
Tikhomirov, M, *Rossiiskoe gosudarstvo XV-XVII vekov,* Moscow, 1973.
Tikhomirov, M, *Russkaia kultura X-XVIII vekov*, Moscow, 1968.
Tretiakov, P, *Vostochnoslavianskie plemena*, Moscow, 1953.
Tretiakov, P, *U istokov drevnerusskoi narodnosti*, Leningrad, 1970.
Troitskii, E, *Russkaia natsia: istoricheskoe proshloe i problemy vozrozhedenia*, Moscow, 1995.
Khrestomatiia po drevnerusskoi literature, Prosveshchenie, 1973.
Shakhmatov, A, *Razyskania o russkikh letopisyakh*, Kuchkovo pole, Moscow, 2001.
Sharapov, S, Aksakov, N, *Germania i Slavianstvo*, Moscow, 1909.
Fedotov, G, *Sud'ba i grekhi Rossii*, St.-Ptersburg, 1992.
Chertkov, A, *Opisaniie drevnikh russkikh monet*, Moscow, 1834.
Chertkov, A, 'O yazyke pelasgov, naselivshikh Italiiu, i sravnenie ego s drevneslovenskim,' *Vremennik Moskovskogo Obshchestva istorii drevnostei Rossiiskikh*, 23, Moscow, 1855.
Cherepnin, L, *Istoricheskie usloviia formirovania russkoi narodnosti do kontsa XV veka*, Moscow, 1957.
Cherepnin, L, *Russkaia Istoriografiia do XIX veka*, Moscow, 1957.
Udal'tsov, A, 'Osnovnye voprosy etnogeneza Slavian,' *Sovetskaia Etnografiia*, 1947, 6-7.
Ukrainskii separatism v Rossii: ideologia natsionalnogo raskola, ed. by Smolin, Moscow, 1998.
Khara-Davan, E, *Chingiz-Khan kak polkovodets i ego nasledie*, Belgrade, 1929.
Yanov, A, *Posle Eltsina*, Moscow, 1995.

Yanov, A, *Rossiia protiv Rossii*, Sibirskii khronograf, 1999.
Iakubovskii, A, 'Feodal'noe obshchestvo Srednei Azii i ee torgovlia s vostochnoi evropy v X-XV' in *Materialy po istorii Uzbekskoi, Tadzhikskoi i Turkmenskoi SSR*, 3, 1, Leningrad, 1932.

Secondary Sources Published Outside of Russia:

Aron, L, 'Russia's revolution', *Commentary*, Nov 2002, v114, n4.
Abu-Lughod, Janet, L, *Before European hegemony: the world system A. D. 1250-1350*, Oxford University Press, Oxford, 1991.
Alter, P, *Nationalism*, Edward Arnold, 1989.
Anderson, B, *Imagined Communities*, Verso, London, 1983.
Auty, R, and Obolensky, D, (eds), *An introduction to Russian History*, Cambridge University Press, Cambridge, 1976.
Bassin, M, 'Russia between Europe and Asia: The Ideological Construction of Geographical Space', *Slavic Review*, 1991, v50, n1.
Bassin, M, '*Asia*' in Nicholas Rzhevsky (ed), *Modern Russian Culture*, Cambridge University Press: Cambridge, 1988.
Bassin, M, 'Turner, Soloviev and the 'Frontier Hypothesis': The Nationalist Significance of Open Spaces', *The Journal of Modern History*, September 1993, v65, n3.
Birch, A, *Nationalism and National Integration*, London, Unwin Hyman, 1989.
Black, J, *G.F. Mueller and the Imperial Russian Academy*, McGill Queen's University Press, Kingston and Montreal, 1986.
Bray, W, *Russian Frontiers from Muscovy to Khrushcev*, Bobbs-Merrill Company, 1963.
Browne, E, *A History of Persian literature under Tartar Dominion*, Cambridge University Press, 1920.
Brandenberger, David, *National Bolshevism: Stalinist mass culture and the formation of modern Russian national identity, 1931-1956*, Harvard University Press, Cambridge, MA, 2002.
Brass, P, *Ethnicity and Nationalism: Theory and Comparison*, Sage publications, 1991.
Brzezinski, Z, 'The Premature Partnership', *Foreign Affairs*, March/April 1994.
Breuilly, J, *Nationalism and the State*, Manchester University Press, 1982.
Brubaker, R, *Nationalism Refrained. Nationhood and the National Question in the New Europe*, Cambridge University Press, Cambridge, 1996.
Brudny, Y, *Reinventing Russia: Russian Nationalism and the Soviet State, 1953-1991*, Harvard University Press, Cambridge, Massachusetts, 1998.
Byrnes, R, *V. O. Kliuchevskii. Historian of Russia*, Bloomington, 1995.
Cameron, D, *Nationalism, Self-Determination and the Quebec Question*, Macmillan, Canada, 1974.
Canovan, M, *Nationhood and Political Theory,* Cheltenham, 1996.
Canovan, M, 'The State of the Nation: Ernest Gellner and the Theory of Nationalism', *American Political Science Review*, Dec 1999, v93, n4.
Carr, F, *Ivan the Terrible*, Barnes and Nobles, Totowa, New Jersey, 1981.

Carr, E.H, *What is History?* Penguin, Harmondsworth, 1964.
Chinn, J, and Kaiser, R, (eds), *Russians as the new minority: ethnicity and nationalism in the Soviet successor states*, Westview Press, Boulder, 1996.
Chulos, C, and Piirainen, T, *The Fall of an Empire, the Birth of a Nation: national identities in Russia*, Ashgate, Aldershot, 2000.
Christian, David, *Russia, Central Asia and Mongolia*, Blackwell Publishers, Malden, 1998.
Clark, K, *The Soviet novel: history as ritual*, Indiana University Press, Bloomington, 2000.
Cleaves, Francis Woodman (ed), *The Secret History of the Mongols*, Harvard University Press, Cambridge, Massachusetts, 1982.
Connel, C, 'Western views of the origins of the 'Tatars': an example of influence of the myth in the second half of the thirteenth century', *Journal of Medieval and Renaissance Studies*, 1973, v3.
Cresson, W, *The Cossacks – Their History and Their Country*, Brentano's, New York, 1919.
Cross, S, Sherbowitz-Wetzor, O, *The Russian Primary Chronicle*, Laurentian text, The Medieval Academy of America, Cambridge, Massachusetts.
Curtiss, J, *The Russian Army under Nicholas I 1825-1855*, Duke University Press.
Daniels, V. N. *Tatishchev: Guardian of the Petrine Revolution*, Franklin Publishing Company, Philadelphia.
Davidson, H, *The Viking Road to Byzantium*, Allen and Unwin, London, 1976.
Davies, N, *Europe: a history*, Oxford University Press, Oxford, 1996.
Davies, S, *Popular Opinion in Stalin's Russia: terror, propaganda, and dissent, 1934-1941*, Cambridge University Press, Cambridge, 1997.
Davies, R, *Soviet History in the Yeltsin Era,* Macmillan, Basingstoke, 1997.
Devlin, J, *Slavophiles and Commissars: Enemies of democracy in modern Russia,* Macmillan: Basingstoke, 1999; St. Martin's Press, New York, 1999.
Dimnik, M, *The Dynasty of Chernigov 1146-1246*, Cambridge University Press.
Dmytryshin, B, *Medieval Russia 900-1700*, Holt, Rinehart and Winston, 1973.
Duncan, P.J.S. and Rady, M, (eds), *Towards a New Community: Culture and Politics in Post-Totalitarian Europe*, LIT Verlag, Hamburg and Munster.
Ely, C, *This Meager Landscape: Landscape and National Identity in Imperial Russia*.
Fedotov, G, *The Russian Religious Mind,* Harvard University Press: Cambridge, 1966.
Fennel, J, *Prince Kurbsky's History of Ivan IV*, 1965, Cambridge University Press.
Fennel, J, *Crisis of Medieval Russia, 1200-1304*, Longman, London, 1983.
Franklin, S, and Shepard, J, *The Emergence of Rus, 750-1200*, Longman, London, 1996.
Gellner, E, *Encounters with Nationalism*, Blackwell, 1994.
Gellner, E, *Nations and Nationalism*, Blackwell, 1983.
Gleeson, W, 'The course of Russian History According to an eighteenth Century layman'', *Laurentian University Review*, 1977, v10, n1.
Greenfeld, L, *Nationalism: Five Roads to Modernity*, Harvard University Press, Cambridge, Mass, 1992.
Grekov, B, *Kiev Rus*, trans. by Sdobnikov, Foreign Languages Publishing House, Moscow, 1959.
Gvosdev, N, 'The Slavophiles speak to America', *Journal of Church and State*, Winter

2000, v42, n1.
Gumilev, L, *Searches for an imaginary kingdom: the legend of the kingdom of Prester John*, translated by R.E.F. Smith, Cambridge University Press, Cambridge, 1987.
Halperin, C, *The Tatar Yoke*, Slavica Publishers, Inc., 1985.
Halperin, C, *Russia and the Golden Horde: the Mongol impact on modern medieval history*, Indiana University Press, Bloomington, 1985.
Harris, N, *National Liberation*, Penguin Books, 1990.
Hastings, A, *The construction of nationhood: ethnicity, religion, and nationalism*, Cambridge University Press, Cambridge, 1997.
Hertz, F, *Nationality in History and Politics*, London, Routlidge and Kegan, Paul Ltd, 1966.
Hobsbawn, E, *Nations and Nationalism since 1780: Program, Myth, Reality*, Cambridge University Press, 1990.
Hobsbawn, E, and Ranger, T, (eds), *The Invention of tradition*, Cambridge University Press, Cambridge, 1983.
Hoffman, D, and Kotsonis, Y, (eds), *Russian Modernity: Politics, Knowledge, Practices*, St. Martin's Press, New York, 2000.
Hosking G, and Schopflin, G, *Myths and Nationhood*, Hurst and Company, London, 1997.
Hosking, G, *Russia and the Russians*, Harvard University Press, Massachusetts, 2001.
Hosking, G, *The Russian Constitutional Experiment*, Cambridge, 1973.
Hosking, G, *Russia. People and Empire 1552-1917*, London, 1997.
Howe, S, *The False Dmitri*, London, Williams and Norgate, 1916.
Howes, Robert Craig, *The Testaments of the Grand Princes of Moscow*, Translated and edited with commentary by Robert Craig Howes, Ithaca, N.Y: Cornell University Press, 1967.
Hurwitz, E, *Prince A. Bogoliubskii: The Man and the Myth*, Firenze, 1981.
Johnston, R, Kofman, E, Knight, D, *Nationalism, Self-Determination and Political Geography*, Groom Helm, 1988.
Keenan, E, 'On Certain Mythical Beliefs and Russian Behaviors', in *The Legacy of History in Russia and the New States of Eurasia*, ed. S. Frederick Starr, Armonk, NY, M.E. Sharpe, 1994.
Kennan, G, *The Decline of Bismarck's European Order 1875-1890*, Princeton University Press, 1979.
Kerblay, B, *Modern Soviet Society*, London, Methuen, 1983.
Khazanov, A, 'Ethnic nationalism in the Russian Federation', *Daedalus*, summer 1997, v126, n3.
Khazanov, A, *After the USSR: Ethnicity, Nationalism, and Politics in the Common-wealth of Independent States* (Madison, WI: University of Wisconsin Press, 1995).
King, D, *The Commissar Vanishes: the falsification of photographs and art in Stalin's Russia*, Henry Holt and Company, New York, 1997.
Kohn, H, *The Idea of Nationalism: A Study in its Origins and Background*, NY, The Macmillan Company, 1945.
Koretskii, V, 'Mongol Yoke in Russia', in *Modern Encyclopedia of Russian and Soviet History*, vol. 23.
Koutaissoff, E, Tatishchev's 'Joachim Chronicle', *University of Birmingham Historical*

Journal, 1951, v3, n1.
Khrushcheva, N, 'Solzhenitsyn's History Lesson', *The Nation*, 1999, v268, n16.
Kupchan, C, (ed.). *Nationalism and Nationalities in the New Europe*, Ithaca, 1995.
Kuzmina, E, and Mair, V, *The Prehistory of the Silk Road*, University of Pennsylvania press, 2007.
Lacqueur, W, *Russia and Germany: A Century of Conflict*, Weidenfeld and Nicholson, 1965.
Lacqueur, W, *The Black Hundred*, Harper Collins publishers, 1993.
Laxdaela saga, translated by M. Magnusson and H. Palsson, Penguin books, 1969, 1972, 1975, 1976.
Lieven, D.C.B, *Russia and the origins of the First World War*, Macmillan Press, London, 1983.
Marsden, John, *Harald Hardrada*, Sutton, Oxbow books, 2007.
Martin, Janet, *Medieval Russia 980-1584*, Cambridge University Press, 1995.
Martin, M, *The Soviet Tragedy. A History of Socialism in Russia, 1917-1991*, New York, The Free Press, 1994.
Massie, R, *Peter the Great*, London, 1981.
Masson, J, Smith Jr., 'Nomads on Ponies vs. Slavs on Horses,' *The Journal of the American Oriental Society*, Jan-March 1998, v118, n1.
Melvin, N, *Russians Beyond Russia. The Politics of National Identity*, London, 1995.
Mendelson, S, 'Russians' Rights Imperiled. Has Anybody Noticed?' *International Security*, 2002, v26, n4.
McDaniel, T, *The Agony of the Russian Idea*, Princeton University Press, 1996.
Morgan, David, *The Mongols*, Basil Blackwell, 1986.
Neumann, I, *Russia and the Idea of Europe*, London and New York, 1996.
Nodia, Gia, 'Nationalism and Democracy,' in L. Diamond & M. F. Plattner (eds), *Nationalism, Ethnic Conflict, and Democracy*, Baltimore, 1994.
Noonan, T, Rus', 'Pechenegs and Polovtsi: Economic Interaction along the Steppe Frontier in the pre-Mongol Era', *Russian History*, 1992, v19, n1-4.
Ostrowski, D, *Muscovy and the Mongols. Cross-cultural influences on the steppe frontier, 1304-1589*, Cambridge University Press, Cambridge, 1998.
Paul, M, 'The Military Revolution in Russia, 1550-1682' The *Journal of Military History*, January 2004, v68, n1.
Payne R, and Romanoff, N, *Ivan the Terrible*, Cooper Square Press, 2002.
Paszkiewicz, H, *The Making of the Russian Nation*, Greenwood press, 1977.
Perry, M, *The Image of Ivan the Terrible in Russian Folklore*, Cambridge University Press, 1987.
Perrie, M, *The Cult of Ivan the Terrible in Stalin's Russia*, New York, Palgrave, 2000.
Petrovich, M, *The Emergence of Russian Panslavism, 1856-1870*, Columbia University Press, 1966.
Pingrose, M, Lerner, A, *Reimagining the Nation*, Open University Press, 1993.
Poe, M, *A People Born to Slavery, Russia in early modern European ethnography, 1476-1748*, Cornell University Press, Ithaca, 2000.
Plumb, J, *The Death of the Past*, Macmillan, London, 1969.

Pritsak, O, *Studies in medieval Eurasian history*, Variorum Reprints, London, 1981.
Rambaud, *History of Russia*, AMS press, New York, 1970.
Riasanosvky, N, *Russia and the West in the Teaching of the Slavophiles*, Gloucester, Mass., Peter Smith, 1965.
Riasanovsky, N, *Nicholas I and official nationality in Russia, 1825-1855*, University of California Press, Berkeley, 1959.
Riasonavsky, A, 'Pseudo-Varangian Origins of the Kievo-Pecherski Monastery: The 'Finger in the Pie' Hypothesis', *Russian History/Histoire Russe*, 7, Pt.3, 1980.
Rogers, G, 'An examination of historians' explanations for the Mongol withdrawal from East Central Europe', *East European Quarterly*, spring 1996, v30, n1.
Rogger, H, *National Consciousness in Eighteenth Century Russia*, Cambridge U.P, Cambridge, 1960.
Rogowski, R, Tiryakian, E, *New Nationalisms of the Developed West*, Boston, Allen Unwin, 1985.
Rowley, D, 'Imperial versus national discourse: the case of Russia,' *Nations and Nationalism*, 6 (1), 2000, 23-42.
Said, E, *Orientalism*, Penguin, London, 1995.
Salisbury, H, *War Between Russia and China*, New York, 1969.
Schwab, G, 'Traveling literature, traveling theory: literature and cultural contact between East and West', *Studies in the Humanities*, June 2002, v29, n1.
Seaton, A, *The Horsemen of the Steppes: The Story of the Cossacks*, Hippocrene books, New York, 1985.
Seton-Watson, H, *Nations and States*, Methuen, London, 1982.
Silverstein, B, 'Islam and Modernity in Turkey: Power, Tradition and Historicity in the European Provinces of the Muslim World', *Anthropological Quarterly*, Volume 76, Number 3, Summer 2003.
Sinor, D, 'Horse and Pasture in Inner Asian History', *Oriens Extremis*, 19, 1972.
Shetelig, H, and Falk, H, translated by E. Gordon, *Scandinavian Archaeology*, Oxford, Calrendon Press, 1937.
Shlapentokh, D, 'Eurasianism: past and present,' *Communist and Post-Communist Studies*, 1997, v30, n2.
Shlapentokh, D, 'Russia on the Eve. The Illusions and Realities of Russian Nationalism', *The Washington Quarterly*, 2000, v23, n1.
Shlapentokh, D, 'Russian nationalism today: the views of Alexander Dugin,' *Contemporary Review*, July 2001, v279, n1626.
Shnirelman, V, *Who gets the Past? Competition for Ancestors among Non-Russian Intellectuals in Russia*, John Hopkins University Press, 1996.
Shnirelman, V, Panarin, S, 'Lev Gumilev: His Pretensions as a Founder of Ethnology and his Eurasian theories', *Inner Asia*, 2001, n3.
Skrynnikov, R, *Ivan the Terrible*, edited and translated by Hugh F. Graham, Gulf Breeze, FL, Academic International Press, 1981.
Slezkine, Yu, 'Who Gets the Past: Competition for Ancestors Among Non-Russian Intellectuals in Russia (book review)', *The Journal of Modern History*, Sept 1998, v70, n3.

Solonari, V, 'Creating a 'People': A Case Study in Post-Soviet History-Writing', *Kritika: Explorations in Russian and Eurasian History*, 2003, v4, n2.
Smith, A, *Theories of Nationalism*, Gerald Duckworth and Company Limited, 1971.
Smith, A, *The Ethnic Revival*, Cambridge University Press, 1981.
Smith, A, *Nationalism in the twentieth century*, N.Y. University Press, 1979.
Smith, A, *Nationalist Movements*, the Macmillan Press, Ltd, 1976.
Smith, A, *The Ethnic Origins of Nations*, Oxford University Press, 1986.
Szporluk, R, 'The Ukraine and Russia', in R. Conquest (ed.), *The Last Empire, Nationality and the Soviet Future*, Stanford University Press, 1986.
Szporluk, R, 'After Empire: What?', *Daedalus*, Summer 1994, v123, n3.
Snyder, L, *Global Mini-Nationalisms: Autonomy or Independence*, Greenwood Press, 1982.
Stender-Petersen, A, *Varangica,* Aarhus, 1953.
Sturluson, Snorri, *Heimskringla*, translated with an introduction by Magnus Magnusson and Hermann Pálsson, Penguin, Harmondsworth, 1966.
Suny, R, *The Revenge of the Past*, Stanford, 1993.
Tamir, Y, 'The enigma of nationalism', *World Politics,* April 1995, v47, n3.
Thaden, E, *Conservative Nationalism in Nineteenth Century Russia*, University of Washington Press, Seattle, 1964.
Thaden, E, 'V. Tatischev, German Historians, and the St-Petersburg Academy of Sciences,' *Russian History*, 13, 4, winter 1986.
Thaden, E, *The Rise of Historicism in Russia*, Peter Lang, NY, 1999.
The Mission to Asia: narratives and letters of the Franciscan missionaries in Mongolia and China in the thirteenth and fourteenth centuries, translated by a Nun of Stanbrook Abbey, ed. by Christopher Dawson, Sheed and Ward, London, 1955.
The Mongol Empire and its Legacy, ed. by David Morgan and Amitai-Preiss, Brill, Leiden-Boston-Koln, 1999.
Thomsen, V, *The relations between ancient Russia and Scandinavia and the origin of the Russian state,* B. Franklin, New York, 1877.
Tishkhov, V, *Ethnicity, Nationalism and Conflict in and after the Soviet Union: The Mind Aflame*, London, 1997.
Tismaneanu, V, 'Discomforts of victory: democracy, liberal values and nationalism in post-communist Europe', *West European Politics*, April 2002, v25, n2.
Tolz, V, *Russia: Inventing a Nation*, Arnold, Hodder Headline group, 2001.
Tolz, V, 'Forging the nation: National identity and nation building in post-Communist Russia', *Europe-Asia Studies*, Abingdon, September 1998, 50, 6.
Toledano, R, 'The 'Mystery' of Christopher Columbus', *Midstream*, Feb 2001, v47.
Toynbee, A, *A Study of History*, Oxford University Press, Oxford, 1934, 1935 and 1945.
Trubetskoi, N, *The Legacy of Chengiz-Khan*, Michigan Slavic Publications, Ann Arbor, 1991.
Tuminez, A, 'Nationalism, Ethnic Pressures, and the Breakup of the Soviet Union', *Journal of Cold War Studies*, Sept 1, 2003, v5, I4.
Verdery, K, 'Whither "nation" and "nationalism"?' *Daedalus*, summer 1993, v122, n3.
Vernadsky, G, *A History of Russia: Russia and the Mongols*, vol. 3, Yale University Press,

1952.
Vernadsky, G, *Kievan Russia*, Yale University Press, New Haven and London, 1948.
Volkogonov, D, *Stalin: Triumph and Tragedy*, edited and translated by Harold Shukman, Weidenfeld and Nicolson, London, 1991.
White, H, *Metahistory: the historical imagination in nineteenth-century Europe*, Johns Hopkins University, Baltimore, 1973.
Windschuttle, K, *The Killing of History: How a Discipline is Being Murdered by Literary Critics and Social Theorists*, Macleay, Paddingtone, 1994.
Yanov, A, 'Russian nationalism in Western studies: misadventures of a Moribund paradigm', *Demokratizatsiya*, Fall 2001, v9, n4.
Yurganov, A, 'The Father of Tsarism', *Russian Life*, Jan 1997, v40, n1.

SOVIET AND POST-SOVIET POLITICS AND SOCIETY

Edited by Dr. Andreas Umland

ISSN 1614-3515

1 *Андреас Умланд (ред.)*
Воплощение Европейской конвенции по правам человека в России
Философские, юридические и эмпирические исследования
ISBN 3-89821-387-0

2 *Christian Wipperfürth*
Russland – ein vertrauenswürdiger Partner?
Grundlagen, Hintergründe und Praxis gegenwärtiger russischer Außenpolitik
Mit einem Vorwort von Heinz Timmermann
ISBN 3-89821-401-X

3 *Manja Hussner*
Die Übernahme internationalen Rechts in die russische und deutsche Rechtsordnung
Eine vergleichende Analyse zur Völkerrechtsfreundlichkeit der Verfassungen der Russländischen Föderation und der Bundesrepublik Deutschland
Mit einem Vorwort von Rainer Arnold
ISBN 3-89821-438-9

4 *Matthew Tejada*
Bulgaria's Democratic Consolidation and the Kozloduy Nuclear Power Plant (KNPP)
The Unattainability of Closure
With a foreword by Richard J. Crampton
ISBN 3-89821-439-7

5 *Марк Григорьевич Меерович*
Квадратные метры, определяющие сознание
Государственная жилищная политика в СССР. 1921 – 1941 гг
ISBN 3-89821-474-5

6 *Andrei P. Tsygankov, Pavel A.Tsygankov (Eds.)*
New Directions in Russian International Studies
ISBN 3-89821-422-2

7 *Марк Григорьевич Меерович*
Как власть народ к труду приучала
Жилище в СССР – средство управления людьми. 1917 – 1941 гг.
С предисловием Елены Осокиной
ISBN 3-89821-495-8

8 *David J. Galbreath*
Nation-Building and Minority Politics in Post-Socialist States
Interests, Influence and Identities in Estonia and Latvia
With a foreword by David J. Smith
ISBN 3-89821-467-2

9 *Алексей Юрьевич Безугольный*
Народы Кавказа в Вооруженных силах СССР в годы Великой Отечественной войны 1941-1945 гг.
С предисловием Николая Бугая
ISBN 3-89821-475-3

10 *Вячеслав Лихачев и Владимир Прибыловский (ред.)*
Русское Национальное Единство, 1990-2000. В 2-х томах
ISBN 3-89821-523-7

11 *Николай Бугай (ред.)*
Народы стран Балтии в условиях сталинизма (1940-е – 1950-е годы)
Документированная история
ISBN 3-89821-525-3

12 *Ingmar Bredies (Hrsg.)*
Zur Anatomie der Orange Revolution in der Ukraine
Wechsel des Elitenregimes oder Triumph des Parlamentarismus?
ISBN 3-89821-524-5

13 *Anastasia V. Mitrofanova*
The Politicization of Russian Orthodoxy
Actors and Ideas
With a foreword by William C. Gay
ISBN 3-89821-481-8

14 Nathan D. Larson
Alexander Solzhenitsyn and the
Russo-Jewish Question
ISBN 3-89821-483-4

15 Guido Houben
Kulturpolitik und Ethnizität
Staatliche Kunstförderung im Russland der
neunziger Jahre
Mit einem Vorwort von Gert Weisskirchen
ISBN 3-89821-542-3

16 Leonid Luks
Der russische „Sonderweg"?
Aufsätze zur neuesten Geschichte Russlands
im europäischen Kontext
ISBN 3-89821-496-6

17 Евгений Мороз
История «Мёртвой воды» – от
страшной сказки к большой
политике
Политическое неоязычество в
постсоветской России
ISBN 3-89821-551-2

18 Александр Верховский и Галина
Кожевникова (ред.)
Этническая и религиозная
интолерантность в российских СМИ
Результаты мониторинга 2001-2004 гг.
ISBN 3-89821-569-5

19 Christian Ganzer
Sowjetisches Erbe und ukrainische
Nation
Das Museum der Geschichte des Zaporoger
Kosakentums auf der Insel Chortycja
Mit einem Vorwort von Frank Golczewski
ISBN 3-89821-504-0

20 Эльза-Баир Гучинова
Помнить нельзя забыть
Антропология депортационной травмы
калмыков
С предисловием Кэролайн Хамфри
ISBN 3-89821-506-7

21 Юлия Лидерман
Мотивы «проверки» и «испытания»
в постсоветской культуре
Советское прошлое в российском
кинематографе 1990-х годов
С предисловием Евгения Марголита
ISBN 3-89821-511-3

22 Tanya Lokshina, Ray Thomas, Mary
Mayer (Eds.)
The Imposition of a Fake Political
Settlement in the Northern Caucasus
The 2003 Chechen Presidential Election
ISBN 3-89821-436-2

23 Timothy McCajor Hall, Rosie Read
(Eds.)
Changes in the Heart of Europe
Recent Ethnographies of Czechs, Slovaks,
Roma, and Sorbs
With an afterword by Zdeněk Salzmann
ISBN 3-89821-606-3

24 Christian Autengruber
Die politischen Parteien in Bulgarien
und Rumänien
Eine vergleichende Analyse seit Beginn der
90er Jahre
Mit einem Vorwort von Dorothée de Nève
ISBN 3-89821-476-1

25 Annette Freyberg-Inan with Radu
Cristescu
The Ghosts in Our Classrooms, or:
John Dewey Meets Ceauşescu
The Promise and the Failures of Civic
Education in Romania
ISBN 3-89821-416-8

26 John B. Dunlop
The 2002 Dubrovka and 2004 Beslan
Hostage Crises
A Critique of Russian Counter-Terrorism
With a foreword by Donald N. Jensen
ISBN 3-89821-608-X

27 Peter Koller
Das touristische Potenzial von
Kam''janec–Podil's'kyj
Eine fremdenverkehrsgeographische
Untersuchung der Zukunftsperspektiven und
Maßnahmenplanung zur
Destinationsentwicklung des „ukrainischen
Rothenburg"
Mit einem Vorwort von Kristiane Klemm
ISBN 3-89821-640-3

28 Françoise Daucé, Elisabeth Sieca-
Kozlowski (Eds.)
Dedovshchina in the Post-Soviet
Military
Hazing of Russian Army Conscripts in a
Comparative Perspective
With a foreword by Dale Herspring
ISBN 3-89821-616-0

29 Florian Strasser
    Zivilgesellschaftliche Einflüsse auf die
    Orange Revolution
    Die gewaltlose Massenbewegung und die
    ukrainische Wahlkrise 2004
    Mit einem Vorwort von Egbert Jahn
    ISBN 3-89821-648-9

30 Rebecca S. Katz
    The Georgian Regime Crisis of 2003-
    2004
    A Case Study in Post-Soviet Media
    Representation of Politics, Crime and
    Corruption
    ISBN 3-89821-413-3

31 Vladimir Kantor
    Willkür oder Freiheit
    Beiträge zur russischen Geschichtsphilosophie
    Ediert von Dagmar Herrmann sowie mit
    einem Vorwort versehen von Leonid Luks
    ISBN 3-89821-589-X

32 Laura A. Victoir
    The Russian Land Estate Today
    A Case Study of Cultural Politics in Post-
    Soviet Russia
    With a foreword by Priscilla Roosevelt
    ISBN 3-89821-426-5

33 Ivan Katchanovski
    Cleft Countries
    Regional Political Divisions and Cultures in
    Post-Soviet Ukraine and Moldova
    With a foreword by Francis Fukuyama
    ISBN 3-89821-558-X

34 Florian Mühlfried
    Postsowjetische Feiern
    Das Georgische Bankett im Wandel
    Mit einem Vorwort von Kevin Tuite
    ISBN 3-89821-601-2

35 Roger Griffin, Werner Loh, Andreas
    Umland (Eds.)
    Fascism Past and Present, West and
    East
    An International Debate on Concepts and
    Cases in the Comparative Study of the
    Extreme Right
    With an afterword by Walter Laqueur
    ISBN 3-89821-674-8

36 Sebastian Schlegel
    Der „Weiße Archipel"
    Sowjetische Atomstädte 1945-1991
    Mit einem Geleitwort von Thomas Bohn
    ISBN 3-89821-679-9

37 Vyacheslav Likhachev
    Political Anti-Semitism in Post-Soviet
    Russia
    Actors and Ideas in 1991-2003
    Edited and translated from Russian by Eugene
    Veklerov
    ISBN 3-89821-529-6

38 Josette Baer (Ed.)
    Preparing Liberty in Central Europe
    Political Texts from the Spring of Nations
    1848 to the Spring of Prague 1968
    With a foreword by Zdeněk V. David
    ISBN 3-89821-546-6

39 Михаил Лукьянов
    Российский консерватизм и
    реформа, 1907-1914
    С предисловием Марка Д. Стейнберга
    ISBN 3-89821-503-2

40 Nicola Melloni
    Market Without Economy
    The 1998 Russian Financial Crisis
    With a foreword by Eiji Furukawa
    ISBN 3-89821-407-9

41 Dmitrij Chmelnizki
    Die Architektur Stalins
    Bd. 1: Studien zu Ideologie und Stil
    Bd. 2: Bilddokumentation
    Mit einem Vorwort von Bruno Flierl
    ISBN 3-89821-515-6

42 Katja Yafimava
    Post-Soviet Russian-Belarussian
    Relationships
    The Role of Gas Transit Pipelines
    With a foreword by Jonathan P. Stern
    ISBN 3-89821-655-1

43 Boris Chavkin
    Verflechtungen der deutschen und
    russischen Zeitgeschichte
    Aufsätze und Archivfunde zu den
    Beziehungen Deutschlands und der
    Sowjetunion von 1917 bis 1991
    Ediert von Markus Edlinger sowie mit einem
    Vorwort versehen von Leonid Luks
    ISBN 3-89821-756-6

44 Anastasija Grynenko in
    Zusammenarbeit mit Claudia Dathe
    Die Terminologie des Gerichtswesens
    der Ukraine und Deutschlands im
    Vergleich
    Eine übersetzungswissenschaftliche Analyse
    juristischer Fachbegriffe im Deutschen,
    Ukrainischen und Russischen
    Mit einem Vorwort von Ulrich Hartmann
    ISBN 3-89821-691-8

45 Anton Burkov
    The Impact of the European
    Convention on Human Rights on
    Russian Law
    Legislation and Application in 1996-2006
    With a foreword by Françoise Hampson
    ISBN 978-3-89821-639-5

46 Stina Torjesen, Indra Overland (Eds.)
    International Election Observers in
    Post-Soviet Azerbaijan
    Geopolitical Pawns or Agents of Change?
    ISBN 978-3-89821-743-9

47 Taras Kuzio
    Ukraine – Crimea – Russia
    Triangle of Conflict
    ISBN 978-3-89821-761-3

48 Claudia Šabić
    "Ich erinnere mich nicht, aber L'viv!"
    Zur Funktion kultureller Faktoren für die
    Institutionalisierung und Entwicklung einer
    ukrainischen Region
    Mit einem Vorwort von Melanie Tatur
    ISBN 978-3-89821-752-1

49 Marlies Bilz
    Tatarstan in der Transformation
    Nationaler Diskurs und Politische Praxis
    1988-1994
    Mit einem Vorwort von Frank Golczewski
    ISBN 978-3-89821-722-4

50 Марлен Ларюэль (ред.)
    Современные интерпретации
    русского национализма
    ISBN 978-3-89821-795-8

51 Sonja Schüler
    Die ethnische Dimension der Armut
    Roma im postsozialistischen Rumänien
    Mit einem Vorwort von Anton Sterbling
    ISBN 978-3-89821-776-7

52 Галина Кожевникова
    Радикальный национализм в России
    и противодействие ему
    Сборник докладов Центра «Сова» за 2004-
    2007 гг.
    С предисловием Александра Верховского
    ISBN 978-3-89821-721-7

53 Галина Кожевникова и Владимир
    Прибыловский
    Российская власть в биографиях I
    Высшие должностные лица РФ в 2004 г.
    ISBN 978-3-89821-796-5

54 Галина Кожевникова и Владимир
    Прибыловский
    Российская власть в биографиях II
    Члены Правительства РФ в 2004 г.
    ISBN 978-3-89821-797-2

55 Галина Кожевникова и Владимир
    Прибыловский
    Российская власть в биографиях III
    Руководители федеральных служб и
    агентств РФ в 2004 г.
    ISBN 978-3-89821-798-9

56 Ileana Petroniu
    Privatisierung in
    Transformationsökonomien
    Determinanten der Restrukturierungs-
    Bereitschaft am Beispiel Polens, Rumäniens
    und der Ukraine
    Mit einem Vorwort von Rainer W. Schäfer
    ISBN 978-3-89821-790-3

57 Christian Wipperfürth
    Russland und seine GUS-Nachbarn
    Hintergründe, aktuelle Entwicklungen und
    Konflikte in einer ressourcenreichen Region
    ISBN 978-3-89821-801-6

58 Togzhan Kassenova
    From Antagonism to Partnership
    The Uneasy Path of the U.S.-Russian
    Cooperative Threat Reduction
    With a foreword by Christoph Bluth
    ISBN 978-3-89821-707-1

59 Alexander Höllwerth
    Das sakrale eurasische Imperium des
    Aleksandr Dugin
    Eine Diskursanalyse zum postsowjetischen
    russischen Rechtsextremismus
    Mit einem Vorwort von Dirk Uffelmann
    ISBN 978-3-89821-813-9

60 Олег Рябов
«Россия-Матушка»
Национализм, гендер и война в России XX века
С предисловием Елены Гощило
ISBN 978-3-89821-487-2

61 *Ivan Maistrenko*
Borot'bism
A Chapter in the History of the Ukrainian Revolution
With a new introduction by Chris Ford
Translated by George S. N. Luckyj with the assistance of Ivan L. Rudnytsky
ISBN 978-3-89821-697-5

62 *Maryna Romanets*
Anamorphosic Texts and Reconfigured Visions
Improvised Traditions in Contemporary Ukrainian and Irish Literature
ISBN 978-3-89821-576-3

63 *Paul D'Anieri and Taras Kuzio (Eds.)*
Aspects of the Orange Revolution I
Democratization and Elections in Post-Communist Ukraine
ISBN 978-3-89821-698-2

64 *Bohdan Harasymiw in collaboration with Oleh S. Ilnytzkyj (Eds.)*
Aspects of the Orange Revolution II
Information and Manipulation Strategies in the 2004 Ukrainian Presidential Elections
ISBN 978-3-89821-699-9

65 *Ingmar Bredies, Andreas Umland and Valentin Yakushik (Eds.)*
Aspects of the Orange Revolution III
The Context and Dynamics of the 2004 Ukrainian Presidential Elections
ISBN 978-3-89821-803-0

66 *Ingmar Bredies, Andreas Umland and Valentin Yakushik (Eds.)*
Aspects of the Orange Revolution IV
Foreign Assistance and Civic Action in the 2004 Ukrainian Presidential Elections
ISBN 978-3-89821-808-5

67 *Ingmar Bredies, Andreas Umland and Valentin Yakushik (Eds.)*
Aspects of the Orange Revolution V
Institutional Observation Reports on the 2004 Ukrainian Presidential Elections
ISBN 978-3-89821-809-2

68 *Taras Kuzio (Ed.)*
Aspects of the Orange Revolution VI
Post-Communist Democratic Revolutions in Comparative Perspective
ISBN 978-3-89821-820-7

69 *Tim Bohse*
Autoritarismus statt Selbstverwaltung
Die Transformation der kommunalen Politik in der Stadt Kaliningrad 1990-2005
Mit einem Geleitwort von Stefan Troebst
ISBN 978-3-89821-782-8

70 *David Rupp*
Die Rußländische Föderation und die russischsprachige Minderheit in Lettland
Eine Fallstudie zur Anwaltspolitik Moskaus gegenüber den russophonen Minderheiten im „Nahen Ausland" von 1991 bis 2002
Mit einem Vorwort von Helmut Wagner
ISBN 978-3-89821-778-1

71 *Taras Kuzio*
Theoretical and Comparative Perspectives on Nationalism
New Directions in Cross-Cultural and Post-Communist Studies
With a foreword by Paul Robert Magocsi
ISBN 978-3-89821-815-3

72 *Christine Teichmann*
Die Hochschultransformation im heutigen Osteuropa
Kontinuität und Wandel bei der Entwicklung des postkommunistischen Universitätswesens
Mit einem Vorwort von Oskar Anweiler
ISBN 978-3-89821-842-9

73 *Julia Kusznir*
Der politische Einfluss von Wirtschaftseliten in russischen Regionen
Eine Analyse am Beispiel der Erdöl- und Erdgasindustrie, 1992-2005
Mit einem Vorwort von Wolfgang Eichwede
ISBN 978-3-89821-821-4

74 *Alena Vysotskaya*
Russland, Belarus und die EU-Osterweiterung
Zur Minderheitenfrage und zum Problem der Freizügigkeit des Personenverkehrs
Mit einem Vorwort von Katlijn Malfliet
ISBN 978-3-89821-822-1

75 Heiko Pleines (Hrsg.)
Corporate Governance in post-
sozialistischen Volkswirtschaften
ISBN 978-3-89821-766-8

76 Stefan Ihrig
Wer sind die Moldawier?
Rumänismus versus Moldowanismus in
Historiographie und Schulbüchern der
Republik Moldova, 1991-2006
Mit einem Vorwort von Holm Sundhaussen
ISBN 978-3-89821-466-7

77 Galina Kozhevnikova in collaboration
with Alexander Verkhovsky and
Eugene Veklerov
Ultra-Nationalism and Hate Crimes in
Contemporary Russia
The 2004-2006 Annual Reports of Moscow's
SOVA Center
With a foreword by Stephen D. Shenfield
ISBN 978-3-89821-868-9

78 Florian Küchler
The Role of the European Union in
Moldova's Transnistria Conflict
With a foreword by Christopher Hill
ISBN 978-3-89821-850-4

79 Bernd Rechel
The Long Way Back to Europe
Minority Protection in Bulgaria
With a foreword by Richard Crampton
ISBN 978-3-89821-863-4

80 Peter W. Rodgers
Nation, Region and History in Post-
Communist Transitions
Identity Politics in Ukraine, 1991-2006
With a foreword by Vera Tolz
ISBN 978-3-89821-903-7

81 Stephanie Solywoda
The Life and Work of
Semen L. Frank
A Study of Russian Religious Philosophy
With a foreword by Philip Walters
ISBN 978-3-89821-457-5

82 Vera Sokolova
Cultural Politics of Ethnicity
Discourses on Roma in Communist
Czechoslovakia
ISBN 978-3-89821-864-1

83 Natalya Shevchik Ketenci
Kazakhstani Enterprises in Transition
The Role of Historical Regional Development
in Kazakhstan's Post-Soviet Economic
Transformation
ISBN 978-3-89821-831-3

84 Martin Malek,
Anna Schor-Tschudnowskaja (Hrsg.)
Europa im Tschetschenienkrieg
Zwischen politischer Ohnmacht und
Gleichgültigkeit
Mit einem Vorwort von Lipchan Basajewa
ISBN 978-3-89821-676-0

85 Stefan Meister
Das postsowjetische
Universitätswesen zwischen
nationalem und internationalem
Wandel
Die Entwicklung der regionalen Hochschule
in Russland als Gradmesser der
Systemtransformation
Mit einem Vorwort von Joan DeBardeleben
ISBN 978-3-89821-891-7

86 Konstantin Sheiko
in collaboration with Stephen Brown
Nationalist Imaginings of the Russian
Past
Anatolii Fomenko and the Rise of Alternative
History in Post-Communist Russia
With a foreword by Donald Ostrowski
ISBN 978-3-89821-915-0

FORTHCOMING (MANUSCRIPT WORKING TITLES)

Margaret Dikovitskaya
Arguing with the Photographs
Russian Imperial Colonial Attitudes in Visual Culture
ISBN 3-89821-462-1

Sergei M. Plekhanov
Russian Nationalism in the Age of
Globalization
ISBN 3-89821-484-2

Robert Pyrah
Cultural Memory and Identity
Literature, Criticism and the Theatre in Lviv - Lwow -
Lemberg, 1918-1939 and in post-Soviet Ukraine
ISBN 3-89821-505-9

Andrei Rogatchevski
The National-Bolshevik Party
ISBN 3-89821-532-6

Zenon Victor Wasyliw
Soviet Culture in the Ukrainian Village
The Transformation of Everyday Life and Values, 1921-1928
ISBN 3-89821-536-9

Nele Sass
Das gegenkulturelle Milieu im postsowjetischen Russland
ISBN 3-89821-543-1

Julie Elkner
Maternalism versus Militarism
The Russian Soldiers' Mothers Committee
ISBN 3-89821-575-X

Alexandra Kamarowsky
Russia's Post-crisis Growth
ISBN 3-89821-580-6

Martin Friessnegg
Das Problem der Medienfreiheit in Russland seit dem Ende der Sowjetunion
ISBN 3-89821-588-1

Nikolaj Nikiforowitsch Borobow
Führende Persönlichkeiten in Russland vom 12. bis 20. Jhd.: Ein Lexikon
Aus dem Russischen übersetzt und herausgegeben von Eberhard Schneider
ISBN 3-89821-638-1

Andreas Langenohl
Political Culture and Criticism of Society
Intellectual Articulations in Post-Soviet Russia
ISBN 3-89821-709-4

Thomas Borén
Meeting Places in Transformation
ISBN 3-89821-739-6

Lars Löckner
Sowjetrussland in der Beurteilung der Emigrantenzeitung 'Rul', 1920-1924
ISBN 3-89821-741-8

Ekaterina Taratuta
The Red Line of Construction
Semantics and Mythology of a Siberian Heliopolis
ISBN 3-89821-742-6

Bernd Kappenberg
Zeichen setzen für Europa
Der Gebrauch europäischer lateinischer Sonderzeichen in der deutschen Öffentlichkeit
ISBN 3-89821-749-3

Siegbert Klee, Martin Sandhop, Oxana Schwajka, Andreas Umland
Elitenbildung in der Postsowjetischen Ukraine
ISBN 978-389821-829-0

Elise Luckfiel
Zwischen Staat und externer Förderung - zivilgesellschaftliche Akteure in der Ukraine
Eine empirische Untersuchung von Kiewer NGOs
ISBN 978-3-89821-852-8

Eva Fuchslocher
Georgiens Nationenbildung
ISBN 978-3-89821-884-9

Oleh Kotsyuba
Ukrainian versus Russian Literature in the Post-Soviet Period
Overtaking and Surpassing America?
ISBN 978-3-89821-914-3

Mieste Hotopp-Riecke
Die Tataren der Krim zwischen Assimilation und Selbstbehauptung
Der Aufbau des krimtatarischen Bildungswesens nach Deportation und Heimkehr (1990-2005)
ISBN 978-3-89821-940-2

Alexander Schrepfer-Proskurjakov
Terror in Russland
Geschichte und Gegenwart
ISBN 978-3-89821-945-7

Quotes from reviews of SPPS volumes:

On vol. 1 – *The Implementation of the ECHR in Russia*: "Full of examples, experiences and valuable observations which could provide the basis for new strategies."

Diana Schmidt, *Неприкосновенный запас*, 2005

On vol. 2 – *Putins Russland*: "Wipperfürth draws attention to little known facts. For instance, the Russians have still more positive feelings towards Germany than to any other non-Slavic country."

Oldag Kaspar, *Süddeutsche Zeitung*, 2005

On vol. 3 – *Die Übernahme internationalen Rechts in die russische Rechtsordnung*: "Hussner's is an interesting, detailed and, at the same time, focused study which deals with all relevant aspects and contains insights into contemporary Russian legal thought."

Herbert Küpper, *Jahrbuch für Ostrecht*, 2005

On vol. 5 – *Квадратные метры, определяющие сознание*: „Meerovich provides a study that will be of considerable value to housing specialists and policy analysts."

Christina Varga-Harris, *Slavic Review*, 2006

On vol. 6 – *New Directions in Russian International Studies*: "A helpful step in the direction of an overdue dialogue between Western and Russian IR scholarly communities."

Diana Schmidt, *Europe-Asia Studies*, 2006

On vol. 8 – *Nation-Building and Minority Politics in Post-Socialist States*: "Galbreath's book is an admirable and craftsmanlike piece of work, and should be read by all specialists interested in the Baltic area."

Andrejs Plakans, *Slavic Review*, 2007

On vol. 9 – *Народы Кавказа в Вооружённых силах СССР:* "In this superb new book, Bezugolnyi skillfully fashions an accurate and candid record of how and why the Soviet Union mobilized and employed the various ethnic groups in the Caucasus region in the Red Army's World War II effort."

David J. Glantz, *Journal of Slavic Military Studies*, 2006

On vol. 10 – *Русское Национальное Единство*: "Pribylovskii's and Likhachev's work is likely to remain the definitive study of the Russian National Unity for a very long time."

Mischa Gabowitsch, *e-Extreme*, 2006

On vol. 13 – *The Politicization of Russian Orthodoxy*: "Mitrofanova's book is a fascinating study which raises important questions about the type of national ideology that will come to predominate in the new Russia."

Zoe Knox, *Europe-Asia Studies*, 2006

On vol. 14 – *Aleksandr Solzhenitsyn and the Modern Russo-Jewish Question*: "Larson has written a well-balanced survey of Solzhenitsyn's writings on Russian-Jewish relations."

Nikolai Butkevich, *e-Extreme*, 2006

On vol. 16 – *Der russische Sonderweg?:* "Luks's remarkable knowledge of the history of this wide territory from the Elbe to the Pacific Ocean and his life experience give his observations a particular sharpness and his judgements an exceptional weight."

Peter Krupnikow, *Mitteilungen aus dem baltischen Leben*, 2006

On vol. 17 – *История «Мёртвой воды»*: "Moroz provides one of the best available surveys of Russian neo-paganism."

Mischa Gabowitsch, *e-Extreme*, 2006

On vol. 18 – *Этническая и религиозная интолерантность в российских СМИ*: "A constructive contribution to a crucial debate about media-endorsed intolerance which has once again flared up in Russia."

Mischa Gabowitsch, *e-Extreme*, 2006

On vol. 25 – *The Ghosts in Our Classroom*: "Freyberg-Inan's well-researched and incisive monograph, balanced and informed about Romanian education in general, should be required reading for those Eurocrats who have shaped Romanian spending priorities since 2000."

Tom Gallagher, *Slavic Review*, 2006

On vol. 26 – *The 2002 Dubrovka and 2004 Beslan Hostage Crises*: "Dunlop's analysis will help to draw Western attention to the plight of those who have suffered by these terrorist acts, and the importance, for all Russians, of uncovering the truth of about what happened."

Amy Knight, *Times Literary Supplement*, 2006

On vol. 29 – *Zivilgesellschaftliche Einflüsse auf die Orange Revolution*: „Strasser's study constitutes an outstanding empirical analysis and well-grounded location of the subject within theory."

Heiko Pleines, *Osteuropa*, 2006

On vol. 34 – *Postsowjetische Feiern*: "Mühlfried's book contains not only a solid ethnographic study, but also points at some problems emerging from Georgia's prevalent understanding of culture."

Godula Kosack, *Anthropos*, 2007

On vol. 35 – *Fascism Past and Present, West and East*: "Committed students will find much of interest in these sometimes barbed exchanges."

Robert Paxton, *Journal of Global History*, 2007

On vol. 37 – *Political Anti-Semitism in Post-Soviet Russia*: "Likhachev's book serves as a reliable compendium and a good starting point for future research on post-Soviet xenophobia and ultra-nationalist politics, with their accompanying anti-Semitism."

Kathleen Mikkelson, *Demokratizatsiya*, 2007

Series Subscription

Please enter my subscription to the series *Soviet and Post-Soviet Politics and Society*, ISSN 1614-3515, as follows:

❏ complete series   OR   ❏ English-language titles
                                   ❏ German-language titles
                                   ❏ Russian-language titles

starting with
❏ volume # 1
❏ volume # ___
  ❏ please also include the following volumes: #___, ___, ___, ___, ___, ___, ___
❏ the next volume being published
  ❏ please also include the following volumes: #___, ___, ___, ___, ___, ___, ___

❏ 1 copy per volume   OR   ❏ ___ copies per volume

Subscription within Germany:

You will receive every volume at 1st publication at the regular bookseller's price – incl. s & h and VAT.

Payment:
❏ Please bill me for every volume.
❏ Lastschriftverfahren: Ich/wir ermächtige(n) Sie hiermit widerruflich, den Rechnungsbetrag je Band von meinem/unserem folgendem Konto einzuziehen.

Kontoinhaber: _____ Kreditinstitut: _____
Kontonummer: _____ Bankleitzahl: _____

International Subscription:

Payment (incl. s & h and VAT) in advance for
❏ 10 volumes/copies (€ 319.80)   ❏ 20 volumes/copies (€ 599.80)
❏ 40 volumes/copies (€ 1,099.80)
Please send my books to:

NAME_____ DEPARTMENT_____
ADDRESS _____
POST/ZIP CODE_____ COUNTRY _____
TELEPHONE _____ EMAIL_____

date/signature_____

A hint for librarians in the former Soviet Union: Your academic library might be eligible to receive free-of-cost scholarly literature from Germany via the German Research Foundation. For Russian-language information on this program, see
http://www.dfg.de/forschungsfoerderung/formulare/download/12_54.pdf.

Please fax to: **0511 / 262 2201 (+49 511 262 2201)**
or mail to: *ibidem*-Verlag, Julius-Leber-Weg 11, D-30457 Hannover, Germany
or send an e-mail: ibidem@ibidem-verlag.de

ibidem-Verlag

Melchiorstr. 15

D-70439 Stuttgart

info@ibidem-verlag.de

www.ibidem-verlag.de
www.ibidem.eu
www.edition-noema.de
www.autorenbetreuung.de

www.ingramcontent.com/pod-product-compliance
Lightning Source LLC
Chambersburg PA
CBHW070541300426
44111CB00028B/1907